Osler, Hoskin & Harcourt

*Portrait
of a
Partnership*

OSLER, HOSKIN & HARCOURT

Portrait of a Partnership

Curtis Cole

McGraw-Hill Ryerson Limited

Toronto   New York   Auckland   Bogotá   Caracas   Lisbon   London   Madrid
Mexico   Milan   New Delhi   San Juan   Singapore   Sydney   Tokyo

Portrait of a Partnership: A History of Osler, Hoskin & Harcourt
Copyright © 1995 Osler, Hoskin & Harcourt

Care has been taken to trace ownership of copyright material contained in
this text. The publisher will gratefully accept any information that will
enable it to rectify any reference or credit in subsequent printings.

First published in 1995 by
McGraw-Hill Ryerson Limited
300 Water Street
Whitby, Ontario, Canada
L1N 9B6

1 2 3 4 5 6 7 8 9 0 EB 4 3 2 1 0 9 8 7 6 5

Canadian Cataloguing in Publication Data

Cole, Curtis, 1953-
Portrait of a partnership : a history of Osler, Hoskin & Harcourt

Includes bibliographical references and index.
ISBN 0-07-552579-8

1. Osler, Hoskin & Harcourt (Firm) — History.
2. Law firms — Ontario — Toronto — History.
3. Lawyers — Ontario — Toronto — Biography.
I. Title.

KE397.T6C6 1995   338.7'6134009713541
KF345.C6 1995   C95-931127-0

Publisher: Joan Homewood
Production Coordinator: Sharon Hudson
Cover Design: Marc Mireault
Page Makeup: Computer Composition of Canada, Inc.
Editorial Services: Don Loney/Word Guild

Printed and bound in United States

CONTENTS

FOREWORD

Why a history of Osler, Hoskin & Harcourt? Why at this time?

When we embarked on our firm history project in 1987, we were conscious of the fact that we were exploring, at least in the Canadian context, some new territory.

Canadian lawyers have not tended to view their law firms as institutions which have histories. Many lawyers see their own careers as being somewhat ad hoc. They could have attended a variety of schools, joined a number of different firms or practised in a variety of places. Even when they are established, they will view their work, like the work of all people in service industries, as being fundamentally responsive to client needs. Viewed from this perspective, a law firm may appear to be a happy coincidence of the idiosyncratic interests of the people who make it up — not an organism with its own evolution, cycles of development and patterns of growth. Looking at a law firm as an institution which transcends the lives of its members, which progresses over time, and which, indeed, has a history, requires patience, imagination and insight.

Our work was influenced at the outset by some histories of other law firms. When we were starting out, the history of the New York firm of Sullivan & Cromwell, *A Law Unto Themselves*, had just been published. It was an independent, highly critical and enormously entertaining history; however, when looked at from the perspective of a practitioner in a large organization, it was curiously unconnected with the issues and decisions which make day-to-day life in a modern legal partnership so challenging and rewarding.

Some members of our firm had also read privately prepared histories of major firms in Toronto and Montreal that had been published for the edification of the members of their respective firms and close colleagues. These histories appeared to depend largely on anecdote and legend. We wanted something more.

While we might quickly conclude that we wanted something more, it was not easy to decide what that "something more" was. We wanted a writer to have a degree of independence and objectivity. After some consultations, we selected Dr. Curtis Cole, an academic and historian specializing in legal history, as our researcher and author. We wanted an analysis that went beyond the anecdotal and colourful. We asked Dr. Cole to review the firm files, comb the partnership ledgers, analyze the minutes of partnership meetings and consider the record of the comings and goings of partners and associates.

We were, of course, required to respect our obligations — and the obligations of the lawyers who had gone before — to clients and the confidential information which they had given to us. It would be pointless to try to discuss a law firm as if it had not been fundamentally shaped, and sometimes directed, by its clients and their relationship to the firm. At every point in the project, we asked ourselves whether the events we were describing would bring a client's confidential affairs into public view.

Because we were substantially unaware of what our firm history would contain, we embarked upon the enterprise with some reservations. What if Dr. Cole turned up evidence of wrongdoing or information damaging to the firm or its former members? What if an objective review of our files suggested that our history was not always an honourable one?

Two sets of events tested our resolve on this point. Older members of the firm, particularly the generation of partners who are recent retirees, would sometimes speak in hushed tones of Walter Reid, a partner who had "stolen from his clients." The event is now several decades in the past, and the shame and embarrassment which the firm felt has turned into a sort of rueful amusement. The story appears in Chapter Five in all of its gory detail.

H.S. Osler, a nephew of our founder Britton Bath Osler and a managing partner in the early decades of this century, presented a much more subtle challenge. The role which H.S. Osler played in the 1920s in a corporate transaction which, almost by accident, became an element in the Teapot Dome scandal in the United States, was roundly criticized in the Toronto press and has been commented upon unfavourably in books published about Teapot Dome. Would we, as his successors at his firm, have new insights to provide? As you will see in Chapter Four, the point that became pre-eminent in our discussions with Dr. Cole was the role that the preservation of client confidences played in both H.S. Osler's professional life and in the continued success of the firm, despite a storm of public abuse.

If our reservations about the project proved unfounded, not all of our ambitions for it were attainable. All of the members of the firm take enormous pride in the excellence of the work it produces, its prestige, and its growth over the last two decades. Could a firm history document, in some objective manner, a pattern of activities, a firm ethos or some deeply held common values which would show the world why we flourished when other firms languished and died? Somewhat to our surprise, evidence of this sort proved to be beyond our reach. The fundamental values were there and were undoubtedly broadly held; an ethos was unquestionably shared by the partnership when the firm was small. These qualities do not, however, show up in correspondence or memoranda; they are much too subtle to be captured and, for the most part, too fleeting to be preserved in documents. After all our work, our firm's values remain an article of faith, and not a matter of record.

As you will note in Chapter Six, the question of the fundamental values shared by the firm several decades ago may bear some reflection. The values most widely affirmed were probably those of the men who formed the senior level of the partnership. Not all of the values of that time would have our approbation today, but with the passage of years, the firm has developed a more open and inclusive group of value systems. We may never again enjoy the security of an organization each of whose members shared a world view too profound to be debated. What we look for now is a means of using all the values that our members espouse in the service of a common cause.

Another of our ambitions was to somehow create windows into the practice of law at various times in the firm's history. What was it like for B.B. Osler to have a sole practitioner's office in Dundas, Ontario in the 1860s? What was it like to practise law in downtown Toronto before telephones were common? What was it like to carry on a barrister's practice in the years before pleadings and records could be typed and photocopied? Once again, these details eluded us. In part, the hard evidence which we had hoped to find was simply not there. B.B. Osler may have been, as we stoutly believe, the greatest advocate of his time, but the arguments, interchanges, correspondence and pleadings of his day-to-day work have disappeared. He comes to life in his courtroom appearances through newspaper accounts of sensational trials, but we can only speculate on his ordinary tasks.

Fundamentally, a firm history provides a link between the current members of the firm and all the lawyers, clients and staff who have shaped the enterprise; the past connected with the present can give insights into the organization which we now are and the challenges which we will face in the future. So some of the impetus for the history project was a sense that the changes in the firm in recent years have been so dramatic that a whole new point of reference must be found.

Appendix II sets out the stark facts: in 1992 the firm had 285 lawyers; in 1982 it had 103 lawyers; in 1972 it had fifty-four lawyers; and in 1962 it had thirty-three lawyers. At any given time, approximately half the lawyers would have been partners in the firm. A partnership of two dozen people can reasonably assume that its members have a fairly intimate knowledge of both the lives and values of the other partners. A partner in the 1960s would expect invitations to the weddings of the children of other partners and would, in turn, extend such invitations. A partnership with one hundred or more members can make no such assumptions. As noted above, it is only by a patient and consistent fostering of the new values which must guide such a large organization that we can maintain a sense of community.

The changes we face are more than simply the changes created by radical growth and enormous size. We perceive that the world around us has changed, that the marketplace for professional services is less courteous, more crowded and more competitive. Consequently, our clients are less patient and more demanding.

By any standards, the work being performed at Osler, Hoskin & Harcourt, and at any of the other large firms in Canada, is more complex than it ever has been. Part of this complexity has its roots in the legal system. Provincial and federal legislation has burgeoned in the past two decades. Our youngest associates cannot remember a time when legislation protecting the environment was not a central element in a client's industrial strategy. Older members, however, will remember a time when there was no provincial sales tax and the Personal Property Security Act was still a matter of debate. Our history takes us back to days when divorces were obtained by Order in Council from the Dominion government, labour law was in its infancy and income tax was just being introduced. Each piece of legislation creates a new need among our clients and demands new expertise among our colleagues.

Complexity also arises out of our client community. The statutory imposition of taxes has, quite naturally, led to tax planning. Tax planning has led to transactions structured with two and three levels of ownership interests, each level having its own tax rationale. Each level of ownership, once more, requires special legal treatment. In a spectacular recent example, the transfer and financing of an interest in a major development in downtown Toronto had a closing agenda which was over one hundred pages long and which listed over one thousand documents. Our history takes us back to a time when a land acquisition and assembly not a hundred yards from our one thousand-document development could be done with a couple of dozen pieces of correspondence, a deed and a file that barely takes up one envelope.[1]

Complexity, however, is not an end in itself. The complexity imposed by the legal system, augmented by the complexity demanded by the tax and financial structures which clients need, can become both unwieldy and expensive. The firm's newest challenge is to review the work it does for clients and its own internal procedures to ensure that each legal step does, indeed, provide the value that the modern client requires from professional advisers. The pressure of assessing value — not merely from the point of view of exacting professional standards but also from the point of view of the commercial needs of clients dealing with cyclical economic forces — is new in the experience of the firm.

Or is it?

Once again, our history provides a point of reference. Our modern firm makes "client development" a central element in both its planning and its commitment to quality service. We have administrative staff responsible for marketing and legal education to develop seminars and written materials for the benefit of clients. We have a calendar of social, cultural and sporting events to which clients are regularly invited, and we encourage every member of the firm to get to know each client well enough that every aspect of the professional experience, including dissatisfactions, can be easily and frankly discussed.

We like to think of this as a world our forebears never knew. Our history, however, provides us with the curious example of H.C.F. "Hal" Mockridge, the benevolently autocratic senior partner during the 1940s, 1950s and 1960s. Hal Mockridge had a dazzling list of corporate directorships and so much work to choose from that when he was forced to pick between two corporate boards, he gave up the one that was more lucrative in order to retain the one that was more interesting. We will never know what Hal Mockridge would have made of the term "client development," and he undoubtedly would have bridled at the suggestion that his profession could be "marketed." He was probably, however, a more commanding presence among his colleagues in the firm than any single individual before or since. Our history suggests that the means whereby we compete, not competition itself, is the new phenomenon.

A final word; by bringing our history up to the present day, we had to recognize it would remain incomplete. The reader will note that we have allowed ourselves a long and relatively judicious look at the firm in its formative years and during the period leading up to its amazing spurt of growth after 1975. The closer the history gets to our own day, the more difficult the task of assessing the firm became. The descriptions and interpretations of events during this time are necessarily spare and oblique.

What we came to realize in the course of this enterprise is that a healthy partnership is always a work in progress. New challenges are always arising, the solutions of last year will not meet them, the wisdom of the past decade is never adequate. If the firm is a work in progress, so must its history be. We offer this effort with affection for our forebears and colleagues, pride in our collective enterprise, and the certain knowledge that partners we have not yet met will be taking their roles in expanding, and perhaps even rewriting, this history for decades to come.

J. Edgar Sexton
Chair
Osler, Hoskin & Harcourt

Laurence D. Hebb
Managing Partner
Osler, Hoskin & Harcourt

Toronto, December 1994

PREFACE

In late 1987, I received a note from David H. Flaherty of the Department of History at the University of Western Ontario. He mentioned that Brian Bucknall, a partner at Osler, Hoskin & Harcourt, had called him to ask if he knew of anyone who might be interested in writing a history of the firm. As the editor of the first two volumes of *Essays in the History of Canadian Law*, Flaherty was then one of a small number of acknowledged experts in Canadian legal history.[1] Bucknall was a member of the board of directors of the Osgoode Society, the publishers of Flaherty's *Essays*, and a published legal historian in his own right.[2]

Flaherty, who had supervised my doctoral thesis on the history of the Ontario legal profession completed that year, suggested my name to Bucknall.[3] I was intrigued with the idea; the opportunity to study a law firm as large and venerable as Osler, Hoskin & Harcourt was very attractive. I was also sceptical; what archival materials and information would remain available? And, more importantly, what records would I have access to? A commissioned biography which is intended only to sing the praises of the subject, regardless of the truth, is of little value to history or the historian.

As Flaherty put it, however, Bucknall told him that they wanted "a serious history, not a pot-boiler." Bucknall pointed out to me in discussions shortly thereafter that Oslers wanted the whole story, "warts and all." In answer to the question as to why the firm wanted to set down its own history, he explained that the partners felt that it was important that the firm preserve its past, in order to "know itself." When, a few decades ago, the firm was comprised of a small group, it was easy to maintain an unspoken sense of community. In recent years, however, it had grown to an unprecedented size. The partners felt, therefore, that it was important to understand and preserve the firm's history in order to maintain a sense of identity within the firm. There might also be an external marketing value to a published history of the firm, for both potential clients and potential recruits. The firm was willing, therefore, to commission a full-scale study and underwrite the associated research costs.

Nevertheless, there were still difficulties to be worked out. Although both the firm and I approached our discussions prior to reaching an agreement with the assumption that each was negotiating in good faith, neither of us knew what would happen if I uncovered some unexpected skeleton in the historical closet. Would they be willing to let some damning evidence about the firm or its members be published? Moreover, how close to the present could the study go without breaching the confidentiality of clients and privacy of the individual members of the firm?

Happily, we were able to come to a workable agreement on these points, and over the course of the project our faith in each other's good will proved to be justified. With respect to the latter issue, we decided that the book's chronology would extend into the 1990s, but in order not to violate the privacy of living persons, it would not go into topics such as individual earnings in the most recent years. Beyond that, with respect to the former issue, the firm lived up to its commitment to a complete history, "warts and all." I was provided with virtually unlimited access to firm records dating back well into the nineteenth century, and some seventy extensive interviews with current and former members of the firm were, almost without exception, extremely candid.

There are four main themes in *Portrait of a Partnership*. The first relates to a fundamental question: What is the secret of success behind one of the largest and oldest law firms in Canada? As might be expected, it is a combination of things: a little of who you know (having the right social, political and business connections has always been important); a little of what you know (without knowledge and skill, connections mean very little); and a little luck (being in the right place at the right time has played a part in the firm's success on more than one occasion).

Most importantly, however, Osler, Hoskin & Harcourt, like many other successful and long-lived institutions, has consistently shown an ability to adapt to fundamental change. This was as much true during the late nineteenth century, when the rise of Canadian industrial capitalism greatly increased the demand for corporate legal expertise, as it was during the late twentieth century, when changes such as the evolution of global capital markets transformed the business law environment. For over 130 years the firm has maintained an ability to adapt to these changes.

The second theme is also related to success; it is less obvious, but no less important. During the twentieth century especially, the leaders of the firm have been able to foster a sense among the members that the collective, institutional interests of the firm must remain paramount to those of the individual partners. In other words, they were able to establish a maxim that "the whole is greater than the sum of its parts."

The third theme is directly related to the second. Beyond the fact that the partners, as a whole, accepted the logic that subordinating their own, individual interests to those of the firm would, in the long run, be in each member's own financial best interest, the leaders relied on the fact that the firm had an established culture of community. It had an institutional personality of its own, and the partners could share in a sense of belonging.

The final theme explains how that personality evolved over time through four distinct eras. During the period prior to 1916, the firm was a compact between two great courtroom lawyers, and ultimately two great families. In 1916, however, the two families went their separate ways, and from that year until the decade of the 1950s, the firm was a clan, with its most significant partners being members of a single, extended family.* From the 1950s through the early 1970s, the firm was a club, with membership extending beyond the clan, but not beyond its socio-economic circle. And finally, during the most recent decades, the firm has become a virtual corporation. It is not a corporation in the legal sense. In those terms, and in many significant others, it remains a partnership. It is, however, a corporation in the sense that it is governed by a committee management structure, and it is often difficult to maintain a sense of intimate community. In fact, maintaining that sense of community, which is a strength the firm relied on throughout its history, is one of the greatest challenges of the future.

---

* A partial Osler family tree, outlining the family relationships of individuals referred to in the text and notes, appears as Appendix III.

ACKNOWLEDGEMENTS

There are a number of people whose contribution to this project deserve acknowledgement. First among these are the members of the Osler, Hoskin & Harcourt Firm History Committee: W. Lee Webster (Chair), Brian Bucknall, Larry Hebb and, at different times, Arthur Peltomaa and George Vesely. Their advice during the research process and comments on successive drafts were invaluable. Second, my friend and colleague Frank Clifford, who in many ways was the real father of this project, has been a constant source of information and advice in his unofficial capacity as firm historian and archivist. Third, my research assistants, Victoria Coombs of Osgoode Hall Law School and Dan Byers of Wilfrid Laurier University, provided essential help, as did the library staff at Osler, Hoskin & Harcourt, the Faculty of Law of the University of Western Ontario, and the Archives of The Law Society of Upper Canada. Fourth, the dozens of people whose names appear in the endnotes as interviewees were very generous with their time as well as their memories and insights.

I would also like to extend my gratitude to Margaret McFetridge, who co-ordinated many of the administrative functions of the project and transcribed over one hundred hours of taped research interviews and archival notes, and Don Loney for his expert editorial and production guidance. Wendy Rickey's assistance was essential to the completion of Appendix I. An earlier version of Chapter Two appeared as "McCarthy, Osler, Hoskin & Creelman, 1882-1902: Establishing a Reputation, Building a Practice," in *Beyond The Law: Lawyers and Business in Canada, 1830-1930*, Carol Wilton, ed., (Toronto, 1990), 149-66.

Finally, without the constant support and encouragement of my wife Joanne Cole, and our children Ryan and Christen, none of this would be worth doing.

London, Ontario

April 1995

A TRADITION OF "AFFECTION AND ESTEEM"

Thursday, November 24, 1994 was rather cold in Toronto, and at the end of the day most downtown bank tower office workers heading for their cars or joining the stream of commuters in the underground concourse to Union Station to catch the subway or the Go Train were dressed for the weather. It was the American Thanksgiving, and some were stopping off at local watering holes to catch the last half of the Dallas-Green Bay NFL game on television. But around 6:30, a few small groups of people in tuxedos and formal dresses could be seen exiting the revolving doors on the east side of First Canadian Place and crossing Bay Street to the National Club.

The people in formal wear were all lawyers; they were partners in Osler, Hoskin & Harcourt, and they were going to a special dinner to honour one of their own. A group of lawyers in black tie going to dinner at the National Club is not surprising. Osler, Hoskin & Harcourt is one of Canada's oldest and largest law firms, and the National Club is one of Toronto's establishment private clubs. Its dark-panelled dining rooms with portraits of long dead Ontario premiers and lieutenant-governors have hosted meetings of the Bay Street élite for over a century.

But this dinner was different; it was for Peter Dey, who in fact was no longer a member of the firm. It was not, however, a retirement dinner. At only fifty-three, Dey had resigned his partnership in the firm earlier that year to become president of Morgan Stanley Canada, the investment bank. The official purpose of the dinner was to make him an Honourary Partner in the firm. But rather than lamenting the loss of someone who had been one of the most significant contributors to the firm's growth during the 1970s and 1980s, his former partners were holding a dinner to honour him.

With the exception perhaps of Peter Dey, who once served as Chairman of the Ontario Securities Commission, few of the people in the dining room at the National Club that evening could be considered a public figure. Despite the fact that many of them had been intimately involved in some of the most significant and newsworthy events in recent Canadian business history, corporate lawyers are anything but media stars. Compared to their generally less influential, and often less well-rewarded professional brethren who take up other legal specialties, corporate lawyers are typically reserved.

This shyness is traditional. Partly it stems from the privacy dictated by solicitor-client privilege. But with the exception of a few courtroom specialists — and despite the common "Perry Mason" public image of lawyers, this is a small and atypical group — the legal profession is anything but flamboyant. Those who are well known usually appear in the public eye through some other non-legal role such as politics or business.[1]

Even those corporate lawyers whom the financial and legal communities reverentially label "deal makers," those who engineer the multimillion-dollar transactions, are relatively unknown outside of these circles. The more senior members of the securities bar, such as Peter Dey, have developed some degree of prominence through regular appearances before the Ontario Securities Commission — whose proceedings are public. Their names appear occasionally in the financial press.

Regardless of its source, this relative anonymity surrounding most Canadian lawyers has meant that a fascinating — and historically significant — story has gone largely untold. There are a number of law firm histories, mostly of American firms, in existence, but almost without exception, none has been written by a professional historian.[2] They all serve a useful purpose; they tell stories which are interesting and informative. They present engaging biographical sketches of some leading lawyers and offer explanations as to how some firms changed over time, but they do not adequately analyze why these firms evolved in the ways they did.

For example, Robert T. Swaine, the author of a history of Cravath, Swaine, Moore (perhaps the best-known American law firm history) pointed out in the foreword to his two-volume study published just after World War II:

. . . these volumes are intended to record, for the benefit of the men who have been in the office and for those to follow, something about the men who built its traditions and about the practice in which those traditions were built. They make no pretence either of popular interest or of philosophical interpretation.[3]

Mr. Swaine was, of course, being overly modest in denying his work's popular interest. It is a very interesting study of a firm whose most prominent partner was William H. Seward, Abraham Lincoln's secretary of state. He was, however, correct in noting his work's lack of interpretation, other than the inevitable, implicitly sympathetic viewpoint of a retired partner in the firm.

In addition, the authors of the existing law firm histories, Swaine included, almost invariably examine their subjects from what legal historians term an internal perspective. They generally do not take external economic, social, and political factors into account in explaining how the firms evolved.[4] For example, major economic events and trends such as the Great Depression of the 1930s and the globalization of trade during the late twentieth century clearly affected legal practice. Some firms were able to adapt to the dramatic changes in the economy and business climate, while others were not. A thorough historical analysis must take externalities into account in trying to understand why.

Of course, not all of the literature on the history of law firms is guilty of the shortcomings described above. Erwin O. Smigel's *The Wall Street Lawyer: Professional Organization Man?* goes well beyond the internal perspective of most traditional studies and analyzes the subject in light of its broader intellectual, political and social context.[5] Similarly, *A Law Unto Itself: The Untold Story of The Law Firm of Sullivan & Cromwell* by Nancy Lisagor and Frank Lipsius, the former a sociologist and the latter a journalist, presents a fascinating look at one of New York's largest and most influential firms.[6]

Although these works deal quite well with the external questions surrounding their subjects, they can do only that. They were written without access to the law firms' internal sources. The Lisagor and Lipsius book, although it offers some excellent insights into the origins and early evolution of the firm, lapses into little more than a spirited indictment of John Foster Dulles, the Sullivan & Cromwell senior partner who served as Eisenhower's secretary of state, when it covers the middle part of the twentieth century.[7] The result is a story which is, necessarily, incomplete.

Portrait of a Partnership makes an attempt to tell both the internal and the external story of one of Canada's largest and oldest law firms — Osler, Hoskin & Harcourt. It was possible only with the complete cooperation of the firm itself. Although they were very careful to maintain solicitor-client confidentiality, the partners in the firm have been fully supportive of the scholarly aims of this research project. They are, of course, more interested than anyone else in learning about and preserving the history of their own firm.

To an outside observer, the dinner at the National Club that evening in November 1994 was not so much to fête Peter Dey as it was to celebrate the firm itself. The members of Osler, Hoskin & Harcourt share a special spirit. It is partly a sense of professional pride because they belong to one of the most successful law firms in Canada, but it is also a sense of community, and a sense that the collective value and success of the firm as a whole is more enduring than any individual partner. The partners sitting around the tables at the National Club that evening seemed to feel it, and that was the implicit theme of most of the after-dinner speakers. Moreover, the former partners — including Peter Dey — felt it as well.

After dinner, there were a number of affectionate and heartfelt speeches about Peter Dey and his time with the firm. Tim Kennish, a senior partner in the Corporate Department who joined the firm a few years prior to Dey, teased him about his athletic career, when he demonstrated both dynamic leadership and bizarre play-calling as the Oslers* quarterback in Sunday morning contests with other law firms, and he highlighted some of Dey's many professional accomplishments, including his highly regarded tenure as chairman of the Securities Commission. But the tone of the speeches, although directed personally to Dey, was a collective one. The speakers and the dinner guests took pride in Peter's accomplishments because they shared in them.

One of the most significant speakers in this respect was Purdy Crawford, who spoke on behalf of the other Honourary Partners. Crawford is acknowledged to have been one of the most important

---

* When Canadian lawyers refer to law firms they often seem to use a short form which adds an "s" to the first surname of the firm name. Osler, Hoskin & Harcourt becomes "Oslers," and McCarthy, Tétrault (formerly McCarthy & McCarthy) becomes "McCarthys." The originally proper spelling was probably the possessive "Osler's" or even the plural possessive "Oslers'" because it was a shortened version of "the Osler brothers' firm." The apostrophe has apparently disappeared in recent years.

leaders of the firm in terms of practice and practice development as well as firm management during the crucial growth years of the 1960s, 1970s and 1980s, and like Dey had left the firm in his early fifties to join the management of a client company. In 1985, Crawford accepted an offer to become president of Imasco Ltd. To most observers the loss of Crawford or Allan Beattie, who left the firm in 1987 to become vice-chairman of Eaton's of Canada Ltd., would be a devastating blow.

But in fact the firm continued to grow and prosper. The fact that each of them joined client companies was significant. As Oslers lawyers will explain, the firm will often serve clients with a team of lawyers. The senior people, like Purdy Crawford, consciously brought along the younger Peter Deys in the 1970s, just as Dey and his contemporaries brought along their juniors in the 1980s. In turn, they passed on the team-oriented firm approach to the next generation in the firm.

Peter Dey said exactly this when he spoke to thank the firm for his appointment as an Honourary Partner. He said:

> If I had to identify the characteristic of the firm which I think has contributed and continues to contribute most to the firm's success it's the ability of the OH&H lawyers to function as a team. I know that this concept of team work is almost trivialized because it is such an overused concept. It's prominently featured in the recruiting materials of all the service organizations. The real question is, of course, how teamwork is practised, and translating this value into practice is the real challenge, even for the most confident of individuals. . . . Team playing means different things to different people, but most will agree that it requires . . . that individuals be able to delegate or be delegated to in either direction, both vertically and horizontally; and ultimately the ability of the group to function as a team depends upon the confidence or the faith of the group that their efforts will be fairly recognized.

Dey was right when he noted that this concept of team playing has become a truism among professional service firms. Most accounting and law firm members today would agree that it is an ideal to strive for, but most would also agree that it is very difficult to attain.

By all accounts Osler, Hoskin & Harcourt has been successful in establishing a team orientation because of its firm culture — and this is not something which has developed only recently. As Peter Dey put it:

> I don't want to forget the generosity of spirit that characterizes members of the firm. I experienced it virtually every day of my tenure at Oslers. . . . There is a willingness to understand, accommodate and provide support and sensitivity to individual circumstances that is not present in all organizations. When the firm makes extra demands on its members, my experience has always been that members responded enthusiastically and wanted to help. This generosity of spirit is greatly assisted by a sense of humour. . . . [You] must never lose sight of the values with which the firm was built. These values have been tested over and over again. . . . Firm culture is not just important internally to the management and growth and development of the firm. It is equally important to clients. Clients want to know and understand the firm's culture, and ultimately they must be comfortable with it. A number of us will recall discussions we had with the people from a leading American investment bank — which will remain nameless — who said that they had done a survey of leading Canadian business law firms, and ultimately they had chosen Oslers because we had a teamwork approach. The lack of jealousy among the people who worked on their account reflected the investment bank's culture and provided them with a level of comfort that was not available from other law firms.

In concluding, he reminded his former partners: "We must never lose sight of our roots, the foundation upon which the firm has been built and the foundation upon which its growth will be based."

The roots which Dey spoke of go back over 130 years. Osler, Hoskin & Harcourt was founded in the small Ontario town of Dundas, on the edge of the Niagara Escarpment, in the autumn of 1862. Its founder was a twenty-three-year-old lawyer named Britton Bath Osler. Osler, the son of the local Anglican minister, had just been called to the bar; apparently unwilling or uninvited to join a firm in the larger provincial centres of Hamilton or Toronto, he decided to hang out his shingle on his own in his home town.

If B.B. Osler could have joined the private dinner party at the National Club that night in November 1994, he would have recognized little of the firm which he founded over a century earlier. What began as a small town, one-man law office had grown to become one of the largest law firms in Canada. By 1994, Osler, Hoskin & Harcourt had close to three hundred lawyers, and in addition to occupying the better part of the top ten floors of the prestigious First Canadian Place in downtown Toronto, it had an office in Ottawa, and, in partnership with the Montreal-based firm Ogilvy, Renault, operated an international affiliate known as Osler Renault with offices in London, Paris, New York, Hong Kong and Singapore.

The changes in this law firm over the course of over 130 years involved more than growth, however. In fact, the firm has gone through a number of metamorphoses involving its practice and its membership since Britton Bath Osler commenced practice in Dundas in 1862. Throughout this evolution, however, some very important things have remained constant. One of the overriding themes in the history of Osler, Hoskin & Harcourt is the interplay between continuity and change.

Had he joined the dinner party at the National Club, Osler likely would have been surprised by the presence of women lawyers in the group. Osler had, in his time, been a bencher of the Law Society of Upper Canada when it considered the admission of Clara Brett Martin into the profession. Indeed, his vote helped to secure Martin a position as the first female lawyer in the British Empire. In 1892, Osler voted in favour of a motion to admit women to practise as solicitors. The motion passed by a margin of twelve votes to eleven, with Osler's partner John Hoskin voting in favour and his other partner D'Alton McCarthy voting against it.[8] But his firm did not employ a woman lawyer until more than fifty years after his death. The first woman lawyer at Osler, Hoskin & Harcourt was Bertha Wilson, who later became the first woman justice of The Supreme Court of Canada.

B.B. Osler might also have been offended by the affectionate roasting which Peter Dey received from some of the speakers, and it would have surprised him that junior and senior lawyers called one another by their first names. But if Osler could look beyond these differences, he would see something familiar.

In addition to the fact that the group of lawyers seemed happy and collegial, Osler would have noticed something else. They were at ease and relaxed as a group. This is a strength which, to a large extent, goes back a long way in the history of the firm. Law firms, like most institutions, seem to have personalities of their own. Davies, Ward & Beck, twenty floors below Oslers in First Canadian Place, was at one time known among articling students as "The Sweat Shop." In the early 1980s, students sometimes called Osler, Hoskin & Harcourt "Camp Osler." In each case the terms have been used both affectionately and derisively, depending upon the observer's perspective, and in each case the firm seemed to some extent to cultivate the image.

In the Oslers case, the tradition of getting along with one another dates back to the nineteenth century. In 1897, Britton Bath Osler wrote to his partners to thank them for a wedding gift. He was honeymooning in New York following his second marriage — his first wife having died some years earlier. In the formal style typical of his generation, Osler thanked them for their thoughtfulness and described why their firm was surviving while others were breaking apart. "Its strength is not only in its good business basis but in the existence of affection and esteem between its members." The lawyers at the National Club almost a century later might have chosen different words, but would not have disagreed.

When asked to describe what makes their firm different from the other Bay Street law firms, most lawyers at Osler, Hoskin & Harcourt will use terms like friendly, cooperative, team oriented, or even "Camp Osler" to explain what they see as a firm culture. Of course, to identify a corporate personality or culture in an organization of close to three hundred lawyers and an even greater number of support personnel spread over a number of office locations is very difficult; there is no doubt, however, that most of the lawyers at Oslers believe this characterization, and they would like to keep it that way.

From an outsider's point of view, whether the Osler firm is such an idyllic place to work may be debatable. The average workweek is generally well in excess of fifty hours, and in some cases approaches seventy. Moreover, the implicit and overt pressure placed on lawyers, particularly the younger ones, to conform to what many observers would consider a workaholic lifestyle, is great.

The question of long hours and pressure and their effect on the quality of work — and quality of life — of the lawyers in the firm is one with which many firms — Osler, Hoskin & Harcourt included — are wrestling. There is no question that working an extraordinary number of hours is a tradition in the legal profession, and probably more so in the large firms. Where this tradition comes from is not as clear. Obviously, individual economic self-interest plays a major role; "the more hours you work, the higher your income" tends to be the rule. But the marketplace for legal services is also a fluctuating one, and it is client driven.

In corporate law, the business cycle has a very direct effect on the number of hours lawyers work. During good times, clients seek more legal advice, and law firms' billable hours go up. Conversely, during economic downturns, hours are reduced. Of course, like any other enterprise, the more diversified a firm is, the more it can protect itself against the negative effects of the economic cycle. For instance, during the recession which began in 1990 the Bankruptcy and Insolvency group at Oslers got busier while the Mergers and Acquisitions group slowed down.

In addition, the pressure which the partners put on young lawyers to work hard is the pressure of example. It is not a case of working extremely long hours in order to make partner, and then sitting back and enjoying life. In fact, the average workweek for a partner at Osler, Hoskin & Harcourt is little shorter than the average workweek for an associate lawyer.

To an historian, another important question to ask about this institutional culture is, "Where did it originate?" In the early years of the firm, when it was still relatively small, certainly the individual personalities of the senior partners played a major role in establishing and maintaining firm culture. In more recent years, the question becomes more clouded. Law firms are tradition-bound institutions, and particularly when they are successful they tend to keep things the same. This accounts in part for the maintenance of the firm's self-image, but leadership also plays an important role.

In some firms, the senior partners covet the prestigious clients and lucrative files. This is partly because of the way many firms divide income, but it is also closely linked to professional status, both within the firm and outside of it. At Osler, Hoskin & Harcourt, however, the culture discourages partners from coveting clients for themselves individually. Although one lawyer is responsible to oversee a client's legal affairs on behalf of the firm, his or her most important function is often to be the team captain and marshall the appropriate talents within the firm to work on a particular file. This is especially true when the client requires a wide range of expertise.

This means the lead partner not only has to be able to recognize individual talent among his or her colleagues, and what mix of those talents will best serve the client's legal needs, he or she must put the client's needs above those of his or her own ego. Rather than holding the client's hand alone, he or she must be able to take the client's hand and place it in hands of the people in the firm who are best able to solve the problem. Lawyers in other firms would probably agree that this standard is one to strive for, but this is much easier said than done.

In any case, although most have difficulty in articulating their feeling about it, the people who work at Osler, Hoskin & Harcourt are proud of their law firm. They believe there are qualitative differences between Oslers and the other big firms, and they want it to stay that way. Certainly, this was the feeling of the group enjoying dinner that night at the National Club. The man who opened his law office in Dundas, Ontario over 130 years earlier would agree on both counts.

CHAPTER

1

BEGINNINGS: 1862-1882

In the fall of 1862, when Britton Bath Osler began to practise law in the village of Dundas, Upper Canada, forty miles west of Toronto, he was twenty-three years old. The second of Ellen and Reverend Featherstone Osler's eight children, he was born on June 19, 1839 near the village of Bond Head in rural Simcoe County, some thirty-five miles north of Toronto.

Osler's parents were remarkable people. His father, born in Falmouth on the south coast of England in 1805, took to the sea at the age of sixteen. He spent ten years as a sailor, first in the merchant marine and later as an officer in the Royal Navy. His letters home during those years offer fascinating accounts of voyages throughout the Mediterranean and Caribbean seas, sailing down the Atlantic coast of South America while Brazil and Argentina were at war, and around the Cape of Good Hope to the Pacific and on to the Indian Ocean. In 1832, partly because a new Whig government at Westminster meant that most of his friends in the Admiralty were gone and his chances of advancement in the navy were therefore very limited, he decided to make a radical career switch. He resigned his commission and began study for the ministry.[1]

Britton Bath Osler's mother was born Ellen Free Picton just outside of London, England in 1806. Her parents were apparently unable to care for her, however, and she was adopted and raised by a Captain and Mrs. Britton of Falmouth.[2] She met young Featherstone Osler shortly after he returned from the sea and married him in February of 1837. Two months later, after his ordination as a priest in the Church of England, they set sail for Canada. Featherstone Osler was, of course, an experienced sailor, but his wife was ill-prepared for the seven-week voyage from Falmouth to Quebec, including a near ship-wreck in the Gulf of St. Lawrence.[3]

If Ellen Osler was ill-prepared for an Atlantic crossing, she was even less prepared for life as a pioneer. Her husband had accepted a post as the minister for West Gwillimbury and Tecumseth townships, which turned out to be 240 square miles of desolate Upper Canadian wilderness. The parsonage was a log cabin which Mrs. Osler described as "a shed . . . in a clearing in the wood, one room upstairs and one down, in which the cattle had been wont to shelter. . . . The horses used to come and look in at the window as much as to say, 'Why have you taken our stable and shut us out?' "[4]

In this environment, Ellen Osler bore and raised eight children. The first of these was born less than a year after the Oslers arrived in Canada. Featherston Osler, named for his father although he dropped the final, silent "e" from the spelling of his first name, was born June 4, 1838. (He was called to the bar in 1860 and later went on to serve on the Ontario Court of Appeal.[5]) Britton Bath followed a year later; Ellen was born in 1841 and Edward in 1842.[6]

The Oslers' fifth child, Edmund Boyd, was born in 1845. He began his career as a clerk in the Bank of Upper Canada shortly before its collapse in 1866; by the turn of the century, he was the president of the Dominion Bank, a director of the Canadian Pacific Railway, and owner of one of the largest stock brokerage houses in North America. He was knighted by King George V in 1912, and assumed the title of "Sir."[7]

Twins Charlotte and Frank were born in 1847, and the youngest, William, was born in 1849. Perhaps the most famous of the family, William Osler graduated from McGill University Medical School in 1872 and served on the faculty of his alma mater as well as the University of Philadelphia, Johns Hopkins and Oxford. In 1911, he became Sir William when he was created a Baronet by George V.[8]

Britton Bath Osler's initial education came as a boarder at local grammar schools in Barrie and nearby Bradford. He was apparently a typical teenager; when he was fifteen, he wrote from school to his elder brother Featherston, then a law student articling in Barrie, to tell him:

On Friday last Diny and I put some gun powder in Small's pipe and it blew up and sent the pieces all about, singed his eyelashes and set him crying. He threw a stick at Diny for doing it. Diny got up and gave him an awful licking. Miss Small came up to put Barklay's trunks to rights and to comb the bugs out of his head. . . .

Hoping you are quite well I remain your affec. brother,

Britton Bath Osler[9]

The young Osler was also a resourceful and enterprising school-boy; years later a fellow student remembered him as the classroom capitalist.

There being no shop nearer than Bradford, three miles away, Britton once a week, on allowance day, opened a shop in the schoolroom. . . . He had a small cupboard in a corner with shelves filled with bread, cakes, sugar sticks, molasses and other sweets, and our weeks' allowances were soon spent — much to the satisfaction of the shop-keeper and his young customers.[10]

Flushed with this mercantile success, Osler apparently decided on a career in commerce. In 1857, when his father was transferred to a parish in Dundas, he took a short bookkeeping course in Hamilton and found a position keeping accounts for a Dundas dry-goods mer-chant.[11] In a letter to Featherston he described a job which was anything but exciting:

The business which . . . occupies my attention at present is to keep I.S. Meredith's accounts straight, in other words I am [his] book-keeper. He is a hardware importer and merchant . . . [and] he does a large business, keeps 2 salesmen and a man to do the dirty work. . . .

We are most gloriously dull here at present. Owing . . . to the harvest, the source of money appears to have dried up. But we do credit enough to keep me on the stool from 8 to 7 o'clock.[12]

He soon realized that a life spent on a high stool hunched over a ledger book wasn't for him, and in October 1858 he wrote to Feath-erston to ask his advice on how to become a lawyer.[13]

For Osler, not having a university degree would generally mean spending five years as an articled clerk in a lawyer's office and writing a series of examinations administered by the governing body of the legal profession, the Law Society of Upper Canada. Under the Law Society rules, however, students who held university degrees would only have to serve a three-year clerkship before being called to the bar. If Osler chose the former route, it would be five years before he could begin to practise, and if he took the latter option, it could take a total of six — three to get a degree and three more as an articled clerk.[14]

But Osler was in too much of a hurry to wait five or six years before being able to earn a living. He decided to enrol at the University of Toronto and earn a degree at the same time as he served his articled clerkship. In this way, he could be called to the bar after only three years. Featherston either approved of his younger brother's plan or knew he could never persuade him otherwise, and he wrote back to Britton that the next Law Society entrance exam for students would be held in Toronto in February:

> [The time] is short enough to give you as much as you can do to be ready . . . but a little hard work ought to accomplish it. You may leave out Greek, which I fear would prove a stumbling block, and take French. The Horace and Latin Prose translation will be most troublesome for you. If, however, the other subjects are done well, this, I believe, is not so much pressed.[15]

Britton got right down to work, and a month later wrote to his brother that "Since Monday I have been at my books 9 and a half hours per day and am getting on better than I expected. The French master says I can easily do the French; I think Algebra and Euclid I can master. The balance, Latin and Blackstone are the stiffest fences I have to surmount."[16]

Osler apparently was able to surmount the fences, because in February, 1859 he passed the Law Society entrance examination and in March started as an articling student with the two-man firm of Notman & Barton in Dundas.[17] Osler obviously worked hard to get through the entrance examination, but influence may also have played a role in his success. As Osler jokingly related to Featherston, the surest way for aspiring lawyers to get in is to:

> Get a good bench. If [they] know a bencher (like old Notman) let them join his artillery corps, tell him the last 18 pounder he got from the Govt. makes the loudest report of any you ever heard — and hint that in your opinion the whole Macdonald party [is] rotten, that Brown is a trump — and that it is no harm to drink Scotch whisky [before] going to bed. They will probably get the gent to assist them through and pass them even if they had only been studying Horace for 2 months and had a natural antipathy to it to commence with.[18]

The phrase "Get a good bench" was a pun. It meant get a good place to article — bench in this sense meaning the apprentice's workbench — but the directors of the Law Society, the body which governed the legal profession, were also known as "benchers." And both William Notman and George Barton were benchers.

Notman was also a lieutenant-colonel in the provincial militia and commander of the Dundas volunteer foot artillery, hence Osler's reference to the loud 18-pounder, and he represented the riding of North Wentworth as a member of the Reform faction in the Canadian Legislative Assembly.[19] John A. Macdonald was then the leader of the Tories in the Assembly, and George Brown was the leader of Notman's Reformers.

Political acumen and influence were important, but they were not the only reasons for Osler's success. His younger brother Edward, who was also promised an articling position with Notman & Barton, failed the Law Society's entrance exam in February 1858 and again when Britton wrote it in February 1859. In fact, Edward did not pass it until 1861.[20]

B.B. Osler's combined program as an articled clerk and university student was not as rigorous as it might seem. Because he was a candidate for a degree in law at the university, he was not required to attend any lectures there, and the university accepted his passing grades on the annual Law Society examinations in lieu of writing university exams. In fact, it appears that he and the others who were able to take advantage of this concurrent studies loophole before it was abolished in 1860 got a university degree without doing anything other than paying fees.[21]

Although Osler began his term as an articled clerk in Dundas, he finished it in Toronto. In the summer of 1860, only sixteen months after joining Notman & Barton, his articles were assigned to the Honourable James Patton. Featherston Osler had apparently articled with Patton in Barrie, and when Patton moved his practice to Toronto in 1860, he invited the elder Osler brother to join his firm. Featherston then convinced Patton to take his brother on as an articling student.[22] Like Notman, Patton was an influential member of the profession. He was also a bencher of the Law Society, and he sat in the upper chamber of the Canadian colonial parliament, the Legislative Council. Unlike Notman, however, Patton was a Tory.[23]

B.B. Osler obviously learned an important lesson while he was a law student. By articling with the Reformer Notman and the Tory Patton, he learned that it was important to maintain bipartisan political connections. Throughout his career, he maintained close associations with active members of both political factions, and his practice prospered. He may have learned this lesson directly from Patton, whose third partner in the firm of Patton, Osler & Moss was Thomas Moss, who sat as a Liberal in the House of Commons after Confederation.[24]

When B.B. Osler was called to the bar in 1862, he decided to return to his home town of Dundas and set up shop on his own. Quite likely Patton felt that with Featherston Osler, who was called to the bar in 1860, and Thomas Moss, who was called in 1861, there was no more room in the firm for junior lawyers. The fact that Osler's father was the local Church of England rector was obviously an advantage in setting up a practice in a small community, but as a letter which the young lawyer received a few years later poignantly demonstrated, not even local prominence could guarantee success:

Quebec, 2nd Feb. 1865

My Dear Brit
    I was served last night at the suit of Adam Crooks & Co. with a summons in the County Court (of Toronto) upon three of the notes I took for Barton's debt.
    Meredith will show you the summons. As I cannot raise the funds to meet it — I thought it advisable to avoid increase of costs and allow judgement to be taken. This painful situation will overtake me sooner or later and the consequences that . . . are about to enshroud me — it is discouraging.

Yours very truly,
Wm. Notman[25]

Shortly after writing this, Notman, who was then attending the winter sessions of the Canadian Legislative Assembly at Quebec, suffered an attack of what the newspapers cryptically termed "softening of the brain" and had to be brought back to Dundas.[26] Seven months later he was dead.[27]

Although practising law was obviously a risky business, Osler was able to survive, partly perhaps because his brother's firm sent him business. Although no firm records from this era seem to have survived, the Osler family papers in the Ontario Archives contain some correspondence from the early 1860s on Patton, Osler & Moss letterhead addressed to B.B. Osler in Dundas. Featherston Osler and his partners apparently used B.B. whenever they needed some legal work done in Dundas. Similarly, Britton Bath Osler listed his brother's firm as his Toronto agent in the *Law List*.

For three years, B.B. Osler practised on his own in a small office on Main Street in Dundas.[28] It is not entirely clear what his practice consisted of, but he was apparently successful enough to get married in 1863. Interestingly, he and Featherston, the brother with whom he was very close, married sisters. Featherston married Henrietta Smith of nearby Ancaster in 1861, and two years later Britton Bath married her sister Caroline.[29]

Because no office records survive, it is impossible to reconstruct Osler's early practice. It is, however, most likely that his practice was much like that of other small town Canadian lawyers of the time. If that was the case, he would have been a general practitioner dealing in property conveyancing, personal matters such as estates, and some litigation. It certainly appears from evidence of later years that he took an early liking to litigation, as some of this work is shown in the case reports of the time.

His first reported case involved a patent dispute. In 1868, he represented a defendant accused of infringement of a patent for a direct-drive, water-powered saw mill. In his submission at trial, Osler claimed that the original patent was not valid because it represented only a simple improvement on existing methods. Although he lost the suit, the jury awarded only one dollar to the plaintiff in damages.[30]

Osler was also involved in a particularly distasteful bit of litigation in 1871. The case of *In Re: Hutchison And The Board of School Trustees of St. Catharines* arose when a black student was refused admission to a public school. When Richard Hutchison's thirteen-year-old son was turned away from the local public school in St. Catharines, he filed suit against the school board.

Acting for the school board, Osler argued that the Common Schools Act, which granted the board the authority to establish any "kind or description of schools," gave it the power to dictate a racially segregated school system.[31] He further argued that, as the local school which had turned young Hutchison away was already overcrowded and the so-called "colored school" on the other side of town was not, the board was legally justified in its decision. The underlying basis of Osler's argument was painfully clear, however, when he submitted an affidavit from the Local Superintendent of Schools stating that "compelling the trustees to admit the colored children of the town into the several ward schools at the present time would be attended with evil consequences from a sanitary point of view.''[32]

But Justice J.C. Morrison, who wrote the judgement for the Court of Queen's Bench, rejected this argument:

> We see no reason why, because the applicant's son happens to be colored, that on that account he should be refused admittance to a common school situate in the ward in which his family resides, and most convenient for his child to go to, upon the same terms as his neighbor's children, and that he should be restricted to one school where only colored children are taught.

With respect to Osler's argument for a permissive interpretation of the school board's powers under the Common Schools Act, Justice Morrison also found that,

> We cannot entertain any doubt that the Legislature never intended by the expression ''kind'' of schools used in that subsection to mean or provide that the trustees could determine that in any particular school only children of any particular race should be admitted. If so, then upon the same reasoning the trustees might order that in certain schools none but natives of Scotland or Ireland, &c., or the children of parents of such and such religious sects, should be educated in certain schools, a system and powers totally at variance with the principles upon which our common school legislation is founded. We read the words ''kind and description of schools,'' as used in that subsection, as being more applicable and as referring to the plan and materials upon and of which the schools may be constructed.[33]

Had Morrison stopped at that point, his judgement might have been a remarkable expression of tolerance for nineteenth-century Canada, but he was not about to offend the sensibilities of white Ontario, or the autonomy of the St. Catharines school board, by forcing it to admit a black child into a public school. He came up with a solution to this dilemma by accepting the board's contention that there simply wasn't any room for the boy in the public school. Perhaps to sooth his conscience, however, Morrison ruled that the entire cost of the application be borne by the school board.[34]

The fact that the school board's decision to refuse a black child admission to the public school was racist, as was its legal argument in defence of the decision, should not be surprising. Nineteenth-century white Canadians were, on the whole, intolerant. This is not to justify their actions, but merely to place them in context. As Chapter Two describes, anti-French and anti-Roman Catholic sentiments were endemic among late nineteenth-century English-speaking Protestant Canadians, and very few would have argued in favour of complete equality of the races; it is highly unlikely that B.B. Osler was among those who would.

As a litigator, Osler might have been content to work on his own, but until he established a solid track record in the courtroom he wouldn't necessarily be able to count on regular briefs. Apparently, in an effort to maintain some form of steady income, he brought in a partner to do solicitor's work. In 1865, Osler was joined by a young man with the unlikely name of Theophilus H.A. Begue, and the two formed a firm known as Osler & Begue.

At the time, the Ontario legal profession was still divided — on paper at least — between an upper branch and a lower branch. Although today most lawyers still use the terms barrister and solicitor (particularly on letter head and business cards), the profession in Ontario, like most of the rest of Canada, is fused.[35] The terms are rooted in the English tradition, where barristers — the upper branch of the legal profession — are qualified to plead before the superior courts, but may not deal directly with clients; solicitors — the lower branch — provide direct legal advice to clients and act as intermediaries between clients and barristers when litigation becomes necessary.[36]

During the early nineteenth century, when the Upper Canadian legal profession, like the rest of the colonial society, was still in its formative stages, a number of lawyers who served in the provincial administration as well in the Law Society wanted to follow the home country's model and create a divided profession. In 1797, when the Law Society was established by statute, it was given authority over all branches of the legal profession; in 1822, the province passed another statute which took away the Law Society's authority over solicitors.[37] From then until 1857, the provincial government maintained authority over the lower branch of the profession while the Law Society was responsible for barristers only.

Unlike the system in England, where a lawyer may be either a barrister or solicitor, but not both, there was nothing in Upper Canadian law to prevent a man from practising as both. The admission requirements for each were different, but most lawyers in the province gained both qualifications. As the nineteenth century progressed, the number of lawyers who held only one or the other designation became smaller and smaller. In 1857, the Law Society regained authority over admission of attorneys and solicitors and began to reduce the differences between the qualification requirements.[38] Until 1889, when the Law Society founded its own law school at Osgoode Hall, there were separate examinations for admission to practice as a solicitor and for call to the bar. At that point, however, the benchers removed the remaining distinction between the two branches of the legal profession. Since then, all lawyers admitted to practice in Ontario have been qualified as both barristers and solicitors.[39]

During the 1860s, most Ontario lawyers were both barristers and solicitors. A small number wrote both examinations at the same time and were admitted to practice and called to the bar at the same time. Britton Bath Osler was among this group when he began practice in 1862. Most, like B.B.'s brother Featherston, wrote the barrister's exam a year or so after writing the solicitor's exam, but almost all obtained both qualifications.[40] Theophilus Begue, however, was only a solicitor.[41] After he was admitted to practice as a solicitor in the late fall of 1863, he either didn't write, or failed, the barrister's examination. When he joined Osler in 1865, therefore, he was not qualified to appear in court. Presumably Begue looked after the solicitor files in the office and Osler focused his efforts more on litigation.

A year after the formation of Osler & Begue, when Osler's brother Edward finally gained admission to practice, B.B. opened an office in Hamilton for him. Not surprisingly, given the trouble Edward had with the law student's entrance exam, he also had great difficulty with the final examination for admission to practice. In May 1866, Britton wrote to Featherston: ''Edward is going up soon for his Exam. which I sincerely trust he will pass this time. It will be such a relief to us all.''[42] In fact, he did pass the solicitor's examination but, wisely, apparently did not attempt the barrister's exam. Like Theophilus Begue, therefore, Edward was a solicitor only.

Part of the reason B.B. Osler opened the office in Hamilton was to give his younger brother a job; then, as in later years, family considerations played a large part in the firm's growth, but if that was the only factor in his decision he could have simply put him at a desk in the office in Dundas. It is likely that Osler had wanted to branch out from Dundas for some time; he would be able to attract some litigation clients in Dundas, but the Wentworth County Court and the assizes were seven miles away in Hamilton.

It was not uncommon for law firms to branch out from one centre and establish another office in a nearby town. The main office was usually located in the larger centre, and the branch office was opened in a smaller town. The branch office would be manned by junior lawyers or even students, and the senior lawyers would remain in the main office, travelling to the branch office only when necessary. In this case, Osler was doing things the other way around. His Hamilton office was manned by the junior in the firm — his brother — but he was moving up rather than down in terms of size of community.

In addition to having the courts, Hamilton was also a much larger centre and offered greater opportunities for general legal work. As a major port at the western end of Lake Ontario and a railway terminus, it served a multi-county hinterland. It also had a population of close to 16,000 compared to Dundas's 3,200. At the same time, however, the competition in Hamilton was probably much stiffer. With forty-five lawyers in town, Hamilton's ratio of lawyers to population was roughly 355:1. Dundas, with only five lawyers, had a ratio of 640:1.[43]

The fact that Osler decided to open a Hamilton office manned by his brother Edward is, therefore, perhaps a little surprising. Edward was known as the black sheep of the family. Besides repeatedly failing his Law Society exams, five years after his brother set him up in practice he walked out on his wife and two small children, leaving them destitute. According to a family biographer, one of his daughters remembered her mother searching desperately for some letter of explanation, and even more desperately for the family savings, but those too had disappeared.[44] Shortly after that, Edward fled to what was then the frontier town of Winnipeg and tried to establish a practice there. He stayed in Manitoba for some twenty years, but never had any success at his practice. In 1895, he returned to Ontario to live with his recently widowed mother, but by that point he had apparently given up on law.[45]

Interestingly, the Hamilton office was not just a branch office of the Dundas firm. It was, in fact, a separate partnership. The firm in Dundas was still known as Osler & Begue; the Hamilton firm was Osler & Osler. Britton Bath Osler was the senior partner in both firms, but Begue was a member of only the Dundas firm and Edward Osler was a member of only the Hamilton firm. The senior Osler maintained his residence in Dundas, but presumably divided his time between the two offices. It was not uncommon at the time for lawyers to maintain partnerships in more than one firm. In the twentieth century, lawyers have tended to maintain exclusive partnerships, although the recent trend towards international partnerships such as Osler Renault bears some resemblance.

While Osler's practice was growing enough to bring in two more partners and expand to Hamilton, he still found time to be involved in local politics. He had learned at an early age that political connections were important, and during the late 1860s and early 1870s he sat on the Dundas Town Council as an alderman for the Canal Ward.[46] Although his legal papers from that era have, unfortunately, not survived, he undoubtedly included the town of Dundas among his growing list of clients.

Clearly, during those years Osler's firm was doing very well in both its Dundas and Hamilton offices, and in 1871 he was able to bring another family member into the firm. Herbert C. Gwyn, known as "Charlie" within the family, was a student in the Osler & Begue Dundas office when he and Osler's sister Charlotte were engaged. They were married a year after he was admitted to practice and joined the firm, which became known as Osler, Begue & Gwyn.[47]

Like Begue and Edward Osler, Gwyn was a solicitor only when he joined the firm. He was not called to the bar until 1876. Also like Edward Osler, H.C. Gwyn was not a terribly successful lawyer. He suffered from financial troubles throughout his career, and as some of B.B. Osler's private papers indicate, he was very often dependant on his brother-in-law's generosity to get by.[48] Gwyn was, of course, not the success that B.B. Osler was, but he was not nearly as much a failure as Edward Osler turned out to be. Perhaps at his brother-in-law's urging, he tried to maintain some political contacts. In fact, for a time he was the treasurer of the North Wentworth Conservative Association, and even served as mayor of Dundas for a year in 1887-88. By the turn of the century, he was also the town solicitor.[49]

After Gwyn joined the firm, it remained intact for two years. Britton Bath Osler, Theophilus Begue and Herbert Gwyn were in the Dundas office and Osler's brother Edward manned the Hamilton office; in July of 1873, however, Begue decided to leave the firm and practise on his own. Unfortunately, there is no evidence to indicate why Begue left. The *Law Lists* of the time indicate that he continued to practise on his own in Dundas for another thirty years before finishing his career in Hamilton, but the only explanation of the split appeared in a terse notice placed in the local newspaper on July 16, 1873:

Notice of Dissolution

The firm known . . . as Osler, Begue & Gwyn [is] dissolved by
mutual consent, Mr. Begue resigning from said firm. The business will be continued by B.B. Osler and H.C. Gwyn, under the
firm name of Osler & Gwyn. All liabilities of the late firm will
be paid by them and all accounts are to be settled by them.

B.B. Osler
T.H.A. Begue
H.C. Gwyn[50]

Perhaps as the only non-family member in the firm — including
Edward Osler in the Hamilton office — Begue felt like an outsider.
Certainly, family relationships played a significant role within the
firm for three more generations. But Begue may also have been
interested in becoming a litigation specialist, something which only
B.B. Osler was qualified to do in the firm; although Begue was still
a solicitor only when he left Osler, Begue & Gwyn in 1873, he was
called to the bar in the spring of 1876.

Seven months after Begue left, Osler had much more serious worries than the loss of one of his partners. In February of 1874, he
rescued his wife from a near fatal fire in their home in Dundas. Osler
apparently went down to the basement to investigate an odour of gas.
He was standing fifteen feet away from a gasoline-powered gas gen-
erator when it exploded. His hands and face were severely burned,
and by the time he made his way back upstairs, the main floor was
in flames. He managed to get himself, as well as his wife and their
house maid, both of whose clothes were on fire, out of the house.
The house was saved, and neither his wife nor the maid suffered
permanent injury, but Osler bore the scars of the fire on his hands
and face for the rest of his life.[51]

By the spring, Osler had fully recovered from the fire and he was
able to turn his energies back to his legal career. In April, he announced plans to build his own two-storey office building on Main
Street just down from the Dundas Town Hall, and in May he was
appointed a Crown attorney. Once again his political connections
may have been helpful; he had served for some time as secretary of
the North Wentworth Reform Association, which was the local Liberal riding association, and when Samuel Freeman, the Crown Attorney for Wentworth County, died, Osler was appointed to replace
him.[52] The Ontario provincial government, led by Oliver Mowat, was

Liberal at the time. It was still Liberal two years later when Osler received his appointment as Queen's Counsel.[53]

In the nineteenth century, the post of Crown Attorney was a part-time one; it did not mean that the incumbent had to give up his practice, and it was paid on a fee-for-service basis rather than by salary. It was a little like being appointed counsel to the Ministry of the Attorney-General to prosecute criminal trials.

While Osler was spending increasing amounts of his time in court, he was not devoting all of his energy to his legal practice. He was taking his earnings and becoming an active investor. In addition to the office building on Main Street in Dundas, in 1875 he and his brother Edmund started a very ambitious project — they incorporated the Hamilton and Dundas Railway Company. As a regular commuter between his offices in Dundas and Hamilton, B.B. Osler knew there was a market for a passenger rail line between the two centres, but the capital outlay for such a project must have been substantial. Nevertheless, the brothers obviously had the ability to raise the amount required, because by 1879 the line was operating.[54]

In the meantime, Britton Bath Osler's work in Hamilton was sufficient to justify selling his Dundas home to his brother-in-law H.C. Gwyn and moving to Hamilton in 1876. This was the first of Osler's two career moves to successively larger centres. He made the choice to set up shop in his home town when he started out in 1862, but by 1876 his practice had outgrown the small centre. Six years later he would make another, much more significant move.

The move to Hamilton was partly prompted by Edward's departure for Manitoba; B.B. Osler took over the Hamilton office, but he brought in another lawyer to take his place in Dundas. Alexander Stronach Wink, who was admitted to practice as a solicitor in 1870 and called to the bar in 1875, joined the Dundas office in 1876. The firm was then known as Osler, Gwyn & Wink. Wink, however, stayed with the firm for only four years, and by 1880 it was once again Osler & Gwyn, with Herbert Gwyn managing the Dundas office and B.B. Osler operating the one in Hamilton.[55]

The year 1880 was significant for Osler also because he was elected a bencher of the Law Society of Upper Canada. In addition to success in his practice, he was gaining recognition within the profession. Throughout his career, Osler was involved in activities to promote his profession. He remained a bencher from 1880 until his death in 1901, and in 1885 he helped found the County of York Law Association. He also served as this organization's first president.[56]

Some time during the following year, Osler decided to bring in another partner, and he offered a position in the Hamilton office to James Vernal Teetzel. Teetzel, who later became a judge of the High Court of Ontario, had been practising in Hamilton since his call to the bar in 1877. He was also a Liberal; he served as mayor of Hamilton from 1899 to 1901 and ran unsuccessfully as a Liberal in the riding of Hamilton in the federal election of 1900.[57]

As Osler, Gwyn & Teetzel, the firm was very prosperous. In 1882, Osler recorded its steadily rising income in the back of his appointment book. In the first year after Osler moved to Hamilton, the firm earned just over $11,000. In 1878 and 1879, its earnings were in excess of $14,000; in 1880, topped $15,000; and in 1881, the figure was almost $19,000.[58]

Even while his law firm was prospering, Osler was involved in other things. The Hamilton and Dundas Railway, of which he was still president, was very successful; in 1882 it grossed over $21,000.[59] And he was still involved in politics. In the spring of 1882, the Liberal Association of the riding of Welland persuaded him to run in the upcoming federal general election. It was not, however, a good year to be a Liberal in Canada. The country was enjoying a time of prosperity after the recession of the 1870s, and the Conservative government of Prime Minister John A. Macdonald was taking the credit.

Macdonald had been in power since 1878, when he recovered the office he lost after the Canadian Pacific Railway Scandal in 1873. Liberal leader Alexander Mackenzie, who had served as prime minister from 1873 until 1878, had retired in 1880. He was replaced as leader by a very reluctant Edward Blake, the patriarch of the Toronto law firm of Blake, Kerr, Lash & Cassels.[60]

When Macdonald dissolved Parliament on May 18, 1882, there were 137 Conservatives and 69 Liberals in the 206-seat House of Commons. When the votes were counted on the evening of June 20, 1882, Macdonald had increased his Conservative majority to 139, and Blake had only 71 Liberals in the expanded 210-seat House.[61] The Liberals did gain eight seats in Ontario, but Welland was not one of them. Osler lost to the Conservative candidate, a medical doctor from Niagara Falls named John Ferguson; Osler polled 1,833 votes but Ferguson polled 1,965.[62]

Whether his election disappointment had anything to do with it is not clear, but very shortly afterward B.B. Osler decided to make another significant career move. In September of 1882, he moved his practice to Toronto and formed a partnership which very quickly became one of the most successful law firms in Canada.

CHAPTER

2

THE COMPACT: 1882-1902

Britton Bath Osler's move to Toronto in 1882 was, perhaps, predictable. As his career as a courtroom lawyer progressed, it was only natural that he would gravitate towards the next larger judicial centre. He began in Dundas, moved on to Hamilton, where the county court and assizes sat, and finally to Toronto, the home of the provincial superior courts. It was undoubtedly the increased availability of litigation work which prompted his moves, but at each level his firm maintained a diversified workload with both general solicitor's and barrister's files. As his reputation — and income — from courtroom work grew, so too did the firm's corporate client list. It was litigation that made his personal career, but as the following chapters show, in the long run it was corporate counselling that made his firm.

The man with whom Osler went into partnership was one of the few Canadian lawyers of the late nineteenth century who would rank as his equal. At forty-five, D'Alton McCarthy was two and a half years older than B.B. Osler when they formed McCarthy, Osler, Hoskin & Creelman in 1882. McCarthy was born near Dublin in 1836; his father was an Irish barrister, but was apparently not particularly successful because he decided to emigrate to Canada when D'Alton was a child. The family settled near Barrie, Upper Canada — not far from the Oslers — and the senior McCarthy tried his hand at farming. He was apparently not terribly successful at this either, because in 1855 he decided to go back to his old profession and was admitted to practice as a solicitor in Upper Canada.

Three years later D'Alton McCarthy took his call to the bar and joined his father in a small practice in Barrie. It is quite likely that B.B. Osler knew McCarthy at the time because his brother Featherston was an articling student in Barrie when McCarthy began his practice. At the time there were only two three-man law firms and two sole practitioners in Barrie.[1] McCarthy remained in Barrie until 1879 when he moved to Toronto, like Osler in search of more litigation work.

Although still a relatively young man, by 1882 McCarthy was generally acknowledged as one of the most prominent appellate counsel in the country. In that year, he appeared in no less than twelve of the seventy-five appeals reported in the *Ontario Reports*.[2] He was first elected as a bencher of the Law Society of Upper Canada in 1871 and he became a Q.C. in 1872. But while McCarthy made an impressive mark in the courts, he made a much more public reputation for himself as a politician. A Conservative, he sat as a member of the House of Commons from 1878 until his death in 1898. He was very influential in the Conservative Party, and during the 1880s he was widely touted as a likely successor to John A. Macdonald, although despite Macdonald's urging he never accepted a cabinet position, choosing instead to devote most of his time to his lucrative law practice.[3]

In politics, McCarthy was best known as the strident champion of Anglo-Protestantism in a series of clashes between French and English interests during the 1880s and 1890s. McCarthy would have felt quite at home in the late twentieth-century debate over language rights in Canada. Unlike the modern situation, however, where the particularly virulent Anglo-Canadian backlash against francophone self-determination was limited, during McCarthy's time anti-French sentiment was very widespread; it was not only socially acceptable in English-speaking Canada, it was a real political force. More than anyone else, D'Alton McCarthy personified that force.

In addition, unlike today's language rights debate, which is entirely secular in nature, the French-English battles of late nineteenth-century Canada were religious as well as linguistic. Multiculturalism is very much a creature of recent decades in Canada. D'Alton McCarthy and his followers, who on this issue were probably among the majority of English-speaking Canadians, saw the ideal Canada as a unilingual English Protestant member of the British Empire. McCarthy in particular saw the political partnership of English and French Canadians in the Conservative Party under John A. Macdonald and Hector Langevin as a necessary, but hopefully temporary, evil. He very strongly argued that French Catholic interests be granted no concessions beyond those which were politically unavoidable.

He undoubtedly held these views during the early years of his career at Barrie when the Legislative Assembly of the old Province of Canada passed the Scott Act granting extensive government concessions to Roman Catholic separate schools in Upper Canada in 1863, and when the British North America Act embodied the terms of Confederation in 1867.[4] He did not enter politics, however, until 1872, when he ran as a Conservative in his home riding of North Simcoe in the second federal general election after Confederation. Although Prime Minister John A. Macdonald's Conservatives won a majority of seats in the House of Commons, D'Alton McCarthy's was not one of them.[5]

McCarthy tried again two years later, when the Pacific Railway scandal precipitated another election. This time he lost again, but so did a majority of other Conservatives, and Macdonald sat as leader of the opposition while Alexander Mackenzie led Canada's first Liberal government. In 1876, when long-time Conservative John Hillyard Cameron died, McCarthy won the resulting by-election in Cardwell, northwest of Toronto, and joined Macdonald on the opposition benches.[6]

In the 1878 general federal election, Macdonald was returned to power and McCarthy joined him, this time representing his home riding of North Simcoe. Rather than join Macdonald's cabinet, however, McCarthy chose to focus his energies on his growing legal practice. By 1877, he had branched out from his Barrie office and opened an office in Toronto; he continued to live in Barrie for two more years, but in 1879 he moved to Toronto.[7] He continued to represent North Simcoe at Ottawa, however, as he did until his death in 1898.

The reason for Osler's and McCarthy's decision to go into partnership in 1882 is not as clear as it may seem. On the surface, the motivation seems obvious; they would be uniting two of the most lucrative counsel practices in the country. There is no reason to assume, however, that this in itself would increase their income; in fact, it may have tended to decrease their litigation opportunities because it would create conflict situations. As partners, they would not be able to appear against each other in court.

The real reason for their decision to come together had more to do with laying a foundation for an equally lucrative corporate practice. In July of 1882, the Canadian Pacific Railway set up a separate company — the Canada North-West Land Company — to distribute 25 million acres of western land promised it by the Canadian government under the contract to build a transcontinental railway.[8] With an initial capitalization of $3 million, the new company would represent a very prestigious account for whoever did its legal work.

The Canada North-West Land Company was originally incorporated in England, and the London solicitors firm of Freshfields & Williams did its initial legal work; however, much of the company's activities would take place in Canada, and it would need a Canadian law firm. One of the two Canadian managing directors was Edmund Osler, and he apparently sought to have his brother appointed Canadian solicitor to the company.[9] B.B. Osler was a very prominent counsel, but he was practising in Hamilton and didn't have the right political connections. If he could form a partnership with a Toronto lawyer who did have the right connections, however, the deal might go through.

On August 23, 1882, B.B. Osler and D'Alton McCarthy met at McCarthy's office in Toronto and agreed to go into partnership, and eight days later, on September 1, the new firm of McCarthy, Osler, Hoskin & Creelman came into being.[10] On the same day, the newly created firm received the Canada North-West Land Company's retainer.[11] Interestingly enough, only two months earlier Osler and McCarthy had been candidates on opposite sides of a federal election campaign — Osler as a Liberal in Welland and McCarthy as a Conservative in North Simcoe — but they obviously had enough in common to establish a very lucrative law partnership. Most likely Osler was not as strong a Liberal as McCarthy was a Conservative. In fact, after 1882, Osler consistently described himself as a political Independent, and in 1896 he declined Conservative Prime Minister Sir Charles Tupper's invitation to join his cabinet as minister of justice.[12]

McCarthy and Osler were obviously the leaders, but the firm had four other members, two of whom were included in its name. Like McCarthy and Osler, John Hoskin was in his forties and was a Queen's Counsel, but unlike his two illustrious partners, he was not a courtroom specialist. Hoskin was born in Devon, England in 1836, and emigrated to Canada when he was eighteen. There is, unfortunately, no evidence to indicate what career he tried at first, but like B.B. Osler, in 1858 he decided to go into law.

Because Hoskin, unlike Osler, did not have a university education, the Law Society rules required that he apprentice himself to a practising solicitor for five years, and he entered a local barrister's office in Bowmanville, just east of Toronto, as an articling student. In 1860, however, like Osler, he decided to move to Toronto and continue his articling period there. He was called to the bar in 1863 and began practice in Toronto with the firm of Gwynne, Armour & Hoskin. His partners were John Wellington Gwynne, who later served on the Ontario court of Common Pleas and the Supreme Court of Canada, and Robert Armour, the lawyer whom he began with as a student in Bowmanville. Although Armour was a member of the firm, he apparently remained in Bowmanville and continued a separate practice there.

Gwynne, Armour & Hoskin lasted only five years and, when John Gwynne was appointed to the Common Pleas in 1868, Hoskin set out on his own. He practised by himself in Toronto for ten years and built up a substantial practice in corporate law and estates. He was appointed Queen's Counsel in 1873, and in 1876 he was first elected a bencher of the Law Society of Upper Canada. It was through his activities with the Law Society that he probably first came in contact with D'Alton McCarthy, who was also first elected as a bencher in 1876. At any rate, a year later McCarthy asked Hoskin to join him in a firm he was planning to set up in Toronto.

In Hoskin's work in the estates field he was often appointed by the Court of Chancery as a guardian *ad litem* to act on behalf of otherwise unprotected infant estate holders in litigation affecting their interests. In 1881, when the Judicature Act created the office of Official Guardian, he was appointed the first incumbent. Like Osler's earlier work as a Crown attorney, Hoskin's position as Official Guardian was a fee-for-service appointment, and the fees he earned for this work were pooled with those of the rest of the firm and divided among the partners according to their partnership agreement.[13]

The fourth member of the firm, and the last of those included in the firm name, was Adam Rutherford Creelman. Creelman was born at Richibucto, New Brunswick on September 21, 1849. Sometime in the 1860s, his family moved to Ontario. When Creelman decided to go into law, he found an articling position with Adam Crooks, who later held various cabinet posts in successive Ontario Liberal governments. Creelman, who was called to the bar in 1875, practised at first with Adam Crooks in a firm known as Crooks, Kingsmill & Cattanach in Toronto, but in 1877 joined Hoskin in McCarthy's new firm. Unlike McCarthy, Osler and Hoskin, Creelman was purely a corporate specialist. In fact, soon after McCarthy, Osler, Hoskin & Creelman was formed in 1882, he took on much of the day-to-day work for the Canada North-West Land Company. The two junior partners in the firm were Thomas Plumb, who was thirty-two years old and had been in practice in Toronto since his call in 1876, and William H.P. Clement, who was twenty-four and had been called to the bar in 1880.

There was also one young man who occupied what would in the twentieth century be called an associate lawyer's position with the firm. Frederick Weir Harcourt acted as John Hoskin's assistant on Official Guardian matters. Harcourt was a large, burly man, who was very fond of sports. Born in June, 1854 near the village of York on the banks of the Grand River in Haldimand County south of Hamilton, he played flying wing for the Hamilton Tigers football team and rowed for the Hamilton Rowing Club.[14]

Harcourt came from a very distinguished political family. His father, Michael Harcourt, represented Haldimand in the old Canadian Assembly prior to Confederation, and his older brother Richard sat in the Ontario Legislature from 1878 until 1908, serving as minister of education from 1899 until 1905. Unlike his father and brother, however, Frederick Harcourt was apparently not interested in politics.

Harcourt began his legal career in 1875 as an articling student with the Hamilton firm of Burton & Bruce. Like Hoskin, he did not hold a university degree, and would, therefore, have to article for five years before entering practice. Shortly thereafter, however, he moved to Toronto, and finished his articles with John Hoskin. He was admitted to practice as a solicitor in February 1880, but apparently did not write the barrister's examination until 1886, when he was called to the bar.

Although Harcourt later became very prominent in the profession and served as Official Guardian after Hoskin's retirement in 1902 and as Treasurer of the Law Society of Upper Canada during the 1920s, he did not become a partner in the firm until 1901. Prior to that date he was paid a fixed salary, initially by Hoskin out of his share of the firm's profits, and after Harcourt's call to the bar in 1886, by the firm directly.[15]

McCarthy and Osler were clearly the leaders of the firm in terms of their expected contribution to revenue because they were to take the greatest share of the firm's profits. Under the articles of partnership establishing the firm on September 1, 1882, its profits were to be divided into 130 shares. Of those, McCarthy was to receive forty-eight, Osler thirty-four, Hoskin twenty-two, Creelman thirteen, Plumb eight, and Clement five.[16] During its first year of operation, the new firm earned a net profit of some $55,000. McCarthy's share of this was over $20,000, Osler's was $14,400, Hoskin's $9,300, Creelman's $5,500, Plumb's $3,400, and Clement's $2,100.

It is not clear what other lawyers earned at the time, but by any estimation these were substantial incomes. At the same time a common labourer in Ontario could expect to earn about $350 per year if he was lucky enough to work all fifty-two weeks. A skilled worker like a millwright would earn about $650.[17] Today, an annual income comparable to McCarthy's of 1882 would be close to a million dollars. Moreover, prior to 1917, there was no income tax in Canada.

Although it is not clear what lawyers at other firms earned in 1882, with six lawyers McCarthy, Osler, Hoskin & Creelman was certainly one of the largest firms in Toronto. Only two firms in the city were larger. Blake, Kerr, Lash & Cassels, the predecessor of the modern Blake, Cassels & Graydon, had nine lawyers, including Edward Blake, the Leader of the Liberal Party of Canada; and Featherston Osler's old firm of Bethune, Moss, Falconbridge & Hoyles had seven, including two future chief justices of Ontario and a future principal of the law school at Osgoode Hall.[18]

The majority of Toronto lawyers practised on their own or in two-man partnerships in 1882. Of the 284 lawyers in the city, 111 were sole practitioners and sixty-four practised with one other partner. There were fifteen three-man firms, eight four-man firms, and two had five partners. This pattern remained roughly the same over the next twenty years. In the *Law Lists* of 1882, 1892, and 1902, roughly 60 per cent of Toronto lawyers were in one or two-man firms, about one-third practised in firms with from three to six partners, and 5 per cent to 7 per cent were members of firms with more than six lawyers. In each case, McCarthy, Osler, Hoskin and Creelman was in the largest group of firms, but it was always slightly smaller than Blake's.[19]

The firm's main office was in the Temple Chambers, number 23 Toronto Street. The building was on the east side of the street, just around the corner from the York County Court House, which was on the south side of Adelaide Street, between Toronto and Church Streets.[20] In addition to the Toronto office, McCarthy, Osler, Hoskin & Creelman also opened an office in Regina to look after local conveyancing work for the Canada North-West Land Company. Although this office had its own letterhead, it was manned only by John Hoskin's younger brother Richard, who was neither a barrister nor a solicitor.[21] The land company paid Hoskin's salary and all of the office expenses.[22]

In addition to the main Toronto office and the Regina branch office, McCarthy and Osler maintained a professional presence in the cities where they practised before moving to Toronto. Interestingly, it seems that law firms of the late nineteenth century were more like co-ventureships than exclusive partnerships. Under the firm's first partnership agreement, both McCarthy and Osler were permitted to retain membership in their Barrie and Hamilton/Dundas firms, and their income from those firms would not be included with that of the new firm. The agreement also included a clause indicating that "it is understood so long as [McCarthy] continues to be a Member of the House of Commons of Canada he is to be permitted to attend the Sessions of that House."[23]

The time McCarthy spent on politics must have been more than his partners anticipated, however, because in the next partnership agreement, signed May 1, 1886, his share in the profits was reduced from 48/130 to 48/140, and he was required to pay back ten of his forty-eight shares "if and so long as [he] shall continue to be a Member of the House of Commons of Canada." Similarly, Osler was forbidden to enter politics and agreed "that he will not during the term of these Articles become a candidate to election as a Member of the House of Commons of Canada or of the Legislature of Ontario."[24] Political connections were valuable, but it was apparently also important to place limits on what today would be termed non-chargeable time.[25]

For this and other reasons, the new firm prospered. In the first few years after 1882, the Canadian economy was in a boom period. Much of this economic growth was attributable to an explosion in railway construction, not least of which was the Canadian Pacific project. This expansion of the transportation network was accompanied by a boom in manufacturing within Macdonald's protective National Policy tariff wall, and both sectors contributed to a tremendous demand for financing. Then, as now, lawyers and law firms took an active, and lucrative, part in this corporate expansion.

The firm's ledger books indicate that its corporate clients during these years included banks, railways and shipping companies, insurance companies, lumber companies, and industrial interests. During the early years, the largest account was, predictably, the Canada North-West Land Company, and although it remained one of the firm's most important clients, over the course of the next two decades other corporate clients, particularly the lumber companies, became even more valuable.

While the firm's corporate accounts were growing, so too were its more traditional litigation accounts. McCarthy and Osler continued to take on counsel work and appeared in trials throughout the courts, from relatively minor local disputes all the way to the Privy Council in London. The account books show that the firm acted in a total of twenty-six disputed election cases arising out of the February, 1883 Ontario election; they also indicate that the St. Catharines Milling and Lumber Company paid $3,500 in 1887 and $5,500 in 1888 to have McCarthy take its case against the Ontario government to the Privy Council.[26]

Although McCarthy ultimately lost this battle with Ontario premier Oliver Mowat, he further aided his own, and his firm's, growing reputation for high-profile constitutional and corporate litigation. At the same time, however, both he and Osler were continuing to build their general legal reputation — and in the process making sure their names would be known to prospective clients — by taking part in a number of sensational trials. In 1882 alone, McCarthy got acquittals for the defendants in three murder trials.[27] In an age before mass electronic media, murder trials were an even greater source of public entertainment than they are today, and the lawyers taking part very often became celebrities.

In one of these trials, McCarthy defended a seventeen-year-old Dufferin County boy accused of murdering his uncle. In January the man had been killed and his farmhouse set on fire. His nephew, who lived with him, claimed that shots had been fired through an open window and couldn't account for the fire. He was known to have purchased a pistol some days prior to the murder, but the weapon was never found. Some cartridges and an empty pistol box were found near the remains of the house, but a box alleged to have contained some $10,000 belonging to his uncle was missing. The coroner testified that the man had been beaten to death with a club, but no blood was found on the boy's clothes or money in his pockets. In spite of this somewhat damning evidence, when the case came up for trial before Osler's brother Featherston, McCarthy was able to convince the Court that Aemelius Irving, who appeared for the Crown, had not proved his case, and the boy was acquitted.[28]

In another trial, McCarthy gained an acquittal for a brother and sister charged with murder while apparently defending the woman's honour. In August 1882, Chester and Maria Spearman of Ottawa were charged with the murder of Robert McCaffrey, who had been found shot in the heart. Maria Spearman confessed to having fired the shot, but claimed that McCaffrey had seduced her under promise of marriage. When she and her brother had confronted him "with the intention of inducing him to fulfil the engagement," she took out a rifle and pointed it at him. When McCaffrey tried to wrench it from her grasp, it discharged. McCarthy was able to convince the jury that the woman was telling the truth, and she and her brother were acquitted.[29]

During the same years, Osler was involved in equally public and sensational trials. In 1883, he represented A.H. Marsh, Prime Minister John A. Macdonald's law partner, in a suit against L.U.C. Titus, an infamous solicitor from Brighton, Ontario. In 1882, Titus had defended Marsh's aunt, Miss Harriett Wright of Belleville, on a charge of murder. She had shot a man whom she believed to have broken into her house. When the trial began, Titus told Miss Wright that there were other ways besides "legitimate ways to manage these things." He then asked her for one hundred dollars "to salt the jury with." Later in the trial, he asked for a further hundred dollars because only three jurors had been "fixed" with the first hundred.

His efforts at jury tampering apparently failed, however, because Wright was convicted. She was later pardoned, but in the meantime Titus accepted a retainer from the family of the man she shot in a civil action for wrongful death.

Marsh, quite understandably, accused Titus of unprofessional conduct and threatened to have him disbarred for conflict of interest and jury tampering. Titus replied by laying a formal criminal charge against Marsh of sending a threatening letter. This resulted in Marsh's arrest, but when the charge was dismissed Marsh retained B.B. Osler and sued Titus for unlawful arrest. Osler obtained a verdict of $500 for his client, and in a separate action before the discipline committee of the Law Society, Titus was disbarred.[30]

The Titus affair was, of course, widely reported in the press, as was a celebrated murder trial in Huron County a year later. A long-standing feud between two farm families near Blyth apparently erupted into deadly violence in May 1884. In the brawl between William Maines and James Beamish and their sons, Maines was killed. Beamish and his two sons were charged with murder and hired B.B. Osler to represent them. At the trial, which took place in Goderich in September, Osler kept his clients from the gallows, but all three were convicted of the reduced charge of manslaughter. Beamish and his oldest son were sentenced to twenty years in prison, and the younger son received a sentence of five years.[31]

These sensational trials probably did not bring in much direct income to the firm.[32] What the firm did gain, however, from the two senior partners' involvement in these highly publicized trials, was recognition. How important this type of recognition was in the firm's attraction of clients during this period cannot be accurately measured, but it was undoubtedly of some influence. Whatever the reason, the firm's net income increased from $55,000 in 1882-83 to $70,000 in 1883-84, and almost $80,000 in 1884-85.

One of the most significant events of the 1880s for Canada was the ill-fated North-West Rebellion of 1885. The resulting trial of Louis Riel for treason was, likewise, one of the most significant events for McCarthy, Osler, Hoskin & Creelman. Although the federal government paid a total fee of less than $6,000 to Osler for his role in the prosecution, while during the same year (1885-86) he contributed four times as much to the firm's income, the value of the public recognition he received was probably much greater for both himself and the firm.

Louis Riel was one of the great symbols in Canadian history. In life he represented the clash between the native frontier and the relentless westward march of European settlement; in death he represented the clash between French and English Canada. As a Métis, a people descended from French fur traders and Native women, he led two separate rebellions which tried to stop the expansion of settlement into the Prairies.[33]

In November 1869, shortly after the Canadian government took over the territory known as Rupert's Land (which included all of the land north of the U.S. border between Ontario and British Columbia) from the Hudson's Bay Company, Riel and his supporters occupied Fort Garry (Winnipeg) and established a provisional government which denied Canadian authority in the region. They held the fort and acted as the local authority throughout the winter, largely because in the era before the transcontinental railway Canadian military authorities were unable to travel there to dislodge the rebels.

Riel knew that he could not hold out against a military force once spring came, so he negotiated with the federal government for terms which would grant his people some guarantee that they could continue their lifestyle under the new Canadian authority. In March 1870, however, he made a colossal error which would eventually bring about his own death.

Not all of the residents of the Red River settlement surrounding Fort Garry sympathized with Riel's provisional government. There was a small, but very vocal, minority known as the Canadian Party. Primarily English-speaking immigrants from Ontario, they wanted a British government in the territory, and more importantly, they wanted the land which the Métis were occupying. The most vocal of these was an Ontario Orangeman named Thomas Scott.

Scott was among a group of men who tried to storm the fort and were taken prisoner. He was a particularly unruly prisoner, continually insulting and provoking his guards, and even threatening to kill Riel. Scott was put on trial by the provisional government and sentenced to death. Riel, either to ''make Canada respect us,'' as he later claimed, or as some historians have surmised, to maintain his own authority within the settlement, upheld the sentence, and Scott was shot by a firing squad on March 4, 1870.

In the end, Canada did respect the Métis government; at least, Prime Minister John A. Macdonald continued to negotiate with it. He did not do this, however, because he respected a government which could carry out an execution; he did it because he wanted to pacify the west without having to resort to a very expensive military occupation. The result of these negotiations was the Manitoba Act of 1870, which granted the Red River settlement provincial status, and provided to some degree cultural and land tenure guarantees for the Métis. Riel, however, fearful of being charged with treason or for the killing of Scott, fled to the United States when the Canadian militia arrived in the early summer.

Riel spent the next fifteen years in various forms of exile. He returned to Manitoba in 1873 and was elected to Parliament, and in 1874 he even stole into Ottawa and signed the Members' register, but fled before he could be arrested.

During the mid-1870s, he began to experience religious visions and became convinced that God had chosen him ''prophet of the New World.'' Not surprisingly, he spent the months between March 1876 and February 1878 in two different insane asylums in Quebec. In 1881, Riel moved back to the American plains and taught at a mission school in Montana. He also married and began a family.

During the 1870s, despite the guarantees of the Manitoba Act and the government's assurances that the Métis would maintain their land in the Red River settlement, the new province of Manitoba was overrun by English-speaking settlers, and the Métis were quickly displaced. They retreated further west, and tried to maintain their lifestyle in what would later become Saskatchewan. By the mid-1880s, however, western settlement was encroaching there as well.

In the summer of 1884, therefore, Gabriel Dumont, the Métis leader in the Batoche area, travelled to Montana to ask Louis Riel to return to lead them again. To Riel this was the fulfilment of his prophecy.

He travelled with Dumont back to Canada and began his mission. His first tactics were like those he employed during the Red River rebellion fifteen years earlier; he began to negotiate with the federal government. In December 1884, he sent a petition to Ottawa calling on the government to redress a number of Métis grievances. Macdonald, once again prime minister after his brief term in opposition during the 1870s, acknowledged receipt of the petition, but made no promise of action.

Riel waited throughout the winter, but in March he established another provisional government for the territory; he appointed himself as president and Gabriel Dumont as adjutant-general. He set up an armed camp at Batoche in hopes of duplicating his success at Red River a decade and a half earlier. Unfortunately for Riel and his supporters, he grossly underestimated the changes which had taken place during the interval.

In 1870, Riel and his rebels were relatively safe in Fort Garry because it was hundreds of miles from any significant Canadian military forces. By 1885, however, a sizeable police force was stationed in the North-West, and more importantly a largely completed transcontinental railway provided quick transportation of more troops from the east if they were needed.[34]

On March 26, a band of armed Métis led by Gabriel Dumont engaged a contingent of North-West Mounted Police at Duck Lake, about midway between Saskatoon and Prince Albert. The Mounties were routed and retreated to Prince Albert. Shortly thereafter, a band of Crees led by Poundmaker attacked and laid siege to Battleford about a hundred miles west of Duck Lake, and a band led by Big Bear killed nine settlers near Frog Lake.

When word reached Ottawa, the government dispatched a force of some three thousand troops under the command of General Frederick Middleton. Because the railway provided swift transportation, Middleton and his troops were stationed in the west within a month. The two sides first met on April 24 at Fish Creek, just south of Duck Lake. This battle ended with no clear winner. A week later Middleton's forces relieved Battleford, but Poundmaker won a major battle at Cut Knife Hill.

The largest battle began on May 9 at Batoche, where Riel had established his headquarters. The fighting lasted three days, and ended when the Métis fighters ran out of ammunition and were overrun by Middleton's troops. On May 12, Riel and the other Métis leaders fled to the poplar bluffs north of Batoche in hopes of rallying their guerrilla forces, but this hope was quickly dispelled. On the night of the 13th, Gabriel Dumont began his flight to the United States, and Riel decided that he would surrender. If he couldn't win a military battle in the field he would win the political battle in the courtroom. Early in the morning on Friday, May 15, 1885, Louis Riel came out of the woods and surrendered to a passing police patrol.

He was taken to Middleton's camp, and from there a military escort of sixteen soldiers took him by river steamer to Saskatoon, and from Saskatoon overland by wagon to Moose Jaw. At first, Ottawa instructed the soldiers to deliver Riel to Winnipeg, but en route they received another telegram ordering that the prisoner be taken to Regina. The government decided, just in time, to have Riel tried in the territorial capital, where North-West law would apply, rather than at Winnipeg. Under the Manitoba Act, Riel would have a right to jury which was half francophone, and Prime Minister John A. Macdonald and Sir Alexander Campbell, his minister of justice, were not going to take any chances on an acquittal.

On May 23, Riel was placed in the custody of Inspector Richard Burton Deane, the commanding officer of the North-West Mounted Police barracks at Regina. He spent the next eight weeks there writing and praying; when he was allowed out to exercise in the barracks yard, he wore a ball and chain. As Inspector Deane explained to Ottawa, this was as much to assure any would-be assassin that there was no chance of escape as it was to confine his prisoner. Deane also observed later that he was convinced that Riel was ''cracked,'' as he watched him pour out religious poetry and letters and memoranda to various government officials. At one point, Riel even suggested that he be photographed holding the ball and chain, and the photographs be sold to raise money to support his wife and children.

For its part, the government wanted a quick trial and conviction. Macdonald wanted no part of Riel's planned political theatre — he wanted a scapegoat. If Macdonald and his ministers were to continue the country's westward growth and economic expansion, and more importantly maintain national unity, they had to prove that Riel was a traitor and bring the North-West under control. To do so, Macdonald chose two of the best lawyers in the country to lead the prosecution.

Christopher Robinson, the senior partner in the Toronto law firm Robinson, O'Brien, Gibson & Lefroy, had impeccable Tory credentials. Among other things, he was the son of Sir John Beverley Robinson, the architect of the Family Compact who had, coincidentally, served as Crown prosecutor in an early set of infamous treason trials, the Ancaster Assizes of 1814.[35]

Robinson was to lead the prosecution team, but to marshall the evidence and examine the witnesses, the government chose Britton Bath Osler. Although Osler's political stripe was not of great notice since his defeat as a Liberal candidate three years earlier, his reputation as a criminal prosecutor was much more important than his politics. The other three government lawyers were Deputy Minister of Justice G.W. Burbidge, Thomas-Chase Casgrain, a young partner in Sir Alexander Campbell's Montreal law firm, and D.L. Scott, the mayor of Regina.

Although Riel was penniless, he had some powerful, albeit personally self-interested, allies. The Quebec Liberals, led by Honoré Mercier, saw Riel as the ideal *nationaliste* symbol with which to attack their Conservative opponents. If they could portray Riel as the francophone martyr of the west, Macdonald and the Conservative Party, provincially and federally, would be the anglophone oppressors.

The defence was led by a brilliant criminal lawyer and member of the Quebec legislature, François-Xavier Lemieux. Lemieux, who would later serve as chief justice of Quebec, was assisted by Charles Fitzpatrick, the Quebec City lawyer who eventually served as federal minister of justice and later became chief justice of Canada. The other two defence counsel were James Greenshields, an established Montreal lawyer, and T.C. Johnstone, a Winnipeg lawyer who also later served on the Manitoba provincial judiciary.

The judge was Hugh Richardson, a sixty-four-year-old English immigrant who had practised law in Woodstock, Ontario for twenty five years before accepting a government posting as a territorial stipendiary magistrate. Although his judicial experience consisted mainly of police court public drunkenness charges, he had presided at one murder trial and a cannibalism trial. Also sitting with Richardson in the tiny courtroom was a territorial justice of the peace and a jury of six men.[36]

In fact, the trial was not held in a regular courtroom. Richardson's normal court was in the North-West Mounted Police barracks, but it was far too small, so the government rented an oversized office from the Canada North-West Land Company, undoubtedly with the assistance of Osler and Richard Hoskin. As it was, the space they had was very cramped. Richardson, the justice of the peace and the clerk sat at one end of the room, with the six jurors behind them. Directly across from the bench was a temporary prisoner's dock, and on either side of that the prosecution and defence tables. Jammed in every other square inch of space in the room were the dozens of press and spectators.

When the trial opened on the morning of Monday, July 20, 1885, the court clerk read the indictment, which was formally laid under the five-century-old Statute of Treasons of 1352. The indictment alleged that:

> Louis Riel, not . . . having the fear of God in his heart, but being moved and seduced by the instigation of the devil as a false traitor against our said Lady the Queen . . . together with . . . divers other false traitors . . . armed and arrayed in a warlike manner, that is to say with guns, rifles, pistols, bayonets, and other weapons, being then unlawfully, maliciously and traitorously assembled and gathered together against our said Lady the Queen most wickedly, maliciously and traitorously did levy and make war against our said Lady the Queen . . . and did then maliciously and traitorously attempt and endeavor by force and arms to subvert and destroy the constitution and government of this realm as by law established, and deprive and depose our said Lady the Queen of and from the style, honor and kingly name of the Imperial Crown of this realm, in contempt of our said Lady the Queen and her laws, to the evil example of all others in the like case offending . . . against the form of the statute in such case made and provided, and against the peace of our said Lady the Queen, her Crown and dignity.

The indictment contained six specific charges; there was one each for the skirmishes at Duck Lake, Fish Creek and Batoche, which identified Riel as,

> a subject of our Lady the Queen, not regarding the duty of his allegiance . . . and wholly withdrawing the allegiance, fidelity and obedience which every true and faithful subject of our Lady the Queen should and of right ought to bear towards our said Lady the Queen.

The final three were identical, but identified him as,

then living within the Dominion of Canada and under the protection of our Sovereign Lady the Queen, not regarding the duty
of his allegiance . . . and wholly withdrawing the allegiance,
fidelity and obedience which he should and of right ought to
bear towards our said Lady the Queen.

Robinson and Osler were covering their bases. Although Riel was
born in St. Boniface, under the British flag, during his exile in Montana he had taken out American citizenship. The government would
go after him both ways. If he was still a British subject, he was a
traitor. If he was an American citizen, he had illegally taken up arms
against the Crown. In either case, he was guilty.

After the indictment was read, the defence tried two different
motions to have the indictment thrown out. The first, that the court
did not have the constitutional jurisdiction to hear the case, Richardson quickly threw out by simply citing the current North-West Territories Act. The second, in which the defence claimed that the indictment was void because it failed to identify the prisoner as a citizen
of a specific country not then at war with Her Majesty, Richardson
also threw out, citing an 1866 case from Upper Canada involving one
of the Fenian raiders.[37]

After Richardson dismissed the defence's opening motions, Osler
called on the clerk to have the prisoner enter a plea, and Riel replied,
simply, "I have the honor to answer the court I am not guilty." After
some further procedural wrangling, the court adjourned for the day.
When they resumed the next morning, Fitzpatrick asked for a further
adjournment of a month to summon and prepare witnesses for the
defence. Richardson gave him a week.

When the trial resumed on Tuesday, July 28, Osler opened for the
Crown: "May it please your Honors, gentlemen of the jury: the
prisoner stands before you charged with the highest crime known to
the law, and you are charged with passing upon his life or death."[38]
He then went through a long and detailed outline of the facts the
Crown intended to prove — that Riel led his guerrilla warriors on
three separate occasions in attempts to subvert the legitimate authority
of the government.

For two days, the Crown brought forth a stream of witnesses,
including General Middleton, to document the case against Riel. The
only thing the defence could do to help their client was to prod the
witnesses to admit that Riel had acted strangely. They were going to
try to obtain an acquittal on the basis of insanity, but Riel would have

nothing to do with it. At one point, he tried to interject and question a witness directly in spite of his own lawyers' pleas that he be quiet. Osler calmly assured the court that the Crown had no objection to the prisoner examining the witness, but Richardson instructed Riel: "If there is any question not put to this witness which you think ought to be put, tell it to your counsel and they will say whether it should be put." After a brief adjournment, during which Fitzpatrick and the others threatened to resign the case if Riel did not sit quietly, he agreed.

On Thursday, July 30, the defence opened its case. The chief defence witnesses were two psychiatrists: Dr. François Roy, superintendent of the Beauport Asylum, where Riel had been a patient in the 1870s, and Dr. Daniel Clark of the Toronto Insane Asylum. Both testified that Riel was clearly a madman. Osler cross-examined the witnesses, and according to most observers succeeded in thoroughly discounting the defence of insanity.

With Roy on the stand, Osler questioned the doctor not only about Riel's mental health, but also about the administration of the Beauport Asylum. If he wasn't able to put a question in the jurymen's minds about the prisoner's insanity defence, he surely was able to taint the psychiatrist's credibility. The asylum was a private institution, which as Osler's questioning (when he could get it in over Fitzpatrick's objections) insinuated, and a subsequent Royal Commission's findings substantiated, returned a substantial profit for its investors and little more than brutality and neglect for its patients.[39]

When Clark took the witness box, Osler focused his questioning on the heart of the insanity defence. Under the M'Naghten rule, which provided the legal definition of insanity, an accused could be found not guilty if he did not understand the nature and quality of his act when he committed it; in other words, he did not know right from wrong. To everyone who had observed Riel, including the jury, he was a very clever man. Although Clark insisted that Riel was, in the doctor's professional opinion, insane, he admitted under Osler's intense cross-examination that the Métis leader's actions could be interpreted as a cunning deception. When Richardson excused Clark, the case was won.

On Friday, July 31, Fitzpatrick and Robinson presented closing arguments, and Richardson charged the jury late Friday afternoon and Saturday morning. At 2:15 p.m., the jury went out; an hour later, they were back. When all six were seated, the clerk asked: "Gentlemen, are you agreed upon your verdict? How say you, is the prisoner guilty or not guilty?'' The foreman, weeping visibly, answered simply, ''Guilty,'' but then he added, ''Your Honors, I have been asked by my brother jurors to recommend the prisoner to the mercy of the Crown.''

Richardson thanked them, and bluntly acknowledged their recommendation of mercy: ''I may say in answer to you that the recommendation which you have given will be forwarded in proper manner to the proper authorities.'' Robinson then asked: ''Do your Honors propose to pass sentence now? I believe the proper course is to ask the sentence of the court upon the prisoner.'' Richardson then looked toward the prisoner's box and asked: ''Louis Riel, have you anything to say why the sentence of the court should not be pronounced upon you, for the offence of which you have been found guilty?''

Riel took his opportunity to make the political speech he had been rehearsing for months, but the moment was anticlimactic; no one listening was interested in the grievances of the Métis, or Riel's interpretation of the events of 1870 and 1885. The crush of reporters and onlookers wanted to hear Richardson pronounce his sentence. At one point, when Riel paused for a moment, Richardson asked, ''Is that all?'' but the prisoner answered, ''No, excuse me, I feel weak and if I stop at times, I wish you would be kind enough to . . .'' and then he continued with his interpretation of the Manitoba Act.

Finally, when Riel finished, it was Richardson's turn. He looked directly at the bearded man, who was still standing in the prisoner's box:

> Louis Riel, after a long consideration of your case, in which you have been defended with as great ability as I think counsel could have defended you with, you have been found guilty by a jury who have shown, I might almost say, unexampled patience, guilty of a crime the most pernicious and greatest that man can commit. You have been found guilty of high treason. You have been proved to have let loose the flood-gates of rapine and blood-shed. . . .
>
> For what you did, the remarks you have made form no excuse whatever. For what you have done the law requires you to answer. It is true that the jury . . . have asked Her Majesty to give your case such merciful consideration as she can bestow upon it. . . . But in spite of that, I cannot hold out any hope to you that . . . Her Majesty will, after what you have been the cause of doing, open her hand of clemency to you.

> For me, I have only one more duty to perform, that is, to tell
> you what the sentence of the law is upon you. . . . All I can
> suggest or advise you is to prepare to meet your end. . . . It is
> now my painful duty to pass the sentence of the court upon you,
> and that is, that you be taken now from here to the police guard-
> room at Regina, which is the gaol and the place from whence
> you came, and that you be kept there till the 18th of September
> next, that on the 18th of September next you be taken to the
> place appointed for your execution, and there be hanged by the
> neck till you are dead, and may God have mercy on your soul.

Riel was taken from the temporary courtroom at the Canada North-
West Land Company back to the barracks gaol, and the reporters
rushed to the telegraph office.

But the convicted prisoner did not hang on September 18. As with
any high-stakes litigation, there would be an appeal; for his part, if
B.B. Osler celebrated his victory, he did not record it in his diary or
in any of his letters home. He had to prepare for the appeal. In a letter
to his brother, Featherston, he made his own opinion about Riel's
sanity clear. The man he had just convinced a jury to convict of high
treason was, "a man whose leading idea is personal sainthood, fed
for years by priests for their own ends. A man, I should judge, of no
personal courage and a good deal of sneak."[40]

Osler travelled to Winnipeg to argue the appeal, because the North-
West Act allowed for an appeal to the Manitoba Court of Appeal, but
on each of the defence's arguments, the jurisdiction of Richardson's
court, the size of the jury, and the method of recording evidence, the
court rejected the appeal.[41] Still, there was at least a possibility of a
further appeal to the Privy Council, so the government stayed the
execution pending a decision from London.

Osler returned to Toronto and prepared for a trip to England. In
the meantime, the political battle heated up. For the Liberals, particularly the Quebec provincial wing led by Honoré Mercier, Macdonald
and his Orange Order henchmen were using a francophone lunatic as
a scapegoat for their own frontier mismanagement. To Ontario, Riel
was a self-interested rebel who would turn the west into a bloodbath
in search of his own glory.

During the rebellion, and even during the trial, the government's
main concern was law and order on the prairies. During the months
following Riel's conviction, however, national unity became a much
bigger problem. On October 22, Osler learned that he would not have

to travel to London when the Privy Council denied leave to appeal. The ball was now back in Macdonald's court.

With each call for executive clemency from Quebec, a louder one would echo from Ontario demanding Riel's death. Macdonald was caught in the age-old Canadian dilemma. On one side was much of French Canada, including (in private at least) his most powerful francophone ministers, and on the other were the traditional Orange Order supporters of his own party in Ontario who insisted that Riel hang "though every dog in Quebec bark!" One of the most notable among this group was Osler's partner, D'Alton McCarthy.

Macdonald ultimately sided with the court's finding, however, and decided to allow Riel's execution to go forth. On the morning of November 16, 1885, Riel and a small party, including two priests and the deputy sheriff, walked out of the barracks to a scaffold in the yard. As the rope was adjusted around Riel's neck, the deputy sheriff asked, "Is there any reason why the sentence should not be carried out?" Riel asked one of the priests, "Should I speak?", but his confessor answered, simply, "No." Finally, Riel and the priest began to recite the Lord's Prayer. When they reached the line, "Deliver us from evil," the hangman opened the trap and Riel fell.

For B.B. Osler, the Riel trial was a career highlight. It was not a particularly complicated or difficult criminal prosecution; certainly, it was much less complex than many of the other trials he was involved with. It was, however, one of the most significant events in Canadian history. Osler did his job efficiently and professionally, but the political and national implications of the trial were not so cut and dried.

Relations between French-Canadians and English-Canadians have been difficult to varying degrees since 1759. The Canadian body politic has a wound which never seems to heal. There have been times when it seems like the wound is closing, but then something like the events of the summer and fall of 1885 will open the wound once again.

Four years after Riel's execution, D'Alton McCarthy poured some salt into that wound. In the course of the debate over a resolution in the House of Commons to disallow an otherwise obscure Quebec statute, McCarthy thundered away at all of the old conspiracy theories about the Roman Catholic Church. Unlike the risks a lawyer who evinces a strong political and religious bias would run today, in late nineteenth-century Toronto, McCarthy's very public role in the Jesuits Estates Act controversy was anything but a detriment to his legal career and his firm's fortunes.[42]

In 1888, the government of Quebec passed the Jesuits Estates Act to clear up a century-old dispute about the title to certain lands in the province which had, prior to the British conquest of New France in 1763, belonged to the Society of Jesus.[43] The Quebec government's solution to the problem was to pay a settlement of $400,000 to the Roman Catholic Church, and let the Pope decide how to divide the money between the Jesuits and the rest of the church. When the most virulent of anti-Catholics in English Canada saw this, they demanded that the federal government use its constitutional power to disallow the legislation. To McCarthy, a statute with which a government under the British Crown acknowledged the authority of the Papal anti-Christ was next to blasphemy. Macdonald, however, could not disallow it without offending a greater number of voters in French Canada, and he held steadfast against McCarthy's railings.

While these controversies were going on, McCarthy, Osler, Hoskin & Creelman's annual profits were increasing from the $70,000 range to $85,000, and Britton Bath Osler was continuing to get involved in attention-getting murder trials. The most sensational of these was the notorious Burchall trial of 1890.

Reginald Burchall was a talented, English conman charged with murder. He had devised a scheme to convince wealthy Englishmen to invest in his fictitious lucrative Canadian horse farm in Oxford County, Ontario. Once in Canada — and once he had their money — he would kill the naive investors. The first of his victims was found at the edge of Blenheim swamp near Woodstock in February 1890. When the case came up for trial in September, the Crown prosecutor was B.B. Osler.

The trial attracted world-wide attention; the *Times* of London devoted more space to the story than almost any other that month and, in fact, printed the entire text of Osler's address to the jury. The details of the crime were not as lurid as some others Osler was involved with, but the aristocratic connections of the victim were enough to gain it notoriety. Whatever the cause, Osler's name was once more very prominent.[44]

Helped by the prominence that both Osler and McCarthy had achieved, the firm continued to grow. In the early 1890s, its gross annual income exceeded $100,000. In 1891-92, the firm earned $117,002.17. Significantly, just over half of this amount came from general, non-litigation files.[45] At the same time, the firm was adding to its personnel. Predictably, the lawyers who joined the firm during these years were particularly noted more for their corporate work than for litigation.

One of the most significant corporate lawyers to join the firm in the 1880s was a young man named Wallace Nesbitt, who came to McCarthy, Osler, Hoskin & Creelman in 1883. Nesbitt, who in later life sported a Van Dyck beard and pince-nez glasses, was an avid sportsman whose interests included golf and boxing. He was significant because he would eventually become one of two former members of the firm to serve on the Supreme Court of Canada.

Nesbitt was born near Woodstock, Ontario in 1858. Like many nineteenth-century Ontario lawyers, he did not attend university. Instead, when he graduated from high school in Woodstock, he served a five-year articling term with a local lawyer and received his call to the bar in 1881.

Nesbitt then joined his older brother, J.W. Nesbitt, in a two-man firm in Hamilton, where he met and apparently impressed B.B. Osler. Some time in early 1883, a few months after he had moved to Toronto to go into partnership with D'Alton McCarthy, Osler invited the young Nesbitt to join them. Nesbitt acted as a junior to Adam Creelman on a number of corporate files, but he also assisted both Osler and McCarthy in litigation matters.

Wallace stayed with the firm for almost ten years, but in 1892 he took an opportunity to play a larger role in another Toronto law firm. At McCarthy, Osler, Hoskin & Creelman, he knew that it would be many years before he could rise above any of the four name partners, in income or recognition. In addition, in an era when family connections meant a great deal in law firms, he could see a number of younger Oslers and McCarthys rising behind him.

In 1892, therefore, Nesbitt accepted an offer from his father-in-law W.H. Beatty to join the firm of Beatty, Blackstock & Chadwick, which was soon renamed Beatty, Blackstock, Nesbitt, Chadwick & Riddell.[46] During the ten years which Nesbitt practised with this firm, he rose to considerable prominence in the profession. He continued as both a corporate practitioner and a litigator, and in 1896 he became a Queen's Counsel.

In 1903, Wallace Nesbitt left practice when he accepted Prime Minister Wilfrid Laurier's invitation to join the Supreme Court of Canada. This appointment was noteworthy, not just because Nesbitt was only forty-five years old and had no judicial experience, but because he was an active and outspoken member of the Conservative

Party. This was an era when the government's appointments to the Supreme Court were often politically partisan. Just three years later, Laurier appointed his own minister of justice, Charles Fitzpatrick, as chief justice.[47]

Laurier apparently had to put considerable pressure on Nesbitt to accept the appointment. Nesbitt was then at the height of this career; he was earning a great deal of money, and a move to Ottawa would mean quite a change in lifestyle. Although the prime minister was able to convince him, Nesbitt's fears were accurate. He hated Ottawa, and he hated being a judge.[48] In 1905, therefore, he resigned to return to practice. He did not, however, return to his own firm. Instead, he went back to his original Toronto firm and became senior counsel at the firm then known as McCarthy, Osler, Hoskin & Harcourt.[49] He remained with the firm in this capacity until his death in 1930.[50]

Next to Nesbitt, the most important lawyers to join the firm during the 1880s and 1890s were members of the next generation of Oslers and McCarthys. Henry Smith Osler, generally known as "H.S." or "Hal," joined the firm in 1889, and his younger brother, Britton Osler, joined in 1897. Both men, who were the sons of B.B. Osler's older brother, Featherston, articled with the firm and joined as partners after being called to the bar.[51] Leighton McCarthy, who was D'Alton McCarthy's nephew, joined in 1892, and D'Alton Lally McCarthy, D'Alton McCarthy's son, joined the firm in 1895.[52] Both of these men had also articled with the firm. Unlike their illustrious uncles and father, these young men apparently made their marks in the boardroom as well as the courtroom, and it appears that this is why the firm was able to survive the deaths of the two founders.

The deaths of D'Alton McCarthy and B.B. Osler, coming as they did so close together, were traumatic events for the firm. On Saturday, May 8, 1898, McCarthy's horse bolted at the sound of church bells and threw him from his carriage near the corner of Queen and Beverley streets. His head struck a telephone pole and he was severely injured. He never regained consciousness and died three days later at the age of sixty-two.[53]

B.B. Osler's appointment diaries tell the poignant story of the last few months of his life. Up to April of 1900, he led a very busy, perhaps too busy, professional life. His practice took him all over North America and occasionally to Europe. In 1885 alone, the year of the Riel trial, he travelled some seventeen thousand miles. His entry for Thursday April 19, 1900 reads: "Phila. . . . 2nd attack nervous prostration.'' He apparently suffered what we would now call a nervous breakdown while on business in Philadelphia.[54]

He left for Toronto by train the next day and arrived home on Saturday. He stayed away from the office the following week, but his diary entry for Thursday April 26 reads: ''3rd attack nervous p. 8 P.M. till 4 A.M. — Dr. McPhedran, Dr. Walker.[55] There is nothing more in his diary until Monday, June 18 when he wrote: ''Moved to Dr. Walker's hospital'' and listed the names of his nurses. The next entry is for Friday, September 7, and reads: ''Moved from Dr. Walker's to house in ambulance.''[56]

Osler remained at his home on Queen's Park Crescent under the care of a personal nurse for the rest of the fall, and he was apparently making plans to return to work in the new year. In December, however, his health took a turn for the worse and he decided to seek further treatment and rest at a sanatorium in Clifton Springs, New York.[57] The only entry in his 1901 diary is ''Tues. Jan. 1 — At Sanatorium, Clifton Springs.''[58] He died on February 5, 1901 at Atlantic City, New Jersey. He was sixty-one years old.

3

CRISIS, STABILITY AND DIVISION: 1902-1916

Word of B.B. Osler's death reached the firm in the form of a telegram from Elizabeth, his wife, shortly after 10:00 a.m. on Tuesday, February 5, 1901. Although he had not practised for almost a year, Osler's partners were holding out some hope that he would return. Ironically, later that same Tuesday afternoon they received a letter his wife had written only the day before telling how the sea air was doing him good and that he was feeling better than ever.[1]

Osler's partners knew that his death would bring great changes to the firm; they may have even feared for its survival. Despite the turmoil and controversy of the political side of D'Alton McCarthy's career, he and B.B. Osler had been able to maintain a healthy working relationship between each other and what Osler called a "strength of . . . affection and esteem" within the firm.[2]

That affection and esteem was a practical necessity for the firm; it was, in fact, what allowed Osler and McCarthy to forge what was a mega-firm of its day — and they knew it. The best example of their understanding of this was the fact that they refused to allow individual partners to covet clients within the firm. Although both Osler and McCarthy had maintained membership in their original firms outside of Toronto — Osler's in Hamilton and Dundas and McCarthy's in Barrie — they were wise enough to make sure that there was no conflict between their local firms and the Toronto partnership.

The local firms dealt with local matters only. All work done by the firm of McCarthy, Osler, Hoskin & Creelman, whether originally generated by the local firms or not, would be shared according the talents of all members of the firm, and the fees would be shared according to the partnership agreement. Both Osler and McCarthy had learned at a very early stage that if a firm like theirs was to survive, its members could not covet clients. With both of them now gone, the question was whether the next generation could maintain the "affection and esteem" they had established. Ultimately, they could not.

According to a story published in *The Globe*, when Britton Bath Osler died in February, 1901, he and Mrs. Osler had been staying at the Hotel Shelburne in Atlantic City for about ten days. They had travelled there from Clifton Springs, New York, where they had been since December. On Monday evening, February 4, he had gone out for a walk on the boardwalk and had retired early. At about six o'clock the next morning, however, he woke his wife and told her he was feeling "oppressed." Shortly after eight o'clock, he suffered what Mrs. Osler called a fainting spell and she called a doctor. When the doctor arrived, however, there was nothing he could do, and Osler died "as if in a sleep."

The headline in *The Globe* read: "HEART FAILURE CAUSE OF DEATH", but the more telling one appeared over the *Star* editorial: "GENERALLY BELIEVED DEATH DUE TO OVERWORK".[3]

Britton Bath Osler was, undoubtedly, what would later be termed a workaholic. Although the surviving records do not indicate his billable hours (in fact, there is no evidence to indicate whether clients were billed by the hour or simply by the case or transaction), Osler's diaries show that he travelled constantly to appear before various courts; in 1899, the year he turned sixty years old, he travelled over fifteen thousand miles by train and spent at least 118 days in court! Moreover, those were the days when the courts did not sit at all during July and August.

Osler had begun the year 1899 in Baltimore, visiting his younger brother William (later Sir William), who was then professor of medicine at Johns Hopkins University. After spending New Year's Day with his brother and two young nephews, Osler took the evening train to Philadelphia. He spent Monday January the second in Philadelphia and then New York, and took the overnight train to Toronto, arriving home at eleven o'clock in the morning on Tuesday the third.[4]

He spent Tuesday afternoon at the McCarthy, Osler, Hoskin & Creelman offices in the Freehold Loan & Savings building at the corner of Adelaide and Victoria streets, but on Wednesday the fourth he left for a court appearance in Sarnia. He spent the night in Sarnia and arrived home in Toronto at nine o'clock on Thursday evening.

He then spent all day Friday and Saturday morning at the office in Toronto, but on Sunday he left for Hamilton to attend the assizes.

The assizes Osler attended at Hamilton on Monday, January 9, were local sittings of the Ontario High Court of Justice. Each county in the province had its own court, but the High Court, one level above the county courts in the provincial judicial structure, also held sittings outside of Toronto on a regular basis.[5] Although, unlike their predecessors, lawyers like Osler did not travel an assize circuit on horseback with the judges, a prosperous litigation practice did mean spending a great deal of time away from home.[6] He also made regular trips throughout the year to Ottawa to appear before the Exchequer Court of Canada and the Supreme Court.

On Monday, January 16, 1899, a week after travelling to Hamilton for the assizes, Osler was in Ottawa to hear the judgement of the Exchequer Court in *The American Dunlop Tire Co.* v. *Goold*. The case involved an alleged breach of a patent for pneumatic tires by Osler's client, The Goold Bicycle Company. Osler left Ottawa disappointed, however, because the court found in favour of the plaintiff in the case, which was represented by Zebulon Lash of the Blake firm.[7]

Osler arrived back in Toronto at 6:15 p.m. on Wednesday, January 18, and went immediately to the office to begin preparations for two cases to be heard in the Ontario Court of Appeal on Friday. In the first case, *Dueber Watch Case Manufacturing Company* v. *Taggart*, Osler's client was a discharged bankrupt who won his case at trial against a former creditor. In the second, *Bicknell* v. *Grand Trunk Railway Company*, Osler represented the railway, which was appealing a trial judgement finding it at fault in a train crash.

Interestingly enough, one of the five justices who listened to Osler's arguments in those cases was his brother, Featherston.[8] Although there appears to be no case law or specific rule prohibiting a Canadian judge from hearing a case argued by his brother, such a circumstance would be considered highly improper, if not unethical, today.[9] At the turn of the century, however, it was quite common. Whether the fact that his brother was making the arguments was a factor or not, Featherston wrote the judgements in both cases, and both judgements found in favour of B.B. Osler's clients.[10]

Unfortunately, Osler did not have time to rest after his appearance in the Court of Appeal on Friday; he spent all day Saturday and Sunday in the Great Library at Osgoode Hall preparing for a labour arbitration on Monday the twenty-third in which he was to sit as a member of the board with Sir William R. Meredith, then chief justice of the Common Pleas Division of The High Court, and another man named F. Balfour. Osler was apparently the management representative, while Balfour was the labour appointee.

The arbitrations, which involved the telegraphers' union, lasted until the following Saturday. Osler spent the next three weeks in Toronto, with only two day trips to Hamilton, but he was only in the office for parts of four days during that time. He spent the rest of the time at the Toronto assizes and the Court of Appeal. On Monday, February 20, he travelled to Ottawa, returning two days later to prepare for court in Toronto on Monday the twenty-seventh. This pattern continued for the rest of the winter and into the spring. He would spend a day or so in the office in Toronto, then one or two days at an assize sitting in one of the county towns or in Ottawa, then return to Toronto to appear before the Court of Appeal or the High Court.[11]

In April, however, Osler began to show the strains of his workload. He spent Monday, April 17 in Ottawa at the assizes, took the overnight train back to Toronto arriving home at seven in the morning, spent the Tuesday in the office, and left for Hamilton in the evening. He spent all day Wednesday at the Hamilton assizes, but recorded in his diary the next day that he had been awake at 4:00 a.m. with congestion and chills. His diary for the next three weeks consists of simple one- or two-word entries for each day. Most simply say "ill — bed." On Friday, May 12, he left for Kionontio, his summer home on Blue Mountain near Collingwood, with his wife and doctor, and a nurse. He remained there for two weeks and returned to Toronto on Friday, May 26.

He stayed home for the weekend, and even went to the horse races at Woodbine on Saturday afternoon, but on Monday morning he was back at Osgoode Hall to appear before the Court of Appeal, and the next day he was off to Guelph for the assizes there. Over the course of the next five weeks, he travelled to Niagara-on-the-Lake, Penetang, Bracebridge, Sarnia, Peterborough, Dundas, and Hamilton and Ottawa twice each. The only evidence of anything but work was his diary entry for Sunday, June 11, which reads "home — first outdoor roses." The entry for Monday June 19, his sixtieth birthday, reads simply "office."

Remarkably, despite his incredibly busy schedule of the winter and spring, Osler took almost all of the summer off. This was standard practice in turn-of-the-century Canada; the legal and business world virtually shut down for the months of July and August. With the exception of two brief visits to the office, Osler spent the seven and a half weeks between Wednesday, July 5 and Sunday, August 27 at Kionontio. At 9:00 a.m. on Monday, August 28, however, he boarded a train for Buffalo to attend the annual meetings of the American Bar Association. He returned to Toronto on Wednesday afternoon, and on Friday night, September 1, he took the overnight train to Montreal to begin preparations for what would prove to be the last lawsuit of his life.

In September 1892, the Canadian Department of Railways and Canals awarded a contract to build a portion of the Soulanges Canal on the St. Lawrence River, just west of Montreal, to Archibald Stewart, a construction engineer. Under the terms of the contract, the work was to be completed by October 31, 1894. In November of 1897, however, the work was only about half finished, and the government terminated the contract. According to the minister of Railways and Canals, the contractor was responsible for the construction delays, but in Stewart's view it was the government itself which was at fault, and he brought suit in the Exchequer Court of Canada for breach of contract.[12]

Osler arrived in Montreal at 7:00 a.m. on Saturday, September 2, 1899. On Sunday he went out to Cascades Point to inspect the canal for himself and that evening took the train to Ottawa. On Wednesday the sixth, the trial began with opening statements from Osler and Samuel Hume Blake, Q.C., the senior partner in Blake, Lash & Cassels, who was representing the government. The first sitting lasted until Saturday morning and the case was adjourned until January 1900. Osler returned to Toronto and resumed the same schedule of assize, High Court, and Court of Appeal appearances that he maintained in the winter and spring. He spent Christmas and New Year's at a resort at Old Point Comfort on the Virginia shore, returning to Toronto by way of Baltimore as he had the year before. In January, he was back in Ottawa for the *Stewart* case.

The court sat to hear the case from January 25 through February 1, 1900, and again from the third to the twelfth of March. At some point during the March sitting, however, Osler collapsed in the middle of his argument and couldn't continue. His collapse apparently took place on Wednesday, March 7 or Thursday, March 8; his diary entries for Monday, March 5 through Thursday, March 8 simply say ''Ottawa Exch. Ct.'' The entry for Friday the ninth reads ''Train O. at 11 a.m. — home 8 p.m.''

It is not clear whether he was able to continue work at that point or not, but his diary reads ''office'' for each day from Tuesday, March 13 through to Thursday, March 22. There are no entries between then and Wednesday April 4, when he took an overnight train for Philadelphia. The April 5 entry reads ''Philadelphia,'' and the pages covering April 6 to April 19 have been ripped out. The entry for Thursday, April 19, 1900 reads ''Phila. — closed arbitration — Balt. & Ohio Railroad — 2nd attack nervous prostration.'' He never worked again.[13]

Following a third attack after his return to Toronto, Osler was completely incapacitated.[14] He was recovering somewhat during the early winter of 1901, but died before he was able to return to the firm. His partners closed the office and met the train carrying his body on Wednesday morning, April 6, when it arrived at Union Station in Toronto. The next afternoon, he was buried in the family vault in St. James cemetery in Toronto; the pallbearers included Sir William Ralph Meredith, Aemilius Irving, the treasurer of the Law Society of Upper Canada, Christopher Robinson, Wallace Nesbitt, John Hoskin and Adam Creelman.[15]

For McCarthy, Osler, Hoskin & Creelman, despite the fact that he had not worked for almost a year, Osler's death was a shattering blow. Coming so close on the heels of D'Alton McCarthy's death in 1898, it might have destroyed the firm, which was founded on the strength of those two great litigators — but it did not. The remaining partners, particularly Osler's nephews and McCarthy's son and nephews, were able to maintain the balance the two founders had established, but fifteen years later it was gone.

When Osler died, there were ten lawyers left in the firm, five of whom had more than ten years' experience at the bar. John Hoskin, Frederick Harcourt and Adam Creelman had been with the firm since its formation in 1882; W.B. Raymond had been there since his call to the bar in 1885; and B.B. Osler's nephew, H.S. Osler, since 1889. Of the other five, D'Alton McCarthy's nephew, Leighton McCarthy, joined the firm when he was called to the bar in 1892; D'Alton McCarthy's son, D'Alton Lally McCrathy, joined when he was called in 1895; Charles MacInnes and H.S. Osler's brother, Britton Osler, both joined when they were called in 1897; and Andrew M. Stewart had been with the firm for less than two years. More importantly, four of the ten had family associations to the founders. As the following chapters will demonstrate, this would be a very significant phenomenon for a number of decades to come.

With ten lawyers, the firm was the third largest in the city, and in fact the third largest in Canada. Only Beatty, Blackstock, Nesbitt, Chadwick & Riddell, with fifteen, and Blake, Lash & Cassels, with thirteen, were larger. In this regard, very little had changed over the previous twenty years. In 1882 McCarthy, Osler, Hoskin & Creelman was the third largest behind the Blake firm and Featherston Osler's old firm of Bethune, Moss, Falconbridge & Hoyles. As of 1892, it had stood second behind only Blake's, and in 1912 it was again third behind the Beatty firm and the Blake firm.[16]

None of the lawyers in the firm was an established courtroom lawyer, let alone of the reputation of B.B. Osler or D'Alton McCarthy. Creelman, Raymond and H.S. Osler were, however, well-established corporate specialists. During the two decades since the formation of the firm, its senior partners, most notably B.B. Osler and D'Alton McCarthy, made a deliberate effort to build up the corporate side of the firm's practice. As noted in the preceding chapter, throughout the 1880s and 1890s, although the firm's most publicized work took place in the courtroom, roughly half of its income came from non-litigious, general work. It was the solid base of corporate clientele which they built up during that period which allowed the firm to weather the storm of its founders' deaths.

Nevertheless, when the partners met shortly after B.B. Osler's death to discuss a new partnership agreement, the first thing they decided to do was to ask a senior, and prominent, litigator to join the firm as counsel. They were very pleased when Christopher Robinson agreed to do so. Robinson was nearing the end of a long and very distinguished career at the bar; among other things, he had been the senior prosecutor, along with Britton Bath Osler, in Louis Riel's treason trial in 1885.[17] He was also a member of one of the most prominent families in nineteenth-century Canada.

The addition of Christopher Robinson as counsel to the firm started a trend which continued for a number of decades. In the following years, the firm had a former justice of the Supreme Court of Canada, Wallace Nesbitt, and a former prime minister, Arthur Meighen, join it as counsel. Under the new partnership agreement, signed on February 15, 1901, Robinson's name would appear on the firm's letterhead, but he would keep his own fees and would not share in the profits of the firm. He was not a partner in the firm, but he was willing to lend it the cachet of his name.

Despite having the credibility of Robinson's name on the letterhead, the partners had another problem to deal with. Adam Creelman, who was the senior corporate lawyer in the firm and was responsible for some of the most important clients, including the Canada North-West Land Company and the Canadian Pacific Railway, had decided to accept an offer to leave the firm and become general counsel to the C.P.R. at its head office in Montreal. He would join the railway as of July 1, 1901, but he was willing to remain a member of the firm until June 30, 1902 in order assist with the transition period.

During the 1890s, the firm had been very prosperous. Its net earnings between July 1897 and June 1898 were $65,000, but as pointed out in the previous chapter, half of that amount came from D'Alton McCarthy and B.B. Osler's counsel fees. After McCarthy died, the firm was able to maintain its income, partly because of Osler's increased workload but also because it was fortunate enough to get all the legal work surrounding the collapse of the Farmers' Loan and Savings Company. The fee for that account alone exceeded $20,000. After Osler died, however, the firm's income declined substantially. By 1902 it was down to $40,000.[18]

The firm continued under the name McCarthy, Osler, Hoskin & Creelman until July 1, 1902 when it became McCarthy, Osler, Hoskin & Harcourt. Under the partnership agreement which came into force on that date, the nine remaining members of the firm agreed to divide its profits into one hundred shares. Of these, H.S. Osler would receive seventeen shares, Leighton McCarthy sixteen and a quarter, W.B. Raymond thirteen and a half, D'Alton Lally McCarthy twelve and a quarter, John Hoskin eleven, Britton Osler, Charles MacInnes and Andrew Stewart eight each, and Frederick Harcourt six.

Then, as now, the choice of the firm's name was very important for many reasons. Marketing, although it was not a term which turn-of-the century lawyers would have used, was probably foremost among these, but the partners' egos were also a factor. The continued inclusion of the names McCarthy and Osler in the firm name was obvious; they represented the firm's illustrious history, and there were still two McCarthys and two Oslers in the firm. Moreover, the two partners with the highest share interest in the firm's profits were named McCarthy and Osler. Similarly, Hoskin's name would logically continue in the firm's name. He was at that point the senior partner in terms of years at the bar, and he was the only remaining member of the 1882 partnership.

The choice of the fourth name, however, would prove to be problematical. Logically, they should have chosen Raymond's name; he had been with the firm since 1885 — a year longer than H.S. Osler

— and was responsible for some very important corporate clients, including the Windsor, Essex and Lake Shore Rapid Railway Company. But Raymond seems to have been a bit of an outsider; he was not a member of either of the two founding families, and he apparently did not get along well with his partners.

They also skipped past MacInnes' and Stewart's names and chose Harcourt's. Although he had been with the firm since his call to the bar in 1886, and in fact had articled there, Frederick Harcourt did not become a partner until B.B. Osler's death in 1901. He had acted as John Hoskin's assistant in the latter's capacity as Official Guardian, and succeeded Hoskin in the post in 1902. This, as much as anything, was probably why they chose his name.

During the first few years after B.B. Osler's death, the firm was going through some difficult changes. The partners were trying to work out an acceptable hierarchy of authority among themselves, and in the process some of them decided to leave. Not surprisingly, perhaps, within four years of being passed over in the choice of names for the firm, Raymond, Stewart and MacInnes would all leave. In addition, the firm was having a troubled time in the marketplace. This was a time of tremendous economic growth in Canada and the rest of the world. The discovery of gold in South Africa and the Yukon brought huge infusions of capital into the world economy and business was eager to exploit Canada's natural resources.

Despite the opportunities this boom created, McCarthy, Osler, Hoskin & Harcourt's net earnings continued to decline and reached a low of $36,000 in 1906. Not surprisingly, there were many changes in the firm's personnel during these years as well. In 1904, both Charles MacInnes and Andrew Stewart left the firm. MacInnes joined a firm which became known as Ryckman, Kerr & MacInnes, and Stewart set out on his own. Two years later, as the firm's income hit its lowest point, W.B. Raymond left to join E.E. DuVernet in a firm which became DuVernet, Raymond, Ross & Ardagh.[19]

Christopher Robinson died in 1905, but the firm was lucky enough to convince a retired Supreme Court justice, Wallace Nesbitt, to take his place as counsel to the firm. As noted in Chapter Two, Nesbitt was a partner in the firm during the 1880s, but had left in 1892 to join Beatty, Blackstock & Riddell.[20] During the 1890s, he was a very prominent counsel, and in 1903 the Laurier government appointed him to the Supreme Court of Canada. Like many of his fellow justices at the time, however, he disliked working on the Court and hated Ottawa, and he resigned in 1905.[21] When he came back to Toronto, he accepted an offer to join McCarthy, Osler, Hoskin & Harcourt as counsel. Like Robinson, he was not a partner and he did not pay any fees to the firm or receive any shares.

A year later, shortly before W.B. Raymond's departure, the firm added one more partner. Leighton McCarthy's younger brother Frank began his articles with his uncle's old firm in Barrie, but finished with McCarthy, Osler, Hoskin & Harcourt in Toronto. When he received his call to the bar in 1905, he stayed on with the firm. With Raymond's departure, there were eight lawyers left at the firm, and this number remained constant for five more years. The eight lawyers who made up the firm from 1906 until 1911 were Frederick Harcourt, John Hoskin, D'Alton Lally McCarthy, Frank McCarthy, Leighton McCarthy, Wallace Nesbitt, Britton Osler and H.S. Osler.

During this period of relative stability the firm began to prosper once more. From a low of $36,000 divided among eight partners in 1906, its net income steadily increased to $40,000 in 1907, $45,000 in 1908, $50,000 in 1909, $62,000 in 1910, and $85,000 divided among seven partners in 1911. In addition, and most significantly, the bulk of the firm's income during these years of growth came from general corporate accounts rather than litigation. During 1908, for instance, only about 11 per cent of the firm's $45,000 net income, or $5,000, came from litigation files. The remainder came from general accounts.

Not surprisingly, with one exception, the members of the firm were not appearing in court on a regular basis either. Except for D'Alton Lally McCarthy, whose name appeared as counsel in some ninety-one reported decisions published in the *Ontario Law Reports* between 1901 and 1915, none of the McCarthy, Osler, Hoskin & Harcourt partners appeared in court with any regularity. In addition, the bulk of cases in which D'Alton Lally McCarthy was involved seem to have been industrial negligence claims against corporate clients such as the Toronto Street Railway.[22]

The firm's clients during those years included many of those whom B.B. Osler and Adam Creelman had brought in during the early years, including the Canada North-West Land Company, the Canadian Pacific Railway, and a number of insurance companies, but they also included banks, manufacturing interests and resource companies.[23]

The firm continued to prosper during the years leading up to World War I. In 1912, its net income was $89,000; in 1913, it was $95,000; and in 1914, it reached $104,000. The leaders of the firm during those years were the nephews of its founders. According to the partnership agreement, signed in 1913, the firm's profits would be divided into 110 shares. H.S. Osler and Leighton McCarthy received thirty shares each, D'Alton Lally McCarthy received twenty-one, Britton Osler eighteen, Frank McCarthy seven, and Frederick Harcourt four.[24]

Despite this prosperity, there were divisions beginning to form within the firm. During the previous generation, B.B. Osler and D'Alton McCarthy had been able to smooth over their political differences and accommodate each other's ego enough to maintain relatively equal prominence within the firm. Their nephews were apparently having difficulty doing so.

Leighton McCarthy, like his uncle, was very politically active. In fact, after D'Alton McCarthy's death in 1898 Leighton won the resulting by-election in North Simcoe and took over his uncle's seat in the House of Commons. He sat as an Independent and won re-election in the general elections of 1900 and 1904 without officially supporting either party, but he was well known to be a close confidant of Liberal prime minister Wilfrid Laurier. McCarthy chose not to run in the 1908 election, but when Laurier called another election in 1911 he persuaded McCarthy to run again — this time as a Liberal.

The issue in the 1911 federal election was free trade. The Laurier government was entertaining the offer of a reciprocity treaty with the United States, and the Conservative Party, under Halifax lawyer Robert Borden, was determined to defeat the government and reject the offer. Much like the free trade debate of the late 1980s, the election campaign of 1911 was very heated, particularly in Toronto. A group of prominent Liberals known as the "Toronto Eighteen," led by Blakes lawyer Zebulon Lash, denounced the treaty and broke with the party to support Borden. Leighton McCarthy remained loyal to Laurier, but both he and the party went down to defeat. Laurier retained his own seat, but Robert Borden became prime minister and formally rejected the treaty offer.[25]

For McCarthy, Osler, Hoskin & Harcourt, the political battle brought some undesirable publicity. Unlike the political controversies of the 1880s and 1890s, in which D'Alton McCarthy played a very prominent role, political activity was not good for business — at least in H.S. Osler's view. He apparently feuded with his partner over this issue, but was unsuccessful in persuading him to keep a lower profile.

The firm stayed together for five more years, but in 1916 Leighton McCarthy, his brother Frank, and their cousin Lally decided to leave and form their own firm. The acknowledged reason for their move was the fact that they would be able to take one very important client with them.[26]

The Canada Life Assurance Company was founded in the Confederation era, but during the late nineteenth century it was built by George Cox, a former railway ticket salesman from Peterborough, Ontario, into one of the largest insurance companies in North America; in fact, it was an insurance conglomerate. Its main focus was life insurance, but under Cox's direction it became the parent company for a number of fire and marine insurance companies.[27]

During the 1880s, D'Alton McCarthy's younger brother, Dr. John Leigh Goldie McCarthy, was the medical examiner for Canada Life. Partly on the basis of this connection, George Cox began to use McCarthy, Osler, Hoskin & Creelman for much of his company's legal work. D'Alton McCarthy was clearly the lawyer in charge of the file, but the fees he earned in overseeing the file were, like all others in the firm, divided according to the partnership agreement.

As Canada Life grew and acquired more subsidiaries, it became one of the firm's most important clients. B.B. Osler helped cement the relationship between the firm and the company in 1897 (two years after his first wife's death) when he married Elizabeth Mary Ramsay, whose father was A.G. Ramsay, president and managing director of Canada Life.[28] By the time of Osler's death, it was by far the largest client. For the first six months of 1902, its bill was $2,500.[29] But over the course of the next few years, it virtually disappeared from the firm's ledger books. In 1903 and 1904, it was not billed by the firm, and in 1905 it paid a bill of twelve dollars.[30] From then until 1910, it paid nothing to the firm, but in that year, its bill was once again $2,500.[31] That same year, Leighton McCarthy became a director of Canada Life.

The following year, Canada Life's bill was $1001.40, but in 1912 it shrunk again to only $275, and in 1913 and 1914 it was only $200.[32] In 1915, it paid $1,000, but by then it was too late.[33] Leighton McCarthy was apparently breaking the most important principle his uncle and B.B. Osler had laid down — he was coveting a very important client for himself rather than for the firm. The key to this situation lies in a two-word difference in a paragraph of the firm's partnership agreement between the McCarthy, Osler, Hoskin & Harcourt version in force prior to the 1916 split, and the Osler, Hoskin & Harcourt version agreed to after the split.

Paragraph seven of the old partnership agreement read: "Any of the parties hereto shall be entitled to his own use to all emoluments received by him from any Company or Corporation of which he is a Director."[34] When the remaining partners got together to draft a new partnership agreement for Osler, Hoskin & Harcourt after the McCarthys had left, they kept this paragraph intact, but they added two very important words. This paragraph in the new agreement read: "Any of the parties hereto shall be entitled to his own use to all emoluments received by him from any Company or Corporation of which he is a Director *as such*."[35]

The difference was that under the new agreement, a partner who served as a director of a company which was a client could keep his director's fees — usually an honorarium in the neighbourhood of fifty to one hundred dollars, but he was obliged to share the legal fees paid by the company with his partners on the basis of the partnership agreement. Under the old agreement, Leighton McCarthy was free to keep the Canada Life legal fees for himself. He was shrewd enough — or gave in to his partners enough — to put some of them into the pot, but he apparently did not see fit to put them all in.[36]

The strain created by this situation finally became too much for the others to bear, and the Oslers and McCarthys agreed to end the partnership when the then current Articles of Partnership expired on May 31, 1916.[37] The partnership B.B. Osler and D'Alton McCarthy created in 1882 lasted thirty-four years, but in its death the lawyers who formed the new Osler, Hoskin & Harcourt relearned a very important lesson.

4

THE CLAN: 1916-1943

When the three McCarthys moved out at the end of May 1916, the firm was left with six lawyers; that is, there were six names on the new Osler, Hoskin & Harcourt letterhead. In order of seniority, the letterhead listed John Hoskin, K.C., Frederick Weir Harcourt, K.C., Henry Smith Osler, K.C., Britton Osler and Wellington Ault Cameron. On a separate line, Wallace Nesbitt, K.C. was listed as "Counsel."

In fact, however, only three of the men listed on the firm's letterhead were active partners. John Hoskin was retired; W.A. Cameron, although he had been with the firm for five years and a member of the bar for almost twenty-five, was still an associate lawyer; and as counsel to the firm, Wallace Nesbitt did little more than lend the credibility of his name.[1]

The departure of the McCarthys may have literally cut the firm in half, but it had only a small impact on the firm's income. The first ledger for the new firm included a very telling income statement which compared Osler, Hoskin & Harcourt's income for the first six months of its existence — from June 1 to November 30, 1916 — to that of the old firm of McCarthy, Osler, Hoskin & Harcourt during the corresponding period of 1915.

Between June 1 and November 30, 1915, the old firm earned a net profit of some $32,500. During the same period of 1916, the new firm estimated its profits at $24,000, a decline of just over 25 per cent. In 1915, however, the profits were split among six partners. In 1916, they were split only three ways. Under the old partnership agreement, the three McCarthys claimed $16,614, or just over half; the Osler brothers and Frederick Harcourt divided the remaining $15,886. The three partners in the new Osler, Hoskin & Harcourt, therefore, immediately saw an increase of over 50 per cent in their net profits![2]

The reason for the fact that the firm's net income declined by only a quarter when the McCarthys — who had been drawing half of its profits — left, is obvious in a comparison of the client dockets before and after the split. During the six-month period from June 1 to November 30, 1915, McCarthy, Osler, Hoskin & Harcourt's gross billings totalled $43,012.30. During the same period in 1916, Osler, Hoskin & Harcourt's gross billings totalled $39,094.86, a decline of less than 10 per cent.[3]

The reason for the differential between a 25 per cent decline in net income and a 10 per cent decrease in gross billings is that most of the firm's expenses, including the salaries of the non-partners and non-professional staff, remained constant. Much more interestingly, however, the reason that both the gross billings and net income declined by so little is that most of the largest clients stayed with the firm.

The firm sent bills to 244 clients for work docketed between June 1 and November 30, 1915. The bills ranged from twenty-five cents charged to D.B. White, a lawyer who practised in Niagara Falls, to $5,129.85 charged to the Toronto Railway Company, the company which operated the city's street cars. The average bill was for $176.28.[4] White's bill was included in a column headed "Agency," which meant that the twenty-five-cent fee was for filing a document on his behalf in one of the Toronto courts or government agencies.

For work docketed during the June 1 through November 30, 1916 period, the firm sent bills to 214 clients. These bills ranged from the fifty-cent kind sent to five different lawyers, including D.B. White, to the $4,248.50 billed to the New York law firm of Cravath & Henderson.[5] The average bill in 1916 went up slightly, to $182.69.

The most telling evidence, however, lies in the list of clients who were billed in both 1915 and 1916. Of the 244 billed in 1915, only one hundred stayed with the firm, but the average bill among these was $254.08.[6] Moreover, the top four and eight of the top twelve clients (in terms of amounts docketed during the 1915 period) stayed with the firm. In addition to The Toronto Railway Company, these included the Borden Company Limited, United Cigar Stores, the Bank of Hamilton, the Dominion Bank, and Cravath & Henderson. The only major clients who did not stay with the firm were Dominion Mines and Quarries, Union Carbide Company, William H. Biggar (the senior partner in the Ottawa law firm of Bell & Biggar) and the estate of the late Senator George A. Cox who, until his death in 1914, had been president of the Canada Life Assurance Company.[7] On the whole, industrial clients and financial institutions seemed to stay with the new Osler, Hoskin & Harcourt, while clients who were lawyers or law firms went with McCarthy & McCarthy.[8]

This division seems to support the notion that, when the McCarthys left, the firm's old practice was divided between litigation and corporate work, with the litigation side following D'Alton Lally McCarthy to the new McCarthy & McCarthy, and the corporate side staying with what became known as Osler, Hoskin & Harcourt. Of course, there were exceptions to this generalization. As noted above, Canada Life went with the McCarthys, as did Union Carbide.

The major exception among law firms which stayed on as Osler, Hoskin & Harcourt clients was Cravath & Henderson. The fact that this New York firm — the predecessor of the firm later known as Cravath, Swaine & Moore — paid a bill of over four thousand dollars in 1916 indicates that it was doing substantially more than sending routine document filing work to the Osler firm.

It is possible that part of this bill included some litigation work, although there is no evidence to support this. More likely, especially given the type of work the Oslers were specializing in, the Cravath firm was using Osler, Hoskin & Harcourt as its expert consultant on Canadian corporate law. Cravath corporate clients, who were interested in expanding into Canada, were going to the New York firm, and in turn the Osler firm would be called.

That Cravath & Henderson stayed with Osler, Hoskin & Harcourt is very important in understanding the growth and direction of the firm's practice during the twentieth century. Most of its largest long-term clients — such as the Borden Company, General Motors and International Nickel — were American-based multinational corporations, which came to Oslers either directly or indirectly through a New York law firm.

Even more important than Cravath & Henderson in this regard was another New York firm whose name first appeared in the Osler ledger book in the fall of 1916 — Sullivan & Cromwell. This Wall Street firm was the American counsel to International Nickel, and although Sullivan & Cromwell did not receive a bill directly from the Osler firm until 1916, it had apparently been directing its clients to McCarthy, Osler, Hoskin & Harcourt for some time. The most important of these were International Nickel and its subsidiaries, including the

Upper Spanish River Improvement Company and Canadian Copper Limited.

International Nickel became a McCarthy, Osler, Hoskin & Harcourt client in 1906; its bill that year was seventeen dollars. By 1920, however, it was by far the largest single client for Osler, Hoskin & Harcourt; its bill that year totalled $24,581.10, or about 15 per cent of the firm's total revenue![9] When Sullivan & Cromwell first directed the nickel company to the McCarthy, Osler firm, it was looking for someone to advise on Canadian corporate law as it sought to acquire a group of companies, including Canadian Copper, which held the mining rights to the area around Sudbury, Ontario. The lawyer they went to was a relatively young Britton Osler.

Over the course of the next few years, International Nickel succeeded in acquiring these companies, and Britton Osler was appointed to its board of directors. Significantly, however, the company remained the firm's client, not Britton Osler's. Osler kept whatever honorarium he received as a director of the company, but the legal fees he charged it went into the firm's general ledger book.

In terms of seniority — and for a short time in terms of the partners' share of the firm's profits — Britton's brother, H.S., was the leader of Osler, Hoskin & Harcourt. H.S., known as Hal, was born on November 8, 1862; he articled with McCarthy, Osler, Hoskin & Creelman, and began practising with the firm in 1889. He received his K.C. in 1902. Britton was six years younger than Hal, born on July 5, 1874, and was called to the bar in 1897. When Osler, Hoskin & Harcourt came into being in 1916, the younger Osler was not yet a King's Counsel, and would not receive the honour until October of 1921.

Under the partnership agreement which the new Osler, Hoskin & Harcourt partners signed after forming the firm, the profits would be divided into 300 shares; H.S. Osler would receive 130 of those, and Britton would receive 113. Frederick Harcourt was to receive twenty shares, and two new partners would receive the remaining thirty-seven. The two new partners were Harold Shapley, who was to receive twenty-one shares, and A.W. Langmuir, who was to receive sixteen.[10]

Within a few years, however, H.S. Osler went into semi-retirement, and it was Britton Osler who actually led the firm. In fact, he was the de facto leader from the moment the McCarthys left. In the ledger for the June–November period of 1916, the first six months of the new firm, someone — presumably George Loveys, the firm accountant — pencilled in the initials of the partner in charge of the file next to each client entry. The letter "B" appears next to by far the largest number of client names, and "H.S." appears next to only a few. Moreover, most of the largest clients, including International Nickel, and Canadian Copper — still operating as a wholly owned subsidiary of Inco — were Britton Osler's clients.

A small number of clients in the ledger were identified by the letter "L." This represented the newest lawyer in the firm — A.W. Langmuir. Archibald Woodburn Langmuir joined Osler, Hoskin & Harcourt as an associate lawyer in June of 1916, just a few days after the new firm was born. He quickly became a very important member of the firm — a fact reflected in his being made a partner the following year. Langmuir's specialties eventually grew to include all of the firm's patent files, and his most important clients included the International Playing Card Company, and Coca-Cola Limited.[11]

The other lawyer to join the new firm almost at the point of its birth was Harold Shapley. Unlike Langmuir, however, Shapley was relatively senior already. He had been called to the bar in 1907 and was a rising partner in the old Toronto firm of Mulock, Milliken, Clark & Redman. Shapley's specialty was banking law, and it was this which brought him to the Osler firm. Oslers and Mulock, Milliken had been appointed joint solicitors for the Dominion Bank, and Shapley was doing much of the bank's work assigned to the Mulock firm. Shortly after the new Osler firm was formed, Britton Osler apparently persuaded Shapley to join them, and he became a partner on August 1, 1917.[12]

During the years following the split with the McCarthys, in addition to maintaining most of the clients which the firm had prior to 1916, Osler, Hoskin & Harcourt developed some important new ones. These included a number of significant Canadian subsidiaries of American corporations, such as Canadian Kodak Company, Borden Milk and International Petroleum, a subsidiary of Imperial Oil — which was, in turn, a subsidiary of Standard Oil of New Jersey. Other new clients included the paper manufacturer Kimberley Clark Company, Hudson Bay Mining and Smelting Co. Ltd. and automobile manufacturer Sam McLaughlin, through whom the firm eventually acquired General Motors of Canada as a client.

Most were corporate clients, although for some litigation was still a significant service. One of the most interesting of these was the Bayer Company Ltd. Bayer, a German company, was the manufacturer of Aspirin. In 1899, Fargenfabriken vormals Fridrich Bayer and

Company of Elberfeld, Germany registered the word ''Aspirin'' as a trade mark for the sale of pharmaceuticals in Canada. In 1913, the German company assigned its Canadian trade mark to its wholly owned American subsidary, the Bayer Company Inc., a New York registered company.[13]

Following the American entry into World War I, the United States government Alien Property Custodian seized all of the American assets of the German Bayer company, including the Bayer Company Inc. In 1918, the Alien Property Custodian sold the Bayer Company Inc. to Sterling Products, an American company which happened to be an Osler, Hoskin & Harcourt client. Sterling incorporated the Bayer Company, Ltd. in Canada in 1919 as a subsidiary of the Bayer Company Inc., and it assigned the Canadian trade-mark to the word ''Aspirin'' to the new company.

In 1923, The American Druggists' Syndicate launched an action in the Exchequer Court of Canada to expunge the trade-mark on the grounds that the name had lost its distinctive character, because the public had come to use the name to describe a number of products based on the same chemical compound. At trial, the court found in favour of the Druggists' Syndicate.[14] On appeal to the Supreme Court of Canada, however, where Bayer was represented by Wallace Nesbitt, the court reversed the trial judgement and allowed the appeal, with costs. Nesbitt's counsel fees, because he was not a participating partner, do not appear in the firm's ledgers. The fact that the company's name does appear in the ledgers throughout the 1920s, however, indicates that the firm was also doing a substantial amount of corporate work for it.

As a result of accounts like Bayer, during the thirteen years between the 1916 split with the McCarthys and the great crash of 1929, Osler, Hoskin & Harcourt posted impressive gains. In the twelve months following the split in 1916, the firm's gross income amounted to some $90,000.00; in the calender year 1918, gross earnings amounted to almost $113,000, which, after expenses, was divided among five participating partners.[15] Ten years later, just before the crash, the firm's earnings had more than doubled. In 1928, the firm earned over a quarter of a million dollars.[16] By comparison, during the same ten-year period, the Canadian cost-of-living index rose by only about 1.8 per cent.[17]

Undoubtedly, the person most responsible for the firm's success during the 1920s — and its survival during the Depression of the 1930s — was Britton Osler. He is generally remembered as a quiet, modest man, who presented a conservative, even austere image. He tended towards dark, three-piece suits and kept a strait-stemmed briar pipe clenched in his teeth, and he could be very strict around the office. But underneath that appearance was a kind man with a warm sense of humour. He looked the other way when students Hal Mockridge and Bob Ferguson played hallway golf using a ball made from an India rubber eraser, and he enjoyed a good joke, particularly at his own expense.[18]

Britton Osler was also a very private man who preferred to keep his legal practice and personal life separate. He almost never had lunch with a client; like most of his contemporaries, he would likely have considered it somehow unprofessional to socialize with a client or potential client. Similarly, he made it a practice never to discuss his work at home. During the late 1920s, he was apparently representing a client whose name had been associated with a particularly juicy society scandal in the press. At one point, his wife Marion received an invitation to tea with some ladies she knew only in passing. When she arrived at the home of one of the ladies on the appointed afternoon, she no sooner had removed her coat when she was asked to tell them all about Mr. "So and So." They were very disappointed to learn that she did not even know that the man was her husband's client, let alone any of the scandalous details.[19]

Most importantly, Britton Osler maintained the loyalty of both the lawyers in the firm and the clients during some very trying times during the years between the wars. The 1930s were difficult, as they were for everyone, but perhaps the most trying time for the firm was during the mid-1920s when an American scandal known as Teapot Dome extended a part of its black cloud north to hang for a time over both the firm and the family.

On the morning of June 2, 1924, a man got off the elevator at the eighth-floor offices of the firm in the Dominion Bank Building, introduced himself as William Houghton of Washington, D.C. and presented credentials from the United States Treasury Department Secret Service. He wanted to see H.S. Osler.[20]

In the early summer of 1924, Henry Smith Osler was sixty-one years old. Although H.S. Osler generally went by his initials, to his friends he was "Hal." In public, however, he was a very formal, even imperious man. In his report to Washington, Secret Service agent Houghton wrote:

Mr. Osler is a man of about 50 or 55 years of age; born in Canada, but with all the mannerisms of an Englishman. He is a nephew of Sir Edmund B. Osler, president of the Dominion Bank of Canada, which is a very large banking institution. He is also related to Sir William Osler, the famous physician.[21]

By 1924, H.S. Osler was the most senior lawyer in Osler, Hoskin & Harcourt, but he was no longer in full-time practice, having left the management of the firm, in 1920, in the hands of his younger brother Britton. He had gone into semi-retirement.[22] He spent only part of his time in Toronto; he also maintained a Mediterranean villa in Nice and he spent a few months every year hunting big game on safari in Africa.[23]

Secret Service agent Houghton was on a special assignment from President Calvin Coolidge to investigate the affair known as Teapot Dome. He had reason to believe that Osler could provide him with some very important information regarding a complex conspiracy of public fraud and cover-up which might be described as the "Watergate" of the 1920s.[24]

Teapot Dome was the name of a ten-thousand-acre tract of federal land in rural Wyoming which was estimated to hold one of the largest untapped reserves of crude oil in the United States. During World War I, the American government introduced a naval oil reserve policy in order to maintain security of supply for military purposes. Shortly after the turn of the century, the U.S. Navy completed a conversion from coal-fired to oil-fired engines on its vessels. Even before the U.S. entered the war in 1917, the navy was one of the largest consumers of American petroleum products. During the war, therefore, the government placed certain tracts of oil-bearing land, including Teapot Dome, in reserve for the exclusive use of the navy if the need should arise.[25]

After the war, private oil companies began to put considerable pressure on Washington to lease some of these lands, but the government decided to keep the oil in reserve in the ground as a hedge against price increases in addition to maintaining security of military supply. The theory was, if market prices began to rise too fast, the navy could simply begin to tap some of its own reserve oil.[26]

In the spring of 1922, however, U.S. Secretary of the Interior Albert B. Fall, whose department had control over the naval reserve lands, agreed to lease the oil rights to Teapot Dome to the Mammoth Oil Company.[27] This company was registered in Delaware and owned by a man named Harry F. Sinclair.[28] Fall, the former U.S. Senator from New Mexico, had been appointed to newly elected President Warren Harding's cabinet less than a year earlier.[29] Harding, a Republican, was elected in 1920; he was an old-style, backroom politician from Ohio, best known for rewarding his friends.[30]

Like other presidents whose administrations have been tainted by scandal, Harding may have been guilty of little more than not keeping close enough tabs on his friends once he put them in office. Two months before his death in August 1923, he was quoted as saying, "My God, this is a hell of a job. I have no trouble with my enemies. . . . But my friends, my God-damned friends . . . they're the ones that keep me walking the floor nights."[31] The most notorious of Harding's friends was his former Senate seat-mate, Albert Fall.[32]

Albert Bacon Fall was a fascinating character, almost a caricature of American history. Born in the hills of Civil War Kentucky, with little or no formal education, he made his way west to the New Mexico Territory in the early 1880s. There he worked as a cowboy, a prospector and a miner, and in his spare time studied law. In 1891, he was admitted to the territorial bar.[33] During the 1890s, he was very successful as a frontier lawyer, mining promoter, rancher and politician. In his early career he was a Democrat, serving in the territorial legislature, but in 1906 he switched parties to become a Republican, and when New Mexico became a state in 1912, the legislature elected him to the United States Senate.[34]

In the Senate, Fall was a strident spokesman for the aggressive, expansionist frontier. Around Washington he was easily recognizable in his black Stetson hat and string tie; according to one national newspaper columnist, "With a long drooping mustache, he looks like a stage sheriff of the Far West in the movies. His voice is always loud and angry. He has the frontiersman's impatience. From his kind lynch law springs."[35] Apparently, this analogy placed Fall on the wrong side of the law.

Like Fall, Harry Sinclair was a ruthless businessman. Born in West Virginia and raised in Kansas, he began his career as a pharmacist, but at an early age he went into the oil business and made his fortune. He also invested in a number of sports enterprises; he was a part-owner of the American League's St. Louis Browns, and in 1923 a horse he owned won the Kentucky Derby. Sinclair was a large, balding and robust man with a winning smile; he was also, as subsequent events would show, thoroughly corrupt.[36]

Even before the government's April, 1922 announcement that the Teapot Dome lands had been leased, there were questions raised. American conservationists were alarmed in early 1921 when then President-elect Harding had announced that Senator Albert Fall of New Mexico, known as anything but sympathetic towards a conservationist policy, would be his Secretary of the Interior. They were still further alarmed when Fall convinced the president to transfer control over the oil reserves from the Department of the Navy to Interior.[37]

Mammoth Oil's lease of the Teapot Dome lands was signed on April 7, 1922.[38] Nevertheless, three days later, when Senator John B. Kendrick of Wyoming, a Democrat, who had received a number of telegrams from constituents regarding rumours of the lease, asked the Interior Department for information, he was told that no such deal had been made.[39] When the rumours persisted, Kendrick rose in the Senate chamber on April 15 and introduced a resolution that the secretaries of the Navy and the Interior "inform the Senate, if not incompatible with the public interests [about] all proposed operating agreements" regarding the Teapot Dome lands.[40]

On April 18, the Department of the Interior made a formal announcement of the lease, and on April 21 Interior officials sent the Senate a copy of the leasing contract with the Mammoth Oil Company.[41] The official reason for changing the government's policy and leasing the reserve to private interests was that the oil was draining into adjacent property, and would be lost if not drilled.[42]

The conservationists were very sceptical about Fall's reasoning and decided to pursue the matter further. On April 21, 1922, Republican Senator Robert M. La Follette of Wisconsin introduced a resolution that the Senate Committee on Public Lands and Surveys "be authorized to investigate this entire subject of leases upon naval oil reserves," and described the Department of the Interior as "the sluiceway for a large part of the corruption to which this government of ours is subjected."[43] In particular, Senator La Follette pointed out that he had specific geological evidence which proved that the Teapot Dome deposit could not be drained by adjacent wells; that excuse was an old and specious ruse of the developers. When the vote was taken on La Follette's resolution, it passed by a margin of 58-0.[44]

Although the Public Lands Committee's investigation started slowly — largely as a result of delaying tactics by administration supporters — over the following months the evidence against Albert Fall began to mount up. In January 1923, the White House announced that Secretary Fall was resigning.[45] In an effort to shore up his own political fortunes, with his own re-election a little more than a year and a half away, Harding was apparently trying to clean up his administration's image.[46] As it turned out, however, the President would not stand for re-election. On August 2, 1923, while in San Francisco on a cross-country speaking tour, Harding suffered a heart attack and died.[47]

Some weeks after Harding's death and the inauguration of Vice-President Coolidge, the Senate Public Lands Committee's investigation of Teapot Dome uncovered some interesting evidence. Committee member Senator Thomas J. Walsh, a Democrat from Montana, learned from sources in New Mexico that during 1922, Albert Fall, who was well known to be in financial difficulty, made some very substantial improvements to his ranch. It was also revealed that Harry Sinclair had been a guest at Fall's ranch in late 1921.[48]

In answer to the question of where he got the money to make the improvements to his ranch, Fall explained that he had borrowed $100,000 in cash from his friend Edward B. McLean, publisher of the Washington *Post*, and added that Sinclair had simply visited him in New Mexico; this, he said, "invited some evil-minded persons to the conclusion that I must have obtained money from Mr. Sinclair."[49] But when Walsh went to Palm Beach, Florida to ask McLean to verify Fall's story about the loan, the publisher told him that he had never loaned Fall any money.[50]

In early 1924, under intense pressure from the Democrats, and from members of his own party who feared that the scandal would damage the Republicans in the elections coming in November, Coolidge agreed to appoint special counsel to investigate the matter.[51] He also assigned a team of four Secret Service agents to assist them.[52] It was one of those Secret Service agents who visited H.S. Osler in June.

During the course of the investigation, the special counsel found records at the First National Bank of Pueblo, Colorado, indicating that some $230,000 in World War I U.S. Liberty Bonds had gone through Albert Fall's account there in May of 1922. These bonds were numbered securities; they might, therefore, be traceable. Unfortunately, they were not registered securities; that is, there was no central registry of their ownership which would provide a record of each time they changed hands. There was, however, a record of their original purchase kept by the Treasury Department in Washington, where they were first issued.[53]

A search of the records at the Treasury department indicated that Fall's bonds were originally part of a $2-million block, first purchased by an Atlanta, Georgia-based steamship company in 1917. By searching the records of the steamship company, a bank and a brokerage house, the investigators traced the bonds to the New York City office of the Dominion Bank of Canada. The Bank purchased them on April 13, 1922, and they were deposited to Fall's First National account in Colorado on May 29, 1922. The special counsel strongly suspected that the bonds had passed through Harry Sinclair's hands during the intervening six weeks.[54]

At the Dominion Bank in New York, the Secret Service agents were told that the bonds they were interested in were purchased on behalf of the Continental Trading Company, Ltd., whose offices were in the Dominion Bank Building in Toronto. The purchase order had been placed by H.S. Osler, K.C., of the same address. Agent Houghton then made his trip to Toronto.[55]

When Houghton asked Osler what happened to the bonds, he replied that he could not give him an answer because that information was subject to solicitor-client privilege, and he was forbidden by professional ethics to reveal it. When Houghton asked him the name of the client whose information he was protecting, he told him that too was privileged.[56] Solicitor-client privilege is the long-standing rule which provides that a lawyer cannot reveal — and cannot be compelled to reveal — the content of any communication with his or her client, without the client's permission. The theory behind the rule is that in order to provide adequate professional advice, the lawyer must have the complete confidence of the client, and the client must be assured that his or her privacy will be maintained. In fact, as another Congressional investigation would later confirm, Osler was protecting the privacy of a number of clients, one of whom was Harry F. Sinclair.[57]

In early 1921, a Colorado oil man named Colonel A.E. Humphreys had a major strike in west Texas. His land, known as the Mexia field, was estimated to hold over a hundred million barrels of high grade, crude oil. On Tuesday, November 15, 1921, Humphreys had a meeting in New York with Colonel H.M. Blackmer, president of the Midwest Refining Company of Denver, Colorado, whose controlling stockholder was the Standard Oil Company of Indiana. Colonel Humphreys indicated that he was willing to sell Midwest thirty million barrels of oil at $1.50 per barrel.[58]

The following day, Blackmer invited Humphreys to lunch to meet two associates who wanted in on the deal. They were James E. O'Neil, president of the Prairie Oil and Gas Company, a subsidiary of Standard Oil of New Jersey, and Harry F. Sinclair, who introduced himself as the president of the Sinclair Crude Oil Purchasing Company. Sinclair himself owned half the stock of this company; the other half was owned in part by the Standard Oil Company of Indiana. On Thursday morning, the four men met again, this time in Blackmer's suite in the Vanderbilt Hotel. Also in attendance was Colonel Robert W. Stewart, chairman of the board of the Standard Oil Company of Indiana.[59]

Colonel Humphreys had brought a draft contract with him which called for the sale of 33,333,333.33 barrels of oil at $1.50 per barrel to the Sinclair Crude Oil Purchasing Company and the Prairie Oil and Gas Company. After some discussion, they came to an agreement, but Blackmer asked Humphreys to change the name of the purchaser to read The Continental Trading Company of Canada.[60]

Humphreys, understandably, had never heard of the Continental Trading Company, but the others assured him that there was no need to worry, because the contract would be guaranteed by both Sinclair Crude Oil Purchasing and Prairie Oil and Gas. When Colonel Humphreys asked who would sign the contract on behalf of this unknown Continental Trading Company, Blackmer informed him that the president of the company would be in New York on Friday.[61] The president of the Continental Trading Company of Canada was H.S. Osler.[62] Osler was known to the men because his firm served as counsel to another subsidiary of Standard Oil of New Jersey, Imperial Oil.[63] It also appears that Osler did some legal work for Blackmer's company, Midwest Refining, about a year earlier.[64]

In fact, the Continental Trading Company had been incorporated the day before in Toronto on behalf of Harry Sinclair, Robert Stewart, H.M. Blackmer and James O'Neil. Although none of their names appeared on the documents of incorporation, later evidence would indicate that they were the controlling stockholders of the company.[65]

On Friday, November 18, Colonel Humphreys met again with Stewart, Sinclair, Blackmer and O'Neil in Blackmer's suite at the Vanderbilt, and they introduced him to H.S. Osler. After some preliminary discussions they signed the deal Humphreys had agreed to the day before, and the Colonel left. Osler then drew up another contract of sale for 33,333,333.33 barrels of oil from the Continental Trading Company to the Sinclair Crude Oil Purchasing Company and the Prairie Oil and Gas Company for $1.75 per barrel, the same 33,333,333.33 barrels of oil it had just agreed to purchase from Humphreys for $1.50 per barrel. In the space of a few minutes, the Continental Trading Company, owned by Sinclair, Blackmer, O'Neil and Stewart, made a profit of $8,333,333.33.[66] It was later suggested that the shareholders of the Sinclair Crude Oil Purchasing Company and the Prairie Oil and Gas Company had thereby been defrauded.[67]

An accusation of fraud is, of course, a very serious one. There is nothing to indicate that $1.75 per barrel was not a fair market value for the oil. In fact, crude oil of the same grade had been selling for $2.00 per barrel earlier that fall.[68] Moreover, each of the four men could argue that he was acting not as an officer of his company, but as a private individual. In the case of O'Neil and Sinclair, this is very difficult to accept. They were the chief executive officers of the ultimate purchasers of the oil. They could have bought it for their companies at $1.50 a barrel, but they chose to buy it for themselves at that price and sell it to their companies for $1.75, and keep the profit.

Stewart's conflict of interest was not quite as direct as O'Neil and Sinclair's, but as the chairman of Standard Oil of Indiana, which had a 50 per cent interest in the Sinclair Crude Oil Purchasing Company, his interest conflicted with that of his own company. Finally, Blackmer, whose company Midwest Refining did not take part in the deal, is perhaps least culpable. It was offered the oil at $1.50, but Blackmer chose to change the terms.

If this kind of deal were arranged today, the participants would most likely be found to be in conflict of interest; by accepting what would amount to a secret commission, they would be in breach of a fiduciary duty owed to their companies and shareholders. From an historical perspective, however, one might legitimately ask whether this kind of behaviour would be more acceptable in the 1920s. According to Harvard professor Carl F. Taeusch, who published *Policy and Ethics in Business* in 1931, this behaviour — which he termed "double agency" — had unfortunately become more common. However, he quoted John D. Rockefeller, Jr., whose family maintained substantial control over most of the Standard Oil companies, speaking bluntly about these affairs when he appeared before the Senate Committee on Public Lands and Surveys: "No officer of any company would have any right to make a profit out of a company which he was paid to protect the interests of."[69]

Whether H.S. Osler should be painted with the same brush is another matter. Assuming for the moment that he knew of each of his client's corporate positions, and that he agreed with Rockefeller's opinion regarding conflict of interest, his role certainly appeared suspect, particularly with respect to O'Neil and Sinclair. But it is important to place these events within the context of the time, not simply in terms of the relative standard of business ethics of the day, but of the relative infancy of the corporate and tax law environment.

It had only been a decade since the 1911 forced break-up of Standard Oil into its various state-based component companies, and although U.S. income tax dated to the Civil War, only since the Sixteenth Amendment to the Constitution in 1913 had the federal power to tax income been clear, and Canadian income tax dated only to World War I.[70] Seen in this light the illegitimacy of the Continental Trading Company is not as clear.

Moreover, the fact that the only publicly identified shareholders of the company were not its real owners or controllers may not have been as questionable as it seems to the layman. Today, it is quite common for clients to ask lawyers to incorporate companies for tax purposes or other reasons. It is also common for clients to ask lawyers to establish corporate share ownership arrangements using trustees and nominees in order to protect the identity of the beneficial owner. The client many have perfectly legitimate business reasons for maintaining his privacy, and there is no obligation on the lawyer to question or investigate the client's motives. In fact, Osler's clients told him that the profits from the Continental Trading Company would go to its rightful owners.

Regardless of the propriety of their motives, or Osler's understanding of its propriety, the four apparently instructed him to incorporate a Canadian company to earn the 25-cent-per-barrel profit on their behalf. Osler used the money to purchase U.S. Liberty Bonds at the New York office of the Dominion Bank, and over the course of the following months he delivered each of the four principals his share of the bonds. In February 1922, Albert Fall agreed to lease the Teapot Dome drilling rights to Harry Sinclair's company, Mammoth Oil, and in May Sinclair gave Fall a total of $233,000 in Liberty Bonds.[71]

Between May 1922 and June 1924, when Agent Houghton came to see H.S. Osler, the investigators had largely pieced the story together. What Houghton wanted from Osler was confirmation that he had given Sinclair the bonds which ended up in Secretary Fall's bank account in Colorado. But as Osler explained, he could not supply that kind of information because it would breach an ethical duty to his client. Houghton therefore returned to New York to continue the investigation.[72]

Later in the summer, Houghton and an associate returned to Toronto to see H.S. Osler. This time the lawyer was a little more candid, explaining that he had organized the Continental Trading Company in the late fall of 1921 to conduct some business on behalf of his client. He had incorporated it as a Canadian company because if all of its business was conducted in the United States and it was registered in Canada, it would be subject to neither American nor Canadian taxes. In addition, under Canadian law the company would not be required to disclose the owners of its stock. As Houghton put it in his report, ''Whether this latter feature was stated to him to be of importance or not, he cannot be sure, but he has a sort of hunch it was desired.''[73]

The officers and directors of the company, all associated with his law firm, were named only to comply with Canadian company law; they had no interest or control in its affairs but simply followed the instructions of their clients.[74] Yes, it was true that the Continental Trading Company had only one contract for purchase of oil, and one for the immediate resale of the same oil, and even that contract had been sold prior to its completion.[75] Beyond that, Osler politely explained, ethics would not permit him to tell them anything.

In the meantime, the United States government filed suit against the Mammoth Oil Company in the Federal District Court in Cheyenne, Wyoming, to cancel the lease on Teapot Dome on the grounds that ''said lease was executed as the result of a conspiracy to defraud the plaintiff, between one Albert B. Fall, the then Secretary of the Interior, and one Harry F. Sinclair, who negotiated the lease on behalf of said Mammoth Oil Company.''[76] The trial of this suit was scheduled for October 1924, and the special counsel very much wanted Osler to testify at the trial.[77] If they could establish that Osler had given bonds to Sinclair which bore the same serial numbers as those found in Fall's bank account, they could connect both alleged conspirators to the alleged bribe and go a long way towards convincing the court that the lease was obtained fraudulently.

The problem was that Osler would not testify because he refused to breach his ethical duty to his client, which prohibited him from revealing either his client's instructions or identity. The U.S. government lawyers then obtained an order from the judge in the Wyoming case against Mammoth Oil appointing a commissioner, Harold

Shantz, the U.S. Consul in Toronto, to take evidence from Osler. When Osler refused to acknowledge the authority of the American court, the government lawyers obtained an order from the Supreme Court of Ontario confirming the appointment. Osler then appeared before Shantz and read a prepared statement, but he refused to take an oath or answer any questions.[78]

The U.S. government then retained E.G. McMillan of the Toronto firm Rowell, Reid, Wood, Wright & McMillan and filed a motion in the Supreme Court of Ontario to have Osler committed to jail for contempt of court.[79] When that motion was heard on September 27, Osler was represented by Arthur W. Anglin of Blake, Lash, Anglin & Cassels, and McMillan was accompanied by his senior partner, Newton Wesley Rowell.[80] Justice William Renwick Riddell granted Anglin an adjournment, but as he did so he looked down from the bench and commented — apparently in jest — "I am deprived of sending my friend Mr. Osler to jail today." Osler replied, "If it will give your Lordship any pleasure I will go this afternoon."[81] Osler was, of course, very well known to Riddell. In addition to being a prominent K.C., he was the son of Riddell's former colleague on the bench, Featherston Osler, who had died only eight months earlier.[82]

After a series of procedural manoeuvres, the case once again came before Justice Riddell on Wednesday, December 10; this time Osler was represented by his colleague Wallace Nesbitt.[83] In response to a question from Riddell, Rowell and McMillan admitted that they were really not interested in having Osler committed to jail for contempt. They simply wanted "an opinion of the Court as to the propriety of the refusal on the part of the witnesses to answer the questions specified."[84]

Nesbitt then submitted a statement to the court on Osler's behalf, in which Osler admitted only what was already public knowledge. He had been retained by an individual — whom he was not permitted to identify — to provide some legal advice regarding the purchase and resale of a large quantity of crude oil. His client had instructed him that, as the oil business was a very speculative and competitive business, secrecy was of the utmost importance. He had incorporated the Continental Trading Company in order to conduct this transaction. Beyond that, on his client's specific instructions, he was unable to provide any information.[85]

The judge disagreed with Osler's interpretation of professional ethics under these circumstances. In his judgement issued on Saturday, December 13, Riddell gave a detailed explanation of the law of solicitor-client privilege, and ruled that as Osler's client's name was apparently known to him prior to becoming his client — at least he did not claim that he only learned it as a result of becoming the man's solicitor — he could not refuse to name him. More importantly, however, Riddell went on to rule that

> The authorities seem to be uniform that it is only facts which come to the knowledge of a solicitor from his client, and not facts obtained on information *aliunde** that are excluded from disclosure.
>
> This rule applies also to the acts of the solicitor. The acts of the solicitor are facts which indeed may proceed from the instructions of the client, but are in no wise confidential communications by the client to the solicitor. I have no doubt whatever that what was done by Mr. Osler, his associates in his office, and by the company, in the way of obtaining money and disbursing it, the persons to whom it was paid, and all the particulars about such transactions, must be disclosed and are not covered by the privilege. . . .
>
> The result is that I think the questions which have been objected to must be answered, and the plaintiffs will have costs.[86]

The Globe carried the story of Riddell's ruling on its front page on Monday with the headline ''OSLER MUST RELATE ALL ABOUT SCHEMES AND PLANS OF 'MR. X','' but added ''APPEAL SEEMS PROBABLE.''[87]

In fact, Osler did appeal the ruling, but even before Wallace Nesbitt had filed the papers, Osler set sail for Africa for another safari.[88] In the meantime, however, the trial in the U.S. government's suit against Mammoth Oil was set to begin in Wyoming. The judge there had already granted the plaintiff's request for a delay pending Osler's hearing in Toronto, but he was unwilling to wait while Osler exhausted the appeal process. The trial was scheduled to begin in Cheyenne on March 8, 1925.[89] Unless the Court of Appeal worked very quickly to deal with Nesbitt's appeal, it was unlikely that the U.S. government counsel would be able to use Osler's evidence in the case against Sinclair's company. The appeal of Riddell's ruling was set for February 9 in Toronto.[90]

The hearing for the appeal, in which A.W. Anglin spoke for Osler and N.W. Rowell represented the U.S. government, lasted two and a

---

* From another source.

half days; and on the afternoon of Thursday February 11, the court reserved its judgement. Rowell politely reminded the judges about the trial in Wyoming, and "hinted that their Lordships could aid matters by delivering an early judgement."[91]

Their Lordships released their decision four weeks later and upheld Riddell's ruling. However, they did so for different reasons. In his judgement, Justice William N. Ferguson explained that when Osler learned his clients' names was irrelevant. If he was acting as their solicitor their identities and instructions were privileged. However, Ferguson continued, "I am not satisfied that Mr. Osler was retained at a place or under circumstances or for a purpose that gave or entitled him or his client to claim that in reference to the business in hand Mr. Osler had the status of professional legal adviser. . ."[92] Osler was not a member of the New York State bar, and his clients were not Canadians. The meeting at which they originally disclosed the nature of the business which Osler claimed was confidential took place in New York City, and he was not, at the time, advising them on Canadian law. "The formation of the Canadian corporation known as the Continental Trading Company Limited was an afterthought."[93]

After dismissing Osler's appeal, however, Ferguson went on to comment on what he personally thought about the propriety of Osler's conduct:

> I do not think that I should leave this case without saying that in disclosing the facts and submitting them to this Court for consideration and direction, before answering the questions in dispute, Mr. Osler only performed what his duty to the Court and to his client required him to do, and that the conclusion at which I have arrived should not be interpreted as indicating that I doubt the propriety of Mr. Osler's conduct in the transactions sought to be investigated or the propriety of his claim of privilege or the propriety of his conduct in prosecuting this appeal. It was not in argument suggested that Mr. Osler had been a party to any wrongdoing; and, in my opinion, his duty to the Court and to his client required that he raise the question of privilege and not abandon it until thoroughly satisfied that he had been rightly directed by the Court. For, as I understand it, the rule is a rule of public policy established in the interest of justice rather than a rule established for the protection of particular persons such as the solicitor or his client, and rather than as a rule granting the solicitor or his client the right to claim some priv-

ilege or protection, and therefore is a rule which the Court must enforce unless its enforcement be waived by the client.[94]

The trial of *U.S.* v. *Mammoth Oil* began as scheduled on March 8, but when the Ontario Court of Appeal judgement dismissing Osler's appeal was released three days later, the government lawyers in Cheyenne told the press that it was too late to use the evidence. Any evidence they could obtain from Osler regarding the Liberty Bonds could only be used in the event of a retrial.[95] Even if they wanted to, however, the government lawyers would not be able to take any testimony from Osler. He was still in Africa, and had apparently been admitted to a Cairo hospital suffering from blood poisoning.[96]

The trial ended in Cheyenne on March 28, and on April 14 *The Globe* reported that Osler had returned from safari in Africa.[97] In June, Judge T.B. Kennedy of the U.S. District Court in Wyoming released his decision; he found that the government had failed to prove fraud in awarding the lease, and dismissed the suit.[98] But the special prosecutors were not about to give up. They immediately filed an appeal with the Eighth Circuit Court of Appeals in St. Louis, and there they had more luck. Although in general an appeal court cannot overrule a trial court's finding of fact, the Circuit Court ruled that the trial judge's finding that the government had failed to prove fraud was a mixed ruling of law and fact. The appeal judges then went on to find that the government had indeed provided sufficient circumstantial evidence to prove fraud, and they invalidated Mammoth Oil's lease of the Teapot Dome lands.[99]

With conflicting judgements in the lower courts, Sinclair decided to take the final step and appeal to the Supreme Court. But that court's judgement, released in October 1927, not only upheld the Circuit Court's finding of fraud, it also denounced the Continental Trading Company as "illegitimate." In his decision, Justice Pierce Butler wrote:

> The creation of the Continental Company, the purchase and resale contracts enabling it to make more than $8,000,000 without capital, risk or effort, the assignment of the contract to the resale purchasers for a small fraction of its probable value, and the purpose to conceal the disposition of its assets, make it plain that the company was created for some illegitimate purpose.[100]

But the court battles over Teapot Dome did not end there. Having succeeded in regaining government control of the oil reserves, the special prosecutors were also intent on criminal punishment for Fall and Sinclair. In 1927 the two were charged with conspiracy.[101]

Fall and Sinclair went on trial in Washington on October 17, 1927 in the Supreme Court of the District of Columbia. At that trial the prosecutors did not try to get H.S. Osler to testify. They apparently felt that the Supreme Court's finding in the civil suit against Mammoth Oil would be enough to convince the jury. Two weeks into the trial, however, the judge stunned the courtroom by declaring a mistrial; Sinclair had been interfering with the jury.[102]

The retrial of Fall and Sinclair on the conspiracy charges was set for the spring of 1928, but in April Fall sent word from his ranch in New Mexico that he was too ill to go on trial. The court granted him a delay, but the government prosecutors decided to go ahead against Sinclair alone.[103] To the prosecutors' amazement, however, the jury ignored the Supreme Court's finding and acquitted Sinclair.[104] Senator Gerald Nye, a Republican from North Dakota, retorted "this is emphatic evidence that you can't convict a million dollars in the United States."[105] Senator George Norris, a Republican from Nebraska, exploded:

> Why, everybody in the United States and even the Supreme Court knows he is guilty. The whole transaction has been held to be fraudulent and it could not have been fraudulent except for Sinclair. He has too much money to be convicted. We ought to pass a law now to the effect that no man worth a hundred million dollars should ever be tried for any crime. That would make us at least consistent.[106]

The New York *World* published an editorial cartoon over the caption "The Empty Cell." The cartoon pictured four jail cells labelled "Rich Man, Poor Man, Beggar Man, Thief." The last three had occupants, but the first one was empty.[107]

In October 1929, Albert Fall finally appeared in the District of Columbia Supreme Court on a charge of bribery. After a trial lasting two weeks, the jury found him guilty.[108] In light of his health they recommended mercy, but the judge sentenced him to a year in prison and fined him $100,000. The District of Columbia Appellate Court upheld the verdict, and the Supreme Court refused to hear a further appeal. In July 1931, he began serving his sentence in the federal prison at Santa Fe, New Mexico.[109]

While the conspiracy trials were going on in Washington, the Senate Public Lands Committee launched another investigation, this time specifically into the affairs of the Continental Trading Company. On January 4, 1928, Senator Norris introduced a resolution that the Senate direct the Public Lands Committee to investigate "the transactions and activities of . . . the Continental Trading Company [to] trace all the Government bonds held and dealt in by said corporation [in order to learn] the beneficiaries of all the illegal transactions connected with the fraudulent and dishonest sale or leasing of the . . . naval oil reserves.[110] The Senate passed Norris' resolution on January 9, and two weeks later the Committee began its hearings.[111]

Over the course of the next four months, the Public Lands Committee heard from a number of oil men and politicians. The Committee members eventually learned that the Continental Trading Company had amassed some $3,000,000 during its short existence. Harry Sinclair had used some of his share to bribe Albert Fall, and he had made some very large donations to both the Republican and Democratic parties.[112] During 1923 and 1924, however, Harry Blackmer, James O'Neil and Robert Stewart had all returned their shares to their respective companies.[113]

It was also calculated from the Liberty Bond transaction records at the Dominion Bank in New York that H.S. Osler's share of the proceeds was 2 per cent.[114] His earnings from the affair were, therefore, some $60,000. Of this amount, the firm's ledgers indicate that the Continental Trading Company paid just over $24,000 to the firm in legal fees.[115] The remaining $36,000 were either Osler's commission for handling the funds or his dividends as a shareholder.

During the early stages of the hearings in January, 1928 the Committee members tried to get H.S. Osler to come to Washington to testify, but like the prosecutors in the Cheyenne oil lease trial, they were unsuccessful. They persuaded Vice-President Charles Dawes to appoint a commission to take evidence from Osler in Canada, but when it was learned that he was in Europe, nothing more was done.[116] Two weeks later the committee issued a subpoena calling on Osler to testify on Saturday February 11, but as he was under no legal obligation to abide the subpoena, he did not appear.[117]

At the conclusion of its hearings, the Committee came to a very damning conclusion about the Continental Trading Company. In his report to the Senate, Senator Thomas J. Walsh wrote:

It seems now, however to have been the ill-gotten gains of a contemptible private steal, the peculations of trusted officers of great industrial houses, pilfering from their own companies, robbing their own stockholders, the share of the boodle coming to one of the freebooters serving in part as the price of the perfidy of a member of the President's cabinet.[118]

In the end, there was no doubt of the guilt of some of the men involved in the sordid affair. Albert Fall was convicted of accepting a bribe and ultimately spent nine months in prison and, although Harry Sinclair was acquitted of paying the same bribe, he went to jail for contempt of court in connection with his tampering with the jury in the first conspiracy trial.

But despite the damning conclusions of the United States Supreme Court and the Senate committee, no charges were ever laid in connection with the Continental Trading Company. Harry Blackmer and James O'Neil were in self-imposed exile, and Robert W. Stewart, although he was acquitted of perjury following his testimony in the Senate inquiry, was ousted from his position as chairman of Standard Oil of Indiana in a proxy fight with John D. Rockefeller, Jr.[119]

With the exception of Sinclair, all of them claimed that they had intended to give the Continental profits to their companies all along and that they were merely holding the bonds in trust. However, as the Senate committee found, those claims became very difficult to accept when it was learned that they had clipped the maturing coupons from the bonds in June and December of 1922 and 1923, but that after that — as the investigation of Teapot Dome was heating up — they stopped clipping the coupons.[120]

Assessing Osler's role in the affair is more difficult. From one point of view the propriety of his conduct could certainly be questioned. From that perspective he was not simply providing sound legal counsel to a client about whose affairs he would not make a moral judgement. Rather, he was an active advisor and participant in an attempt to defraud. From a more sympathetic perspective, however, he may have been duped by his clients — at least at first. If he honestly believed that the four men either had a legal right to the Continental profits, or that they genuinely intended to give the money to its rightful owners, his role in the affair at its beginning was an innocent, if naive, one.

Moreover, there is no clear basis to assume that Osler was aware that Sinclair intended to use the Liberty Bonds to bribe U.S. government officials or that Osler was in any other way implicated in the Teapot Dome affair. Nevertheless, it is likely that at some point Osler came to realize that his clients were involved in questionable dealings. At that point, he would have found himself in an ethical dilemma. Regardless of his personal feelings, or the negative publicity he received, as Justice Ferguson pointed out, he could not willingly breach his clients' privilege and submit to the questioning of foreign investigators without direction from the courts. As well, if his clients wished, he had no choice but to pursue any right of appeal which remained open.

However, if that was the case, one might legitimately ask: "Why then did Osler not appear before the Commissioner and give a full and complete accounting of himself? And why did he choose not to appear before the Senate Committee on Public Lands and Surveys in the spring of 1928?" There was nothing in law to compel him to answer a foreign subpoena, and the effort to obtain commissioned evidence through Vice-President Dawes was apparently abandoned, but he ignored the opportunity to clear the air and, perhaps, his name.

Perhaps the answer to this question is in what happened to the firm over the years which followed. Despite the negative publicity,[121] the events of the Teapot Dome scandal had little negative impact on the firm. Although Osler, Hoskin & Harcourt's revenues declined somewhat in 1924, they rebounded over the following years.[122] Moreover, there is no evidence to indicate that clients chose not to retain the firm because of H.S. Osler's implication in the scandal. Perhaps most significantly, Imperial Oil remained a client. If John D. Rockefeller had wanted to rid Standard Oil of all connections with the Continental deal, as he did when he ousted Robert Stewart, he could have instructed Imperial to fire Osler's firm, but he did not.

Had H.S. Osler chosen to go public, once the Ontario Court of Appeal removed the ethical roadblock, he might have been able to clear his own name, at least in some people's minds; but the fact that he did not, the fact that he defied a U.S. Senate subpoena, which meant that he could never again enter the United States without fear of being arrested, meant that he could be trusted to keep a client's secrets, regardless of how unsavoury they might be.

Even if this was the case, H.S. Osler apparently did not serve any more clients following the end of the Continental Trading Company affair. Although he remained a minority partner in the firm, he spent virtually all of his time away from Toronto. He died in Montreal in 1933. His younger brother Britton, who had taken over the firm even before the affair began, had more important things to worry about. On October 29, 1929, the New York Stock Market crashed, and many of Osler, Hoskin & Harcourt's clients found themselves in great difficulty.

The collapse of the stock market on "Black Tuesday," as it came to be known, brought disaster for the economies of virtually all of the industrialized world. Canada, as a still largely primary products-based economy, suffered more than most. In the stock markets, Wall Street, where many Canadian-operated companies were traded, saw the biggest losses, but the Toronto and Montreal stock exchanges were also hard hit. Many investors felt that the market would rebound, but the economy continued to decline for four years. It finally reached the bottom in 1933, and began a slow recovery.

In Canada, wheat was a major problem. Prairie farmers who had purchased land and equipment on fixed-interest credit during the boom years of the late 1920s were forced to try to pay off their debts with the price of wheat at a fraction of pre-crash levels. Moreover, on the heels of plummeting prices came drought; hundreds of fore-closed farms simply blew away in the wind.

Overall, the Canadian gross national product fell from a high of over $6 billion in 1929 to $3½ billion in 1933.[123] The value of Canadian exports saw a similar decline, falling from over a billion in 1929 to less than half that amount in 1932.[124] Perhaps the most tangible indicator of the hard time the Depression brought was the unemployment rate. In 1929, some 116,000 Canadians, or roughly 2.9 per cent of the labour force, were out of work. By 1933, some 826,000 Canadians, 19.3 per cent of the labour force, were unemployed.

The one figure which should indicate the prospective health of a corporate law firm was the stock market. The fifty leading stocks on the Toronto Stock Exchange lost 85.9 per cent of their value between October 1929 and May 1932.[125] Under Britton Osler's leadership, however, Osler, Hoskin & Harcourt did not decline nearly as much as most other Canadian enterprises during the Depression. The firm's gross revenue fell from almost $285,000 in 1929 to just over $200,000 in 1932, but by 1933 it had rebounded to $234,000. By 1939, it was back over $284,000.[126]

Perhaps more significant to the long-term health of the firm was the loyalty which Britton Osler engendered among the staff. A number of long-time employees who joined the firm after World War II remember senior staff telling them that, unlike most other employers in the city, Oslers did not lay anyone off or reduce any salaries during the Depression. The story sounds apocryphal, but in fact while other expense items in the firm's annual profit-and-loss statements were going down in the 1930s, the cost of staff salaries remained virtually constant.[127]

As World War II began, the firm was in very good financial condition. With some of the country's most important companies among its clients, and fifteen lawyers — including Arthur Meighen, a former prime minister — on its letterhead, the firm was doing very well. Towards the end of 1943, however, the firm was in for a shock.

5

GROWTH, CHANGE AND BETRAYAL: 1943-1954

Two weeks before Christmas of 1943, Britton Osler died. He went into the office on the ninth of December, a Thursday, to discuss a file with Harold Shapley, but on Friday morning he called to say that he didn't feel well and wouldn't be in. At about six o'clock Saturday night he suffered a heart attack and died. He was sixty-nine years old. He had suffered from phlebitis when approaching sixty and had had gall bladder trouble more recently, but he was in reasonably good health for someone of his years. His death, therefore, came as a real shock to the firm.

Osler had begun to limit his practice somewhat since the war began, but he was still very much the leader of the firm. Since H.S. Osler's semi-retirement in the early 1920s, he was the senior partner and made virtually all of the decisions about matters such as salaries and partners' shares.[1] He was also one of the best-known corporation lawyers in Canada; he had been in practice for over forty-five years and was responsible for most of the firm's important clients. His directorships included Royal Trust, American Bank Note, Hudson Bay Mining and Smelting, the Borden Company and International Nickel.

The rest of the members of the firm, however, were relatively junior. Only two partners had more than twenty-five years of experience at the bar. The senior of these, a very old man named Wellington Ault Cameron, who was called to the bar in 1891 and had joined the firm in 1911, was a fixed-interest partner whose practice was limited exclusively to real estate. Bill Bryden, who was a student in the firm after the war, remembers Cameron as always sitting behind his desk with a blanket over his knees, even in the warmest summer weather.[2]

The other was Harold Shapley, who was then sixty years old. Shapley was called to the bar in 1907 and joined Osler, Hoskin & Harcourt from Mulock, Milliken, Clark & Redman in 1917. He was a highly respected corporate counsel, but by 1943 his practice was confined almost entirely to the Dominion Bank and Borden accounts. Shapley was a large, bald, robust man who could generally be found over lunch in Rutherford's Restaurant on the ground floor of the Dominion Bank Building facing Yonge Street, regaling the juniors with stories about the old days.[3]

Including those of Cameron and Shapley, there were sixteen names on the firm's letterhead, but many of these lawyers were not in active practice. A. Munro Grier, a very senior litigation lawyer, and Arthur Meighen, the former prime minister, were listed as "Counsel to the Firm." Their names added some prestige to the letterhead, but they neither shared in the partnership nor brought in any fees. Of the remaining twelve, five were on active service with the Canadian armed forces, including two of Britton Osler's sons.

The two men who became co-senior partners in the wake of Osler's death were George Meredith Huycke and Harold Charles Featherston Mockridge. Huycke, known universally as "Mossey," was a World War I veteran who was very seriously wounded at the Battle of the Somme in May of 1917. He was brought back to Canada by hospital ship. A piece of shrapnel lodged next to his spine was removed at Toronto General Hospital. When he was discharged, he enrolled in the accelerated course for veterans at Osgoode Hall and articled at Osler, Hoskin & Harcourt; he was called to the bar in 1920.[4]

The origin of Huycke's nickname seems to be a mystery. Some think that it was a diminutive of Meredith, but his son Ed Huycke, a partner with the firm prior to his retirement in 1991, disagrees. He thinks that his father picked it up in the army during the war or afterwards at the fraternity house where he lived while a law student. "It no doubt related to some horrendous evening or something. The fact that he never saw fit to even tell my mother leads me to think that it must have been pretty bad!"[5] In 1943 Mossey Huycke was forty-eight years old and was a well-known corporate lawyer specializing in mining companies.

Mockridge, known as "Hal" to his friends and "The Prince" to some of the less reverent students, was younger than Huycke.[6] Those who knew and worked with Hal Mockridge during his career with

the firm, which spanned six decades, remember him as very businesslike, even severe; he was not an easy person to get to know —
particularly to students, some of whom found him intimidating —
but once you got to know him, he could be very warm and charming.
He was not an especially tall man but he was, nevertheless, an very
imposing presence; he was all business. His one distraction outside
of his work was his cottage on Lake Rosseau in Muskoka, Ontario.[7]

Born in Detroit in 1901, Hal Mockridge was Britton Osler's
nephew. His mother was Osler's older sister, Beatrice; his father,
John Mockridge, was the Rector of St. James Episcopal Church in
Philadelphia. In fact, his father, paternal grandfather and paternal
great-grandfather were all Episcopalian or Anglican clergymen, as
was his maternal great-grandfather, Featherstone Lake Osler. Not
surprisingly, Mockridge attended The Episcopal Academy in Philadelphia before going on to college at Princeton in 1919.[8] Rather than
follow in his father's footsteps to a career in the clergy, however,
young Mockridge chose the other traditional career in his family. His
maternal grandfather, Featherston Osler, and his great-uncle, B.B.
Osler, were both lawyers, as were his uncles H.S. and Britton Osler.

In the spring of 1923, his final year at Princeton, Mockridge began
to think seriously about law as a career. In the United States, this
would mean three more years of full-time study in law school before
being called to the bar. If, as Britton Osler explained to him, he chose
to make his career in his mother's country, however, he could join a
law firm as an articling student and do the three-year part-time law
school program at Osgoode Hall. He accepted his uncle's offer and
joined the firm as a student in the fall of 1923.

After his call to the Ontario bar in the spring of 1927, Mockridge
accepted an offer to stay with the firm as a junior lawyer. His uncle,
who had taken over as senior partner from his older brother, H.S.
Osler while Mockridge was a student, had apparently taken a liking
to his nephew, and took him under his wing and began grooming him
to eventually take over leadership of the firm. In 1929, Mockridge
became a partner. Britton Osler had three sons of his own — all of
whom eventually joined the firm — whom he might have considered
as candidates to succeed him. However, he had married and started
a family relatively late in life, and his sons, the oldest of whom was
nine years younger than Mockridge, would simply be too young to
assume such a position when it came time for Osler to retire.

During the 1930s, Britton Osler increasingly relied on Mockridge
to assist him in the legal work for many of the firm's most important

clients, particularly Inco. Inco was one of the firm's largest clients, and despite the fact that they were happy with Mockridge's work as Osler's junior, there was a real danger that they would take their work to another firm after Osler's death. This would have been a disaster for the firm.

These fears were quickly dispelled, however, by an explicit vote of confidence in the firm which appeared in the business section of the January 4, 1944 *New York Times*, announcing that the board of directors of International Nickel had elected H.C.F. Mockridge to the board in place of the late Britton Osler.[9] In the weeks following, virtually all of the companies for whom Osler had served as a director named either Mockridge or Huycke to their boards, and the firm maintained its client list.[10]

The fact that the firm maintained its clients following the crisis of Britton Osler's death was indicative of the success of one of the policies he insisted on while acting as senior partner. Despite the fact that he was clearly the leader of the firm — in terms of client responsibility and income as well as administration — he made sure that everyone, lawyers and clients alike, knew that clients were considered to have retained the firm as a whole, rather than an individual lawyer. This teamwork approach to practice not only fostered a strong sense of community within the firm, but it made the transition period following the death or retirement of even the most important partner much less traumatic. Mockridge and the others learned from this and continued the policy during the post-war era, when the increasing complexity of the law and consequent specialization in practice made it even more valuable.

The other five lawyers in the firm after Britton Osler's death were Norman Strickland, R.G. Ferguson, Harold Boston, John Hood, and T.D. Delamere. In addition to practising law, Strickland acted as the firm's office manager. He was responsible for hiring and supervising the staff and students and, according to Donald Pattison, a lawyer who joined the firm as a student in the mid-1950s, Strickland ran the office in a style which could best be described as "despotism tempered with anarchy."[11]

Strickland was a fairly short, round man, who chain-smoked Players' Navy Cut cigarettes.[12] He was born in Cornwall, Ontario in 1895 and came to the firm as a fifteen-year-old office boy in 1910. Britton Osler apparently took a liking to him and encouraged him to become a lawyer. Strickland left the firm to serve in the Canadian army during World War I, but when he returned in 1919 he did so as an articled law student. Like Mossey Huycke, Strickland took the short course for veterans at Osgoode Hall and was called to the bar in 1921. He then joined the firm as a junior lawyer and became a partner two years later.

In addition to looking after the interests of his clients, who included the International Playing Card Company of Windsor, Ontario, the makers of Bicycle Playing Cards, Strickland's responsibilities included opening all of the mail addressed to the firm. Until the firm's business grew to such a size that it became impossible (some time in the late 1950s), the partners would gather every morning in Strickland's office to open the mail. Strickland would distribute it according to who was responsible for which client or area of law, and they would often use the occasion to bring each other up to date on what they were doing. These daily sessions were actually informal partnership meetings. Formal partnership meetings were not considered necessary until the firm grew much larger some years later.

Bob Ferguson, who had gone to Princeton with Mockridge, was born in Great Falls, Montana in 1899. His father was a Canadian who had immigrated to the American west to practise medicine. Ferguson's mother was from Alabama; in fact, his maternal grandfather was a Civil War veteran of the Confederate army. When he graduated from Princeton, like Mockridge, he took the advice of a Canadian uncle and came to Toronto to study law. His uncle, Mr. Justice William N. Ferguson of the Supreme Court of Ontario, arranged for him to be articled at Mulock, Milliken, Clark & Redman, and young Ferguson enrolled at Osgoode Hall in the fall of 1924.

Ferguson stayed with the Mulock firm until just prior to his call to the bar in 1927, when he took the advice of Hal Mockridge, with whom he shared a Toronto apartment, and transferred his articles to Osler, Hoskin & Harcourt. He stayed with the firm as a junior lawyer and, in 1929, he joined the partnership along with Mockridge. Unlike his Princeton classmate, Ferguson did very little corporate law, and by the outbreak of World War II his practice was confined almost exclusively to estates work and trademarks.

Harold Boston was not really a part of the group. Born in Toronto in 1902, he graduated from Oakwood Collegiate and took a job as an office boy in a watch factory. Not long after he started, however, he happened to see a payroll list and decided that he would look around for another career. When he saw an advertisement in a Toronto newspaper for a law student at Osler, Hoskin & Harcourt, he applied for the position.[13] In those days a high school graduate could become a lawyer without attending university by articling for five years and attending the part-time lectures at Osgoode Hall during the final three. University graduates like Mockridge and Ferguson could do it in three. Boston started as a student in the firm in 1920 and was called to the bar in 1925.

Oslers apparently didn't have a place for Boston as a lawyer in the firm, but Wallace Nesbitt, the former Supreme Court of Canada Justice who was then counsel to the firm, found him a job with his brother, Montalieu Nesbitt, in Woodstock, Ontario. Boston stayed there for a year and a half, and in 1927 returned to Osler, Hoskin & Harcourt. Unlike Mockridge and Ferguson, who were offered partnerships very quickly, Boston remained an associate lawyer for over sixteen years. It wasn't until after Britton Osler's death in 1943 that he became a partner, and even then it was as a fixed-interest partner.[14]

C.R. Osler, Britton Osler's youngest son, remembers Boston as a bit of an outsider. He was a very quiet man who never really took part in the social activities of the other lawyers in the firm.[15] Like Cameron, Boston did mostly real estate work; as a consequence, he had a lot to do with the students who did most of the title searching in the small commercial and residential conveyancing files he worked on. Allan Beattie remembers him as a very knowledgable teacher and a thoughtful supervisor.[16]

John Hood was even more of an outsider than Boston. He practised for many years in Shelburne, Nova Scotia, but found it virtually impossible to make a living during the Depression. His son, who was the manager of the Bank of Commerce branch in Toronto where Britton Osler did some banking, asked if the firm might be able to find some room for him. Osler apparently felt sorry for the man and offered him a place; he also did mostly real estate, but according to Harold Mockridge, "any job you gave him to do you were treated to about half an hour's disposition as to how it would have been done in Nova Scotia."[17]

T.D. Delamere was very much a part of the firm, and his presence after Britton Osler's death had a great deal to do with its continued success. Delamere, who was known as "Tommy" to his friends, was a labour law specialist, and during the war labour relations became one of the most important areas of the firm's corporate practice. He had articled at Osler, Hoskin & Harcourt along with Harold Boston between 1920 and 1925, but like Boston, there was no room for him with the firm when he was called to the bar. Instead, he joined the two-man firm of Wilkie & Hamilton around the corner on Bay Street.

He maintained contact with the firm, however, because he was Mockridge's brother-in-law, their wives being sisters.[18]

In 1942, when Britton Osler began to cut back on his practice, the firm invited Delamere back and he accepted a partnership. Before the war, labour relations had not been a particularly significant area of corporate legal practice. Labour law in Canada was governed by the 1907 Industrial Disputes Investigations Act and the old common law of master and servant, neither of which made the legal relationship between management and labour particularly complicated. Rather, it was simply economics which governed the labour-management relationship.

During the Depression years, the demand for labour, like all commodities, was down. Organized labour, what there was, had little or no economic leverage to force employers to negotiate or even recognize a union as the workers' collective bargaining agent. With the exception of a few particularly militant strikes among furniture workers in Stratford and auto workers at the General Motors plant in Oshawa, labour problems were the least of Canadian managers' worries during the Depression.[19] When the war came, however, all of that changed. The demand for labour was sharply up, and unions now had some leverage. Industrial employers, whose products were also in high demand because of the war, were anxious to avoid labour disputes, and labour lawyers became much more important.

Even more significant, however, as a factor in the rise of the importance of the labour lawyer during the war, was the revolution in labour law brought about by the federal government's efforts to maintain peace on the domestic labour front in order to avoid work stoppages in essential industries. Over the course of the war, the government introduced a series of orders-in-council under the authority of the War Measures Act regulating labour. These culminated in P.C. 1003 in February of 1944 which, in addition to granting Canadian labour a legal right to collective bargaining, set up a Labour Relations Board to certify unions and arbitrate disputes.[20] As always, more law meant more need for lawyers, and the firm's clients, particularly International Nickel and General Motors, both of whom supplied essential products for the war effort, relied heavily on Tommy Delamere and Hal Mockridge.

Mockridge, in fact, did much of the direct negotiating on behalf of Inco with the union representatives. He didn't particularly enjoy that part of the work, but the client insisted that he be there. Prior to the war, Inco had been an important client, but during the war, largely because of its labour needs, the giant nickel producer became the firm's most important client. This was quite apparent in the annual reports which Inco submitted to the U.S. Securities and Exchange Commission indicating how much they were spending on legal bills.[21]

While Inco was becoming the firm's major client, the overall volume of work for the firm was increasing dramatically. During the war Osler, Hoskin & Harcourt's total billings increased by some 40 per cent. General Motors, which had apparently come to the firm during Britton Osler's time as senior partner, was very much involved in the war production effort.[22] Throughout the war, Hal Mockridge took part in all the contract negotiations between General Motors and C.D. Howe's Department of Munitions and Supply for military vehicles, including tanks, trucks and even aircraft. This type of work involved a great deal of travel — all by train — to places like Ottawa and New York for the firm's lawyers.

At the same time that the volume of work the firm was doing was rapidly increasing, the number of hands to do it was decreasing. As noted above, five of the sixteen lawyers whose names appeared on the letterhead in 1944 were in the Canadian armed forces. Gordon D. ''Swatty'' Wotherspoon, who first came to the firm as a student when he graduated with the gold medal from the Royal Military College in 1930, commanded the South Alberta Armoured Regiment in Normandy.[23] B.M. ''Brick'' Osler, Britton's eldest son, was a major in the Royal Canadian Artillery, also in Normandy; his younger brother, John G., was also a major serving in the R.C.A. in Europe. A. Woodburn Langmuir Jr., a patent and trade mark specialist like his father, was serving in the Canadian army in North America, and W.B. Reid, a young lawyer who had articled with the firm and practised for a year after his call to the bar in 1941, was a lieutenant in the 48th Highlanders. In August of 1944, Reid was taken prisoner in Italy; he spent the next eight months in a German prisoner-of-war camp.

At the time, Osler, Hoskin & Harcourt was the third-largest law firm in Toronto. The two larger firms were Blake, Anglin, Osler & Cassels, and McCarthy & McCarthy. With twenty-four lawyers, Blakes was by far the largest firm in Canada. Led by A.W. Anglin, Walter Gow and Britton Osler's younger brother Glyn, it was also a family-dominated firm with three Anglins, three Cassels and three Oslers, including Glyn Osler's sons Britton Bath Osler and Peter Scarth Osler.[24]

The Blake firm had offices in the Bank of Commerce building on the South side of King Street just west of the Dominion Bank Building, which was at the corner of King and Yonge streets. When Blakes moved into the brand-new building during the early years of the Depression, it was considered a very prestigious address. McCarthy & McCarthy, with offices in the Canada Life Building on University Avenue, had seventeen lawyers. Led by brothers Leighton and Frank McCarthy, both of whom had practised with the old McCarthy, Osler, Hoskin & Harcourt firm prior to the split in 1916, it had six lawyers absent in the armed forces.[25] Blakes were missing seven for the same reason. There were only five other Toronto firms with as many as ten lawyers.[26]

Largely because of Hal Mockridge, Osler, Hoskin & Harcourt was one of the strongest corporate firms of the World War II and post-war era. The firm survived the death of Britton Osler and the demands of the war years, and when the veterans returned the firm was well positioned to profit from the post-war boom in the Canadian economy. Like the decade of the 1920s, when H.S. and Britton Osler had led the firm, the boom of the 1950s was led by the resource sector and by multinational companies. Once again, the firm was particularly strong in this area.

The three largest firms in the city — Blakes, McCarthys and Oslers — were also the three strongest corporate firms. Blakes were led by Allan Graydon, and McCarthys were led by Beverley Matthews. Like Mockridge at Oslers, neither Graydon nor Matthews were the most senior members of their firms. Graydon was called to the bar in 1924, and Matthews began practice in 1930. They were, however, what became known as the "rainmakers" for their firms. They were the best-known corporate lawyers in their firms, and they were the best at attracting new clients or new business from existing ones.

There were more senior corporate lawyers in Toronto, including W. Kaspar Fraser of Fraser, Beatty, who was called to the bar in 1913, and C.C. Calvin of Fasken & Calvin, who was called in 1919, but the post-war era belonged to men like Mockridge and Matthews.[27] The other well-known corporate lawyer of the time was J.S.D. Tory of the firm known as Tory & Associates, the predecessor of Tory, Tory, DesLauriers & Binnington. Tory, who was called to the bar at the same time as Mockridge in 1927, was considered very aggressive in the way he attracted clients.

In this respect Tory was ahead of his time. The traditional style of business among the Toronto legal élite was to let the clients find you. A "gentleman" did not go out and solicit files. From a late twentieth century perspective, when most of the large firms have practice development committees, and even marketing professionals on staff, Tory's approach does indeed seem to have been ahead of his time, but to his more traditional colleagues at the bar, it was unseemly.[28]

Beverley Matthews, who was known as one of the best "rainmakers" himself, remembers Tory as being very aggressive in seeking out clients. Mockridge, on the other hand, didn't have to be so aggressive because he had inherited a blue-chip stable of clients from his uncle, Britton Osler. Although Mockridge was very sensitive to changes in the legal marketplace, and was careful to make sure that the firm was always able to provide the best service to clients whose business environment was changing rapidly, he was a very conservative man in many respects.

Despite this conservatism — or perhaps in some cases because of it — Osler, Hoskin & Harcourt's business grew substantially during the post-war years. Part of this growth involved files dealing with what would today be known as mega-projects. One of the first of these was the project to build an oil pipeline from Alberta to Ontario. When the Alberta oil fields opened up after the war, one of the biggest problems was getting the crude oil from the well-heads in the west to the refineries in the east. Imperial Oil, the Canadian subsidiary of Standard of New Jersey and one of Osler, Hoskin & Harcourt's major clients, set up Interprovincial Pipe Line Ltd. to build and maintain a pipe line east from Alberta to Ontario.[29]

The Interprovincial project, which completed a 1,100-mile line from Edmonton to Lake Superior in 1950 and a further extension through Michigan to Sarnia, Ontario in 1952, provided an enormous financing task for the lawyers at Oslers. Hal Mockridge and Swatty Wotherspoon tackled the corporate side of the project, and Harold Boston tied up the real estate requirements for easements and rights of way for the pipe through four Canadian provinces and three U.S. states. Each of these was assisted by what, in those days, would be considered an army of students and junior lawyers. One of those, Britton Osler's youngest son C.R. Osler, who joined the firm after the war, remembers one of the biggest tasks in the project as trying to produce acceptable copies of reams of documents such as trust deeds. He remembers trying to keep the firm's hand-cranked mimeograph machine working late into the night, with people getting covered in ink. Eventually, the firm bought a state-of-the-art electrically cranked Gestetner machine.[30]

Largely because of the success of the Interprovincial Pipe Lines project, Osler Hoskin & Harcourt attracted an increasing number of very large financing deals during the 1950s and into the 1960s, but the largest area of expansion in the firm's business, as it was for the Canadian economy as a whole during the post-World War II boom, was in American subsidiaries. During those years, the firm attracted a number of international clients interested in setting up Canadian subsidiaries or doing business directly in Canada. Oslers had an excellent reputation for this type of work dating back to the early part of the century, and particularly to H.S. Osler.

Much of the subsidiary work the firm did was for long-term large clients like Imperial Oil and Inco, but small companies like Royal Doulton also came to Oslers, specifically to Mossey Huycke, because of the firm's growing reputation. Ed Huycke, the younger of Mossey's two sons who joined the firm after the war, remembers doing the incorporation work for the English fine china company's Canadian subsidiary.[31] Bill Bryden, another of the post-war students, remembers the firm as having "the strongest lineup of U.S. clients in Toronto."[32]

Much of the firm's work among U.S.-based clients and parent companies came through referrals from American law firms. New York firms including Cravath, Swaine & Moore and Sullivan & Cromwell, who acted as Inco's American counsel, very often recommended Osler, Hoskin & Harcourt to American clients looking for a good Canadian law firm, as did many other large American firms. Bill Bryden remembers one such referral from the Cravath firm in 1950 when Bethlehem Steel wanted to set up an iron mining company in Ontario. Largely because of Mossey Huycke's reputation in the mining field, Hoyt Moore, then the senior partner at Cravaths, recommended Oslers to Bethlehem.[33]

Corporate law, particularly involving mining and other resource-based companies, had been the firm's specialty for many years, but in the years following World War II corporate law was becoming much more complex. Generalists like H.S. and Britton Osler had begun to give way to specialists like T.D. Delamere. In Delamere's case, the federal government's regulation of labour during the war made specialization a necessity, but labour was not the only area in which government regulation provided for more specialized legal work. During the war, in addition to trying to regulate industrial production to manage the war effort, the federal government's own budget requirements shot up dramatically. This meant that income tax, particularly corporate income tax, was a focus of concern, and

in a highly regulated environment, income tax became a very important part of corporate legal practice.

As one of the best corporate lawyers in the country, Hal Mockridge
was considered to be a tax expert, but in addition to being an excellent
lawyer, he was also a very good law firm administrator. He could see
that if the firm was going to succeed in competing with the other
major corporate firms in the city it was going to have to stay ahead
of the law; that is, it was going to need a real tax expert. The problem
was, beyond Heward Stikeman and his partner Fraser Elliott, there
were very few of them around. Mockridge and his partners were
lucky, however; there was one who might be available.

Stuart Thom was born in Regina in September 1906, barely a year
after Saskatchewan joined Confederation. He came east to do a B.A.
at the University of Toronto, but went home to study law at the
University of Saskatchewan. He was called to the bar of that province
in 1930 and joined his father's Regina law firm the same year. He
remembers the boom years of the late 1920s on the prairies when he
was a student, and many of the young lawyers he knew were involved
in speculative land and commodities investments. Most of them were
bankrupt when the ''Dirty Thirties'' hit. Although there was very
little legal work to do in Regina during the Depression, as Thom
rather sheepishly puts it, his father's firm had many of the mortgage
companies and farm machinery dealers as clients, and he spent his
early years in practice as a ''mortgage foreclosure and bankruptcy
lawyer, because that's all the business there was. If you had any
business at all, it meant trying to collect money from poor deadbeat
brokers and farmers and businessmen whose businesses had gone
belly-up.''[34]

Thom practised for ten years in Saskatchewan before joining the
Canadian navy during World War II. In 1945, when the war ended,
he took a job with the Department of National Revenue in Ottawa.
Although he modestly claims that he knew absolutely no tax law at
the time, he acted as legal executive assistant to the deputy minister
of Revenue. He stayed there for two years and in 1947 came to
Toronto to join the law firm of Smith, Rae, Greer. It was while he
was with Smith, Rae, Greer that he developed a substantial reputation
as a tax expert, and in the late winter of 1954 Hal Mockridge, Mossey
Huycke and Tommy Delamere invited him to lunch in the Victoria
Room in the King Edward Hotel. They made him what he considered
to be a very attractive offer, and he was with the firm until his
retirement in 1978.[35]

During the early post-war years the firm occupied the eighth floor and part of the seventh floor in the Dominion Bank Building. Most of the lawyers' offices were on the eighth floor facing south to the lake and east overlooking Yonge Street. The largest office, in the southwest corner of the building, had been Britton Osler's; after his death in 1943 it became the firm's conference room. The students' desks were in the hall outside the eighth-floor offices which faced Yonge St., and the library was on the seventh floor, as were Wellington Cameron's and Harold Boston's offices.

Perhaps the most lasting memory the lawyers who practised in the old Dominion Bank Building have is of the soot which would work its way through the tiny gaps in the window frames and blacken everything that was not covered up. The building was only a few blocks north of the railway lands, and most buildings in the downtown area were still heated with soft coal. The result was that you would go home at night with charcoal grey cuffs on a white shirt.[36]

When Stuart Thom joined the firm in 1954, it had nineteen lawyers. In the years since the war, it had begun the process of growth and transition from a family firm to what today might be recognized as a comprehensive, full-service law firm, but in the process went through a real crisis. In addition to the five war veterans — Swatty Wotherspoon, Woody Langmuir, W.B. Reid, and Brick and John Osler, who returned in 1945 — the firm brought in a number of students in the late 1940s and early 1950s who would have a lasting impact on the firm as it went through the transition.

In the fall of 1945, Britton Osler's youngest son, C.R., had joined the firm as an articling student. Like his two older brothers, he was an officer in the Royal Canadian Artillery during the war. He had originally planned to begin his articles when he graduated from the University of Toronto in 1940, but the war delayed his legal career by five years. He stayed with the firm when he was called to the bar in 1948 and significantly, when he accepted an offer to join the partnership in 1950, he was the last relative of B.B. Osler to do so. Osler, Hoskin & Harcourt had long been a family firm, and during the immediate post-war years it remained so — but it also began to change.

C.R. Osler was one of seven students at the firm in the class of 1948, all veterans. This was far more than the firm had ever had in the past, and probably more than they needed, or even had room for, but in the wake of the war, when the returning veterans swelled classes at Osgoode Hall from fewer than a hundred to well over three hundred, the firm had to do its part. Two of the students had been prisoners of war. Ian Douglas, who stayed with the firm until 1956 and went on to become a partner with McCarthy & McCarthy, was an infantry officer captured in Sicily in 1943; Ivan Quinn, who practised for many years with the Vancouver firm of Bull, Housser & Tupper, was a fighter pilot when he was shot down in 1942.[37]

Of the seven students who articled with the firm and were called to the bar in 1948, only two — C.R. Osler and Ian Douglas — stayed after graduation. The following year's class contained two Osler, Hoskin & Harcourt students, but neither stayed with the firm after graduation. The following year, the class of 1950 saw one Oslers student stay with the firm. Bill Bryden, who retired from practice in 1992, was the son of a faculty member at the Ontario College of Agriculture in Guelph. He originally intended to be a geologist. He studied chemistry and geology at McMaster University in Hamilton, and when he graduated in 1947 his first job was as an exploration geologist in the British Columbia mountains.

After a few weeks in the isolation of the Rockies, however, Bryden decided that this wasn't the career for him. He thought about medicine, but chose law just in time to enrol at Osgoode Hall Law School in September 1947. At the end of his first year, he had to find a firm to article with. He started off in the summer of 1948 with the Guelph firm of Mackinnon & Clare. He had to find a firm in Toronto, however, to join when he returned for his second year at Osgoode. Jim Clare, the partner to whom he was articled, had himself articled at Osler, Hoskin & Harcourt, and he recommended Bryden to Mossey Huycke.

As Bryden remembers it, the senior student got the front desk in the hall on the eighth floor. He also got the telephone on his desk. A year later, in 1949, when Bryden became the senior student, he was joined by three more students. Bryden, of course, had no close connections to the firm, but two of the three who joined in 1949 did. One of them was Mossey Huycke's eldest son, Fred. The other was Allan Beattie, whose father was R. Leslie Beattie, then vice-president and general manager of the International Nickel Company of Canada Ltd. He was, therefore, the senior Inco executive in Canada. The third was Edmund Meredith, whose father was a good friend of Mossey Huycke.[38] Fred Huycke and Allan Beattie stayed with the firm after their call to the bar, but Edmund Meredith chose not to practise law. Instead, he joined his father's real estate firm.

Allan Beattie remembers a humorous, self-deprecating story involving himself and Meredith. When they were in first year law school at Osgoode Hall in the spring of 1949, Beattie and Meredith failed the first-year Real Property course taught by Bora Laskin and had to write a supplemental exam. Failing a course and having to write a "supp" was not unusual in those days. Beattie remembers his first day at Osgoode in September of 1948, when Dean "Caesar" Wright welcomed the first-year class with the old line: "I want you to take a good hard look at the fellow on your left and the fellow on your right because one of you is not going to be here next year." The program was very demanding, and unlike today's law schools, which are very difficult to get into, but where the failure rates are very low, at Osgoode they let virtually anybody in and weeded them out later.[39] Beattie remembers that of a class of about 360 who started in September, about fifty or sixty had withdrawn by Christmas, and of the three hundred or so who wrote the final first year exams in the spring of 1949, fewer than half got through without having to write any supplemental exams.

The Real Property supp which Beattie and Meredith wrote consisted of six questions. Beattie said, laughingly, that he never really understood Real Property with its fee tails and rule against perpetuities, but while they were walking back down to the office after writing the supplemental exam, he and Meredith found, to their horror, that they had given different answers to every question. They were sure that one of them would fail and at the very least have to suffer the indignity of repeating the entire first year. When the results came out a month or so later, they went up to Osgoode Hall where the grades were posted. When they arrived, they found that the list containing the surnames from A-L was on one side of the hall and M-Z was on the other, so they separated to see their own results. After a few minutes, they turned back, each expecting to offer condolences to the other. As it turned out, Laskin had given them both a passing grade of 50 per cent on the exam. The problem was they never knew which 50 per cent of the questions they had answered correctly and which 50 per cent they had fumbled.[40]

In 1951, the most junior desk in the hall belonged to Mossey Huycke's younger son Ed. Huycke had played professional football for the Toronto Argonauts while he was a law student. His football career was cut short, however, when halfway through the 1951 season Hal Mockridge came up to him in the hall and told him to make up his mind between football and law. Although the $1,000-a-season the Argos were paying him was big money compared to the forty dollars a month he was making as a law student, he chose law. His decision was a wise one for many reasons, but Mockridge and his partners rewarded Huycke and the other students shortly afterward by raising their salaries to one hundred dollars a month.[41]

Ed Huycke was called to the bar in June of 1953, in the midst of the greatest crisis in the history of the firm. On Friday, June 5, 1953 the lawyers in the firm were shocked to learn that they had been betrayed by one of their partners. Since some time shortly after his return to the firm in 1945, W.B. Reid had been systematically embezzling from the firm and its clients. Over the course of that time he had stolen close to $40,000.

In the early spring of 1953, Norman Strickland began to suspect that something fishy was going on at the firm. During the winter he had discovered that a few books of firm receipt stubs were missing. The firm's receipts came in two parts separated by perforations; one part was the actual receipt, and the other was a stub for accounting purposes. Both parts bore the same number, and the receipts were numbered sequentially. When Strickland first realized that a large group of stubs were missing, he blamed the printer. He thought that the printer had somehow skipped a series of numbers in preparing the receipts or had simply lost them.[42] A more cynical man might have suspected theft from within the firm, but prior to the Reid incident such a thing would have been unthinkable; afterwards, sadly, it wasn't.

Strickland's suspicions were raised further when he began to receive complaints from clients about late trust fund payments. In all of the cases, the clients' lawyer had promised that they would soon receive the proceeds of the estates, but he kept putting them off. When Strickland checked the firm's records, he found that in each case a cheque had been issued and cashed, but the client claimed to have never received it. The common denominator was that W.B. Reid handled all of the estates.

On the afternoon of Friday, June 5, 1953, Strickland apparently called Reid into his office and asked him about it. Strickland's worst suspicions were true. Reid decided that the jig was up and the whole story came tumbling out. He confessed that for years he had been stealing from clients and even his own partners. Strickland listened for a while and decided that someone else had better hear Reid's confession; he instructed Reid to wait and walked down the hall to ask Hal Mockridge to come down to his office. When Mockridge arrived, a tearful Reid began to recount his story.

In 1947, the firm received a $30,000 trust account for the estate of a recently deceased client. In October of that year, one of the beneficiaries of the estate came in to the office to ask when he could expect his money. Reid told him that it would have to be held in trust until the succession duties and other matters had been cleared up. The man asked him if part of the money could be paid out, and Reid told him he would try to get him something. He then went to the firm accounting department and had them prepare a cheque for $500 made out to the beneficiary, but when he went back to his office he told the man that he couldn't get him anything.[43]

Reid then forged the beneficiary's signature on the cheque and took it downstairs to the main branch of the Dominion Bank and cashed it, telling them that the client preferred cash. In January 1948, he did the same thing with a cheque for $250, and in July he upped the ante to $1,000. This gave him the courage to repeat the procedure roughly once every month over the next six months for $500 or $750 each time. In each case, he forged the name of a beneficiary of the estate and cashed the cheque.

In another case, Reid acted on behalf of a client whose property had been expropriated by the Toronto Transit Commission for the Yonge Street subway line. The docket charges on the file amounted to $225, which Mossey Huycke agreed to write down to $200. The client came in and made out a cheque payable to Reid for this amount, which he simply pocketed. In another situation, the firm received a $2,000 Dominion of Canada bearer bond in trust for a client who was the beneficiary of a very large estate. Instead of passing the bond on to the client, Reid used it as collateral against a personal loan he took out in the summer of 1952 at the Bank of Montreal on King Street. As of June 1953, the bank still held the bond.

In another case, Reid stole from a trust fund for which he, Harold Shapley and Swatty Wotherspoon were the trustees. In the words of Reid's confession:

> The assets of the trust consisting largely of Dominion of Canada Bearer Bonds are kept in a safety deposit box in the Dominion Bank, Toronto Branch. Any two of the trustees have the right of access to the box. Mr. Wotherspoon and I from time to time would go down to the box and clip coupons from the bonds and deposit them with the Dominion Bank in a trust account. On

one occasion in 1951, we went down to clip coupons and Mr. Wotherspoon, when we had opened the box, stated that he also had a safety deposit box and that he was going to clip some of his own coupons and instructed me to finish clipping the trust account coupons. While he was out of the room getting the key for his own box I took two $5,000 and one $1,000 Dominion of Canada bonds and put them in my pocket. One of these $5,000 bonds I shortly pledged against my overdraft at the Dominion Bank; the other two bonds I kept and some months later pledged first the $5,000 bond and then still later the $1,000 bond against loans from The Royal Bank of Canada, Toronto Branch. Subsequently on two or three occasions, when it became necessary, I got back the coupons that had matured, and when attending to clip further coupons with Mr. Wotherspoon was able to include with the coupons so clipped the coupons from the bonds that were missing. I have handed to you one coupon for $75.00 which I was holding in readiness for this.

The Royal Bank called my loan with them and sold the $6,000 worth of bonds which they had in their possession and this included two coupons which I had not been able to get back. This sale occurred in April 1953. The remaining $5,000 bond together with all coupons is still pledged in my name with the Dominion Bank.

Strickland and Mockridge listened to Reid's story in horror. The worst thing they could imagine had happened; one of their partners was a common thief. A law partnership is built on trust; the members of the firm share an intimate professional relationship, and perhaps more important, their stock in trade is largely dependent on their trustworthiness. The only thing worse than stealing from one another was stealing from a client; Reid had done both.

Reid told them that he would cooperate completely, so they sent him home and sat down to try to figure out what to do next. Mossey Huycke was in Ottawa, so they telephoned him there. The three of them decided that they had better convene an emergency partnership meeting that weekend. Shortly after Huycke arrived back in Toronto, the partners met to decide what to do about the situation. Once the shock of having been betrayed by one of their partners had set in, they began to discuss what to do. The publicity would very likely hurt the firm, but they had no choice but to inform the Law Society and the police. Harold Boston wryly remarked, ''Perhaps we had better hire ourselves a solicitor.'' They also decided that they would reimburse everyone Reid had stolen from, as soon as they could determine the extent of his crimes.[44] On Sunday afternoon Hal Mockridge telephoned Joe Sedgwick, the senior partner in Stuart Thom's firm of Smith, Rae, Greer and the chairman of the Law Society's Discipline Committee, to tell him what had happened.

On Monday, Reid came in to the office and dictated and signed a confession outlining what he could remember of his villainy. The confession, headed "To: Osler, Hoskin & Harcourt, and To Whom It May Concern," was nine legal-sized pages long, and itemizing theft, forgery and embezzlement from eighteen different parties, and closed:

> The above constitutes to the best of my memory and belief a full, true and correct statement of the facts in connection with my dealings with other people's funds and to the best of my memory and belief there are no other instances of the same.
>
> And I am signing this statement in the presence of G.M. Huycke and N.E. Strickland after having carefully read over the same.
>
> Dated at Toronto this 8th day of June, 1953.

It was signed in a very shaky hand: "W.B. Reid."[45] That afternoon, Mossey Huycke took Reid's confession over to Sedgwick's office and handed it to him.

In hindsight, the other lawyers at Oslers realized that they had never really known Reid. He was a bit of a loner who generally ate lunch by himself, but he was a very charming and entertaining man. He was tall and good looking, and thought of as a very good lawyer with a bright future. He had worked on a number of tax cases with Hal Mockridge, and most people at the firm assumed that he would eventually become the firm's primary litigator.

Reid was born in Scotland but grew up in Lima, Peru, where his father was a manager for the International Petroleum Company, a subsidiary of Imperial Oil. He came to Canada to go to high school at Trinity College School in Port Hope, Ontario, and from there went on to W.P.M. Kennedy's undergraduate law program at the University of Toronto.[46] He graduated from the U. of T. in 1938 and started law school at Osgoode Hall. He found an articling position at Osler, Hoskin & Harcourt because his father and Britton Osler knew one another.[47] Imperial Oil was one of Britton's clients.

When Reid applied for admission to the Law Society as a student in June of 1938, he had a small problem which was interesting in light of subsequent events. In those days the Law Society required references from two people who had known the applicant for ten years and were not related to him, who could certify that he was "a gentleman of respectability and a proper person to be admitted as a student of the Law Society of Upper Canada with a view of being called to the bar." Reid had not been in Toronto that long, and one of his certificates was from W.P.M. Kennedy, who had known him for only four years. He explained this to Shirley Denison, then the chairman of the Legal Education Committee, and Denison waived the rule.

Reid's career in law school was not particularly outstanding. In first year he stood eighty-seventh in a class of 119 and, interestingly enough, he failed Criminal Law. He passed the supplemental examination, and in second year he stood fifty-first in a class of 109. In third year, he stood forty-eighth in a class of 108. Despite his lacklustre record in law school, the firm offered him a position when he was called to the bar in September of 1941, probably because with Wotherspoon and the two Osler brothers away in the war there was little choice.

Reid stayed with the firm for a year, but in July of 1942 he also decided to join the army and enlisted in the 48th Highlanders. He went overseas in August 1943 and, a year later, on August 27, 1944, he was taken prisoner during heavy fighting near the Gothic Line in Italy. He escaped from his German captors three times during transport, but he was recaptured each time and spent the rest of the war in Stalag 7A in Bavaria. He was liberated by advancing Allied forces in April 1945, and returned to Oslers some weeks later. He apparently was able to fit right in as the firm's business boomed after the war, and in late 1949 he was offered a partnership.

By 1953 Reid and his wife, whom he met when they worked together on the *Varsity*, the student newspaper at the University of Toronto, had moved from their apartment on Bayview Avenue to a house in Leaside, and they had three children. He apparently had everything going for him. He was a rising partner in a prestigious downtown law firm, he had a beautiful family, and he was a well-respected reserve officer in the 48th Highlanders. But he was leading a double life. He was becoming a very accomplished philanderer, and he was stealing more and more from his clients and his partners to support his philandering.

Over the next few days, Joe Sedgwick set the wheels in motion to have Reid disbarred. He called Earl Smith, then the secretary of the

Law Society, and they drew up charges against Reid based on his written confession. In the meantime, Reid's father, who had apparently retired sometime after the war and moved to Toronto, came in to plead with the Mossey Huycke and Hal Mockridge, saying that he would make good everything his son had stolen if the firm would agree not to press criminal charges.[48] He understood that disbarment couldn't be avoided, but if the firm would consider not pressing criminal charges his son might not have to face going to prison. Mockridge and Huycke didn't have to think very long before refusing. The publicity of charges being laid against one of their former partners would, of course, not do the firm any good, but besides the moral outrage and personal betrayal they felt, to even consider covering it up would be much worse for the firm.[49] How the firm came out of this crisis, in the eyes of existing and potential clients, was crucial. So there would be no misunderstanding based on rumour, Mockridge went in person to all of the firm's major clients to explain exactly what had happened and what they were doing about it.[50]

Some time later in the week two Toronto police detectives, William Thompson and Barney Simmonds, interviewed Reid. What they must have told him would be very frightening. He was to be charged with theft, and the penalty upon conviction would be a prison term of up to fourteen years.[51] In the meantime, Sedgwick had arranged a disciplinary hearing for the afternoon of Wednesday the twenty-fourth of June and sent a registered letter to Reid instructing him to appear "in person or by counsel before the Committee with your witnesses, if any, at the time and place aforesaid, and give evidence in your own behalf."

The letter was addressed to Reid's business address: Osler, Hoskin & Harcourt, Room 801, 68 Yonge St., Toronto, and the receptionist signed for it when it arrived on Friday, June 12. On Saturday morning, Norman Strickland gave it to Harold Boston and asked him to deliver it to Reid.[52] When Boston phoned Reid, his wife told him that her husband was sleeping but she would give him the message. Late Sunday morning, Reid phoned Boston and told him he would come over to Boston's house to pick up the letter. He arrived at about one o'clock in the afternoon and Boston gave it to him.

That was the last anyone ever saw of Walter B. Reid. When his father's pleas to Hal Mockridge and Mossey Huycke failed, and when Detectives Thompson and Simmonds told him about the fourteen-year prison term, he decided to run. No one knows how he got out of the country, or even where he went, but it has always been assumed that he fled to South America. He acted as Peruvian Consul in Toronto from 1946 to 1949, and he knew many people doing business in Central and South America. Most likely he found a way to get out of the country using his diplomatic and business contacts.

By Tuesday, June 16, when the story hit the Toronto papers, Reid was long gone. *The Telegram*, which carried a front-page photograph of Reid under the headline "TORONTO LAWYER ACCUSED OF STEALING $33,000," said that "Today, movers were removing the last of the Reids' household effects from their Glenvale Blvd. home. The house has a For Sale sign at the front." The story also indicated that a warrant had been issued for Reid's arrest.[53] Perhaps not surprisingly, when he disappeared he did not take his wife and three children.[54]

On June 24, the Law Society's Discipline Committee met to hear charges of "professional misconduct and conduct unbecoming a barrister and solicitor." Reid was called but, of course, did not answer. Sedgwick then asked Mossey Huycke, whom he had asked to attend along with Hal Mockridge, if he could verify that the confession they had before them had been signed by Reid in Huycke's presence. He testified that it had been, and that Reid had made the confession voluntarily and had, in fact, dictated all but the opening and closing paragraphs. The committee then found Reid guilty of professional misconduct, and Sedgwick sent a formal recommendation to the Benchers of the Law Society that Reid be disbarred.

The Law Society went through the formality of informing Reid by registered letter that Convocation intended to deal with this recommendation at its next meeting and that he would have an opportunity to defend himself then but, of course, this too went unanswered. On July 8, 1953, Walter Brechin Reid was disbarred and his name was struck from the Roll of Barristers and Solicitors of the Supreme Court of Ontario.

For Osler, Hoskin & Harcourt, the events of June and July 1953 were traumatic. The partners had been betrayed by one of their own. They had worked side by side with a thief for at least six years and not known it. Although they hadn't really known Reid very well, he was a very charming and outwardly confident man. In reality he was a simple con artist. In going through Reid's desk after he disappeared, Norman Strickland wasn't surprised to find the missing receipt books.

In future the partners would be much more hesitant to trust people. From that point forward, Hal Mockridge made a habit of examining the back of every returned cheque to make sure that there was nothing unusual about it. Had someone in the firm been doing that when Reid was still there, they would have wondered why so many cheques made out to clients were also being endorsed by one of the lawyers, and they might have been able to catch him sooner.[55]

Outwardly the crisis did not damage the firm. *The Telegram* published the story about the warrant for Reid's arrest as the lead item with a banner headline in the early edition. By the time the final afternoon edition came out, the story was still on the front page, but it was below the fold. More importantly, the name of the firm did not appear in the story in any edition. For a time, there was a story around the firm that Mossey Huycke telephoned or visited John Bassett, the publisher of *The Telegram*, shortly after the early edition came out, to ask that the item be given less prominence. Bassett, who was Huycke's nephew as well as a client of the firm, apparently complied.[56] Interestingly, however, *The Star*, Toronto's other afternoon paper, didn't carry the story at all, and *The Globe and Mail* carried only a short item — with no mention of the firm — on page five of the next morning's paper.[57]

As Beverley Matthews, then the senior corporate lawyer at McCarthy & McCarthy, remembers it, the rest of the downtown bar felt very sympathetic towards Oslers. They realized that the same thing could have happened to any one of them, and they were grateful that it hadn't. He also says that he would be very surprised if the incident had any effect on client confidence in the firm.[58] In fact, the Reid affair appears not to have had any negative impact on the firm's income. Over the four years prior to 1953, the firm's income grew at a rate of just under 7 per cent per year; during the four years following, it grew at over 15 per cent per year. Of course, there were many factors affecting this figure, including the fact that they no longer had someone with his hand in the till, but the bottom-line is that the clients stayed. In fact, none of the clients whom Reid had stolen from took their legal business elsewhere.

Although the incident did not hurt the firm externally, there is no doubt it was damaging internally. As the following chapter will explain in some detail, during the 1950s the firm was going through a process of transition from being a family firm to being a large, comprehensive and diversified firm. The Reid incident made this more difficult because it made the partners much less trusting, and it made them very careful about whom they would welcome into their midst.

CHAPTER

6

THE CLUB: 1954-1970

In the 1950s, the firm — like the rest of the country — stood on the verge of a major transformation. By any measure Osler, Hoskin & Harcourt was still a family enterprise. It was large by national standards; only two firms — the Montreal firm of McMichael, Common, Howard, Ker & Cate, and the Toronto firm of Blake, Anglin, Osler & Cassels — were larger.[1] But of the eleven men who were partners after Stuart Thom joined the firm in 1954, five were either members of, or directly related to, the Osler family, and of the three men who joined the partnership on December 31, 1955, one was the son of a senior Osler partner, and another was the son of the senior Canadian executive of the firm's largest client.[2] Most importantly, the firm's management was almost exclusively in the hands of one man — a great-nephew of Britton Bath Osler. A generation later the firm had grown to well over fifty lawyers, and it was managed by a partly elected executive committee of the partners, none of whom was an Osler.

In mid-century, Toronto was still very much "Toronto the Good." It hadn't been that long since Sunday movies and sporting events were allowed. The mayor of Toronto was Allan Lamport; the premier of Ontario was Leslie Frost, a Conservative; and the prime minister of Canada was a Liberal and former Quebec City corporate lawyer, Louis St. Laurent. Although the post-war wave of immigration was beginning to radically change the ethnic and demographic face of the city, it was still dominated by a small white, Anglo-Saxon, Protestant élite.

Osler, Hoskin & Harcourt, like the other large downtown law firms, was a part of that élite. Every one of the twenty-two lawyers in the firm in 1955 was white and male, and all but two were members of a mainstream Protestant church. Vince Reid, who had been called to the bar a year earlier in 1954, was the only Roman Catholic in the firm, and Frank Mott-Trille, who was called to the English bar in 1953 and the Ontario bar in 1954, was a Jehovah's Witness.

Things were beginning to change, however; people in Toronto could now hear Elvis Presley and Little Richard on the radio, and as of 1954 the city had its own subway and a metropolitan municipal government. In 1955, it elected its first Jewish mayor, Nathan Phillips. For the firm things were also beginning to change, but the change would come slowly. The firm's office was still located in the old Dominion Bank Building on the southwest corner of King and Yonge streets, although the building was renamed the Toronto-Dominion Bank Building in 1955 when the Dominion Bank merged with the Bank of Toronto.[3]

The Dominion Bank Building was a brand new, eleven storey, state-of-the-art structure equipped with electric elevators manned by white-gloved attendants when McCarthy, Osler, Hoskin & Harcourt moved there in 1914. The brochure put out by the bank's leasing agent in 1913 described it as "the most complete bank and office building in Canada, and one that will not be excelled in America in points of arrangement and equipment." By the late 1950s, however, it was beginning to show its age. The firm gained a little more space in the middle of the decade when it moved from the seventh and eighth floors down to the fourth and fifth, but the wide, tiled hallways and dark mahogany trim were still prominent. The lawyers' offices were also dominated by heavy, dark furniture, and globe light fixtures hung from the high ceilings.[4]

If the atmosphere of the firm was old-fashioned, in many ways so was its leadership. In hindsight, of course, there are many good and bad things about being old-fashioned, and this holds true for people as well as furnishings. Clearly, Osler, Hoskin & Harcourt's leader during the 1950s was Hal Mockridge. As Purdy Crawford, the lawyer who took over many of Mockridge's client responsibilities as the senior man began to move into retirement, remembers it, "He would, in effect, defer to Mossey Huycke in many matters, although he could always call the shot if he wanted to."[5]

The portrait which accompanies Mockridge's biography in the 1968 edition of *Who's Who in Canada* shows a rather stern and reserved man, but he also seems to have a bit of a twinkle in his eye. This is also how the people who were students and young lawyers at the time remember him. He was a demanding supervisor and meticulous practitioner, but he enjoyed sharing a few drinks with his partners when the work was finished. He was not a tall man, no more than five-foot-eight or -nine, but most remember him as standing very erect and square-shouldered. He also smoked cigarettes; like Norman Strickland, Mockridge's brand was Player's Navy Cut (Imperial Tobacco was an Oslers client).[6]

The most significant aspects of Hal Mockridge's personality involved his leadership and administrative style. Perhaps the most important decisions made in a law firm are those concerning the division of profits. If a firm is to survive, it is essential that the partners feel that the profits are divided fairly or, perhaps more importantly, that the process is fair. There are numerous examples of law firms which have split up, but the most common reason seems to be the division of profits among the partners.

Certainly, Britton Osler passed on some fundamental values about a partnership to Hal Mockridge. Under both Osler's and Mockridge's leadership, the firm consistently endeavoured to treat clients as the firm's clients rather than individual lawyers' clients. Income distribution among the partners was, therefore, based on overall assessed value to the firm rather than on the amount of fees paid by specific clients. Moreover, the partnership splits were prospectively set; that is, the percentage of profits to be distributed to each partner was agreed upon prior to the start of each partnership term, not after its conclusion. The result was a substantial disincentive for individual partners to covet clients.

One of the practical results of the system of firm-wide clients was a central filing system. Individual lawyers would keep current files and some files relating to clients for whom they did continuing work in or near their offices, but all clients' files were generally available to all lawyers in the firm. No single partner would maintain a proprietary right to a client's files, and therefore its fees.

The fact that the filing procedures in the firm were open does not, however, mean that the firm was run as a democracy; in fact, it was anything but. During the 1950s, Osler, Hoskin & Harcourt was still a dictatorship — a benevolent one — but a dictatorship nonetheless.

Mockridge's proprietorship of the firm was originally based on his ancestry — according to his widow, he always said that "Uncle Britt left him the firm" — but Britton Osler would not have entrusted him with it, nor would the clients have maintained confidence in him, if he was not obviously competent. Moreover, his partners, including his cousins, would not have bowed to his authority if they did not have confidence in his fairness.

The most tangible evidence of Mockridge's fairness was in the partnership splits which he drafted himself. Under the partnership agreement of December 31, 1955, the profits for the period from January 1, 1956 through December 31, 1958 were to be divided into 380 shares. Of these, Mockridge would receive fifty-seven, or 15 per cent. Although the overall profit figures for that time period are not available, this was clearly a great deal of money. Nevertheless, it was not inordinate given his contribution to the firm. In fact, when those who were younger members of the firm at the time look at the partnership splits, they invariably feel that Mockridge's share was substantially below what it would have been if an impartial observer were to divide the profits.[7]

This undervaluing of his own contribution was not simply modesty or unselfishness on Mockridge's part. It is true that he was not an overly acquisitive person; unlike some of his contemporaries in corporate law, he did not capitalize on his insider position and play the stock market, but he purposely diminished his own share of the profits in order to maintain the perception of fairness — within the firm. Moreover, according to many, he also purposely overvalued the contributions of the junior partners in order to establish their loyalty.

Mockridge was, however, a modest man in other ways; despite his renown as a corporate lawyer, he always chose to drive an Oldsmobile rather than a Cadillac, which his friends and relatives felt was more befitting his station.[8] Moreover, if he were to find a reference to himself as the leader of the firm, he would quickly point out that G.M. Huycke was seven years senior to him at the bar, and if he somehow felt it was appropriate to breach the confidentiality of the partnership agreement, that his share of the profits was identical to Huycke's and only marginally greater than T.D. Delamere's.[9] It is true that he continually sought his partners' advice, particularly Huycke's, but according to most observers both within the firm and outside of it, Hal Mockridge's authority was acknowledged.

Mockridge was also insistent on a very high standard of ethics within the firm; the best example of this trait was his attitude towards a practice known as tax stripping. Under the Income Tax Act, corporate profits are essentially taxed twice; the corporation's income is taxed, and when the profits are distributed to the shareholders in the form of dividends, the dividends are taxed. During the post-war years, it was fairly common practice among tax lawyers to devise schemes by which companies could set up complicated paper chains through which taxable corporate profits would enter one end of the chain, and non-taxable profits would end up in the hands of the shareholders at the other. Heward Stikeman, one of the best known of the early tax specialists, once gave a lecture to the Tax Foundation on the procedure.

Hal Mockridge, although he personally felt that the double tax provision of the Income Tax Act was an ill-advised policy, made it clear to his clients that he would simply not do it. Even if tax stripping was not tax evasion, it was a shady form of tax avoidance, and it was certainly contrary to the intent of the law; if they wanted it done, they would have to go to another law firm.[10] Interestingly, Mockridge was vindicated when the Supreme Court of Canada ruled that the practice was contrary to the statute in a case the Department of National Revenue took against Toronto Maple Leaf owner Conn Smythe and his son Stafford in 1969. In the report of the judgement, Heward Stikeman was identified as Conn Smythe's counsel on the case.[11]

All of this makes Hal Mockridge sound a bit like a saint — he was not. He was an excellent lawyer, and generally recognized as a leader of the corporate bar, but he was also a creature of his generation and his class. Among early to mid-twentieth century Protestant Canadians of means, genteel religious intolerance was the norm rather than the exception. Although, unlike D'Alton McCarthy, there is no evidence to indicate that Hal Mockridge or any of his partners was a religious bigot, the fact is that there were no Roman Catholic lawyers at Osler, Hoskin & Harcourt until 1954, and the first Jewish lawyer did not join the firm until 1963.[12]

Oslers was not unique in its ethnic and religious homogeneity at the time. Virtually all of the élite Toronto law firms were made up of white, male Protestants. As the late Senator David Croll, a Jewish graduate of Osgoode Hall Law School in 1924, remembered it, the largely unspoken religious barrier existed until well after World War II. "There were no Jewish lawyers in any of the large firms. They wouldn't let them in. . . . A Jewish lawyer couldn't get near a large firm; they didn't want any of us."[13]

If any of the lawyers at the major Bay Street firms of the 1940s or early 1950s could be asked why this was the case, they would certainly deny that anything as ugly as anti-Semitism was the cause. They would explain that there were Jewish firms and there were gentile firms — much like there were Jewish golf courses and gentile golf courses. In hindsight, we know that this separate but equal argument is just as bankrupt as the doctrine which came out of the U.S. Supreme Court's judgement in *Plessy* v. *Ferguson* in 1896 and the Jim Crow segregation laws which it upheld until *Brown* v. *Board of Education* in 1954, but it was one which many people, perhaps most, in 1950s Toronto would have accepted. By the end of the decade, however, things were about to change.[14]

There were two people who were very much a part of the changes which took place at Osler, Hoskin & Harcourt beginning in the late 1950s. Their names were Purdy Crawford and Bertha Wilson. Coincidentally, both were graduates of Dalhousie Law School in Halifax, and both were called to the Nova Scotia bar just before moving to Toronto to join Oslers. Significantly, both were outsiders — in more than just a geographic sense.

Madam Justice Bertha Wilson, who many would argue did more than anyone else to breathe life into the Canadian Charter of Rights during her eight years on the Supreme Court of Canada, was born Bertha Wernham in the Scottish port town of Kirkcaldy, across the Firth of Forth from Edinburgh, on September 18, 1923. She graduated from the Secondary School ninety miles up the North Sea coast in Aberdeen in 1941; in 1944, she received an M.A. in History and English from the University of Aberdeen and, in 1945, a Teaching Parchment from the Aberdeen Training College for Teachers. In December of that year she married John Wilson, a recently ordained Presbyterian minister who met and courted the young Miss Wernham while he was a theology student at Aberdeen.

Reverend Wilson was posted to Macduff, a rural village overlooking the Moray Firth in the north of Scotland, and at twenty-two Mrs. Wilson found herself the mistress of the parish manse. Whenever she is asked about that time in her life, Justice Wilson says that living and working with the poor people in that fishing village was "the beginning of my education for living."[15] As she said in a convocation address to the graduating class at Dalhousie Law School in Halifax in 1980 — after receiving the first of many honourary doctorates — "It was there that I learned a great deal about people, being privileged to get to know intimately something of the drama of their daily lives and to develop an understanding of their springs of conduct." In an interview for an article in *Saturday Night* magazine in 1985, she said:

> I became intimately involved with the drama of the daily lives of these people, their joys and their sorrows and, at sea, their terrible tragedies. I discovered how lonely proud people are,

how dependent on the rest of us old people are. And how most of us are locked up tight inside ourselves, much of the time, pretending to be something we are not.[16]

Justice Wilson is a religious person; her motivations in life are essentially moral, but even more importantly, she is guided by an enormous faith in the dignity of humankind, and in the same speech to the graduating class at Dalhousie she told them that "God is far more interested in what you *do* when you are behind your desk than He is in what you *say* when you are on your knees." In that sense, Wilson is a social activist, but she is not radical. Her concern for what is right — in the moral and social sense as well as the legal sense — comes through clearly in her judgements, but it is also always placed within the context of her respect for the law — for the rule of law and its institutions. This is not to say that she does not feel that legal institutions should be reformed; on the contrary, that is essential. In her mind, Osler, Hoskin and Harcourt was one of those institutions, and in the long run she had a great deal to do with its reform.

The Wilsons stayed in Scotland for four years after their marriage, but in 1949 they immigrated to Canada and Reverend Wilson became the United Church minister in the Ottawa Valley community of Renfrew, Ontario. When Canada entered the Korean War, however, John enlisted in the Canadian navy as a seagoing padre. While he was away at sea, Mrs. Wilson moved to Ottawa and took a job as a receptionist in a dental office. When John returned from the war in 1954, he stayed in the navy and was posted to Halifax.

When they arrived in Halifax, for the first time in her adult life Mrs. Wilson was without a job. In the navy there was no parish for the minister's wife to tend to, and she was not interested in working in another dentist's office. After some thought she telephoned Dalhousie University and made an appointment to see the dean of law. As she put it, she really had no intention of practising law; she felt that law school was simply a way to return to the liberal education she had left off ten years before.

When Wilson explained her reasoning in applying to law school to Dean Horace Read, he responded, "Madam, we have no room here for dilettantes. Why don't you just go home and take up crocheting?"[17] This was not the first — or last — time Wilson would encounter sexism in her career, but fortunately she did not give up. She convinced Read to give her a chance, and three years later she graduated with an LL.B. and a number of academic awards.

During her time at Dalhousie, Bertha Wilson fell in love with the law, with its intellectual intricacies and its relevance.[18] And at some point in her time there, she reversed her thinking about practising. When it came time to find an articling position, however, being a woman was once again an obstacle. She enlisted the help of the future chief justice of Nova Scotia, Lorne Clarke, then a faculty member at Dalhousie who was also active in Nova Scotia Conservative politics. On Wilson's behalf, Clarke went to see Fred Bissett, a prominent Halifax lawyer and former provincial Conservative Party leader, to ask him to, as she put it, "take this woman in so she can article."[19]

Bissett's was a one-person practice, centred mostly in criminal law, and Wilson's months there were light years away from the peaceful hours in the Dalhousie law library. As she described it,

From the dizzying heights of academia, I was plunged into the stark reality of the police court, with its daily roster of drunks and prostitutes. . . . And when I became too insufferable in my new-found legal knowledge . . . Fred would say to me, innocent-like, "How would you like to work up a defence on this buggery charge?"[20]

Although she finished her articles with Bissett and was called to the bar in late 1957, she never practised in Nova Scotia. During the winter of 1957-58, John decided to leave the navy and accept a job with the national office of the United Church of Canada in Toronto. Once again, the Wilsons picked up stakes and moved.

Despite being a fully qualified Nova Scotia lawyer, if Wilson wanted to practise in Ontario, the rules of the Law Society of Upper Canada required her to article with an Ontario lawyer for another year in order to qualify for call to the bar of that province. Just as it had been when she finished law school, she knew that finding a firm willing to take in a woman student would be a problem. Fortunately, Fred Bissett had a good friend in Toronto, fellow Nova Scotian Arthur Pattillo, then a senior partner at Blake, Anglin, Osler & Cassels.

When she and her husband arrived in Toronto, Wilson telephoned Blakes and asked for Pattillo. She was told that he was unavailable and put through to the managing partner. He told her that Pattillo was away from the firm serving on a commission of inquiry in British Columbia, and would likely be gone for a year or more. She explained that she was a recently called Nova Scotia lawyer and was looking for an articling position to qualify for the Ontario bar. As she remembers it, although he did not sound too enthusiastic, he promised to discuss it with one or two of his partners and call her back.[21]

From the tone of her phone call, however, she didn't hold out too much hope about Blakes, so when she hadn't heard back in a few days she took out the Toronto telephone book and looked up lawyers. She was particularly interested in the larger firms because, as she put it, "In a small firm, they could always fob you off with excuses about not having a ladies' washroom."[22] In truth, she was also interested in a large firm because of the range of practice experience it would offer. As she glanced down the list of lawyers and firms in the Yellow Pages, her finger stopped at one — Osler, Hoskin & Harcourt. The name didn't mean a thing to her, but its list of lawyers was almost as long as Blakes'.

She picked up the phone and called; the receptionist put her through to Ed Huycke, Mossey Huycke's younger son, who was then responsible for students and junior lawyers. Huycke explained that although the firm did not have a vacancy at the moment, he would arrange an interview for her. When she arrived at the Oslers office in the Toronto-Dominion Bank Building and took the old elevator up the fifth floor, Ed Huycke spoke to her briefly in his office, and then took her down the hall to meet Swatty Wotherspoon. It was a very happy coincidence — for Wilson, but more significantly for the firm — that Wotherspoon happened to be in that day. Had Huycke taken her to see one of the other senior partners — particularly Hal Mockridge — the story might have been much different.

Wilson had her transcript from Dalhousie with her, and Wotherspoon was suitably impressed with her grades. "You've done rather well at law school," he mused.[23] Although she had not won the gold medal, she had finished very high in the class of fifty students and received a couple of the graduating prizes. He was much more impressed, however, with Wilson's military connection. Wotherspoon had been an brigadier-general in the Canadian army during World War II and had remained in the reserves after the war, and he was very interested in John Wilson's naval service during the Korean War.

There was more to it than that, however. Despite Wotherspoon's gruff, military manner, he was a very progressive thinker, in many ways in contrast to Hal Mockridge. Wotherspoon knew that the world was changing, and more particularly legal practice was changing, becoming much more competitive. If Osler, Hoskin & Harcourt was to survive and prosper in the new world, it was going to have to be much more forward thinking in a number of ways. One of the most important ways was in its personnel development. It was going to have to look much more at how good a lawyer might be, rather than at who *his* father was. In addition, Bertha Wilson was — and is — a very charming person. A stranger meeting her for the first time cannot help but warm to her. Wotherspoon ended their chat with, ''Well I think, my dear, that you deserve a chance; but I will have to speak, of course, to my colleagues.''[24]

A few days later Wotherspoon called Wilson in again, this time to meet some of the other lawyers in the firm. At the end of this meeting, he told her that there was one senior partner, a man named Mockridge, who was not particularly enthusiastic about the idea of a woman at Osler, Hoskin & Harcourt. Mockridge was away at the head office of International Nickel in New York at the time, and nothing further would happen until he returned. Wilson then told him that she had since then had a call from Blakes inviting her to an interview. Wotherspoon asked that she not go for an interview until after he had a chance to change Mockridge's mind, and she agreed.

Mockridge was anything but a reformer. As Stuart Thom remembers it, ''Certainly Mockridge and I guess Delamere weren't groundbreakers of that sociological type. To them, law was a downtown business for the man, and the lawyer they hired had certain qualities and connections and patterns of behaviour. Women just didn't fit.''[25] When Mockridge returned from New York, however, Wotherspoon was apparently able to convince him that Wilson deserved a chance; they called her in for yet another interview. She had a brief meeting with Mockridge, and then was ''marched down the hall to Mr. G.M. Huycke.''[26]

Huycke explained that the firm would offer her a position, and as the future Supreme Court justice recalls,

> *but* only on the basis that they thought that I deserved a chance to become qualified; they were quite prepared to have me in to article, but as soon as I had completed my articles and got my call to the bar I would be on my own. Their commitment to me was simply that I deserved the opportunity to get qualified. So I said that was fine; I was a little bit irked at that, so I said, ''Well, I think that would be a mutually acceptable arrangement. I might not like it here either.''[27]

Huycke apparently liked her answer and asked her if she could start the following morning.

When she arrived for work the next day she found her office, a tiny, windowless, converted supply cupboard across the hall from Mossey Huycke, and settled in to work. Her first assignment came in a phone call from Swatty Wotherspoon, who opened the conversation with the question, "What is a bond?" Wilson knew perfectly well what a bond was, but was a bit flustered by Wotherspoon's bluntness. She mumbled a little, and he finally said, "Well, why don't you do a memorandum, what is a bond?" She had no idea of the context of the question, if this was related to a client, or why Wotherspoon wanted her to do it, but she went to the firm's library and wrote a detailed memo answering the question.[28]

She remembers getting a number of research assignments like that during the first months at the firm, and slowly realizing that she could learn the context of the research by going to the filing department and pulling the file herself. This was, of course, one of the advantages of working at Oslers, but she was expected to figure it out for herself. In fact, she had almost no face-to-face contact with her superiors at first. She would receive a brief research question and would prepare and send a memorandum back, and that would be the last she heard about it.

On one occasion, however, she got a response from Hal Mockridge, who actually called her down to his office to thank her and discuss a memo she had prepared. She obviously impressed him because he began to send quite a bit of important corporate work her way. She was originally interested in practising in trust law, a field which she particularly enjoyed at law school, but as Mockridge and Wotherspoon began giving her corporate assignments, there was little time for anything else.[29]

One day the following year, when Wilson had almost completed her articling period, Swatty Wotherspoon came into her office with a research assignment. She recalls the incident with some humour; apparently Wotherspoon began by saying,

"Oh I've got a really interesting project for you, you're going to enjoy this one." They all knew, of course, that I loved the law and there was nothing I liked better than to sit down and struggle with some of these problems. So he told me about the project, and I said that this is an ongoing problem, this is going to go on for months. He said, "Oh yes;" and I said I think you'd better get somebody else — you do know that tomorrow is my last day. He said, "What do you mean that tomorrow is your last day?'' I said, "I get my call to the bar tomorrow and that's when I leave." He was just appalled and said, "You mean that no one has spoken to you?" and I said, "No, no one has." He said, "Don't go anywhere, stay there," and off he went and came back and said, "We're just all taking it for granted that you're continuing on." Nobody had ever said anything to me, so of course I did stay on; I stayed on for seventeen years.[30]

Bertha Wilson's tenure with Osler, Hoskin & Harcourt was significant to the history of the firm for many reasons. Obviously the firm was very proud to have one of its alumnae serve on the Supreme Court of Canada, but she had an important impact on the firm in many other ways. Partly because she was a woman, but also because she loved and was exceptionally good at it, she ended up doing almost exclusively research work for the firm. Having her act as a "super student" doing research kept her from having direct contact with traditional male clients who might not have complete confidence in a woman lawyer.

In the process, however, Wilson became what is now referred to as "a lawyer's lawyer." That is, she acted as the adviser to the solicitor on a file. She did not simply research the law; she counselled the lawyer on the advice he should give to the client. In fact, as the firm and its practice continued to grow at a rapid pace, this research function became indispensable to the firm, and Wilson began to attract bright young lawyers from places like the Law Reform Commission to work in her new Research Department. It may have begun as a function of chauvinism which the firm should not be particularly proud of, but the result was an innovation of which it is justifiably proud.

The other very significant outsider to join the firm in the late 1950s was a young Nova Scotian named Harold Purdy Crawford. Purdy, as he was known, did not fit the mould of the traditional Oslers lawyer. He did not grow up in Rosedale and graduate from a private school; he was the son of a coal miner and grew up in tiny Five Islands, Nova Scotia. He attended a two-room rural school up to grade ten and then travelled fifteen miles up the road and lived in a boarding house to finish high school in a four-room school.[31]

When he graduated from high school, Crawford made an unusual decision for those from his community and went west to Sackville, New Brunswick to attend Mount Allison University, which was then, and remains, a very small university with an excellent liberal arts reputation. When Crawford graduated from Mount Allison with a Bachelor of Arts degree in 1952, he went back to Nova Scotia and enrolled in Dalhousie Law School.[32]

At Dalhousie, Crawford really came into his own. Bertha Wilson, who was two years behind him at Dalhousie, remembers Crawford as being a real leader among the students. "He was a very giving type of person and very popular." He would often "hold court" at the top of the library steps and explain a lecture to a group of students who had not understood it.[33] Towards the end of his final year in law school, Crawford, like many other top Dalhousie students, was urged to go on to Harvard to do a graduate degree. As he remembers it,

> At the time when I decided to apply, I probably was ambivalent in my own mind as to whether my future was in teaching or practice, [but] I very deliberately took courses at Harvard that related to what I would want to do if I was going to practise.[34]

At Harvard he took courses with professors including Archibald Cox, a long-time faculty member and expert in labour law who became famous outside of legal circles as the Watergate Special Prosecutor in 1973, Albert Baker, a utilities law specialist, and Louis Loss, a securities law authority.[35]

Although Crawford eventually became a noted securities specialist in his own practice, it was Cox who had the greatest influence on him at Harvard. In fact, when Crawford came back to Canada his initial intention was to become a labour lawyer, and during his first few years at Osler, Hoskin & Harcourt he did quite a bit of labour work for International Nickel and other clients with B.M. Osler and T.D. Delamere.[36]

During his year at Harvard, Crawford made the decision that he would go into practice. He had some offers to go into teaching law, but turned them down. He was interested in law in the fast lane, in the exciting world of corporate law. For most of his classmates at Harvard this meant Wall Street, but at that time if he wanted to practise law in the United States he would have to take out U.S. citizenship. Crawford couldn't live with the idea of giving up his Canadian citizenship; if New York was out, it had to be Toronto.

Before going up to Toronto, however, he decided to return to Halifax to complete the short articling period required for a call to the Nova Scotia bar. Unlike Bertha Wilson, Crawford had little difficulty in finding an articling position. As a top Dalhousie student who was also male, he had many more options, and he ended up with Roland Ritchie, who later served on the Supreme Court of Canada. Ritchie, in fact, wrote the majority judgement in the famous 1969 Supreme Court case of *The Queen* v. *Drybones*, the only case to use the 1960 Diefenbaker Bill of Rights to disallow a piece of federal legislation.[37]

Ritchie's practice was a general and wide-ranging one, and a normal day's docket might include everything from a real estate deal to manslaughter case to an admiralty problem. This was the advantage of practising in Halifax, but Ritchie also had the traditional Nova Scotian's distrust of what Maritimers pejoratively call "Upper Canada." Ritchie and others in Halifax told Crawford that he should think very carefully before deciding to go up to Toronto to practise. As he remembers it, Ritchie said that Toronto was "establishment country . . . those big law firms will let you work for them, but you'll never break through."[38]

To some extent Ritchie was right; Toronto was establishment country, but it was about to change. Crawford was certainly not a member of the establishment, but his record at both Dalhousie and Harvard was very impressive, and when he got to Toronto in August of 1956 he had interviews with many of the old-line firms. In addition to Oslers, he interviewed at Blakes; Borden & Elliot; Fraser & Beatty; and Wright & McTaggert. He ultimately chose Osler, Hoskin & Harcourt because it had a particularly impressive list of blue-chip clients like International Nickel, Procter & Gamble, Coca-Cola, General Motors and Kodak. More importantly, in looking over the *Law List* entry for the firm, which indicated the dates of call of the lawyers, he felt — in the brash confidence of youth — that it offered him the best opportunity to advance.[39]

Crawford joined the firm as an articling student in September of 1956 and stayed as an associate lawyer after his call to the bar in early 1958. During his time as a student and the first couple of years after his call to the bar, he did primarily labour work with Tom Delamere and Brick Osler.[40] Since Delamere joined the firm during World War II, Oslers had built up a sizeable practice in labour law. There were three reasons for this: the first was that the demand for legal advice in labour relations was increasing as the scope of federal and provincial industrial relations regulation grew; the second was that the firm had a large group of established corporate employer clients whose work forces were becoming increasingly unionized; and finally, the Osler lawyers, particularly Delamere, Brick Osler and his brother Campbell, were developing a very good reputation in the field.

While working with Delamere and Brick Osler doing labour work, however, Purdy Crawford learned a very valuable lesson. Both of these men were lone-wolf practitioners. They were excellent lawyers, but they were not very good at delegating work. Allan Beattie remembers this about Delamere in particular with a story from the early 1950s:

> Mr. Delamere as a practitioner . . . tended I think to do a lot himself. He was not what I would call a good delegator, so he didn't particularly use the young lawyers a great deal. If he did use a young lawyer, it was usually to do something very specific, but you didn't get to work hand-in-glove with him very often. I can recall an instance of this. We were working on a transaction that involved American Standard which was one of Mr. Delamere's principal clients, both labour and outside labour, and this was a corporate transaction of some kind. I was asked to help him do this corporate work. We stayed down one evening to work on this and during the evening I recall there was a particular little agreement that had to be done. So he said to me, "You do that and we'll discuss it tomorrow sometime." I went off and I worked away at this and I got a draft of this done. Later the next day, we got together and one of the items that we were to talk about was this agreement. So I said, "Well, I've produced something of a draft." "Oh," he said, "I've already drafted that!" That's an example of how delegation wasn't one of his great strengths.[41]

The result for Crawford was not a very good learning experience. As he puts it, "Quite frankly . . . I could have trained forever and would still only be good enough to go up to Sudbury and sit with them while they argued labour arbitrations [for International Nickel]."[42] The lesson that he learned was that in order to bring junior lawyers along — and ensure that there is someone within the firm qualified to keep up service to existing clients after you are gone — you have to give them responsibility.

In any event, Crawford found that "the first couple of years I spent half my time with labour law and the rest of my time wasn't very busy," so he sought out other work from the other senior partners. He began by assisting Stuart Thom on a number of tax matters, and found that he quite enjoyed it. He also found himself doing quite a bit of securities and other corporate work with Hal Mockridge and trusts and estates with Mossey Huycke. Before long, Crawford was recognized as a rising star in a number of areas of corporate law — both within the firm and outside of it.

Some observers would describe Crawford as primarily a securities specialist, but during the early years of his practice he was equally involved in tax law. During the 1960s, he served on the Ontario Attorney General's Committee on Securities Legislation and both the Ontario and national taxation sections of the Canadian Bar Association. From 1970 to 1972 he was a member of the Board of Governors of the Canadian Tax Foundation. He also taught courses on a part-time basis in income tax and securities at Osgoode Hall Law School from 1964 to 1968, the University of Toronto Law School from 1969 to 1971, and the Law Society's Bar Admission Course from 1969 to 1972.[43]

Crawford apparently had the ability, at a time when the law was becoming more and more complex, to be both a multi-field specialist and a generalist at the same time. He was able to master the intricacies of a number of areas and still see the big picture.[44] This was particularly important as the trend of the 1960s was towards the large, complex transaction requiring legal advice across a range of specialties; this meant that larger numbers of lawyers would be involved on a single file. To use an analogy common on Bay Street, he was a good quarterback on a deal.

There were obviously a number of aspects to Purdy Crawford's practice and personality which had a very significant impact on the development of Osler, Hoskin & Harcourt. Perhaps the most important of these — and the one which best sets him apart from the previous generation — was his skill as what lawyers call a rainmaker.

Lawyers in Ontario have only recently been allowed to advertise, and the Law Society's rules governing professional advertising are very restrictive compared to those governing other service industries. The rule, which was until recently a complete prohibition on the marketing of legal services through advertising, is rooted in the pre-twentieth century professionalization of lawyers. One of the things which lawyers, like other professionals, used to distinguish themselves from the non-professional trades was the fact that clients sought them out because they were known to provide skilled service. They did not "tout their wares."[45]

Of course, as a number of authors have pointed out, this rule did not hurt élite lawyers and firms as much as those at the lower end of the professional ladder.[46] Firms such as Oslers, who by mid-century had a strong stable of corporate clients and whose lawyers were largely members of the social establishment, had little difficulty in making contact with prospective clients. In addition, as discussed in previous chapters, the firm's reputation for competent and creative corporate legal advice, particularly in the international business community, meant that client development did not have to be a priority. Men of Hal Mockridge's generation could mildly disapprove of what would later be considered professional entrepreneurship in men like Beverley Matthews at McCarthys and Pete Elliot at Borden & Elliot.

By the beginning of the 1960s, however, the business environment was starting to change. As the Canadian economy grew and became much more competitive, the old sense of loyalty to a particular law firm began to wane. The result was the clients were increasingly likely to shop their legal business around, and lawyers had to become much more aggressive marketers. Purdy Crawford saw this and acted on it. During those years, the Oslers stable of blue-chip corporate clients grew substantially, and according to most, Crawford had a lot to do with it.

One of the more significant additions to the Osler client list during the 1960s was Molsons, the brewing giant. Molson Breweries maintained its corporate headquarters in Montreal, where the company was founded in 1787, until it moved to Toronto in 1968. Its primary corporate counsel up to that point was the Montreal firm of Chisholm, Smith.[47] Prior to 1953 Molson did not brew beer in Ontario; it had a warehousing and distribution operation in Toronto, and retained Toronto counsel for whatever legal consultation this required.

When Molson began construction of a brewery on Fleet Street, across from the old Maple Leaf Stadium in Toronto, it kept the same arrangement, but in the late 1960s the company began a campaign of substantial growth and diversification. It acquired control of a number of companies, most of which were not involved in the brewing industry, and moved the head office of the company to Toronto. On each of these steps Purdy Crawford acted as legal advisor to the company.

The Osler, Hoskin & Harcourt relationship with Molson actually dated to the early 1960s, when Hal Mockridge went on the board. Unlike some other corporate directorships for lawyers, Mockridge's appointment to the Molson board did not mean that his firm could expect to get legal work from the company. It was not uncommon for a lawyer sitting on the board of a major corporation to also serve as legal counsel to the company, but in this case Hartland Molson made it clear that he was not inviting Mockridge to serve on the board in return for a retainer. In fact, Mockridge would consider it unprofessional to ask that such an understanding be put in place.[48]

Nevertheless, when the company began its diversification program in the late 1960s, it was Purdy Crawford who they looked to for advice. Crawford — and therefore Osler, Hoskin & Harcourt — became Molson's primary corporate counsel and looked after a number of important transactions for the company in the years which followed.

One of the more interesting deals Crawford worked on for Molson involved a loan to Maple Leaf Gardens Ltd. In the late 1970s, Harold Ballard, the principal shareholder of the company which owned Toronto's National Hockey League team and the landmark arena in which they played their home games, needed capital. Molson agreed to provide Ballard with a sizeable, interest free loan, in return for certain marketing privileges within Maple Leaf Gardens, and for an option on 25 per cent of the shares in Maple Leaf Gardens Ltd.[49]

Oslers' acquisition of Molson Breweries as a client may have represented something of a transition from the old style to the new. Hal Mockridge sat on the company's board of directors, but he did not solicit its legal work.[50] Although Mockridge's directorship probably did not hurt, Purdy Crawford — by making his own name and that of his firm well known — attracted the account. Law firm client development tends not to involve traditional forms of advertising, although during the 1980s many firms began to retain professional marketing advice. Even though Oslers hired a client development specialist to act as the firm's director of marketing, Oslers' methods of making prospective clients aware of its services and expertise are rather more subtle.[51]

In the early days of this trend, Crawford saw the benefits of exposure in venues like part-time law school lecturing and bar association activities. As Crawford put it:

> You have to get out from under the bush and make [your firm]
> known a bit. . . . That's why I thought it was important to have
> many people in the firm teaching in law schools, bar courses,
> going to law schools to talk to students, lecturing, involved in
> seminars,in programs involving the business community. The
> more tentacles you can get out there, the better.[52]

Mockridge had some difficulty with this concept. He generally thought of rainmaking as a little unprofessional, and perhaps beneath what he — or his uncle — might have defined as an Oslers standard. On the other hand, he was very much aware of the changing climate of corporate practice, and he had great confidence in Crawford.

Not surprisingly, Crawford also had great confidence in himself and, more importantly, in his partners and the other lawyers in the firm. Also, he was able to convey that confidence to clients. This was essential if he was to be able to delegate this new-found client legal work to the rest of the firm. The ability to delegate is an essential prerequisite to rainmaking; if you do not pass work on to others within the firm, you can only take in as much new work as you can do.

A good example of the new clients which Crawford attracted to the firm was OMERS, the Ontario municipal employees' pension fund. One of Crawford's students at Osgoode Hall Law School in the mid-1960s was very much involved when OMERS was founded some years later, and she sought him out specifically because of their contact at the law school.[53]

The OMERS account represented one type of marketing benefit of Crawford's law teaching, but another, and perhaps equally important benefit, was marketing the firm to potential lawyers. Just as the client market was becoming much more flexible and less tradition-driven, so too was the market for incoming lawyers — and the law schools were the places to start the recruitment process. Until the arrival of people like Bertha Wilson and Purdy Crawford in the late 1950s, Oslers was a family firm. From that point forward, it was moving toward becoming a meritocracy. The process of change was, however, a slow and at times difficult one.

During the 1950s, Crawford and Wilson were the exceptions to the rule. Although the firm recruited some excellent lawyers during the decade, most of them seem to have had some form of familial or other relation to the firm. Fred and Ed Huycke's connection was obvious; Allan Beattie was the son of Leslie Beattie, who was the head of Canadian operations for International Nickel and sat on the Inco board of directors with his close friend Hal Mockridge. And there were others with similar, if not as direct, connections. Jack Ground, who joined the firm as a student in 1957 shortly after his graduation from the University of Toronto Law School, was a fraternity brother of Ed Huycke.[54]

As Ground, who was a partner in the firm until his appointment to the Ontario Court of Justice in 1992, described the firm in the late

1950s, "The place was just at the end of the era of being a gentlemen's club. It was very much, I would say, an old Toronto establishment firm and 90 per cent of the people in the firm had gone to one of the Little Big Four schools and it was . . . very old Toronto."[55] The Little Big Four were the most prestigious of the Ontario private boys' high schools: Upper Canada College, Trinity College School, St. Andrews and Ridley College.[56]

Oslers was not unusual in this regard; most law students found articling positions in firms or with lawyers they were related to or knew in some way. Harry Boylan, for instance, who joined the firm as a young lawyer in 1956, articled with the Toronto firm of Armstrong, Young and Burrows because his father-in-law knew Vernon Armstrong.[57]

Family connections were obviously an advantage to some, but those who had them often had a difficult decision to make. Ed Huycke, for instance, thought hard about whether it would be a good idea to stay with the firm after his call to the bar in 1953. He wondered whether it would be wise to try to practise in his father's shadow, or if he should accept the offer he had from a small firm in Barrie, Ontario.[58] His fears, in fact, were not without foundation; Bertha Wilson remembers Mossey being rather hard on young Ed, probably because they were both in the estates field.[59] Huycke is quick to point out, however, that there were distinct personal benefits as well:

> I am very glad that I made the decision that I did because I think the most rewarding ten or twelve years of my life were my first . . . years of practice when I was able to practise with my father. It was a tremendous learning experience because he was an outstanding lawyer, but it was also a very rewarding experience between father and son.[60]

Ed Huycke obviously credits a good experience with his father with his early training in practice, but there were other advantages to the continuing family nature of the firm. Even as it began to change, the firm was still a close-knit group. Until they moved to the Prudential Building in 1962, most of the younger people ate lunch together almost every day at the same table in Child's Restaurant on King Street next to the Dominion Bank Building.[61]

There were also irregular hockey games played during the late 1950s as challenge matches between the two floors of the Dominion Bank Building. As Allan Beattie remembers, it started with a certain amount of nostalgic stories about school-day exploits, and one group good-naturedly called the other's bluff.[62] As it turned out, a few weeks later the Fourth Floor Flyers took on the Fifth Floor Wolves at Leaside Arena. Bill Bryden, then some twelve years past his playing days on the McMaster University varsity hockey team, kept until his retirement a tomato-can trophy in his office which read "5th Floor Wolves 1959 Champs."[63]

Most of the students and young lawyers in the firm played in the games, with Bill Somers, then an articling student, and John Goodwin, who had also played for the Osgoode Hall Law School Owls, as goalies.[64] Apparently, some of the older lawyers also took part, including Harold Boston, who would have then been almost sixty, and Stuart Thom — although Thom laughingly denies any such foolishness.[65] The games were very competitive; most participants remember Bill Somers being cut for a few stitches in the face (this was the pre-mask era) and Purdy Crawford collapsing from exhaustion on the bench after one of his frantic end-to-end rushes.[66]

Events like the hockey games showed that even as the firm was growing, it was maintaining the closeness which sprang from its family roots. And like an old-style family, the firm was still ruled by a *pater familias* — in this case, Hal Mockridge. In this area, however, things were about to change.

The beginning of the changes in the firm's management structure appeared in the December 31, 1958 partnership agreement. That agreement, signed by sixteen partners, including Ed Huycke and Ed Saunders, who were signing for the first time, provided for the appointment of five "Executive Partners."[67] The five, who were, not surprisingly, the top five in terms of percentage earnings with the firm, were Hal Mockridge, Mossey Huycke, Swatty Wotherspoon, Tom Delamere and B.M. Osler.[68]

Although it was not until some years later that this group became officially named the Executive Committee, it was described as such almost from the start. Under the terms of the agreement, the partnership as a whole formally delegated certain management and administrative duties to the Executive Partners. These included:

> . . . the power to manage and conduct the affairs of the Firm in
> all things; to act on behalf of all the partners in all matters and
> things relating to or in any way concerning the partnership and
> the relationship of the Firm to the public and in particular, but
> without limiting the generality of the foregoing, the Executive

Partners shall have the right and power to . . . terminate the appointment of the Auditors of the Firm and to appoint new Auditors and from time to time to change such appointment; to terminate the appointment of the Bankers of the Firm and to appoint any other chartered Bank as such Bankers and from time to time to change such appointment; to supervise the internal operation and management of the Firm and its employees; from time to time to engage such employees, either professional or otherwise, as the business of the Firm may require and to dismiss such employees with power to appoint an office manager and to delegate to him to such a degree as they see fit the duties of supervising the internal operation and management of the office of the Firm and the power to engage and dismiss any employees other than professional employees. The term "professional employees" shall include solicitors employed on a salaried basis and students-at-law.[69]

In addition to these powers, the Executive Partners had one other very significant responsibility. Under the terms of the partnership agreement, they had the authority to allot 10 per cent of the firm's profits on a discretionary basis. Ninety per cent of the profits were to be divided according to the terms specified in the partnership agreement, but the Executive Partners were to have the discretion to allot the remaining 10 per cent on an annual basis using whatever criteria they felt appropriate.[70]

The purpose of this provision was apparently to allow for some form of retrospective partnership share allotment to take account of changing circumstances. Interestingly, however, the Executive Partners chose not to make any changes to the division outlined in the partnership agreement. At the end of the first year under this system, they decided to allot the discretionary 10 per cent on the same basis as the regular partnership shares.[71] The next partnership agreement, which came into force January 1, 1962, did not contain the discretionary allotment provision.[72]

Also included in the new agreement for 1962 was the addition of Stuart Thom's name to the list of Executive Partners. The 1958 agreement did not specify how many partners would serve on this committee; it simply named the five. The new agreement indicated that there would be no fewer than five and no more than seven.[73] Significantly, the members of this committee were not elected; in theory they were appointed by the partnership as a whole, but in fact they appointed themselves. They were the leaders of the firm, and the more junior partners had neither the inclination nor any reason to challenge their leadership — at least not yet.

The new partnership agreement further gave the Executive Partners the power,

> with or without stating their reasons . . . [to] require a partner to resign from the Firm and if such resignation is not submitted . . . [to] expel such partner, the expulsion to take effect upon ratification of the Executive Partners' action by not less than two-thirds of all the partners excluding the partner in respect of whom the action is proposed to be taken.[74]

Still, the only time the partners met was once a year to review the audited financial statements and sign off on them.[75]

In fact, it was still Hal Mockridge and Mossey Huycke who were making most of the important decisions. As Stuart Thom remembers it:

> Actually, although I was on the Executive Committee, the Executive Committee during the time I was on it was Mockridge in collaboration with Huycke . . . in that order. Not that they were competitors or there was any strain between them, but Mockridge was the senior man and he did what he did or didn't do . . . pretty well on his own. People came or dropped out because they displeased him as much as anything, although I don't doubt that . . . he acted fairly. . . in deciding whether they should come in or not. I can think of a couple of people who left the firm because Mockridge didn't like them and turned out quite well elsewhere. He had certain definite antipathies which were a little hard to discern, to sort of understand, but people would strike him the wrong way and that was the end of that person. It was his show, very much.[76]

Over the course of the next few years, things began to change, albeit slowly. The Executive Partners held regular meetings, roughly once a month, to deal with matters such as lawyers' charging rates, new personnel, and firm procedures. It is obvious from the minutes of these meetings that the committee was trying to respond to the increasing complexity of practice in the 1960s. An interesting example was the system they established to deal with new legislation.

Complaints from lawyers about the volume of law they keep up to date on are not new. The Canadian law journals would often print letters from lawyers bemoaning the increasing weight of law reports and statute volumes in the late nineteenth century. But by the mid-twentieth century, they really did have something to complain about. The 1937 *Revised Statutes of Ontario*, a comprehensive set of provincial legislation then in force, totalled four relatively thin volumes. The next edition, published in 1950, was five volumes. The 1960 edition was also five volumes, but they were each larger, and the 1970 edition was seven volumes.[77] And the intervening annual volumes of new legislation grew larger every year.

In an effort to divide the workload of keeping up with new legislation in a systematic way, and to make sure that the firm as a whole received the full benefit of each of its member's expertise, in May 1962 the Executive Committee approved a procedure whereby new bills introduced in a provincial legislature or at Ottawa would be given to a specific lawyer or lawyers based on the content of the bill. That person would then prepare a memorandum to the rest of the firm summarizing and commenting on the subject matter of the bill.[78]

The membership of the Executive Partners remained the same until early in 1965, when Swatty Wotherspoon submitted his resignation from the partnership — and therefore his position as an Executive Partner — to accept a senior executive position with Eaton's. Wotherspoon's departure was a shock to the firm. Although it has become more common in recent years, his was one of the first instances of a senior law firm partner resigning to become a business executive.[79]

The reasons for his resignation were complicated. He was not an old man; at fifty-six he was in the prime of his legal career. In many ways he was one of the leaders of the firm, and in many people's eyes — including his own — the lieutenant and successor to Hal Mockridge and Mossey Huycke. His clients were among the firm's most important, including *The Telegram*, the Bassett family, Baton Broadcasting and Eaton's, and he was influential in much of the firm's management evolution of the early 1960s, particularly in terms of recruiting young lawyers.[80] Yet he chose to jump ship.

An apparent clue to Wotherspoon's resignation appeared in the Executive Committee minutes of December 16, 1964. At that meeting, Hal Mockridge explained to the committee that Wotherspoon had informed him of a possible conflict of interest involving one of the firm's clients. Apparently, he had recently learned that his wife had an interest in a small parcel of land in northern Ontario, which was the subject of litigation with the Texas Gulf company.[81] The fact that Wotherspoon left the firm a month later seems to indicate that he chose to accept the Eaton offer in order to remove the firm from the apparent conflict situation.

But Wotherspoon's decision to go to Eaton's involved more than that. Purdy Crawford remembers a few specific conflicts between Mockridge and Wotherspoon which made the latter's junior position clear. Moreover, the offer from Eaton's was an apparently very attractive one.[82] But the reason which seems most compelling, particularly in light of the long-term evolution of the firm, was that the writing was already on the wall that Hal Mockridge's successors as the leaders of the firm would be from the next generation, not from Wotherspoon's. The next leaders would be Crawford, Allan Beattie and Fred Huycke.

Two months after Wotherspoon's resignation, on March 10, 1965, Mossey Huycke stepped down from the Executive Committee.[83] Huycke was then just over three months from his seventieth birthday.[84] If there was a point when the firm began to hand over its active management to the next generation of partners, it was probably at that meeting on March 10. The partnership agreement called for a minimum of five Executive Partners; since Stuart Thom's addition in 1962 there had been six, and when Wotherspoon resigned it left five. When Mossey Huycke stepped down, however, they had to add at least one person.

In fact, they added Fred Huycke and Allan Beattie. Had the Executive Partners decided to appoint the next highest share-earning partner they would have simply added Bob Ferguson to the group, but they felt that it was time to bring in the next generation. On the face of it, it seemed as if they simply passed on the positions to each retiring member's designated heir. Fred Huycke was Mossey's eldest son, and Allan Beattie had acted as Wotherspoon's junior for many years.[85] In fact, Beattie took over most of Wotherspoon's client responsibilities, including Eaton's, *The Telegram*, and the various Bassett family companies.[86]

The Executive Committee remained with Hal Mockridge, Tom Delamere, B.M. Osler, Stuart Thom, Fred Huycke and Allan Beattie as its members for the rest of the decade. The partnership agreement, which was renewed every three years, made no changes to the powers of the Executive Partners in either its 1965 or 1968 versions.[87] During those years, however, Hal Mockridge was slowly relinquishing his decision-making authority to the other members of the committee. The minutes of the committee's meetings during those years show an increasing number of sub-committees and greater bureaucracy in the management process. Until Allan Beattie became the chairman in January 1972, however, Mockridge continued to make the most important decisions.[88]

Mockridge, for instance, still apparently decided on what each partner's share of the firm's profits would be. He would inform the other partners and ask for their opinions, but the final decision was clearly his.[89] The process that he used was to draw up a draft of what he thought would be a fair division and then take it to the next senior partner — during the late 1960s, this would be Mossey Huycke — to ask what he thought. He would then work his way down the letterhead (or more likely the existing share division list) through Delamere, B.M. Osler, etc. In later years Beattie followed the same procedure, but as he pointed out, when he did it he was actively trying to build consensus.[90] When Mockridge did it, no consensus-building was necessary; his decision was simply accepted.[91]

One of the most important events for the firm during Mockridge's term as chairman of the executive committee was to leave the old Toronto-Dominion Bank Building and move across King Street to the new Prudential Building. At some point during the late 1950s, the partners held a special meeting of the firm in the fifth-floor board room in the Toronto-Dominion Bank Building.[92] It was this meeting that began a series of events which necessitated a move to much larger premises.

Hal Mockridge had just made a very important decision, and he wanted to discuss the implications of his decision with his partners. Mockridge had recently been asked to serve on the board of directors of Massey-Ferguson Limited, the giant farm implements manufacturer, recently taken over by E.P. Taylor's Argus Corporation. It would, naturally, be a personal plum for Mockridge to serve on another prestigious corporate board, but more importantly for the firm, and in contrast to the understanding when Mockridge went on the Molson board, the offer also implied that Osler, Hoskin & Harcourt would get a significant portion of Massey's legal work.

As he explained at the meeting, however, Mockridge had reluctantly decided to decline the offer. The firm simply did not have the manpower to adequately serve the client. They had some of the best corporate lawyers in the country; they just did not have enough of them to take on another huge client. But nevertheless, he went on to ask the meeting, "What should we do about this?"[93]

As they began to discuss the question, it became clear that their options were either to keep the firm small, and continue as it had for some years, or make a conscious effort to expand. The latter option had many negative connotations. There was great danger in becoming a law factory, the term some critics were using to describe New York firms numbering over fifty lawyers, of losing the sense of professional intimacy which was one of the firm's strengths. A small partnership based on trust and even affection was something radically different from a large organization with complex rules and bureaucracy. And as they had learned from the W.B. Reid debacle of only a few years earlier, it was very important to *know* who your partners were.

Growth would mean a substantial lifestyle change for most of them, but as Mockridge put it, the status quo was not really an option. If they tried to stay the same size and turn down work because they didn't have the manpower, they would inevitably shrink. The message to clients — potential and existing — would simply be, ''We can't do the work.'' Swatty Wotherspoon, in particular, argued that the firm should accept any and all work, and expand whenever necessary to meet the need. In Wotherspoon's view, there certainly were dangers which would have to be dealt with, but the alternative was not an option.[94] This was a critical conclusion for the firm; it meant that Oslers would go forward and remain one of the largest firms in Canada. Other firms made the opposite decision during those years, and their fate was what Mockridge and Wotherspoon predicted.

An eventual result of this decision was the firm's move from the old Toronto-Dominion Bank Building across the street to the brand new Prudential Building at the northwest corner of King and Yonge streets. Mockridge and the other Executive Partners began to seriously discuss the possibility of a move in 1960. Space had been a problem in the Toronto-Dominion Bank Building for a number of years; after the 1960 calls to the bar, there were twenty-nine lawyers in the firm and well in excess of that number in support staff, and the Bank building simply had no more room for expansion. The old building was also beginning to show its age, especially in comparison to some of the new buildings in the city. Without modern amenities such as air conditioning — and most importantly, without sufficient room for expansion of the firm — it was time to look elsewhere.

After a survey of available space, the firm decided on the new building owned by The Prudential Insurance Company of America. At twenty stories, it was one of the tallest of a new wave of buildings in the city, and the firm signed a lease on November 1, 1961 for all of the seventeenth floor and part of the sixteenth.[95]

Swatty Wotherspoon chaired an Accommodations Committee of partners responsible for determining the leasehold improvements the firm would arrange for in its new premises. C.R. Osler, who served on the committee, remembers Wotherspoon asking him to fly down to New York for a tour of Cravath, Swaine & Moore's new offices. Wotherspoon had done a fair amount of referral work for the Cravath firm since the Interprovincial Pipe Line deal some years earlier.[96]

Osler, Hoskin & Harcourt apparently implemented a few of the Cravath designs, but one thing they did not do was establish a stenographic pool. At Cravath, Swaine & Moore, only the very senior lawyers had their own secretaries. The majority of the firm's secretaries worked in a huge typing pool guarded over by a matronly supervisor. Lawyers would simply hand dictaphone tapes to the supervisor and she would assign a secretary to do it. The lawyer would then pick up the finished work when it was ready.[97] This was considered far too factory-like and impersonal for Osler, Hoskin & Harcourt.

The firm's relationship with its clients — particularly the Toronto-Dominion Bank as an existing one and Prudential as a potential one — was a consideration in deciding where to move. The Dominion Bank had been a client going back to when B.B. Osler's brother Sir Edmund Osler was still its chairman, but the firm had largely lost the bank's work, even before the merger with the Bank of Toronto in 1955. Harold Shapley had always looked after the bank's file, but when he died in 1952, it apparently decided to go to Beverley Matthews at McCarthy & McCarthy.[98] The Prudential was not an Oslers client, but significantly, it became one after the move.[99]

The Prudential was a brand-new building, and it offered impressive facilities, but it was not considered the most prestigious address in the city. At least two other new buildings, the Royal Bank Building next door and The Bank of Canada Building at the southwest corner of Queen Street and University Avenue, were more prestigious, but this probably says something about Hal Mockridge and the firm which still reflected his image. He would let Pete Elliot, the senior partner at Borden & Elliot, move his firm into the Bank of Canada Building. The Prudential would do for Oslers.[100]

Borden & Elliot's move to the Bank of Canada Building may have seemed a little pretentious to someone like Mockridge, but it was nothing compared to the move which McCarthy & McCarthy made six years later when the new Toronto-Dominion Centre opened in 1967. The Prudential Building was twenty stories; the TD Centre was over fifty![101] When McCarthys moved from the Canada Life Building to the new TD Centre, it raised a few eyebrows by renting very expensive space with a commanding view of Lake Ontario and spending a great deal of money on leasehold improvements such as a magnificent spiral staircase between floors. According to most observers, this really set the tone for law firm location and decor. Many other lawyers, including those at Oslers, felt that clients might wonder who was going to pay for all this opulence, but the first-class surroundings certainly did not hurt McCarthys' client list and other law firms — including Oslers in 1976 — soon followed suit.

The new downtown buildings — particularly the new Toronto City Hall, which was completed in 1965 — were the most tangible evidence of change.[102] During the latter part of the decade, places like Rochdale College and the Yorkville district, where the drug and counter-culture movement blossomed, showed that the old "Toronto the Good" was gone forever. Osler, Hoskin & Harcourt was changing also, although it was far more than a few blocks from Rochdale College on Bloor Street to the Prudential Building on King Street.

By the Canadian Centennial year of 1967, there were forty-seven lawyers in the firm, eighteen of whom were partners. Of the twenty-nine associates, almost all had articled with the firm. Interestingly, although the range of political views within the firm had changed very little, the religious profile of the lawyers was beginning to change. In the view of the man who was then the office manager and knew all of them well, twenty-six of the forty-seven (55 per cent) would be identified either publicly or privately as Conservative party supporters. The remaining twenty-one (45 per cent) were mostly Liberals, but there may have been the odd quiet supporter of the NDP. This contrasts with the group of twenty-three lawyers in the firm in 1957, seventeen of whom (74 per cent) would be described as Conservatives.[103]

Very few of the lawyers in the firm were active in either party, and those who were generally kept their political involvement at a low profile. Allan Beattie's friends might describe him as a Liberal, but he kept his political views very private.[104] He did not list any political affiliation in *Who's Who*, and many of his most prominent clients, including the Bassetts and the Eatons, were Conservatives. Others, such as Bill Bryden, who served for a time as president of the largely Conservative Albany Club, were more public supporters of a political party. Bryden was listed as a Conservative in *Who's Who*.

Since Leighton McCarthy left the firm along with his brother and cousin in 1916, no one in the firm ran for political office until 1962.

In the Ontario general election of that year, Vince Reid ran as Liberal in the Toronto riding of St. George but lost to the Conservative incumbent, Allan Lawrence. Lawrence later served in the Davis cabinet at Queen's Park and Joe Clark's cabinet in Ottawa.[105]

In other ways, however, the firm was not changing. Nineteen of the twenty-three lawyers with the firm in 1957 were Protestants, and ten years later thirty-seven of the firm's forty-seven lawyers would be described as members of one of the Protestant denominations. Of the remaining ten, four were Roman Catholics, and six would be described as having no religious affiliation. There were no Jews in the firm.

In addition, as of 1957 there were no women lawyers with the firm, and by 1967 there were only two. As previously noted, Bertha Wilson came to the firm as an articling student in 1958 and was called to the bar in 1959. Alicia Forgie, who was called to the bar in 1963, joined the firm in 1966. Neither of these women was a partner in 1967. Wilson was invited to join the partnership on January 1, 1968, and Forgie became a partner in 1971.

It is perhaps significant that these women joined the partnership eight and nine years after their calls to the bar, when the average waiting period was much shorter. Similarly, Jack McTague and Vince Reid, the first two Roman Catholic partners in the firm, were made partners fourteen and eleven years, respectively, after their calls to the bar.[106] More significantly, as will be discussed in the next chapter, Frank Zaid, the firm's first Jewish partner, was called to the bar in 1973 and offered a partnership in 1977.

If the firm's religious and political profile was beginning to change, so too was its practice. After the recession of the late 1950s, the Canadian economy entered a sustained period of growth which lasted throughout the 1960s. By the close of the decade, inflation had become an acknowledged problem, but for a period of about twelve years, the Canadian business world went through a very dynamic period. As business historian Michael Bliss described it, the 1960s saw

> ballooning development of oil and gas; the adoption of modern management techniques and the explosion of business schools; and the beginning of the end of the old ethnic exclusivity as networks and networking crumbled in a world of ready information, fast-moving competition, and ambitious, talented newcomers to business life.[107]

Successful and growing corporate law firms such as Osler, Hoskin & Harcourt took an active part in this boom.

Ironically, however, it was a litigation file, a field which had not been one of the firm's strong points ever since the departure of the McCarthys, which brought the firm its most dramatic public exposure during the 1960s.

In the late winter of 1959, a trapper or pulp wood cutter tramping through the bush just north of Timmins, Ontario might have seen a small helicopter flying back and forth just above the treetops. The aircraft belonged to the Texas Gulf Sulphur Company, and it was carrying sophisticated photographic and electromagnetic survey equipment. Texas Gulf, a large and old American company originally founded in Houston during World War I, had long been one of the world's largest producers of sulphur. During the early 1950s, it underwent some management changes and began to diversify out of sulphur and into other commercial minerals. As a part of this process, it began to conduct serious survey work in eastern and northern Canada — and it became an Osler, Hoskin & Harcourt client.[108]

As the Texas Gulf helicopter flew over a particular spot in Kidd township about fourteen miles north of Timmins, its survey equipment recorded what mining geologists call a significant electromagnetic anomaly. This meant that the rock beneath the thin layer of muskeg below maintained a degree of electromagnetic conductivity which was markedly different from that of the surrounding area. Such an anomaly can mean the presence of marketable minerals, or it can be worthless. The Texas Gulf geologist in the helicopter didn't know it at the time, but he had just flown over one of the richest base metal deposits in the world.

Prospecting for a mine is a long and involved process. It is also much like looking for a needle in a haystack, although the methods of searching are very sophisticated, and the needle can be made of gold. While the helicopter was flying over the muskeg, the geologist aboard was monitoring the readings from an electromagnetometer, a device which produces a strip of paper much like that from a physician's electrocardiograph. The paper strip, which was marked in time intervals, had a continuous line measuring the conductivity of the ground below. He was also keeping an eye on a motion picture camera which was taking a continuous film of the topography below. By combining the output of these two devices, the geologist could later piece together an accurate map of the electromagnetic conductivity

— and if they were lucky — the potential mineral-bearing rock of the area surveyed.

Following the promising results of the aerial surveys, Texas Gulf began more involved ground surveys, and eventually decided to conduct drill tests to obtain core samples. In addition, over the course of the next five years the company conducted negotiations — in large part through their lawyers at Oslers — with four property owners whose land encompassed the area where the geologists felt the ore body lay. In the meantime, Texas Gulf continued its extensive aerial surveying of the surrounding areas.

On one occasion in the summer of 1960, when the helicopter was surveying an area known as Prosser Geary, next to the Kidd discovery, for a number of reasons the geologist decided to fly over the Kidd area again. The electromagnetometer strip and film of this overflight, because it was done during the Prosser Geary surveys, were unfortunately filed with the latter's survey results rather than the results of the Kidd surveys a year earlier.

The Kidd anomaly was by far the most promising, and Texas Gulf was anxious to recoup some return for the expenses it had incurred surveying the other areas which it was less likely to pursue. For that reason, in the winter of 1963, it entered into a contract with a small Canadian company, Leitch Gold Mines Limited, to sell the survey results for much of the area covered in return for a 10 per cent interest in any mine which Leitch might develop on those lands.

The Kidd area was specifically excluded from the areas covered by the agreement. Unfortunately, however, the map which accompanied the contract was rather poorly prepared, and as luck would have it, the Kidd anomaly was within a mile of the boundary between the areas. Moreover, when the Leitch representative picked up the survey data from the Texas Gulf offices in Calgary, he also got the results of the 1960 flight over the Kidd anomaly which had mistakenly been included with the Prosser Geary data.

In April 1964, Texas Gulf made a formal announcement that it had made a major discovery in the Timmins area of northern Ontario, and the company received a letter from Leitch Gold Mines congratulating them on their discovery. The letter also suggested that the discovery might be within the area covered by their agreement of the previous year. Texas Gulf wrote back to thank them for their congratulations, and to say "no, the discovery is definitely not within the area covered by our agreement."

Shortly thereafter, Leitch Gold Mines Limited launched suit in the Supreme Court of Ontario claiming ownership of the mine site, or failing that, damages in the amount of $450 million for breach of contract.[109] Over the course of the next four and a half years, the Osler lawyers, led by Bill Bryden, who was in charge of the Texas Gulf file, as well as Dennis Lane, who later served as a judge on the Ontario Court of Justice, Don Wakefield and Dave Purdy, prepared and argued the case at trial. In addition, many of the lawyers at the firm, including Hal Mockridge and a team of researchers led by Bertha Wilson, helped in preparing the defence.

Significantly, Bryden decided it would be necessary to bring in outside counsel to lead the argument of the case in court. He hired John Arnup, then the senior litigator at Weir & Foulds. At about the same time, Leitch's lawyer, Syd Robinson, one of the senior solicitors at Holden, Murdoch, decided to bring in John J. Robinette from McCarthys. The key issue in the case was whether the parties intended to include the area which turned out to be the Kidd discovery in their agreement, and the resolution of the dispute hinged largely on the admittedly poorly drawn map and whether the court believed Texas Gulf when it claimed that the inclusion of data from the second flight over the anomaly with the package given to Leitch was simply a mistake.

In the end, when Chief Justice Gale announced his decision on November 29, 1968, he sided with Texas Gulf. The deciding factor was largely his view of the credibility of each side's witnesses. The case did not involve a jury, and Gale believed the Texas Gulf people; he did not believe those from Leitch. For Osler, Hoskin & Harcourt, the benefits were substantial, if not entirely tangible. Although unlike similar massive law suits in the United States, the firm's fee was not contingent upon winning the case, the bulk of the fees for the suit went to the firm. Arnup was the only non-Oslers lawyer on the Texas Gulf side. All of the supporting lawyers — and there were many — were from Oslers.

In addition, partly because the case was very much in the public eye — it was the largest lawsuit claim to that date in Canadian history, and there were allegations of insider trading and stock market manipulations surrounding the Kidd strike — the firm gained a great deal of business exposure through the trial. The fact that Texas Gulf had acquired all of the plots of property necessary to put the mine in operation without having to give up much of its potential mineral income was largely credited to Oslers lawyers. Beyond that, however, the case taught the firm that it needed to further strengthen its litigation department; as will be discussed in the next chapter, in the decade which followed, it did so.

In contrast to litigation, an area of practice in which the firm had been very strong during the years since World War II was labour law. One of the more significant events of the transition period, and one from which the firm learned an expensive lesson, was the loss of the International Nickel labour work in 1970. As discussed previously, Osler, Hoskin & Harcourt had been providing Inco with labour relations advice since the company began collective bargaining with its employees during World War II. Hal Mockridge was a long-time director of International Nickel and the senior lawyer on the Inco account, and although his general corporate advice included labour matters, Tom Delamere and Brick Osler had the primary responsibility for this aspect of the client's legal work.

In fact, Mockridge did not particularly enjoy the labour negotiation process, and although the client liked to have him at the bargaining table, he much preferred to leave it to Delamere and Osler. By the late 1960s, Tom Delamere was heading up the contract negotiation team and Brick Osler was doing most of the arbitration hearings.[110] Unlike Mockridge, those two apparently relished the adversarial atmosphere of the process.

Delamere and Osler were also very conservative men whose world views were rooted in a time when workers did not use the power of collective bargaining to gain a greater share of industrial wealth. In many ways, their ideas came from a time fifteen or twenty years earlier, when the fights between labour and management were often clear, ideological battles between left and right. Prior to 1944, Canadian workers did not have a right to collective bargaining, and there were still many in the corporate and legal world who felt that it wasn't such a good idea.

By the late 1960s, however, most younger lawyers and executives had accepted the fact that industrial unions were here to stay, a confrontational approach to labour negotiation was no longer in management's best interest. Unfortunately, Delamere and Brick Osler apparently did not agree. As Purdy Crawford put it, "They were good, but time was leaving them behind; and that's why Inco changed."[111]

Crawford remembers sitting across the table from Lynn Williams, later the president of the United Steelworkers of America, who was a negotiator on behalf of the Inco workers in the late 1960s. Crawford feels that he and Williams developed a good working relationship; they were simply representing competing business interests trying to work out a mutually satisfactory deal. To Delamere and Brick Osler, and to a certain extent Mockridge as well, the union was a political adversary. This is not to say that the fault for the strained relations between the Steelworkers and Inco during that time lay entirely with the company's conservative lawyers, but it certainly didn't help.

In addition to the regular contract negotiations, the company and the union would often enter into arbitration procedures to resolve certain disputes. The agreed-upon procedure called for a three-person arbitration board, with one person appointed by each side and a third acceptable to both. For the Inco side, the Osler lawyers generally appointed one of a group of eight to ten lawyers from various firms in Toronto. One of these was a man named Robert V. Hicks, who headed up the firm known as Hicks Morley Hamilton Stewart Storie.

Hicks was himself a labour specialist, and was apparently of the new school of labour lawyers; he was also a very charming and confidence-inspiring practitioner. The Inco people were impressed with him, and at the same time they were becoming less satisfied with the advice they were getting from Oslers.

In the summer and fall of 1969, Inco was embroiled in a particularly long and bitter strike involving almost eighteen thousand workers at its Sudbury and Port Colborne facilities. In the months leading up to the walkout, and during the strike itself, Brick Osler was putting in twelve to fourteen billed hours per day on the Inco file. As Frank Clifford, then the firm office manager, remembers it, Osler seemed to be constantly flying up to Sudbury for negotiation sessions or meetings with company officials.[112] The strike itself lasted 128 days and was marked by a very hostile atmosphere around the bargaining table. Finally, on November 14, the union members voted to accept the company's offer which would provide an overall wage increase of some 30 per cent. The vote, however, was very close, with only 50.8 per cent in favour. Almost half of the strikers were so angry with the company, they were willing to throw out the tentative agreement and let the walkout go on indefinitely.[113]

Very shortly thereafter, Hal Mockridge called a special meeting of the partnership to drop the bombshell. Inco had decided to take its labour work away from Osler, Hoskin & Harcourt and give it to Hicks Morley Hamilton Stewart Storie. Tom Delamere and Brick Osler were devastated; this was a personal rebuke of their work, and the rest of the partners were shocked.[114]

When word got around that Bob Hicks had "scooped" the Inco labour file away from Oslers, there were a number of eyebrows raised within the labour bar. There is, however, no evidence to suggest that it was Hicks who suggested the move. On the contrary, it was probably Inco which initiated discussions. They were unhappy with Oslers, and they were impressed with Hicks. Nevertheless, in the view of those who still held to the Mockridge-style standards of practice development, it was Oslers who introduced Hicks to the client, and they looked disdainfully at someone who would accept the work under those circumstances.[115]

Almost at the same time as the loss of the Inco labour file, Hal Mockridge did two things that were particularly symbolic of the transition in Osler, Hoskin & Harcourt which had taken place. One came four months after he turned seventy years old when he announced his retirement from the Executive Committee; the second was when he purposely left the room to let his partners discuss the decision to invite his son to become an associate lawyer in the firm. Britton Mockridge was Hal Mockridge's second son. He had attended Trinity College School and Princeton (his father's alma mater), and had graduated from the University of Toronto law school in 1967. He articled at Osler, Hoskin & Harcourt and was scheduled to be called to the bar in the spring of 1969.

A generation earlier, there would have been no question about his joining Osler, Hoskin & Harcourt — if he had wanted to — and of his father's taking part in the decision. As it turned out, he was offered a place in the firm following his call to the bar and did remain as an associate lawyer for two years. In 1971, however, he decided to leave the firm and go into the petroleum industry. The details of the partners' discussion regarding his admission remain confidential to the firm, but the significant fact — in the history of the firm — is that Hal Mockridge took no part in the discussion. In fact, he was not in the room. He knew that times had changed and that it was no longer appropriate for him to be present.

CHAPTER

7

THE TRANSFORMATION: 1970-1980

On June 22, 1970, Frank Clifford, the firm's office manager, sent a memo to all personnel: "The office will be closed tomorrow, Tuesday, June 23rd, from 1:00 p.m. onwards as a token of respect to the late Mr. G.M. Huycke, who passed away yesterday." Mossey Huycke died five days short of his seventy-fifth birthday and fifty years after his call to the bar. His passing was a sad event for the firm, particularly because Fred and Ed Huycke lost their father. The firm's senior partner, though, had been in ill-health for many months and had not been expected to recover. As his career-long friend and colleague Hal Mockridge put it in reply to one of the many telegrams of sympathy, "The end of an association of such length is always sad. . . . However, he had been in very bad shape for a number of months with no hope of recovery, and his actual going was a release."[1]

Mossey Huycke's death was also symbolic of the end of an era for the firm. The transformation of Osler, Hoskin & Harcourt, which began during the 1960s, continued at an accelerated pace during the 1970s. Although as the decade began the firm's management remained in the hands of Huycke's generation, Hal Mockridge was clearly in the process of handing over the reins to the next generation. Within eighteen months of Mossey Huycke's death, Mockridge stepped down as chairman of the Executive Committee, and in 1976 he officially retired as an active partner.[2]

Just as it was for Osler, Hoskin & Harcourt, the 1970s was a decade of enormous change in the Canadian business and legal environment. The country enjoyed substantial economic growth, particularly in the resource and finance sectors, with real growth averaging 3 per cent to 4 per cent during the decade. Naturally enough, this growth attracted investment, particularly off-shore investment.[3] But growth had its downside, including high rates of unemployment — particularly in the poorer regions of the country — and inflation. Inflation was fed by the staggering energy costs brought about by the oil crisis of 1973.

In addition to these economic phenomena, lawyers and business people were faced with an increasing array of government regulation during the 1970s. This included regulation at the municipal level by the City of Toronto and the Metropolitan Toronto government and at the provincial level by William Davis' moderate Conservative administration at Queen's Park, and particularly by the Trudeau Liberal government in Ottawa, which was responsible for measures such as the Foreign Investment Review Agency (FIRA), which came into operation in 1974, and the Anti-Inflation Board, which the government established in 1975.[4]

This bureaucracy made life more difficult for business, but it also made much more work for lawyers. It provided more complexity for commerce, which meant that business needed more expert help to steer around obstacles. Perhaps just as significantly for Osler, Hoskin & Harcourt, it created an excellent prep-school for young lawyers. Two such lawyers, whose careers with the firm will be discussed below, were Bob Lindsay, who came to Oslers from the Department of Finance in 1972, and Brian Levitt, who came from the Anti-Inflation Board in 1976.

Although the growth in the economy and the volume of government regulation meant more work for lawyers, the 1970s also saw tremendous change in the market for legal services. At Oslers this was significantly manifested in what marketers would call a "decline in brand loyalty." Perhaps it was simply a change of generations, or an increase in the general competitiveness of the Canadian economy, but at the same time that the Old Boys' network in law and business was breaking down, so too was the loyalty of large clients to law firms. The first real instance of this phenomenon for Osler, Hoskin & Harcourt was Inco's decision to pull its labour relations work from the firm early in 1970 and hand it over to Hicks Morley.[5]

This incident was traumatic for the firm, but it presaged a trend which would continue throughout the decade. The blue-chip firms like Oslers could no longer count on longtime clients to sustain them. Viewed from one perspective, this phenomenon was very unsettling, but from another, it was an opportunity. The firm may have been in danger of losing some clients, but it might also gain some new ones. In either case, it was going to have to prove that it deserved them.

The fact that Osler, Hoskin & Harcourt was able to adapt to this new and much more competitive market was very significant.

It was not, however, an easy adaptation. Being "competitive" went against one of the strongest traditions in the legal profession. Since the development of the medieval English bar, lawyers have sought to diminish competition among themselves. Beginning with guild-like organizational structures, by the early twentieth century lawyers throughout the common law world had established so-called professional organizations. The codes and canons of ethics these organizations established were, in large part, designed to reduce competition among lawyers.[6] By the mid-twentieth century, the culture of the Canadian bar, particularly among its élite, was anti-competitive. This was why many lawyers disapproved of ploys like Bob Hicks' so-called "scoop" of the Inco labour work.[7] And it was why the move to a more competitive approach was only really possible at Osler, Hoskin when the generational torch was passed.

This is not to say that at this time law firms became competitive in the way that the rest of the marketplace is competitive. In many ways, the old personal relationships between lawyer and client, much like those between patient and physician, remained in place. This was less true as larger corporations moved away from the dominant proprietor models of earlier days, but the personal relationship between a client company's general counsel and the partner in charge of the client's file remained very important.

In addition, even as law firms have become more competitive, they have generally not done so at the level of pricing. This would still be regarded as essentially "unprofessional." They have tried harder to market themselves by emphasizing the "excellence" of their services; this standard is, however, very difficult for a client to objectively assess. In the view of some lawyers, the term "competitiveness," in many cases, simply means "marketing."[8] Regardless of its meaning, however, there is little doubt that it has brought substantial changes.

The increased competitiveness of the market for legal services was revealed in a number of very significant changes in law firm statistics. These included unprecedented growth in the number of lawyers, particularly in terms of the size of the profession relative to that of the population, and an increase in the rate of growth among the largest firms.

During the first half of the twentieth century, the legal profession in Ontario saw relatively stable growth. Between 1911 and 1931, the number of lawyers in the province grew by approximately 5.6 per cent per year, while the population grew at a rate of 3.9 per cent annually. The ratio of lawyers to population rose during those years from 1:1,543 to 1:1,350. Interestingly, the largest law firms did not grow as fast as the profession as a whole. In 1911, there was a total of fifty lawyers in the five largest firms in Toronto; by 1931, the five largest firms totalled sixty-eight. This represented an annual growth rate of only 1.8 per cent. Osler, Hoskin & Harcourt, with nine lawyers, was the third-largest firm in 1911; by 1931, it had fourteen lawyers and ranked as the second largest in the city. This represented an annual growth rate of 2.8 per cent, despite the loss of the McCarthys in 1916.[9]

During the following two decades, between 1931 and 1951, the Ontario legal profession grew by a more modest 2.7 per cent annually, while population growth averaged 1.7 per cent per year. The ratio of lawyers to population continued to rise, therefore, from 1:1,350 to 1:1,169. The growth rate among the five largest firms remained below that of the profession as a whole. The five largest Toronto firms grew from a total of sixty-eight lawyers in 1931 to eighty-four in 1951, an annual growth rate of 1.2 per cent. Osler, Hoskin & Harcourt grew during the same period from fourteen to seventeen lawyers, a growth rate of 1.1 per cent per year. It also remained the second largest in the city.[10]

Obviously, there were many factors affecting these rates of growth in population, the legal profession, and the largest firms — not least of which were two world wars and an intervening economic depression. During the following decade, things began to change. Between 1951 and 1961, a period of relative stability and prosperity, both population and the legal profession grew at an annual average rate of 3.5 per cent, and the ratio of lawyers to population fell marginally from 1:1,169 to 1:1,173. The five largest firms grew, however, from eighty-four in 1951 to 145 in 1961, a growth rate of some 7.2 per cent per year. Similarly, Osler, Hoskin & Harcourt maintained an average annual growth rate of 7.1 per cent during the 1950s, expanding from seventeen to twenty-nine lawyers, although it fell from second largest to third in the city.[11]

During the 1960s, these trends continued. While the provincial population grew at an annual rate of 2.4 per cent, the legal profession grew at a rate of 4.3 per cent per year, and the ratio of lawyers to population rose from 1:1,173 in 1961 to 1:1,102 in 1971. Even more significantly, the five largest firms in Toronto grew from a total of

145 lawyers to 287, a growth rate of 9.8 per cent per year. Osler, Hoskin & Harcourt grew at an annual rate of 7.7 per cent, from twenty-nine lawyers in 1961 to fifty-three in 1971.[12]

The most dramatic changes occurred, however, during the 1970s, when the legal profession in the province grew by over 10 per cent per year, while the population grew at a rate of only 1.2 per cent annually. The ratio of lawyers to population jumped from 1:1,102 in 1971 to 1:564 in 1981. The five largest Toronto firms did not quite keep pace with the rest of the profession, maintaining a growth rate of 7.5 per cent per year, while Osler, Hoskin & Harcourt grew from fifty-three lawyers in 1971 to ninety-seven in 1981, a growth rate of roughly 8.3 per cent annually.[13]

These data of growth rates, percentages and ratios indicate graphically that the market for legal services, particularly for those practising in the larger firms, was changing dramatically during the decades after World War II. Only those law firms that were able to adapt to the rapidly changing environment would survive and prosper.[14] Osler, Hoskin & Harcourt was able to adapt.

In addition to the external changes the firm felt, there were some very significant changes within the firm, including the demographic characteristics of its lawyers. Of the fifty-three lawyers in the firm after Mossey Huycke's death, twenty-three were partners. By 1981, the firm totalled ninety-seven lawyers, of whom fifty-six were partners, thirty-five were associates, and six were retired partners.[15] Of the fifty-three lawyers in the firm in late 1970, forty-three (81 per cent) had articled with the firm.[16]

During the following decade, the firm made some very significant lateral appointments, and by 1981 only sixty-three of the ninety-seven lawyers had articled with the firm (65 per cent).[17] In addition, the lawyers practising with the firm in 1981 were significantly younger than those of 1970. The average experience — measured from date of call to the bar — of the firm's fifty-three lawyers in 1970 was 12.4 years. For partners, this figure was 20.8 years, and for associates, it was 4.9.[18] In 1981, the average experience of all the lawyers in the firm was relatively unchanged at 12.7 years, but when the six retired partners' names are removed from the list, this figure drops to 10.3 years. Most significantly, among the active partners, the average experience in 1981 was only 15.8 years. Among the associates, the figure was only 1.9 years.[19]

Despite these changes, there were still relatively few women in the firm. In 1971, there were three woman lawyers practising with the firm, but only one of them was a partner.[20] By 1981, the total number of women lawyers in the firm was sixteen (16.5 per cent), but only five of these (8.6 per cent) were partners.[21] These numbers were, however, not unusual among the large firms. At McCarthy & McCarthy, for instance, only one of the firm's fifty-seven lawyers was a woman, and by 1981 McCarthys had only ten women among the 112 in the firm (8.9 per cent).[22] There were, however, other very significant changes in the firm during the 1970s, particularly in the growth and diversification of its legal practice, and in its management.

The most significant event in the management of the firm during the 1970s was Hal Mockridge's retirement from the Executive Committee in January 1972. At the meeting of January 12, 1972, the Executive Committee chose Allan Beattie as its new chairman. The other members of the committee were Brick Osler, who had also served as the firm's managing partner since the loss of the Inco labour account in 1970, Harry Boylan, Bill Bryden, Purdy Crawford, Ed Huycke and Fred Huycke.

The two newest members of the Executive Committee were Ed Huycke and Harry Boylan, who joined the Committee in the fall of 1971.[23] They were the first elected leaders of the firm. In addition to Mockridge's passing of the chairmanship to Allan Beattie, the election of a portion of the Executive Committee by the partners as a whole was a significant reform. Harry Boylan later described it as a "push to have other areas of the firm represented, not necessarily those who had the biggest share."[24]

That push to provide representation to the other partners began in the spring of 1971 when discussions began about a new partnership agreement to replace the three-year agreement signed in 1968. Under the old partnership agreement, the Executive Committee consisted of six partners, named in the agreement. The six men named were Hal Mockridge, Tom Delamere, Brick Osler, Stuart Thom, Fred Huycke and Allan Beattie. Not surprisingly, these six had the highest share percentages under the agreement.[25]

In addition, the 1968 agreement stipulated that the Executive Committee was to consist of a minimum of five and a maximum of seven members, and the existing Committee held the power to add members if a resignation reduced their number to less than five or, at their discretion, to increase the size of the Committee to six or seven. In July of 1970, shortly after the loss of the Inco labour work, Tom Delamere resigned from the Committee; the remaining members appointed Bill Bryden and Purdy Crawford to replace Delamere and bring the membership up to seven.[26] Significantly, although Bryden was the next in line in terms of shares in the firm to replace Delamere, Crawford was not. In fact, he ranked twelfth in the firm — behind Delamere and the other Committee members, as well as C.R. Osler, Ed Huycke, Ed Saunders and Jack McTague.[27]

In April of 1971, Hal Mockridge informed the partners that a new partnership agreement was being drafted, and he would see that it was circulated in the very near future.[28] He sent around a draft agreement to solicit comments in June, and called a meeting of the Executive Committee in July to discuss the matter. At that meeting, in addition to setting the partnership shares under the new agreement, the Committee agreed that "membership of the Executive Committee would be a maximum of eight, of which two members would be elected by the partners for a term of eighteen months."[29]

In August, the rest of the partners agreed to the new partnership agreement, which was backdated to January 1, 1971, and in the fall they held their first election. Under the new partnership agreement, the two elected members would serve an initial term ending on December 31, 1973, and thereafter the elected Executive Committee members' terms would last eighteen months.[30] The fact that two of a maximum of eight members of the Executive Committee would be elected was not a particularly radical step.[31] Moreover, when the election took place, the partners chose Harry Boylan and Ed Huycke, two of the next highest share-earners in the firm anyway. Stuart Thom announced his retirement from the Executive Committee as of December 31, 1971, and in January Hal Mockridge stepped down in favour of Allan Beattie.[32] This brought the membership of the Committee to seven — five appointed members: Allan Beattie, Brick Osler, Bill Bryden, Purdy Crawford and Fred Huycke — and two elected: Harry Boylan and Ed Huycke.

If the partnership agreement was the firm's constitution and the partnership meetings its parliament, the Executive Committee was its cabinet, and Allan Beattie was its prime minister. In reading the minutes of both the Executive Committee and the partnership meetings, it is clear that the Executive Committee — skilfully led by Beattie — was making all of the important decisions. It generally met twice a month to deal with everything from assignment of offices and charging rates to admission to the partnership. In dealing with admission to the partnership in particular, the Executive Committee's technical function was to make recommendations to the partners, but in fact the partners generally accepted these recommendations without amendment.

By contrast, the partners met only five times a year, and with very few exceptions made little or no changes to the policy decisions recommended by the Executive Committee. Prior to 1972, Hal Mockridge chaired the partners' meetings, but at the first meeting following his retirement from the Executive Committee he nominated Allan Beattie to act as chair. Out of deference, Beattie suggested that Mockridge continue, but the elder statesman declined.[33]

The transition from Hal Mockridge's benevolent dictatorship to Allan Beattie's consensus management was smooth and relatively painless. In large part, this was because of Mockridge's desire to see the firm evolve as he knew it must, but it was also due to Beattie's personal style. As Jim Kennedy, a young lawyer who was admitted to the partnership in 1971 put it,

I would emphasize Allan Beattie probably as well as part of that. I mean, Allan was such a convivial, easy-going and teasingly humorous guy that it really had a lot to do with the character of the firm at that time. Hal Mockridge was a very austere person in many respects. He didn't mind being ribbed, but he wasn't the sort of person that you thought of as very jovial and slap-on-the-back.[34]

Allan Beattie was born in the northern Ontario mining town of Copper Cliff on March 25, 1926. His father, Leslie Beattie, who started as a clerk with the old Canadian Copper Company prior to World War I, was the senior accounting supervisor of International Nickel's mining operations in the Sudbury area.

In the early part of World War II, when Beattie was in high school in Copper Cliff, his father was promoted to head of Inco's operations in Canada.[35] During the war, Inco's legal requirements were substantial, and Leslie Beattie and Hal Mockridge became quite close. When Allan Beattie graduated from the University of Toronto in 1948 and decided on a career in law, there was little question that he would article at Oslers.

When he was called to the bar in 1951, however, it was not necessarily a foregone conclusion that he would stay with the firm to practise. Only two of the seven Osler students called to the bar in 1948 stayed with the firm, the 1949 class saw none, and only one stayed in 1950.[36] Moreover, if the firm was only going to keep one graduating student in 1951, Beattie assumed that his classmate, Fred Huycke, whose father Mossey was a senior partner in the firm, would likely get the nod.

Apparently being the son of a major client was as important as being the son of a senior partner, however, because both Fred Huycke and Allan Beattie were invited to join the firm. Nepotism was not the only factor involved; it may have helped them get in the door, but both men have since been acknowledged to be outstanding corporate lawyers, who played a very major role in maintaining and building the firm's practice during the transitionary decades of the 1960s, 1970s and 1980s.

As a student and young lawyer with the firm, Beattie was involved in a wide range of practice. He worked with Harold Boston doing real estate work, and with Tom Delamere on labour files, but over a period of time he gravitated more toward general corporate practice, working closely with Swatty Wotherspoon. With Wotherspoon, he provided legal advice to the Eaton and Bassett families, and as discussed in Chapter Six, when Wotherspoon left the firm to go to Eaton's in 1965, Beattie took over responsibility for the Eaton and Bassett files.

By the time Beattie succeeded Hal Mockridge as chairman of the Executive Committee in 1972, he had been in practice over twenty years, but he was not the most senior lawyer in the firm. In fact, including Mockridge, nine of the firm's thirty partners were more experienced. Nevertheless, it was not Beattie's seniority which allowed him to effectively lead — it was his personality.

Allan Beattie was "the consummate diplomat" — that is to say, by all accounts he was able to gauge and articulate the various viewpoints and interests within the firm, rationalize differences and diffuse potential conflict. Frank Clifford, who kept the minutes of both the Executive Committee and partnership meetings throughout the 1970s, described Beattie as a peerless meeting chairman. He had a "profound gift of being able to introduce and outline proposals in a most logical and convincing fashion, and to formulate recommendations for adoption."[37]

More important than Beattie's skill in leading a meeting, however, was his charm and wry sense of humour, which he would often employ to get an important message across. He was also very patient and sincere, but if he had a fault as a leader, it was that he was apt to be a little too sensitive to personality conflicts within the firm. Where another, less sensitive leader might make a quick executive decision without undue regard for everyone's feelings, Beattie would take the time to explain and cajole, and broker conflicting interests where necessary.

Allan Beattie was also an inveterate, sophisticated sports fan. He was a season ticket holder for Toronto Argonaut and Maple Leaf home games; at Leaf games he was one of the people dressed in jacket and tie whom *Hockey Night in Canada* viewers could see sitting in the gold seats near the players' benches in Maple Leaf Gardens. He was also an excellent golfer and avid downhill skier, even after having a hip replaced in 1987.[38]

Beattie was not alone in managing the firm after Mockridge's retirement. In fact, most partners at the time would point to three members of the Executive Committee — Beattie, Purdy Crawford and Fred Huycke — as the power within the firm. Dave Purdy, a young corporate and labour lawyer who served as a junior in the Texas Gulf case, affectionately dubbed them "The Troika," making fun of them at partnership meetings and Christmas parties.[39]

The word *troika* comes from the Russian, where it originally meant a carriage pulled by three horses harnessed abreast, but after the revolution it was generally applied to some type of political trium-virate. Although Purdy's use of the term was affectionate, its accep-tance by others in the firm may have been significant in light of Solzhenitsyn's use of the term in his 1974 bestseller *The Gulag Archipelago*, in which he described ". . . permanently operating troi-kas — panels of three, operating behind closed doors — [which] were created to bypass the courts" and sentence detainees to the Gulag.[40]

Regardless of the level of satire used in the term, each of the members of the Oslers "Troika" had a well-understood role to play in the firm's leadership in the early post-Mockridge era. If Purdy Crawford was the big-picture visionary who provided much of the impetus for the firm's direction toward the future, and Allan Beattie was the good-natured manager of growth, it was Fred Huycke who acted as the anchor with the past.

Fred Huycke, the elder of Mossey's two sons, was a conservative man. In some ways his affinity with Tom Delamere (he called De-lamere "Tom," whereas to Allan Beattie, he was always "Mr. De-lamere") was quite telling.[41] Although he was a year and a half older than Beattie, Huycke had served with the Canadian army in Europe during World War II and had taken a four-year honours degree at the University of Toronto before starting law school in 1948; he was called to the bar, along with Beattie, in 1951.

Fred Huycke was not a dynamic man in public; in a group he was reserved, even shy, but according to most he could be very persuasive in private.[42] He was also a very accomplished general counsel, who was regarded by many as one of the most innovative and incisive corporate lawyers of his generation. During the early years of his practice, he did a fair amount of labour law, working closely with Tom Delamere, but he also worked with Swatty Wotherspoon on the huge Interprovincial Pipe Line deal during the 1950s, and with his father on general corporate work.[43] In fact, he took over prime responsibility for Interprovincial Pipe Line Ltd. when Wotherspoon left for Eaton's and for many of his father's corporate clients when Mossey retired.

Although the lawyers who were partners during the 1970s all point to "The Troika" as the leaders of the firm, it was Allan Beattie who made most of the administrative decisions, and after 1974 he officially reduced his legal practice in order to do so. In Hal Mockridge's day — and certainly in Britton Osler's, when the partners could meet each morning in Norman Strickland's office to open the mail — good firm administration did not have to take away from the leader's time to practise law. By the 1970s, however, it was obvious that a firm approaching a hundred lawyers, even with a structure of committees and sub-committees, could not be efficiently run by a single person who was also one of the leading practitioners.

The problem was who would be willing to sacrifice all or part of a professionally satisfying legal practice, and who would also have the necessary credibility among the partners, to fulfil the role. Since 1970, Brick Osler had acted as managing partner, but the new position would involve substantially more time and administrative responsibility than his had, and in early 1973 he announced his intention to step down from the post. If there was any one person who exercised managing authority — and the problem was this authority was too diffused — it was Allan Beattie acting as chairman of the Executive Committee.

Within a year of his assumption of the chairmanship of the Executive Committee, Allan Beattie raised this problem. In April of 1973, he asked Ed Huycke to speak to Douglas Young, one of his clients, about the matter. Young was a management consultant with Hay Associates Canada Limited, a Toronto consulting firm.[44] Young came to the next Executive Committee meeting and gave them some ideas, then conducted a series of interviews with members of the Committee and other lawyers and staff, including Hal Mockridge and Stuart Thom.[45]

On July 10, Young presented a detailed report to the Executive Committee. He opened this report by noting the firm's historical roots in the nineteenth century coupled with its recent growth. In his view, rationalizing the old and the new was the key to successful growth. ''The partnership . . . may encounter great difficulty in the future in coping rationally with its own growth and the rapidly changing challenges of the environment, within the framework of the loose organizational structure of the firm's formative years.''[46]

Young's report made one key recommendation; the firm should appoint a managing partner who would be expected to spend a maximum of 75 per cent of his time practising law and the remainder on firm management.[47] The main reason for Young's recommendation that the firm appoint a managing partner was his feeling that there were just too many lawyers involved in the administration of the firm. Although he understood that a law firm is a partnership, and therefore decisions are theoretically made by all of the partners, since Mockridge's retirement the theory had become practice. The result, as Young wrote in his report, was a tendency to

> weigh and consider in minute detail all possible alternatives. Whereas management problems, by their nature, usually require decisions and actions based on insufficient data, the firm's style of weighing point and counter-point, opinion and counter-opinion, seduces management into analyzing problems to death rather than engaging in the risk-taking behaviour intrinsic to solving many management problems.

The cure was to delegate much of the decision-making authority back to a senior partner. In a way, this meant a return to the Mockridge era; the difference would be that power would be clearly delegated from the partnership, rather than simply exercised by a benevolent dictator.

The Executive Committee apparently debated Young's recommendations at their meeting on July 10, but two weeks later they met again and decided to accept them. The minutes of the meeting of July 24 explain what happened:

> After full discussion it was agreed to support the principal recommendation which called for the appointment of a managing head or partner supported by an administrative head. The

former appointment, it was agreed, should be given to a senior partner who would combine the function of managing head with the chairmanship of the Executive Committee on the understanding that this responsibility would occupy between 25% and 40% of such partner's time. The administrative head would be a suitably qualified and trained person who would be responsible for the administrative operations of the firm and who would report directly to the managing head. It was also agreed that the overall administrative organizational details required to support this new management concept would have to be worked out when the two main appointments referred to have been made.

The Chairman at this stage indicated that he himself, while not seeking the appointment of managing head, would be prepared to give serious consideration to taking this appointment should it be decided that he was the appropriate person to hold the appointment. The Chairman, Mr. Beattie, then retired from the meeting and Mr. F.A.M. Huycke assumed the chairmanship.

A discussion then took place regarding various aspects of the proposals and recommendations submitted by Mr. Douglas Young of Hay Associates during the course of which discussion it was unanimously agreed that Mr. A.L. Beattie should be requested by the Executive Committee to assume the appointment of managing head in the event that the overall proposals are approved by the full partnership. Mr. B.M. Osler and Mr. F.A.M. Huycke undertook to communicate this to Mr. Beattie.[48]

The formal lawyers' language and procedure belies the fact that it was a foregone conclusion that Beattie would take the job on, but it also subtly indicates the substantial change he was willing to make in his own professional life. A reduction in his own practice of up to 40 per cent was far from insignificant.

At its meeting of September 18, 1973, the Executive Committee formally decided to recommend to the partnership that they approve the Hay Associates recommendations and appoint Allan Beattie as the new managing partner.[49] At the partners' meeting held on October 4, Beattie led the discussion of the recommendations contained in the report, but then left the room and Hal Mockridge took the chair. In Beattie's absence, "It was resolved unanimously that Mr. A.L. Beattie be appointed as the managing partner effective April 1, 1974 for a period at the pleasure of the partnership."[50]

Shortly thereafter, the firm followed up on another of Young's recommendations and hired an administrative head to assist the managing partner in the day-to-day operation of the firm. Young had recommended that they hire someone who would report directly to the managing partner, to take on a significant degree of administrative authority within the firm, much like a university director of administration or a corporate comptroller. The ideal candidate would have a strong track record as a corporate manager, some accounting credentials, and knowledge of computers. Most importantly, however, he or she should have "an understanding of the needs and characteristics of a professional group, [and the] ability to win and keep the willing collaboration of a large group of intelligent, strong-minded, individualistic people."

The person they hired in the summer of 1974 was a forty-three-year-old Scotsman named Peter Lang. A native of Glasgow, after doing his National Service in the RAF, Lang emigrated to Canada in the 1950s. Over the course of some years, he became a chartered accountant and served as comptroller in several Canadian companies. By the summer of 1974, he met all of the requirements which the Hay report identified. As an accountant and corporate comptroller, he was thoroughly qualified for the financial administrative responsibilities and was equally familiar with the then-existing computer systems. What made him most attractive, however, and the quality which placed him first on the short list, was his personality. In the words of Frank Clifford, the office manager who joined the firm some years earlier and who worked closely with Lang over the next few years, he was able to "fit between the upper and lower millstones."[51]

The main recommendation in the Hay Associates report was that the firm place more decision making authority in a managing partner and free up the other lawyers to do what they do best — practise law. This makes perfect sense in theory, but a law partnership is not a corporation where senior executives can issue orders and employees can be expected to carry them out. It is, in fact, a group of owners, often with significant egos, who will carry out directives only if they are convinced to do so. In fairness, Young dealt with this problem in his report, and to some extent probably intended his recommendations to represent an ideal type of management structure. The reality was something less than that. In fact, it turned out to be a balance between an ideal delegation of authority and the near-chaos which Young saw in his study.

Clearly, Allan Beattie understood this balance; as his fellow-Executive Committee member Harry Boylan put it,

Allan was the consummate politician. I used to kid some of the present [Executive Committee members] that sometimes they would go to a meeting not knowing what the outcome would be. But Allan Beattie never had a meeting of the partnership or the Executive Committee that he didn't know what the outcome was going to be. He'd have felt it out and sounded it out before. Allan used Purdy and Fred as sounding boards; before he would make a move that might be at all controversial, he would at least have talked to those two guys as the biggest operators in the firm at that time. . . . that's where "The Troika" came from.[52]

Unlike Hal Mockridge, who ruled the firm with a stern, if benevolent hand, Allan Beattie ruled it by orchestrated consensus, and he did so as the firm's managing partner until shortly before his retirement in 1986.

Beattie's appointment as managing partner was not an end to, but merely a step in, the evolution of the structure of Osler, Hoskin & Harcourt. In fact, that evolution continued throughout the decade. Another step in the evolution began with a memorandum addressed to the Executive Committee which crossed Beattie's desk on July 17, 1975. That memo was signed by Peter Dey, Larry Hebb, Ed Huycke and Bertha Wilson, who described themselves in a covering note to Beattie as "four partners at different levels of experience at the Bar and in the partnership who have tried to put on paper their thoughts on how the existing structure of the Firm might be made more responsive to some concerns which are being expressed by a number of partners."

Indeed, the four did represent different levels of experience, they represented a very important cross-section of opinion within the firm. Ed Huycke, the younger of Mossey's two sons and a former member of the Executive Committee, was called to the bar in 1953; Bertha Wilson, who within a year would accept an appointment to the Ontario Court of Appeal and would go on to become the first woman justice on the Supreme Court of Canada, was called to the Nova Scotia bar in 1957 and the Ontario bar in 1959; Larry Hebb who, in effect, succeeded Allan Beattie as managing partner in 1986, like Wilson, was first called in Nova Scotia in 1963 and Ontario in 1964; Peter Dey, who was well on his way to becoming one of the country's leading securities law practitioners and would eventually serve as chairman of the Ontario Securities Commission, was called to the bar in 1969.

It was significant that the four placed their names on the memo to Beattie in alphabetical order rather than by seniority at the bar or within the firm. What they were suggesting in their memo was further democratization of the firm. The firm's roll of lawyers in the *Canadian Law List* at the time, as was the custom, listed names in order of seniority. In 1977, the Osler roll was changed to alphabetical, although the other large firms continued with listings by seniority.

Although the memo was written in very respectful terms, its intent was quite clear. It opened with a sentence which read: "A number of partners are becoming concerned that the existing structure in the Firm is not as responsive as it might be to the current needs of the Firm and may become even less so over the next decade." After highlighting some of the demographic changes discussed above in this chapter, it went on to note:

> We believe that the time is opportune for a Firm re-appraisal and for the institution of some changes designed to attain a number of objectives on which the concerns of many partners seem to be focusing, [including] an Executive Committee which reflects a wider range of points of view in the partnership.

In a lengthy explanation of their argument in favour of change to the constitution of the Executive Committee, the memo pointed out.

> Until the recent change to permit two elected (as opposed to appointed) partners to sit on the Executive Committee the five or six most senior partners constituted the Executive Committee on a tenure-at-will basis. This approach seemed to have several disadvantages. It meant that persons whose talents and inclinations might not necessarily equip them for Firm management and administration were automatically seized with that responsibility and that others whose talents and inclinations might have developed in that direction were foreclosed.
>
> Moreover, these senior partners were usually at the peak of their professional careers which raised in itself the question whether the Firm was best served by having *all* of them involved in Firm administration. This aspect has, of course, to some degree been resolved by the advent of Mr. Lang and by the focusing of a substantial part of the Executive Committee function in the Managing Partner. Our impression is that this is working well and that the partnership is happy with these changes. We wonder, however, whether the advent of these changes means that the composition of the Executive Committee

can now be a little different and designed to accomplish different things.

The traditional practice of appointing all the senior partners to the Executive Committee tended also, as the Firm increased in size and the Associates were admitted to partnership at an earlier age, to result in a widening gap between the Executive Committee and the younger partners rapidly forming a substantial percentage of the whole.

The recommendations put forward in this memorandum in relation to the restructuring of the Executive Committee are intended to

(a) preserve continuity of policy making and administration;

(b) give more partners an opportunity to develop their administrative skills;

(c) free up some of the senior partners for the development of the Firm's existing business and new business; and

(d) make the Committee more dynamic through a diversified approach to firm problems.

The authors' viewpoint was very clear, also, when they wrote:

There is a growing concern that only a limited number of partners have developed a sense of personal involvement and identification with the Firm. As the Firm gets larger (now 38 partners), its special character is less readily discerned than when it was a group of 10, 15 or even 20 people, and it is not easy for new partners to catch its spirit. A smaller group such as the Executive Committee, which is at the very heart of the life of the Firm, may be quite unaware of the sense of dissociation which comes from non-participation. Yet one of its main tasks and the task of the partnership as a whole must be to try to overcome this. We do not want a Firm in which the ''each man for himself'' philosophy predominates. Nor do we want one in which many partners feel that they are simply practising out of the same office space. While it is recognized that each partner has a proper concern for the development of his or her own career, we want this concern to be wedded to a sense of commitment to the Firm and to all its clients whether we happen to work on their matters or not.

In a sense, this memo and the earlier Hay report represented two swings of the management pendulum. The Hay report, which recommended centralizing decision-making in the Executive Committee and a new managing partner, favoured the efficiency of oligarchy. In their memo, Peter Dey, Larry Hebb, Ed Huycke and Bertha Wilson seemed to favour a much more democratic approach.

Following these sentiments, the memo made some specific recommendations. Under these proposals, the position of managing partner would be continued with little change, except that he or she would hold office for a finite term. Under the existing partnership agreement, the partners had the power to appoint a managing partner "from time to time."[53] Under the proposal recommended in the memo, the partners would elect a managing partner for an initial term of four years, and subsequent terms would last two years.

The most important recommendations the memo included, however, were those involving the Executive Committee. Under the partnership agreement in force at the time, the Executive Committee consisted of between six and eight members, four to six of whom were appointed, and two of whom were elected. As of July, 1975, there were four appointed members — Allan Beattie, Bill Bryden, Purdy Crawford and Fred Huycke — and two elected members — Jack Ground and Ed Saunders. The four appointed members had all been named in the 1971 partnership agreement, and Ground and Saunders had been elected in late 1973 to replace Harry Boylan and Ed Huycke.

The authors of the memo recommended that the Executive Committee structure be changed so that it would consist of seven members, including the managing partner as an ex officio member, four members elected from the partnership as a whole, and only two appointed members. Moreover, apparently in an effort to ensure that the problem of lack of broad representation of the partnership be addressed, they went on to suggest that of the four elected members, one be elected to represent each of three divisions of partners based on seniority at the bar and/or share interest in the firm, and one represent the partnership as a whole. These four would hold office for three-year terms, and would be eligible to stand for re-election at the expiration of their terms; but, in order to create an overlap of terms for sake of continuity, two of them would serve an initial term of four years.[54]

Beattie received the memorandum and placed it on the agenda for the next meeting of the Executive Committee, scheduled for September 11. The minutes of that meeting simply note that the memo was the subject of "full discussion," but there is no indication of the members' opinions. There is evidence of one member's view, however, in a memo which Jack Ground sent to Beattie prior to the meeting. In it, Ground explained:

> I may be somewhat late for the Executive Committee Meeting next Thursday and would like to put forward my ideas re the Dey-Hebb-E. Huycke-Wilson memorandum. I am in agreement with most of the points raised in the memorandum. . . . With regard to the composition of the Executive Committee, I have two thoughts. Firstly, I think that the recommendation is unduly complex, and secondly, I am not in favour of constituencies in the firm which would elect their own representatives to the Executive Committee. I would propose that the Executive Committee consist of the Managing Partner plus six other partners. The six partners should, I suggest, be elected for a three-year term with two of them retiring each year on a United States Senate format. I would suggest that the two partners elected each year be elected by the partnership as whole and that there should not be any restriction on retiring members of the Executive Committee standing for re-election.[55]

The proposal to restructure the Executive Committee was hardly a palace revolt, but it did represent a significant change from the past, particularly from the way the firm had been governed under the previous generation, and it would represent a constitutional levelling of power within the firm which would apparently be in very sharp contrast to the regime common in the other large law firms of the time.

In any case, the Executive Committee could see that it was a serious enough matter to be taken to the partners as a whole to discuss, and they decided to circulate the memo to all of the partners and place it on the agenda of the next partnership meeting. At that meeting, held on September 29, the partners agreed to establish a special committee composed of Peter Dey, Jack Ground, Larry Hebb and Ed Saunders to study the proposals and make recommendations. They also agreed to extend Ground's and Saunders' terms on the Executive Committee, which had expired on June 30, pending any changes.[56]

The special committee deliberated during the rest of the fall and into the winter, and in February, Ed Saunders presented its recommendations to the partners. These recommendations, which the partners adopted, and which appeared in an amendment to the partnership agreement dated March 31, 1976, were very much in line with those contained in the Dey, Hebb, E. Huycke, Wilson memorandum of the previous summer. Under its new makeup, the Executive Committee was to have seven members: the managing partner, who would sit as an ex officio member, two appointed members, who would be the two highest share earners in the firm, and four members elected by the firm. Very significantly, and apparently in response to a question from the floor, the meeting also decided that in the election, "each partner would have one vote for each of the 4 candidates of his choice and that each and every vote cast would be of equal value."[57] The other option would have been to base the value of each vote on the share interest of each partner.

The only variation from the original memo reflected Jack Ground's suggestions. The elected members did not represent any specific constituencies within the partnership, and their terms would have staggered termination dates. Because the Committee had two appointed members and four elected members, rather than all six elected, the elected members' terms lasted two years. At the first election, to be held as soon as possible after the March 31, 1976 amendment to the partnership agreement, four executive members would be elected. The two of these receiving the highest number of votes would sit for a three-year term, and the next two would sit for a two-year term. Beginning in 1978, an election would be held to elect two members every year. Under the share division schedule in force as of March 31, 1976, the two highest earning partners in the firm were Purdy Crawford and Fred Huycke, and at the election held in April, the partners elected Harry Boylan, Jack Ground, Ed Saunders and one new member — Tim Kennish, a young corporate lawyer who had joined the partnership in 1972.[58]

The fact that the firm was able to make an important change in its management structure in an evolutionary and relatively painless way is very significant. Clearly, the stage had been set for change, and many of the partners had expectations of reform, but the tone of the four-partner memo of July, 1975, in particular, seems to indicate that they assumed it could be accomplished in a spirit of community and goodwill. Like much of Canadian society during the 1960s and 1970s, however, the evolution of Osler, Hoskin & Harcourt was not always entirely smooth.

The law and the legal profession have always struggled with a fundamental ambiguity. Richard L. Abel, of the University of California at Los Angeles, wrote in the preface to his 1989 monograph study of the U.S. legal profession, *American Lawyers*:

All law is inescapably two-faced. It reproduces and justifies existing inequalities and injustices; yet it also embodies ideals and offers mechanisms through which they can be pursued. Lawyers display the same moral ambiguity. The legal profession has constructed and defended an elaborate constellation of economic, social and political privileges. It propounds an ideology that allows lawyers to escape difficult moral choices by invoking their technical expertise. Most lawyers persist in seeing their daily work as morally neutral and apolitical. Yet many are attracted to the profession precisely because they embrace law as a "transformative vocation" (to use Roberto Unger's eloquent phrase) and wish to dedicate themselves to "struggle against the defects or the limits of existing society." A few remain committed to that ideal throughout their legal careers."[59]

What Abel wrote was equally applicable to the Canadian legal profession. During the late 1960s and early 1970s, in particular, many students were drawn to law school because it offered the prospect of putting their idealism into action. Consumer advocates like Ralph Nader and civil liberties proponents like those in the A.C.L.U. were lawyers, and they were using the law as a sword to right some of the inequities of the world. At the same time, the law was more often used to maintain the economic and social status quo, and the lawyers who acted in this behalf were paid very handsomely to do so. Unlike the heroic stories of struggles such as the Spanish Civil War, where the forces of good and evil were clearly and sharply delineated, lawyers, and the collective legal profession, were ambiguous about these issues.

The lawyers at Osler, Hoskin & Harcourt during the early 1970s were also ambiguous about the firm's role in society. This ambiguity was clearly evident in 1973 during an extended debate among the partners over what was known as the "Community Law" initiative. During the late 1960s and early 1970s, the legal profession's tradition of *pro bono* service was the subject of considerable discussion in both the United States and Canada.[60]

Within a general social critique of the time period, which ranged from anti-Vietnam War sentiments to consumer protection efforts, the bar's traditional claim that it had a right to professional status in part because its members provided services and advice on a gratis basis as a gesture of social responsibility came under substantial criticism. There was very little evidence to support either the traditional assumption that lawyers did provide such service or the popular critique that they did not. What was clear, however, was that both views were represented within the profession — and within Osler, Hoskin & Harcourt.

In August of 1971, the firm's Executive Committee gave Brian Bellmore, a young associate in the litigation department, permission to participate in a community law and clinical training course run by Osgoode Hall Law School.[61] The course was offered from Osgoode's Parkdale Community Legal Services Clinic, which the law school had opened that year in an inner-city neighbourhood in west-end Toronto. The clinic was very controversial, because in addition to providing clinical training for law students, its implicit raison d'être was social activism. Even with a provincially funded legal aid scheme in place there were a great many people, particularly in low-income neighbourhoods like Parkdale, who for cultural as well as financial reasons did not have access to legal advice. The clinic was intended to deal directly with that need. Many of the more traditional members of the bar, including a number of Law Society benchers, felt that Parkdale's approach was too radical, and in fact at one point a group of benchers threatened to withdraw York University's licence to use the name Osgoode Hall Law School unless it did something to curtail the clinic's activities.[62]

Nevertheless, the Parkdale clinic was very successful, even taking a landlord-tenant dispute to the Supreme Court of Canada, and winning.[63] More importantly, the clinic had some strong support, even within the Bay St. bar. In February 1972, Professor Fred Zemans, the director of the Parkdale clinic, wrote to Purdy Crawford asking if Oslers had a few more lawyers who could volunteer to spend some time at the clinic. Crawford took the request to the Executive Committee, which decided to allow members of the firm to spend up to half a day per week in the clinic.[64] Very shortly thereafter, Peter Dey and Ron Ellis joined Brian Bellmore as Parkdale volunteers.[65]

The support of certain members of the firm for the Parkdale clinic was part of a general move towards what was being called community law. In August of 1971, the Junior Lawyers Committee submitted a report to the Executive Committee regarding the use of non-chargeable time docketing for charitable purposes.[66] The firm was then considering a proposal from Stuart Thom which would see lawyers change from a subjective dollar-based docketing system to a more objective time-based system, as a number of firms had done. Under Thom's proposed system, the partner in charge of determining the billing value of the work completed on a given file or transaction would have regard for the amount of time spent working on the file by each lawyer, multiplied by that lawyer's hourly rate.

The primary purpose of the hourly docketing system was to allow for efficient allocation of resources and planning, but it also provided a method by which the firm could systematically make a charitable contribution of legal expertise. In January 1972, the Executive Committee decided to put the new system in place as of the first of April.[67] At the same time, the committee was looking into the general question of community law. The Junior Lawyers Committee had followed its August 1971 report with another in September calling for a greater commitment by the firm to community law. The issue was the subject of much discussion in late 1971; in January, Allan Beattie told the partners that he "recognized that there was considerable feeling in the firm on this matter and that the Executive Committee would be expected to pronounce upon it in due course."[68]

There was a general feeling among the partners that they should be doing something to support and encourage community law within the firm; the question was, what should that involve? In October 1972, the Executive Committee approved the establishment of a Community Law Committee chaired by Ed Huycke to study "the question of whether the firm should formally engage in community or public interest law and, if so, the manner in which it should do so."[69]

Huycke held several meetings of this committee during October and November to study the experiences of other firms in the field. A number of large American firms had opened up their own community law departments in neighbourhood storefronts, much like the Parkdale clinic.[70] The primary purpose of these firm-sponsored clinics was to serve the *pro bono* tradition, but they also offered an internal marketing advantage. The large American firms (like their Canadian counterparts a few years later) were becoming very competitive about recruiting the top graduates of the best law schools. In an age of increased social activism and awareness among young people, a firm which could boast a storefront community legal clinic would have something more to offer potential recruits.

This notion held some currency for Canadian firms like Oslers, but the members of Huycke's committee were also aware of the fact that Thomson, Rogers, a Toronto litigation firm, had opened a storefront office on Bathurst Street. The Thomson, Rogers office, said to be the brainchild of Ian Outerbridge — who held a reputation for a wide range of law office innovation — came under a great deal of cynical criticism, however. Its location was right across the street from the Toronto Western Hospital, and a number of people in the legal community questioned the appropriateness of a personal injury litigation firm opening a storefront operation in the shadow of a hospital.[71]

At the partners' meeting in December, Ed Huycke reported that his committee had held five meetings during the fall, and they had conducted some discussions with people from Thomson, Rogers about their firm's activities in the area. They intended to solicit comments from the partners during the early winter and submit a report in the spring.[72] In March, however, Huycke made a very significant report to the Executive Committee. It seemed that there was a possible conflict of interest between the activities of the firm's volunteers at the Parkdale clinic and one of the firm's major clients.[73]

Although the minutes do not name the client or provide any detail about the nature of the conflict, this situation highlighted a fundamental problem with the community law idea. To a large degree, the social activist movement of the early 1970s, of which the storefront law clinic was a part, was basically inimical to the capitalist system. At a time when President Richard Nixon was calling on his supposed "silent majority" to support his battles with campus peace demonstrators, it was difficult to see it as anything but an "us versus them" scenario. To a large corporate law firm, whose clients included many of the largest multinational companies, it was hard to see how they could side with both.

In May, Ed Huycke submitted his committee's report; it recommended that the firm establish a community law department which would satisfy the firm's *pro bono* professional obligations by providing low-cost or free legal services in the public interest and/or poverty law areas. This could be accomplished either with a department housed within the firm's regular offices, or by a separate storefront office.[74] On May 29, the Executive Committee held a special meeting to discuss the report.

At the meeting it was obvious that there were some widely different views among the Executive Committee members about community law. On one side was Ed Huycke, who stood behind his committee's recommendation; on the other was his brother Fred, who was convinced that this was not an appropriate thing for the firm to be involved in. In the middle was Allan Beattie, who struggled to find some degree of consensus. In the end, however, the Executive Committee rejected Ed Huycke's committee's recommendation. In ratifying this decision, the partners agreed to acknowledge the firm's commitment to the *pro bono* tradition, but in an unstructured way. They decided to maintain community law as a heading for non-chargeable time docketing, but there would be no public interest department, and no Osler, Hoskin & Harcourt storefront clinic.[75] Nevertheless, community law ended up with a status that it did not previously have within the firm.

Over the course of the following years, the firm did exercise a commitment to public interest law. Ron Atkey, for instance, incorporated the Canadian Civil Liberties Association, but any such activities were entirely voluntary and ad hoc.[76] To some, it must have been a disappointment. Ron Ellis, a strong proponent of the community law initiative, although in later years he was quite philosophical about the firm's decision, took a leave of absence from the firm to succeed Fred Zemans as director of the Parkdale clinic, and eventually resigned his partnership in the firm.[77]

When Ellis looked back on his decision to leave practice at Oslers, he was certain that he had made the right decision. Although he laughingly admitted that his subsequent career in academics and public administration was not nearly as lucrative as a continued partnership would have been, he points out that some people are cut out for the life of the corporate lawyer, and some are not. He counts himself as one of the few lucky individuals who are not only able to recognize their own aptitudes, but are also able to make a choice.

Another Osler alumnus who made the decision not to stay in practice was Ken Dryden, best known as an all-star goaltender with the Montreal Canadiens during the 1970s, and as a bestselling author during the 1980s for his book *The Game*. Dryden, who grew up in Toronto, completed a bachelor's degree in history on a hockey scholarship at Cornell University in Ithaca, New York during the late 1960s. After graduating, he joined the Canadiens organization and was assigned to their American Hockey League farm team — the Montreal Voyageurs. He also enrolled in law school at McGill. Anyone who has tried to combine law school with a part-time job can attest to how difficult it is; to combine law school with a career as a full-time professional athlete, however, was unheard of.

In the spring of 1971, Dryden was called up to join the National Hockey League team, and a few weeks after finishing his first year of law school, he won not only the Stanley Cup but also the Conn Smythe Trophy, awarded to the most valuable player during the playoffs. During his second year in law school, he won the NHL rookie of the year award, but during his final year at McGill, he began to have some contract difficulties with the Canadiens. He had a contract which ran until the end of the 1973-74 season, but he had led the team to a Stanley Cup, and wanted to renegotiate. That winter he had received two letters from Ontario law firms suggesting that if he was considering articling after finishing law school, he should get in touch to arrange an interview. One of the two firms was Osler, Hoskin & Harcourt.[78]

Dryden assumed at the time that he would article after retiring from hockey, and he simply filed the letters away. By the mid-summer of 1973, however, it began to look like the Canadiens might not renegotiate, so he told them that if they did not come up with a new contract, he would sit out the 1973-74 season and spend it as an articling student. The hockey team apparently thought he was bluffing, and they did nothing. At the end of August, Dryden telephoned Osler, Hoskin & Harcourt and was put through to Jim Kennedy, the chairman of the Students Committee.

On the Thursday before the Labour Day weekend, Dryden saw Kennedy for an interview. Kennedy offered him a position and told him he could start on Tuesday. Dryden still felt that the Canadiens would come through, but the hockey team apparently still thought he was bluffing, and on Tuesday morning he began his articling year with the firm.

Dryden enjoyed his year at Osler, Hoskin & Harcourt, but although the firm offered him an associate lawyer's position if he took his call to the bar, he decided to return to hockey in 1974. He signed again with the Canadiens and played five more seasons. His first few games back in the fall of 1974 were not, however, very pleasant. He was rusty after a year spent in a law office, and he played poorly. After one particularly painful game, he received a playful telegram from Peter Dey, with whom he had become friendly during his year with the firm, suggesting that if he should reconsider his decision about hockey, the offer to join Osler, Hoskin & Harcourt still stood.

Like Ellis, Dryden was clear about his decision not to continue with the firm. As those who have read his books or heard him speak can attest, he is a very thoughtful, observant person. His personality was not suited to practising law, at least not to the lifestyle of the Bay Street lawyer. He was not, as he termed it, an "action junkie" — someone who takes enjoyment from being in the thick of the action. He saw this as being entirely consistent with being a goalie — one who sits back and observes, then reacts to what he sees. At any rate, although he took the Law Society's bar admission course after retiring from hockey in 1979 and was called to the bar in 1980, he has stuck with his original decision and has not practised law. For a brief time in the mid-1980s he was an administrator, serving as Youth Commissioner for the Ontario provincial government, but he has primarily pursued a career as a writer. His most recent work, published in 1993, is a nonfiction study entitled *The Moved and The Shaken: The Story of One Man's Life.*

Although the firm had some difficulty, like many others, in adapting to the great social changes and upheavals of the early 1970s, it was clearly able to adapt to the changing economic and business environment of the era. There is no doubt that the Osler, Hoskin & Harcourt legal practice grew substantially during the 1970s. It grew within the firm's established stable of blue-chip clients, but it also grew into new areas — with new clients, and new fields of law. More importantly, however, the firm's practice, like those of all other law firms in North America, went through a transition.

The loss of the Inco labour file in 1970 taught the firm a lesson. Even the blue-chip clients would no longer sit by and continue to give out their legal work because of loyalty. The old norms which applied during Britton Osler's day were gone. If a firm was going to keep its established clients, and better yet attract new ones, it was going to have to be able to adapt to a much more competitive market. It was going to have to keep bringing in — and bringing along — bright young lawyers who could provide service in all of the new areas of specialty, and it was going to have to provide sufficient incentives to attract and keep them.

One of the most significant young lawyers which the firm was able to attract and keep was Brian Michael Levitt, who arrived late in 1976. Over the course of the next fifteen years, Levitt became very important to the firm. Particularly following Purdy Crawford's departure to Imasco in 1985, Levitt played the role of a primary rainmaker.

Levitt, who was twenty-nine years old when he joined the firm, began his university education in engineering. When he graduated from the University of Toronto in 1969, however, he decided that he would not pursue a career as an engineer, and instead took an administrative position at the U. of T. A year later, when he decided to try law school, he chose the University of Toronto because he would be able to keep his administrative job on a part-time basis.

When he graduated with an LL.B. in 1973, he accepted an articling position at Blake, Cassels & Graydon. In sharp contrast to the articling applicants of more recent years, Levitt says that he knew virtually

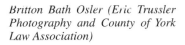

Britton Bath Osler (Eric Trussler Photography and County of York Law Association)

John Hoskin

F.W. Harcourt

Dalton McCarthy (The Law Society of Upper Canada)

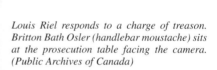

Theophilus H.A. Begue

Louis Riel responds to a charge of treason. Britton Bath Osler (handlebar moustache) sits at the prosecution table facing the camera. (Public Archives of Canada)

James V. Teetzel

John Hoskin

William M. Douglas (Bench and Bar of Ontario)

Leighton McCarthy (Bench and Bar of Ontario)

Wellington A. Cameron (Bench and Bar of Ontario)

Wallace Nesbitt (Law Society of Upper Canada)

H.S. Osler

Britton Osler, the young litigator at the Privy Council, ca. 1909

Harold Shapley

Norman Strickland

Britton Osler, at his desk on the eighth floor of the Dominion Bank Building

Britton Osler on the shore of Lake Scugog

Captains C.R. Osler (l.) and B.M. Osler in Colchester, England, December 1942 (C.R. Osler)

T.D. Delamere

Lieut-Comdr Stuart Thom on the bridge of HMCS Arnprior *(Stuart Thom)*

Photograph taken at Mossey Huycke's cottage at Stony Lake, Ont., in 1952. (l. to r.) Norman Strickland, Swatty Wotherspoon, J.G. Osler, Harold Boston, Mossey Huycke, W.B. Reid (kneeling).

Purdy Crawford at his call to the Nova Scotia bar, 1956

Ed Huycke

Peter White, Sr.

Bertha Wilson

Hal Mockridge

Purdy Crawford in his Montreal office, 1992

Brian Levitt

Peter Dey

Lee Ferrier

Fred Huycke

Jack Ground

Executive Committee, 1963. (l. to r.) Stuart Thom, B.M. Osler, George Mossey Huycke, Hal Mockridge, Swatty Wotherspoon. Absent: T.D. Delamere.

(l.) Ed Saunders, Harry Boylan

(l.) Bill Bryden, Allan Beattie

Temple Chambers — Toronto St., 1882-1894

Freehold Loan & Savings Building — Victoria St. at Adelaide, 1894- 1913 (NAC/PA 45971)

Dominion Bank Building — south-west corner of Yonge and King Sts., 1914-1962 (T.D. Bank)

Canadian Pacific Building — south-east corner of Yonge and King Sts., 1913-1914 (Metropolitan Toronto Reference Library)

Prudential Building — northwest corner of Yonge and King Sts., 1962-1977 (Prudential Insurance Company)

First Canadian Place — northwest corner of Bay and King Sts., since 1977 (Olympia & York)

nothing about the various firms, and as he puts it, "When I articled, I took the first job that was offered to me."[79] Despite that, his experience at Blakes was a good one, and in the spring of 1974, when he was nearly finished his articling year, the firm offered him a position as an associate lawyer on his call to the bar in 1975. It is not clear why he turned down an opportunity to work with the largest law firm in Canada, but there may be a clue in the fact that he chose the opposite extreme and accepted a job in a two-person firm in Shelburne, Ontario, a town of some eighteen hundred people in Dufferin County, northwest of Toronto.[80]

Shelburne may not have been to his liking either, because in September he moved to Ottawa to take on a position with the legal staff of the federal government's newly created Anti-Inflation Board. A year later, however, Levitt felt that he was ready for a move back to Bay Street. Surprisingly, particularly to those familiar with his subsequent career, he was interested in litigation. He contacted Blakes, "But when I applied for a job there, they had a policy that if you had at any time refused a job with the firm then they would never hire you."[81]

He made some other inquiries with lawyers he knew through his work with the Anti-Inflation Board, including Jack Ground, and began to think in terms other than litigation. In answer to the question, "What made you want to come to Oslers?", he rather modestly claimed: "It was the only place I could get a job. I was looking for a job doing litigation and I had a round of interviews, but there were basically no jobs and I needed a job. So I then started to look at corporate work."[82] Levitt's modesty belied his influence and position within the firm. Despite his generally rumpled and sleepy-eyed demeanour, he was responsible for many of the huge files which drove the firm's tremendous growth during the late 1980s.

Despite Levitt's claim that there were no jobs in the mid-1970s, however, Osler, Hoskin & Harcourt was still actively pursuing good young lawyers. At the Executive Committee meeting of October 19, 1976, Jack Ground brought up Levitt's name. He explained that Levitt was then on staff at the Anti-Inflation Board in Ottawa, but was considering moving to private practice. He also mentioned that Levitt was highly recommended by David Johnston, who had taught him at U. of T. before moving to Western to become Dean of the law school there.[83]

Johnston himself had been identified as a possible candidate for recruitment a few years earlier. Purdy Crawford, whose theory was that you took the best people when they were available and then looked for work to keep them busy, rather than expanding the firm only when the volume of work required it, brought Johnston's name up at an Executive Committee meeting in May 1973.[84] Johnston, who was then thirty-two years old, had articled at Oslers, but had never practised law. He was a member of the Ontario Securities Commission, and had been on the faculty at the University of Toronto law school since 1968. Prior to that he held a teaching position in the Faculty of Law at Queen's.

Despite his lack of practice experience, Johnston was exactly the kind of capable, dynamic person Crawford wanted to recruit. A native of northern Ontario, when he graduated from Sault Collegiate in Sault Ste. Marie, Johnston was lured to Harvard — as much to play hockey as to study. He was obviously very successful at both, because in 1962 and 1963 he was selected as an All-American, and when he graduated with an A.B. in 1963 he was accepted to study law at Cambridge University in England.

He received an LL.B. from Cambridge in 1965 and then returned to Canada and received an LL.B. from Queen's University in Kingston the following year. He articled at Osler, Hoskin & Harcourt in 1966-67, but decided to accept a teaching position at the Queen's law school rather than take the bar admission course. He taught at Queen's during the academic year 1967-68, and in 1968 moved on to the University of Toronto. By 1972 — at the age of thirty-one — he had been promoted to full professor, but in early 1973 he was apparently considering some career options — or at least Purdy Crawford hoped he was.[85]

One of the things which apparently made Johnston attractive was the fact that he had published a book entitled *Computers and the Law*, an area which Crawford could see was a very important new field. At the Executive Committee meeting of June 12, 1973, Crawford reported that he had had some favourable discussions with Johnston, but shortly thereafter Johnston decided to stay in academics. A year later Johnston accepted the deanship at Western, and in 1979 he went on to become the principal at McGill University in Montreal.[86]

Oslers was more successful, however, with Brian Levitt. After Jack Ground brought up his name, Tim Kennish also gave him a high recommendation, and the Committee gave Ground authority to pursue the matter.[87] A few weeks later, Levitt joined the firm. David Johnston's recommendation was obviously very accurate, because Levitt went on to become one of the firm's most important corporate practitioners, and he was made partner within two and a half years of joining the firm and only four years from his call to the bar. This was the fastest partnership from date of call since C.R. Osler, who was called to the bar in 1948 and made partner in 1950.

During his rapid rise in the partnership, Levitt became a specialist in mergers and acquisitions. In some respects, he was the beneficiary of history, as the late 1970s and early 1980s became the era of the massive corporate takeover as a business phenomenon. Most observers agree, however, that Levitt likely would have become a dominant force in whatever field happened to be the coming thing.

Nevertheless, he was particularly good at what became known as "mega-deals" such as corporate mergers and reorganizations, because he was what some of his partners described as the best "quarterback on a deal," meaning he was able to effectively marshall teams of literally dozens of lawyers on files which were of enormous importance to the client — and which brought in enormous fees to the firm. Perhaps most importantly, however, Levitt was an excellent "client's lawyer," whose reputation became quickly well known throughout the corporate and financial community; in this way, and in some very important other ways which will be discussed in the following chapter, he was following directly in Purdy Crawford's footsteps.

Another beneficiary of the rise of mergers and acquisitions work and the mega-deal was Peter Dey. Dey, one of the authors of the 1975 memo which helped bring about the restructuring of the Executive Committee, was a securities law specialist. Although, like Levitt, his first degree was in engineering, like Purdy Crawford, Dey was a graduate of the Dalhousie and Harvard law schools, receiving an LL.B. from Dalhousie in 1966 and an LL.M. from Harvard in 1967.[88] Crawford made an effort to maintain his contacts from his own days at Dalhousie and Harvard, and he was always eager to pursue promising recruits. In 1967, he apparently convinced Dey to come to Toronto to article with Oslers; when Dey was called to the bar in 1969, he joined the firm as an associate lawyer.

Both Levitt and Dey rose within the partnership much faster than lawyers of the previous generation, partly because of the M&A phenomenon. In Dey's case, the need for massive financing of these mega-deals created much more work for securities law specialists, but even more importantly, and because of the increase in volume of corporate financing during this era, securities regulation became much more complex. The result was a higher demand for securities lawyers.

Although Dey was an internal recruit — that is, he articled with the firm and stayed after his call to the bar — Osler, Hoskin & Harcourt was equally eager to recruit established lawyers — directly into the partnership, if necessary — on a lateral basis. As noted above, although the growth in the firm remained largely internal during the 1970s, the proportion of external recruits among the firm's lawyers grew from 19 per cent to 35 per cent.

In addition, not all of the internal recruits had been with the firm throughout their careers. Some of them articled with the firm and then returned after practising elsewhere for a time. This seems to indicate something important about the firm — or at least many of those who followed this career pattern believe that it does. There was something attractive about the firm which they saw as articling students, and after experiencing life elsewhere, it brought them back.

The most notable of the lawyers who articled with the firm, then left to practise elsewhere and later returned, was John F. "Jack" Petch. Jack Petch was born in Kitchener, Ontario in 1938. After obtaining his B.A. from the University of Western Ontario in 1960, Petch attended the University of Toronto law school where he excelled academically, earning the Law School Gold Medal and other awards. He articled at Oslers in 1963-1964, and then entered the Law Society's Bar Admission Course where he won the Treasurer's Gold Medal, the First Prize of both the Law Society and the Lawyers Club and other awards in such diverse fields as criminal law and commercial and company law.

Much to the disappointment of the partners of Oslers who felt he had great potential, Petch elected to enter practice, not on Bay Street, but in London, Ontario, where he had attended university as an undergraduate. However, it was not the more sedate pace of practice in a small community that appealed to Petch. By the mid-1960s, a great number of public companies had located their headquarters in London. This was a centre of considerable commercial activity which Petch reckoned would allow him to become quickly involved in significant and interesting corporate and securities work. He joined the firm of Ivey & Dowler, a firm of fifteen lawyers (large by London standards of the time), which specialized in acting for public companies. Among the clients of the firm were Labatt's Breweries, Supertest Petroleum, Silverwood Dairies and Midland Securities. Due to his willingness to take on difficult and challenging assignments,

Petch was soon involved in numerous public offerings and other significant transactions. By the time he left Ivey & Dowler in 1971 to form his own firm, though only thirty-three years of age, he had as much or more experience in the practice of corporate and securities law than many lawyers who had practised in the area for twenty years or longer. After four years of practice in his own firm, which had by then grown to include four partners, Petch realized that London was not likely to continue as a significant centre of public company activity and that his future was in Toronto. His obvious choice was the firm at which he had articled, and the partners at Oslers were delighted to welcome him back. He joined Oslers as a partner in October of 1975. The firm that he had left in 1964 had in the meantime grown from thirty to sixty-five lawyers.

Petch quickly became involved not only in the work of the firm, but also in its administration. By the late 1970s, he had become chairman of the firm's Associate Lawyers Committee, and by 1986 he had become a member of the Executive Committee and chairman of the firm's Corporate Commercial Department. In addition, he enrolled in Osgoode Hall Law School's Master of Laws programme, and obtained his LL.M. in 1980. He also became involved in various professional and community activities outside the firm. He lectured at numerous courses and conferences offered to legal and business audiences. His community activities included serving as a member of the board of directors at St. Michael's Hospital, as a member of committees of the United Way and numerous other charitable organizations, the Canadian Stage Company, the Toronto Pops Orchestra, and as a fundraiser on behalf of his alma mater, the University of Toronto and the University of Western Ontario. Petch's involvement in outside professional and community activities, which was by no means unique to him either within Oslers or the profession at large, did more than satisfy his sense of public obligation — it enhanced his and the firm's profile within the community.[89]

Therefore, given his standing as one of Canada's leading corporate and securities lawyers, it was not surprising that the name Jack Petch was recommended to Wallace McCain when he went looking for a lawyer in 1991 to advise him as to his rights as a shareholder, officer and director of McCain Foods Limited.[90]

Wallace McCain was born in Florenceville, New Brunswick, in 1930. In 1956, after graduating from university, he and his older brother Harrison decided to start a business together. With start-up capital of just $100,000, they purchased a pasture on the banks of the

St. John River at Florenceville and proceeded to construct a plant to manufacture frozen french fried potatoes. During the ensuing thirty-five years, McCain Foods grew to become the largest manufacturer of french fries in the world, while expanding into the production of frozen vegetables, juices, pizzas and desserts. Its sales activities extended to sixty-five countries and it established processing facilities in North and South America, the United Kingdom, Europe and the Pacific Rim. Remarkably, all of this was accomplished without the brothers ever having to raise money from the public. Therefore, McCain Foods was still entirely owned and controlled by members of the McCain family.

Wallace and Harrison McCain, as co-CEOs, had jointly operated McCain Foods as a partnership since founding it in 1956. However, by the late 1980s differences between the brothers began to arise in relation to the issues of succession and corporate governance. Wallace became concerned that Harrison was apparently soliciting the support of other family members. As subsequent events revealed, plans were afoot to oust Wallace from the company. That was when Wallace McCain realized that he needed legal advice. He was at first apprehensive about involving a Bay Street lawyer in what was essentially a personal family dispute. Although he was no stranger to the corporate milieu, having been instrumental in building a multi-billion dollar empire and serving on the board of directors of the Royal Bank of Canada, he had always been an intensely private person who tended to keep things, both business and personal, close to his vest. However, soon after meeting Jack Petch, McCain's notions about the stereotypical corporate lawyer began to fade away. There quickly developed a relationship of trust, confidence and respect between Petch and his client.[91]

After more than three years of legal wrangling, Wallace McCain was eventually removed from the position of co-CEO, although his right to continue as a director and as an officer of McCain Foods until age seventy-five was confirmed. In any event, by the fall of 1994, Wallace McCain had come to the painful realization that his future, and that of his children, did not lie with McCain Foods, and that they would have to look for another business to become involved in. Although he was then sixty-four years of age, McCain was in good health and full of energy and ambition, with no interest in slipping away into a life of leisurely retirement.

McCain then proceeded to investigate various possible food businesses in which he might become involved by way of acquisition or otherwise. One possible acquisition candidate was Maple Leaf Foods Inc., Canada's largest food processor, which was formed by way of amalgamation in 1991 between Maple Leaf Mills Limited and Canada Packers Inc. It had been fairly common knowledge within the food industry that Maple Leaf's majority shareholder, Hillsdown Holdings PLC, a British public company, might be interested in disposing of its 56 per cent interest in the shares of Maple Leaf if a buyer at the right price came along. The first formal meeting between Wallace McCain and Hillsdown concerning a possible acquisition of Maple Leaf occurred in January 1995. Discussion continued periodically over the next two months, and in early March 1995, an agreement was struck whereunder McCain agreed to make an offer to purchase all of the outstanding shares of Maple Leaf at a price of $15 per share, consisting of a combination of cash and shares. The financing for this $1.2-billion takeover bid was to be provided by Wallace McCain, together with the Ontario Teachers' Pension Plan Board which had agreed to make a significant equity investment, with The Toronto-Dominion Bank providing the necessary lending support.

The task given to Jack Petch and his colleagues at Oslers was to make an extraordinarily complicated transaction (which contemplated never-before-tried transactional techniques) happen within what appeared to be the impossibly short time frame of six weeks. Not only did the offering documents have to be prepared and sent to Maple Leaf's shareholders by the following week, but extensive loan documentation had to be prepared, shareholders' meetings had to be called and held, approvals of various securities and competition agencies had to be secured, and court approval of a statutory plan of arrangement had to be obtained, all by the end of April. In quick order, Petch assembled his team. Partners and associates from numerous areas of the firm were mobilized — corporate lawyers, take-over and securities specialists, research lawyers, banking and financ ing experts, a tax lawyer, a litigator to take care of the court application process, a competition lawyer to deal with the competition tribunal, a trust lawyer to advise with respect to the transfer of shares held by various McCain family trusts, and a labour lawyer to give advice as to issues that would arise in connection with the impact of the proposed transaction on the 11,000 employees of Maple Leaf. In addition to the partners and associates involved in the transaction, essential support had to be provided by law students, law clerks, secretaries and other staff. The agenda for the closing exceeded sixty pages in length and contemplated hundreds of steps involving more than a thousand documents, most of which did not exist on March 6 when the bid was publicly announced, but all of which had to be in final form and signed by the closing six weeks later.

The McCain/Maple Leaf transaction in many ways epitomized the concept of teamwork which is essential to the successful execution of modern large corporate and securities transactions. The complexity of the law and broad scope of modern-day governmental regulation of business activities call for the involvement of experts from a number of diverse legal practice specialties. Although Oslers was not unique in this regard, only a relatively few firms in Canada had the personnel and expertise to do this type of work.

Another very significant appointment to the partnership in the 1970s — because his area of expertise involved one of the most important, and certainly the most voluminous, legal change of the 1970s — was tax lawyer Bob Lindsay. During the 1960s, in addition to Stuart Thom's practice, which attracted a significant amount of work directly, much of the firm's tax work was servicing corporate clients. And although tax law was becoming more complicated, it was still possible for corporate lawyers like Fred Huycke, Ed Saunders and Purdy Crawford to do tax work. All of that changed, however, with the federal government's massive tax reform of 1971.

As Purdy Crawford once described it to Bob Lindsay, prior to 1971 roughly 25 per cent of his practice could be described as tax work. He quickly realized, however, that it was now going to have to be either 99 per cent or 1 per cent — and he chose the latter. The new Income Tax Act had created a far too specialized field of law, which the general corporate practitioner would be foolish to try to master on a part-time basis. Although it seems hard to believe, even Stuart Thom claims that he never even bothered to read the new act, but decided to retire from practice instead.[92] Crawford and others realized, however, that the firm was going to need some more tax expertise, and who better to get than one of the lawyers who drafted the awe-inspiring legislation?

Crawford actually tried to recruit Bob Lindsay in the early 1960s.[93] The Executive Committee minutes of April 28, 1965 contain a note which reads: "There was also a Mr. Lindsay concerning whom enquiries were being made," but apparently Crawford had been keeping his eye on Lindsay for some years.

Lindsay, who was born in Toronto in 1936, graduated with a Bachelor of Commerce degree from the University of Toronto in 1958. He stayed at U. of T. for another year to complete a Master's degree in economics, and then decided to go to law school. He chose Dalhousie University in Halifax because, like Peter Dey, he was offered a Sir James Dunn Scholarship. Before leaving Toronto, however, he attended a luncheon sponsored by local Dalhousie graduates, including Purdy Crawford, who were apparently very impressed. Crawford kept tabs on him through his informants at Dalhousie, and when Lindsay was about to graduate in the spring of 1963, he offered him an articling position with Oslers.

Lindsay found Crawford's offer attractive; he knew that he wanted to return to Ontario, and he had already decided that he wanted to specialize in tax law, if possible. Osler, Hoskin & Harcourt had an impressive list of corporate clients, and Stuart Thom had an excellent reputation as a tax lawyer. Nevertheless, he turned Crawford down and accepted an articling position with a local firm in Halifax. His logic made perfect sense. If he articled for the summer in Halifax, as both Crawford and Bertha Wilson had done, he could get a call to the Nova Scotia bar in September. If he went to Toronto, he would have to article for a full twelve months and then attend the bar admission course before he would be eligible to be called to the Ontario bar in 1965.

Moreover, once he was a member of any provincial bar, he could take a job as a lawyer with the federal government in Ottawa, wait three years and apply as a transfer lawyer from another province for call to the Ontario bar; by 1966 he would be able to apply to a Toronto firm with three years of hands-on experience in the tax field. In the United States, it was quite common for young lawyers to do a stint with the federal civil service to gain experience before starting or returning to practice. In Canada, however, it was less common, but in Lindsay's view, it was no less valuable.

He did, in fact, take a job with the Department of National Revenue in Ottawa in the fall of 1963, but he stayed a little longer than he had originally planned. It was five years before he got around to applying for admission to the Ontario bar, and it was more than eight before he had the time to think about going into private practice.

When Lindsay joined the Department of National Revenue in 1963, he began working mostly as a staff lawyer enforcing the Income Tax Act, but he also did some policy work. By 1965, he was considering going into private practice, and it was then that his name came up again at Oslers; he once again opted not to take a position in Toronto, but decided to stay with the federal government and accept a position with the Department of Finance.

While in the Department of Finance, Lindsay helped prepare a government white paper in response to the Carter Commission recommendations. In 1962, Prime Minister John Diefenbaker had appointed a Royal Commission on Taxation, chaired by Toronto accountant Kenneth Carter of McDonald, Currie & Co. In 1966, Carter presented a 2,600-page report to Parliament. The report was considered very controversial, particularly by the business community; among other things, it recommended that capital gains be fully taxed as income.[94]

In November of 1969, Pierre Trudeau's finance minister, Edgar Benson, tabled the White Paper on tax reform which Lindsay had helped to draft. To many observers — although not much of the business community — it was considered "a retreat from Carter," because it watered down the capital gains tax provisions. Lindsay then set to work to help draft a completely new Income Tax Act.

This massive statute, which critics described as a further retreat from Carter, provided for taxation of capital gains, but at a concessionary rate. Corporate taxation in general retained great flexibility.[95] It was much less threatening to business than the Carter recommendations had been, but more significantly — from the perspective of lawyers — it created a much more complex body of law than had been in place before.

Once his huge drafting assignment was completed, Bob Lindsay could once again think about going into private practice; in July 1971, his name again came up again in the Osler, Hoskin & Harcourt Executive Committee minutes, and Purdy Crawford was given the go-ahead to pursue discussions with him. As Stuart Thom and Purdy Crawford well knew, Canadian tax law was going to be an entirely new field once the new law came into effect, and the firm was going to have to be prepared.

At the Executive Committee meeting of September 28 and the partnership meeting of September 30, Crawford reported that he had made Lindsay an offer, but had not yet received a reply. Of course, Lindsay was not just looking at Oslers. As one of the authors of the new legislation, he was apparently in great demand. In fact, on one occasion when Crawford met with Lindsay in Ottawa, he happened to run into John and Jim Tory, Bill DesLauriers and Jim Baillie, then four of the senior partners at the Tory firm, in the lobby of the Chateau Laurier Hotel. Crawford thought to himself, "I wonder what would bring those four guys to Ottawa all at the same time? Could they be here to see Lindsay, too?"

It turned out that they were; they had a lavish room-service meal laid on in their suite in the Chateau Laurier, and made a very attractive offer to Lindsay over dinner. As Lindsay remembers it, he was very impressed with the people from Torys; they had an excellent reputation — as he points out, they still do — but ultimately he chose Oslers. He is not entirely clear as to why. He expected that the practice would be comparable no matter which of the big firms he ended up with; they all had excellent corporate clients, and he knew that he could attract quite a bit of referral work. But he chose Osler, Hoskin because of the people. It was not a calculated judgement as much as it was a gut decision. He just liked the people and the atmosphere of the firm, and he joined Oslers on January 1, 1972. Over the next two decades, Lindsay played a key role in building one of the largest and reputedly one of the best tax departments in all of Canada.[96]

Among the other lateral recruitment successes of the 1970s at Oslers, one stands out. Although the firm was founded on its litigation practice in the late nineteenth century, Osler, Hoskin & Harcourt had not been known as a litigation firm since the departure of the Mc-Carthys in 1916. During the years after World War II, there was some thought that W.B. Reid would become the firm's courtroom specialist, but his dramatic exploits of the early 1950s spelled the end to that.

During the 1960s, a number of young lawyers in the firm gained some valuable experience in litigation in the Texas Gulf suit, but by the 1970s it was obvious that this was an area which the firm should think about expanding. In 1977, Oslers attracted a man who had by then established a reputation as a leading courtroom specialist; by the late 1980s, he was chairman of the Executive Committee.

J. Edgar Sexton was born in Ottawa on October 28, 1936, and grew up in London, Ontario. After he graduated from high school, he decided he wanted to be an engineer. However, unlike many other young Londoners, he chose not to stay at home and go to the University of Western Ontario, instead, he travelled east to Kingston and enrolled at Queen's University. Over the course of the next four years, he came to the conclusion that he did not enjoy engineering; at least, not enough to make a career of it. Ironically, it was a course in the engineering school which gave him an idea.

As a part of his program Sexton took a course in engineering law, and as he put it, "for the first time I started getting interested in university courses."[97] With his interest piqued, he started sitting in on classes in the law school. In 1958, the Queen's law school was brand new; it had only opened its doors a year earlier when the Law Society of Upper Canada relinquished its monopoly over professional legal education in Ontario. The classes which Sexton sat in on were small, and the faculty included some very stimulating teachers.[98] What he found he most enjoyed, however, was studying the cases, particularly those involving a handful of judgements written by Justice Ivan Rand of the Supreme Court of Canada.

A few months before he graduated with an engineering degree in the spring of 1959, Sexton decided to apply to law school; the question was, which one to attend? The traditional law school — in fact, until very recently, the only law school in the province — was the Law Society's Osgoode Hall Law School in Toronto. But the classes at Osgoode were enormous. His other choices were the University of Toronto, the University of Ottawa, and Queen's, whose small classes he was already familiar with.

He was leaning towards staying at Queen's, when he learned that the University of Western Ontario was planning to open a law school in September, with none other than Ivan Rand as its first dean. Rand had announced his retirement from the Supreme Court and agreed to accept the post at Western in the spring of 1959.[99] Sexton decided to return to his home town and join the first class in the UWO law school. His expectations about the small classes at Western, and particularly about Rand, were met; over the course of his three years there, Sexton became quite close to Dean Rand, whom he remembers fondly.

Interestingly, during Sexton's first year at Western, classes were held in the Engineering building across the street from the construction site which would become the new law school. Sexton's engineering degree came in handy, however, because during the summer between his first and second years he got a job as the resident engineer on the law school construction site. Unlike engineering, however, Sexton thoroughly enjoyed law school. He found the material very stimulating and won a number of prizes when he graduated.

Sexton graduated with an LL.B. in 1962, but when it came time to article he once again decided to leave London; he chose Toronto, and ended up at McCarthy & McCarthy. Although it was largely John Robinette's courtroom reputation which attracted him to McCarthys, Sexton assumed, because one of the prizes he won at Western was in tax law, that he would spend most of his time there doing tax work. In fact, although he did rotate through the tax group, he spent over four months working with Robinette on a large fraud case. It was this contact with Robinette which would shape his career.

Unlike the systems put in place more recently, where the large firms announce a specific date when the articling students will be told whether they are being invited back to work for the firm after call to the bar, the process of evaluation and selection of students in the early 1960s was not particularly systematic. Sexton obviously impressed both Robinette and Bill Latimer, then the senior tax lawyer at McCarthys, because both men indicated that they would like to see him stay with the firm. Nevertheless, it was Beverley Matthews who ran the firm and, like Hal Mockridge at Oslers, it was up to him to make the formal offers to students. When Sexton hadn't heard anything official from Matthews by the end of his twelve-month articling term, he accepted an offer to join Giffen & Pensa, a two-man general practice in London.

Apparently both Latimer and Robinette were still assuming that Sexton would be coming back to McCarthys, but when he did get a formal offer from Beverley Matthews, he decided that he would stick with his commitment to Giffen & Pensa. Although he only stayed in London for a year after his call to the bar in 1964, he feels that the general work he did there was good training for the future. In 1965, he made the decision to leave London once again. After doing major litigation in Toronto with John Robinette and general solicitor's work in London with Giffen & Pensa, he decided that he much preferred the former.

He happened to be in Toronto some time later and had lunch with a classmate from law school. He mentioned that he was thinking of coming back to Toronto to practise, although he hadn't gone so far as to put in any applications with Toronto firms. Very shortly thereafter, he got a telephone call from Bert MacKinnon, a litigation lawyer with the Toronto firm Wright & McTaggart. Apparently MacKinnon, whose firm was looking for a junior litigator, happened to meet Sexton's friend on the street one day. The friend suggested Sexton, and he came down to Toronto for an interview. He accepted a position with the firm and stayed for ten years. He later spent two years with Holden, Murdoch prior to joining Osler, Hoskin & Harcourt.

One of Sexton's more interesting cases occurred during the mid-1970s. Unlike some of his cases, it did not involve a highly influential client or a significant amount of money, but it did entail a very important constitutional law issue. On October 31, 1974, two young men in long hair and blue jeans came into his office; they explained that they were musicians, and they wanted to know if they could sue the Liquor Licence Board. They felt that the chairman of the board, former Toronto police chief James Mackey, was unfairly persecuting them.

Blair and Gary MacLean were twin brothers originally from Glace Bay, Nova Scotia. Billed as "MacLean & MacLean," they had a popular singing and comedy act on the university and bar circuit in and around southern Ontario. As they explained to Sexton, in early October they had been booked to play at Fryfogle's Tavern, a London, Ontario nightclub popular with students at the University of Western Ontario. *The Gazette*, the bi-weekly student newspaper at Western, ran an advertisement in its Tuesday, October 8 edition, listing them as appearing "All This Week." The same ad reminded students that the Dundas Street bar offered "Great Food — Dirt Cheap!" The Friday edition carried a full-page advertisement on the back page proclaiming "Tonight and Saturday — McLean & McLean (*sic*) (The Comedy Singing Duo That Was Booted Off The Lighthouse Tour by Labatt's).[100] But, as the brothers explained to Sexton, they had not been not allowed to finish their week at Fryfogle's.

On the Thursday afternoon, when they went to the tavern, the manager told them that he had had a visit from the liquor inspector that morning. The inspector had told them that he thought the brothers' act was obscene, and if they appeared on Fryfogle's stage again, the tavern's liquor licence would be cancelled. The manager said that he was sorry, but there was nothing he could do. The original contract called for a fee of $1,500 for the week; the manager gave the MacLeans $500 and they packed up their instruments.

The brothers were used to controversy; by their own admission their act was raunchy, and many people would consider it offensive. But among the young crowd attracted to the kind of places they played, they were very popular. On college campuses at the time, *National Lampoon* magazine was a bestseller; one of the most popular comedy albums that year was George Carlin's *Class Clown*, which featured a bit called "The Seven Words You Can't Say on Television." As the brothers understood it, a liquor board inspector had happened to see them perform at a club, and he found their act very offensive. And according to their Toronto booking agent, shortly thereafter the Liquor Licence Board had warned all the bars where they might play that if the MacLeans appear on your stage, you will lose your licence.

Their question to Sexton was, "What can we do? We can't earn a living if the bar owners won't hire us because they are afraid of losing their liquor licences." He told them, "I think you've got a good case. I think we can get an injunction restraining the Board from threatening the bars." As he recalled it some years later, "I immediately thought of *Roncarelli*."[101] *Roncarelli* v. *Duplessis* is one of the best-known constitutional precedents in Canadian history.[102] In fact, it was for many years the first case taught to law students in introductory constitutional law courses.

In the years following World War II, the Quebec Provincial Government was waging what many considered a holy war with the Jehovah's Witnesses. The Witnesses of Jehovah are members of a Christian sect who are required by their faith to spread what they believe to be the word of God. When the Roman Catholic Church in Quebec resisted this uninvited theological correction, the Witnesses fought back with the fury of the true believer.

The premier, Maurice Duplessis, saw himself as the staunch defender of French Canadian *nationalisme*. In fact, it was an extremely intolerant, conservative *nationalisme*. Its proponents considered any threat to the state or its supporting institutions a threat to the survival of French Canada. Duplessis and his supporters saw such threats in what they considered radical political ideologies and in "subversive" religious groups. And he was not averse to using the power of the state to defend French Canada against what he loosely defined as "communists," and particularly against the Jehovah's Witnesses.[103]

Duplessis used his authority as provincial premier and attorney general to prevent the Witnesses from holding public meetings and distributing literature by padlocking the homes and offices where they printed their materials. But in a series of cases, the Supreme Court of Canada disallowed this abuse of power.[104] The last of these was *Roncarelli*.

Frank Roncarelli was a successful Montreal restaurateur and a member of the Jehovah's Witnesses. Although, unlike hundreds of his co-religionists, he was not arrested, he did post bail for a great many who were. And Duplessis did not like it. In fact, the premier described Roncarelli's "repeated and audacious" posting of bonds as "a provocation to public order, to the administration of justice and ... definitely contrary to the aims of justice."[105] As punishment for this "provocation," Duplessis ordered the provincial Liquor Commission to cancel Roncarelli's liquor licence and seize his entire stock of liquor.

Although the Quebec Alcoholic Liquor Act gave the Commission the authority to ''cancel any permit at its discretion,'' Roncarelli filed suit against Duplessis for damages amounting to some $118,000 as a result of the cancellation of his liquor licence.[106] At trial, the court found in Roncarelli's favour but awarded him only $8,000.[107] On appeal, the Quebec Court of Queen's Bench overturned this decision and dismissed the suit entirely.[108] Then, represented by Frank Scott, the long-time civil liberties activist and dean of law at McGill University, Roncarelli took the case to the Supreme Court of Canada.

The Supreme Court overruled the Court of Queen's Bench and accepted Roncarelli's appeal, but awarded him only $25,000 in damages. In its decision, however, the Court restated one of the fundamental principles of constitutional law — that a democratic nation must be governed by the rule of law, not by arbitrary power. And the judge who wrote the most often quoted judgement in the case, taught the principle to Ed Sexton in his first year at Western. In his judgement, Justice Ivan Rand, whose portrait still hangs in Sexton's office at Oslers, wrote:

[I]n public administration of this sort there is no such thing as absolute and untrammelled discretion. . . . [If] administration according to law is to be superseded by action dictated by and according to the arbitrary likes, dislikes and irrelevant purposes of public officers acting beyond their duty, [it] would signalize the beginning of disintegration of the rule of law as a fundamental postulate of our constitutional structure.[109]

But as Sexton later explained, high-minded constitutional maxims may mean a great deal in the Supreme Court of Canada or to an eager young law student, but the practising litigator often has to be concerned with more mundane things, such as evidence. Maurice Duplessis, with the righteous arrogance only he could muster, had explained very clearly to the *Montreal Gazette* why he had ordered Roncarelli's liquor licence cancelled. Had he, or perhaps more specifically the Quebec Liquor Commission, claimed that Roncarelli's licence was being revoked because his restaurant was in breach of regulations, it is most likely that his lawsuit would have no chance at all. Unless the MacLeans could prove that the Ontario Liquor Licence Board was acting outside of its mandate in threatening the bar owners, they would have no case.

Before they went any further, Sexton suggested that they simply telephone James Mackey, the Liquor Board chairman, from his office. He assumed, pessimistically, that Mackey would claim that he had simply been interested in the safe service of liquor. He had heard that because of the nature of the MacLeans' act things tended to get out of hand at their performances, and he was simply warning the licence holders to make sure that did not happen. As it turned out, however, Mackey felt he had nothing to hide.

When they telephoned Mackey on the speaker phone in Sexton's office and asked him why he had threatened to cancel the licence of any tavern in which they performed, he told them point blank that he thought their performance was obscene, and he was not going to allow it to take place in any licensed establishment in Ontario. That admission was crucial.

That afternoon, Sexton filed an action in the Ontario High Court of Justice seeking an injunction against the Liquor Licence Board and its chairman and inspectors from interfering with the MacLeans' business interests by suspending or cancelling or threatening to cancel the liquor licences of establishments who might hire the brothers. He also asked for damages for unlawful interference with the MacLeans' business trade. In his statement of claim, Sexton cited *Roncarelli* v. *Duplessis* and argued that neither the Liquor Licence Act nor its regulations gave the Board or its chairman or inspectors the right to cancel liquor licences on the basis of the type of entertainment offered.[110]

In response, Dennis Brown, a staff lawyer with the provincial Ministry of the Attorney-General, admitted that the Act did not grant a specific authority to the Board or its officers to pass judgement on entertainment presented in licensed establishments; but, he argued, such a power was implicit in the statute. Further, the Board was taking action only against holders of dining lounge licences, which permitted minors on the premises.

But Justice Donald Keith rejected this claim. He accepted Sexton's argument that *Roncarelli* was binding, and he quoted from Ivan Rand's judgement in that famous case: "[N]o legislative Act can, without express language, be taken to contemplate an unlimited arbitrary power exercisable for any purpose, however capricious or irrelevant, regardless of the nature or purpose of the statute."[111] He then issued an interlocutory injunction against the Liquor Licence Board, the chairman and inspectors.[112]

The result was that Maclean & MacLean could begin to perform again in Ontario and earn a living. The question of damages was never determined. As Sexton later remembered it, because they had moved so fast with the injunction application, they had very little in the way of provable damages. More importantly, because of the publicity, the brothers probably benefitted from the incident. The exposure and controversy, in fact, increased their popularity. In the scheme of things, it was a very minor piece of litigation, but it was memorable because it involved a fundamental constitutional point of law.

Shortly after the MacLean brothers case, Sexton became involved in what he felt was the most colourful case of his career, although it did not involve litigation per se. He received a telephone call from the very distraught head of a client company. He explained that his company had sold and delivered a large shipment of lumber products to a man named Aziz in Saudi Arabia.[113] Shortly after taking delivery, however, Aziz contacted the client to complain. The delivery was short volume and the lumber was defective.[114]

Sexton's client wanted to maintain a good relationship with Mr. Aziz and other potential customers in Saudi Arabia, so he asked how they could resolve the situation. Aziz explained that he would soon be in London, England on business; could someone meet him there to discuss it? The client said certainly, and a meeting was arranged. When the client's representative met Aziz in London, however, the latter apologized and explained that he had left his file at home. Would he be so kind as to come back to Jiddah on Aziz' private jet to retrieve it? He agreed, and they left for Saudi Arabia.

When they arrived, the company representative examined the lumber personally, but he found that it was in no way short volume or defective. He explained this to Mr. Aziz and left for the airport. Before he could board a commercial flight back to Britain, however, he was stopped by Saudi police officers and arrested. His passport was confiscated and he was informed that he would not be allowed to leave the country until he had paid $500,000 to Mr. Aziz.

At this point, the client telephoned Sexton. The company representative was, in fact, being held hostage by the Saudi government. He was not in police custody; he was staying at a hotel in Jiddah at the company's expense, but without a passport he was forbidden to leave the country. As Sexton soon learned, under Saudi law, a foreign national can be refused exit in order to ensure payment of a legal debt to a Saudi national or corporation. The problem here was that the client did not believe anything more was owed to Aziz. Aziz felt there was, and he had the right connections in the Saudi government to enforce his view of the matter.

Sexton was able to get through to Aziz in Jiddah, but the impression he got was, if you ever want to see your man again, send half a million dollars. After that, Aziz would no longer communicate. Sexton tried the Department of External Affairs in Ottawa; they told them they had an embassy in Riyadh and a consulate in Jiddah through which they could relay messages to the company man, Aziz, or Saudi officials, but beyond that there was really nothing the Canadian government could do.

Sexton felt that they were at an impasse. He wanted to open negotiations; however, without sending the money up front — which Sexton's client was very reluctant to do in the absence of any guarantee of its return — Aziz would not cooperate. But Sexton had an idea which he thought might get Aziz' attention. He suggested they send two messages to their man. The first would be sent in an open cable directly to his hotel; it would simply say, "You have cost us this account, and you are fired for incompetence." They assumed that Aziz would automatically be informed of the content of any messages to the man, and this might make him believe that his hostage might not be worth $500,000. Meanwhile, they quietly sent the other message by way of the Canadian consulate telling their man the strategy and to ignore the direct cable.

The ploy apparently worked, because they soon received a message from Aziz indicating that he wanted to negotiate. As it turned out, among other things, the dispute involved the measurement of dressed lumber. As anyone who buys lumber for a home renovation project learns, a "2-by-4" is not really two inches by four inches in dimension. It starts off that way, but after it is dressed — that is, planed square — it is only about 1.75 inches by 3.5 inches. Aziz felt that the difference in volume meant that he deserved a sizeable refund of the purchase price. Sexton's client did not agree, but was willing to have the dispute resolved in a reasonable forum.

Aziz replied that this would be fine; he would make arrangements to have the issue resolved in a Saudi court as soon as possible. Given what they knew about Aziz' influence over the police, Sexton's client was not willing to do this. Sexton told Aziz that they thought it should be resolved in a Canadian court. But Aziz was unwilling to do that, and they were once again at a stalemate. Sexton then suggested a trial by an impartial tribunal at a neutral site, that they request an arbitration before the International Chamber of Commerce in Paris. Aziz was willing to go before an ICC panel, but he did not want it to take place in Paris; instead, he suggested London.

Sexton agreed to London, but Aziz then asked, "How will I be assured of payment if the panel decides in my favour?" Short of leaving their man in Jiddah until the dispute could be resolved, the client would have to post an irrevocable letter of credit with a Paris bank guaranteeing any award made by the ICC panel. Sexton advised the client to accept this, but drafted the letter of credit to be contingent upon the safe return of their man to Canada. Shortly thereafter, the client's representative got his passport back and came home; in the meantime, a Paris bank had the letter of credit awaiting the decision of an International Chamber of Commerce arbitration panel in London.

Under the terms of the agreement, the arbitration panel would consist of three members. Each side could choose one member, and the third would have to be mutually agreeable. Sexton's choice was Earl Palmer, an expert in company law and one of his professors at Western.[115] Aziz chose a Saudi jurist, and they agreed on an English barrister from Lord Denning's chambers as the third member of the panel.

In preparation for the hearing, Sexton was checking the terms of the letter of credit when he happened to notice something interesting. The contingency terms about the bank transferring funds in the amount of any award the panel might determine were all in order, but the remainder of the letter was a standard form provided by the bank. Included in the standard conditions was a two-year time limit, at the expiry of which the letter of credit was at an end. When he read this, Sexton thought, perhaps, they should use up a little time by presenting a motion for the determination of the panel prior to arguing the main issue in the dispute.

The purpose of the motion was actually two-fold. First, it would use up some time and hopefully make Aziz a little more interested in settling as the deadline got closer; and second, it would give Sexton a feel for the litigation process in an unfamiliar setting. He then wrote to Aziz' lawyer in Jiddah, saying that in his opinion the law which should apply in the arbitration should be the law of Ontario. Aziz' lawyer replied that in his view Saudi law should apply. Sexton then suggested that they have a preliminary motion before the panel to determine what law would apply. This, of course, would take some months.

When they appeared to argue the preliminary motion in London, Sexton had retained a professor of Islamic law from the University of London to accompany him. He told him to bring a law text written in Arabic with him to the hearing and to have it open on the table to a page with something relevant to the issue on it. Aziz was represented by a member of the English solicitors firm Freshfields & Williams, but while the Freshfields lawyer was speaking, Sexton put on his glasses and pretended to read the Arabic text. In fact, he doesn't understand a word of Arabic. After both sides were heard, the panel decided to reserve its decision; when it finally did decide that Ontario law should apply, about a year and a half had gone by.

By that point Aziz was becoming more interested in settling, but as the unspoken deadline for the letter of credit approached, Sexton refused to settle. He told Aziz' lawyer that they should hurry up and set a date for the main hearing before the arbitration panel. The date they agreed on happened to be twenty-five months after the posting of the letter of credit.

At the hearing, the first thing the Freshfields lawyer did was present a motion to have the panel force Sexton's client to renew the letter of credit. Sexton argued that the panel had no jurisdiction to amend the terms of the arbitration agreement by doing so, and the panel members agreed. At that point, Aziz and his lawyer went into conference; when they emerged, they invited Sexton and his client to accompany them to Jiddah to discuss a settlement. Sexton politely suggested that they host such a meeting in Toronto. Finally, they agreed to meet at a hotel in London. Sexton's client wanted to retain good relations with Aziz, because he wanted to sell him more lumber.

When Sexton and the client arrived at the hotel, however, the Freshfields lawyer was there, but Aziz was not. The Freshfields man apologized and explained that Aziz was not well. He asked that the meeting be held in his London flat. Sexton was a little nervous, but the client wanted to be as amicable as possible, so they agreed to accompany the lawyer to Aziz' flat. When they arrived there early in the afternoon, they were given the once-over by an armed guard and a video security camera before being allowed through a steel door into the flat itself. There was Aziz — all smiles and in a jacket and tie — with no sign of ill-health.

Aziz ushered them into the dining room and they all sat down around a massive table with at least five different coloured telephones on it. As the settlement negotiations went on, the phones kept ringing and Aziz would answer each in turn, issue some orders in Arabic, and then hang up. Finally, after some hours of discussion, they reached an agreement. Aziz agreed to drop his claim entirely if Sexton's client would sell him another shipment of lumber at cost. The client company was the sister company of a number of others, and ''cost'' could be virtually anything they wanted it to be. Sexton was sure that Aziz knew this, but it would allow him to save face at home.

They agreed to have the Freshfields lawyer go back to his office to have the agreement typed up and meet at Aziz' flat at 7:00 p.m. Sexton went out for a quick dinner and returned at seven. When they arrived, the man was there with Aziz, but before they could get the signatures on the document and leave, which Sexton was very anxious to do, the doorbell rang. When the door opened there was a tall, very well-dressed man accompanied by five young women. Aziz ushered them in and served drinks.

About an hour later, with the party still going on, Sexton was able to get his client and Aziz back to the dining-room table to sign the settlement agreement. But before they had done so, the doorbell rang again, and more people arrived. When Sexton looked around again, Aziz had disappeared. He asked someone where he was, and was told that he was taking a bath. Finally, after some time, Aziz emerged and sat down and signed the document. Sexton gathered up his client's copy and left.

Some months later Sexton happened to meet the man who had been held in Jiddah until the letter of credit had been posted with the Paris bank. He asked him if he feared that he might never be released. He said that yes he had; in fact, he had already begun negotiations with some fishermen who were willing to sneak him by boat across the Red Sea from Jiddah to the Sudanese coast. Some time after that, Sexton also received a call from the Department of External Affairs in Ottawa. They explained that a Canadian was stuck in Panama as the result of some commercial dispute, and said that they had given the man's employer Sexton's name, but he never heard anything more about it.

During the time Sexton was involved with the Aziz affair, Osler, Hoskin & Harcourt experienced one of the most significant changes, and certainly the most tangible change of the decade, when it moved to First Canadian Place in January 1977. The firm had been in the Prudential Building at the northwest corner of King and Yonge streets since 1962, but in the early 1970s they began to look at other options. In 1971, at the end of the original ten-year lease, the landlord raised the firm's rent from $6.80 to $8.30 per square foot. Even at that figure, the firm was paying less than the going rate in other buildings in the downtown area, and they decided to sign another ten-year lease for some 29,000 square feet on the fourteenth, sixteenth and seventeenth floors, for approximately $240,000 a year.[116] The firm then totalled fifty-six lawyers.

Over the course of the next few years, the firm continued to grow, and it slowly became apparent that the Prudential Building would soon not meet their needs. In October 1974, Allan Beattie wrote a very detailed memorandum to the Executive Committee discussing the firm's future accommodation:

In light of the continuing expansion of the firm and the rate at which we seem to be requiring additional space, I have been wondering recently whether we should be reconsidering longer range plans for either remaining in, or moving from the Prudential Building.

The problem with the Prudential Building, as we all know, is that the per floor area is rather small. We are beginning to find ourselves spread over too many floors in the building. On the other hand, at the moment, we are reasonably comfortable in the Prudential Building and can manage quite nicely at a reasonable rent in today's market. . . .

If we should decide that we should move from the Prudential Building in the next few years, it would not only be important to move only to a first-class building but, if at all possible, also to a building which would have with it an associated client relationship. It could be that the coinciding of these two elements might not fit into our own timing if we delay a decision on moving until we are pressed more heavily than we are at the moment.

In considering where we might move at some future date, the only two buildings that I see in the course of construction or contemplated which might be considered by us are the Bank of Montreal building and the Royal Bank Complex, where the timing of completion of construction might not be too bad for us. I do not see any client advantage in either of these buildings. The new Eaton Centre would have client advantages, but I think the complex is too far from the downtown business district to make this an attractive proposition for our firm.

The only buildings that I see at the moment in the downtown area which combine the two elements of prestige and client relationship are the buildings in the Toronto Dominion Centre. We have already rejected the Commercial Union Tower on the basis that its floor space (approximately 17,000 square feet) is too small.[117] I understand that any new building that might be constructed on the south side of Wellington Street would have the same disadvantage. I understand the original TD Bank tower has approximately 24,900 square feet of rental area, and the Royal Trust Tower has slightly in excess of 22,000 square feet. These floors are in the dimension of close to twice the size of our present floors in the Prudential Building.

For some time, we have been aware that the Toronto-Dominion Bank has been anxious to have our firm in their complex and Dick Thomson has spoken both to Fred Huycke and myself on a number of occasions.[118] Recently, I indicated to Dick Thomson that if any substantial amount of space became available in either the original building or in the Royal Trust Tower, we might be sufficiently interested to the point of at least having a look. I indicated that we were not in any rush, but we appreciated that having regard to the amount of space that we would require, the timing of such space becoming available and an ideal timing from our point of view might not necessarily coincide. Recently, we had been advised that there is a possibility of two floors coming available in the Royal Trust Tower, possibly in April 1976 or perhaps not until October 1977. These floors are the 10th and 11th floors and are presently under option to IBM. There seems to be a real possibility that IBM will not wish to exercise these options.

We are presently renting approximately 40,000 sq. ft. in the Prudential Building, so two floors in the Royal Trust Tower would not be sufficient. We would require at least control over one further floor and probably might require control over a total of four floors for the longer term.

A decision is required as to whether or not we are sufficiently interested in moving to the Royal Trust Tower in two or three years from now, that we should ask the TD Centre people to consider in greater depth whether or not they could accommodate us and suggest to them that they advise us more fully as to what they might offer.[119]

Beattie discussed his memo with the other members of the Executive Committee at their next meeting, but they did not come to any conclusions other than to keep the lines of communication open with the Toronto Dominion Centre.

In January 1975, the Executive Committee authorized Allan Beattie to conduct surveys of space availability and suitability in the TD

Centre as well as the new buildings being built for the Royal Bank and the Bank of Montreal.[120] In March, he presented a report to the Committee comparing hypothetical plans for occupation of two and a half floors in the Royal Trust Tower of the TD Centre, and one and a half floors in the new Bank of Montreal building at the northwest corner of Bay and King streets.

The firm would be spread over more floors in the Royal Trust Tower because the potentially available space was on the lower floors of the building, where there was relatively less interior space. Office towers of that size require banks of elevators which service different ranges of floors. The shafts of all the elevators take up a great deal of space on the lower floors, while those which service the uppermost floors take up considerably less space. In the new Bank of Montreal building, the firm could acquire space in the upper portion of the building.

For this reason, Beattie felt that, of the two buildings, the Bank of Montreal building option was more attractive. On the other hand, because of the client relationship with the Toronto-Dominion Bank, the Committee did not want to rule out the TD Centre too quickly. Perhaps they should stay in the Prudential Building for a few more years and hope that some space on the upper floors of the Royal Trust Tower would come open. The Committee agreed that, whatever their decision, they should make it soon.[121]

Over the summer and into the fall, Beattie and the others continued to discuss the office space situation. They ruled out the new Royal Bank Plaza because the limited space per floor would mean that the firm would be spread over too many floors. The options were really the TD Centre, if and when satisfactory space became available, and the Bank of Montreal building, which they learned would be called First Canadian Place. Allan Beattie favoured the latter option, because it was still under construction and so sufficient space would be available on the upper floors. The problem was that the TD Bank was a very important client; Fred Huycke, who was the partner in charge of the TD Bank file, suggested it might be worth waiting for suitable space in the TD Centre. Beattie pointed out that if they decided on First Canadian Place, there were indications that both the Bank of Montreal and Olympia & York, the owner of the building, "were prepared to give us a certain amount of legal work in the future."[122]

At partners' meetings in late September and early October, Beattie presented what the Executive Committee saw as the firm's three options. They could stay where they were indefinitely; they could move to First Canadian Place "where adequate accommodation is available, and there is some prospect of additional business"; or they could wait, and move into one of the towers in the TD Centre whenever satisfactory space became available. They decided to eliminate the first option, but could not make a decision between the other two. They simply acknowledged the merits of each: on the one hand, "the strong client relations we have with the TD Bank require us to consider seriously the prospect of moving to that complex even though this building is now ten years old and is judged to be inferior in comparison to the newer buildings now being erected." On the other hand, however, "the new Bank of Montreal building, both in terms of floor space facilities and location, would be highly appropriate for our purposes, and prospects for legal work from the Bank of Montreal and from O&Y are thought to be good."[123]

Over the course of the following months, they began to lean heavily towards moving to First Canadian Place. There were no further indications of satisfactory space becoming available in the TD Centre, but Beattie continued to meet with the people from Olympia & York. At a partners' meeting in February 1976, Beattie suggested "the possibility that we might even consider occupancy of two of the uppermost floors as of our options."[124] Such prestigious space would not be cheap, however; as Beattie explained to the partners in a meeting in May, he estimated that the annual rent in the upper reaches of the seventy-one-storey building would be in the range of sixteen dollars per square foot. This would mean over a million dollars a year in rent.[125]

At the partners' meeting in May 1976, they discussed all of their options fully, and passed a motion to move to First Canadian Place. Allan Beattie introduced the motion but, significantly, the seconder was Hal Mockridge.[126] Mockridge was an Oldsmobile man; he let other, more ostentatious lawyers drive Cadillacs. And when Blakes were in the Bank of Commerce building and Borden & Elliot were in the Bank of Canada building, he preferred the Prudential Building for Oslers. Yet here he was, seconding a motion to move his firm into the tallest building in the British Commonwealth.

The question of how big a step the firm was going to take was not, however, entirely finished. At a meeting of the partners on June 4, 1976, they discussed an offer from Olympia & York of a ten-year lease of the sixty-sixth and sixty-seventh floors of First Canadian Place, with an option for future expansion to the sixty-fourth and sixty-fifth floors, for sixteen dollars per square foot. As Beattie explained, the original plan had been to take the sixty-eighth and sixty-ninth floors, but Olympia & York had already completed substantial leasehold improvements on the sixty-eighth floor. If the firm insisted on taking this floor, it would cost an additional $100,000. The Executive Committee felt, therefore, that despite the fact that the view of Lake Ontario from the south side of the building would be somewhat blocked from the sixty-sixth storey down by the new Bank of Commerce building, the extra expense could not be justified.

At that point, a number of partners raised the question of whether the extra expense of leasing the upper floors of the building was justified at all. Rental rates on the lowest floors of the building were only $12.50 per square foot. With an initial occupation of some 60,000 square feet, this would mean a saving of over $200,000 per year. Moreover, was it wise to go against the more frugal traditions of the firm by taking up what was perhaps the most expensive office space available? Apparently it was, because when the question was put to a vote, a majority of the partners favoured accepting the lease proposal for the sixty-sixth and sixty-seventh floors, and in the following January the firm moved.

CHAPTER

8

THE CORPORATION: 1980-1994

By the late 1970s, the transformation of Osler, Hoskin & Harcourt was largely complete. That is not to say that the decade of the 1980s did not bring great changes to the firm, because clearly it did. In particular, the firm grew from fewer than one hundred lawyers in 1981 to almost three hundred in 1991.[1] As indicated in Chapter Seven, in 1981 the firm was at the end of a decade during which its average annual growth rate was 8.3 per cent; between 1981 and 1991, its annual rate of growth averaged almost 21 per cent.[2] Moreover, during the 1980s the number of woman lawyers in the firm grew substantially. In 1981, only sixteen of the firm's ninety-seven lawyers (16.5 per cent) were women; by 1991 seventy-five of the firm's 298 lawyers (25 per cent) were women.[3]

The changes of the 1980s were, however, only possible because of the fundamental transformation of the firm associated with the transition from the Mockridge generation to the Crawford generation. This process, which involved integral changes in the Osler style of practice and the locus of decision-making power within the firm, took place during the 1960s and 1970s.

The structure which allowed for the changes of the 1980s, including growth, was already in place by the late 1970s. Although Allan Beattie was clearly the most significant force in the management of the firm during that period, by the time he accepted an offer to leave the firm and become vice-chairman of Eaton's of Canada Ltd., he had passed the reins of decision-making power on to the entire Executive Committee. In the early 1970s, Beattie inherited Hal Mockridge's authority and exercised it in consultation with Purdy Crawford and Fred Huycke. By the 1980s, that authority — both formal and practical — rested with the Executive Committee in consultation with the rest of the partners.

The best example of that transition was the process of determining partnership splits. During Mockridge's day, he would decide who deserved what part of the firm's profits. When Beattie took over the management function, he approached it — like he did most things within the firm — by building a consensus among those whose opinion he, and the rest of the firm, trusted. He would draw up a handwritten split of the profits among the partners and then begin a process of consultation. He would walk around the partners' offices, beginning with Purdy Crawford and Fred Huycke, and work his way down the list on the existing share division. Not surprisingly, by the time he reached the lower levels there were very few changes made.

Like Mockridge, Beattie's primary goal in this exercise was to maintain a feeling of fairness and approval of the process among all of the partners. Also like Mockridge, Beattie's process involved a high degree of paternalism. Beattie had to work much harder at building a consensus, but the process was a relatively informal one, conducted among intimates. By the end of Beattie's tenure as managing partner, however, the process had, of necessity, become much more formal. The significant point, however, is how smooth the transition from paternal consensus-building to institutionalized profit-division really was.

In the early 1980s, Beattie began to use an ad hoc team of two Executive Committee members to assist him in the process. These two would go around and speak to each partner to get his or her views on how the profits should be divided. Beattie and his two assistants would then produce a first draft of the split. They would then take another tour of the firm to seek comments on their draft. Following this second tour, Beattie would produce the final draft and present it to the partnership for approval. This document would also be in Allan Beattie's handwriting only. Theoretically, all of the partners had the opportunity to express their views on how the profits should be divided, and each would have to initial his or her approval. In practice, however, the more junior partners were implicitly not expected to take part in the process.

In 1983, the firm took the formalization process one step further and made the determination of profit splits an official Executive Committee function. In the process, it also laid down specific criteria which were to be used. These included the amount and type of work each partner conducted, the profitability of that work, his or her involvement in developing new business for the firm, professional reputation and "power in the marketplace," involvement in firm administration, and contribution to "the significance of the firm." The process also became more formalized with the intent of bringing more of the partners into the active decision-making process. Several drafts of the split were produced for distribution, and all of the partners were encouraged to make comments.

The amount of directly generated firm income was obviously the primary criterion in determining the split, but this was tempered somewhat by the fact that the Executive Committee's instructions included a directive to be mindful of the fact that the partners considered Osler, Hoskin & Harcourt a "full-service" firm, meaning that they had a commitment to more than just the most profitable types of legal work. Moreover, contributions to the significance of the firm, which included such things as public speaking and publishing as well as law school and bar association involvement, although they clearly had a marketing function, were also felt to be a fulfilment of the firm's "professional obligation."

These were roughly the same criteria which Beattie, and even Mockridge before him, used to determine the partners' splits, but the key point here is that they had never been articulated before. Fairness, and even more importantly the perception of fairness, was still the goal. But where this had been possible in the old informal system without reducing the procedure to writing, the size of the firm now dictated that a formalized system be used.

Not surprisingly, however, even after the formalized procedure was put in place, the firm maintained the strengths of the old system. The splits were established to divide the profits on a prospective rather than retrospective basis, and even more importantly, all partners were privy to the information. The document was considered highly confidential and open only to the partners (in fact, the document still in the firm's records for the 1986 split is in Allan Beattie's handwriting), but unlike some other firms, every partner knew what every other partner's share was going to be.

In addition to the formalization of the split determination process, changes related to the firm's growth were evident in its practice. During the modern period, the firm's practice grew exponentially. Chris Portner, who joined the firm in 1980 after eight years in practice and business and later served on the Executive Committee, saw a fundamental transformation in the firm's practice. He attributed this transformation to three coincidental events of the 1970s: an explosion in the Canadian capital markets, the reform of securities law and the fact that Purdy Crawford was at the height of his career:

> The real authors of the new securities laws were Purdy Crawford and Howard Beck, of Davies Ward & Beck.* My perception — and it's only a perception — is that those events all coincided probably around the early to mid-seventies. And so with the boom in the capital markets, with the new expertise basically in two firms, Davies Ward & Beck and Oslers, and Crawford's prodigious capacity and ability and gregariousness, that's what transformed the firm, once and for all . . . from the old family compact to an aggressive, transaction-oriented meritocracy. It probably didn't happen in one day, but I suspect it happened within a relatively finite period of time.[4]

Prior to the mid-1960s, the law provided very little regulation of the securities industry in Canada. It is true that Ontario, the jurisdiction which housed the Toronto Stock Exchange and therefore the bulk of the industry, had a Securities Commission since shortly after the crash of 1929, but it had really very little effect on the industry.

In October 1963, less than a month before Texas Gulf made the mammoth strike at Kidd Creek which would eventually result in a storm of controversy surrounding the activities of mining stock promoters like Viola MacMillan, the Ontario provincial government established a special committee on securities legislation.[5] This committee, headed by John R. Kimber, then chairman of the Ontario Securities Commission, included the two best-known securities lawyers in the province: Hal Mockridge of Oslers and R.A. Davies of the firm then known as McDonald, Davies & Ward, as well as Howard Graham, then president of the Toronto Stock Exchange, and W.B. Common, the deputy attorney-general.[6]

Interestingly, while Mockridge and Davies, as the leaders of the securities bar, were perhaps the most influential members of the committee, the secretaries of the committee were the leaders of the next generation of the securities bar. They were Mockridge's partner Purdy Crawford and Davies' partner Howard Beck. In fact, it was these two men who drafted the legislation which Kimber recommended to the government in his report.[7] Following Kimber's report, the government brought in legislation in 1966 which completely

* See the reference to the Kimber Committee, below.

overhauled and expanded the Securities Act.[8] This was followed by a further major revision in 1978.[9]

The net effect of these securities law reforms was, like all other regulations, to provide more work for lawyers. In this case, it placed many more restrictions and limitations on how businesspeople could raise money; it also placed a great deal of discretionary power in the hands of the regulatory body — the Ontario Securities Commission. The intent was to protect the investing public and provide stability for capital markets, but the additional result was a much greater need for legal advice, for both securities issuers and investors.

It was not just legislative reform which brought about changes in legal practice. In the case of the firm's securities practice, changes in the corporate world were also very significant. The 1980s were the age of the corporate take-over. There were very few weeks which would go by without the business media reporting on some new or rumoured merger or acquisition, and each of these would require complex legal advice.

These massive transactions, often involving complicated financing and corporate reorganizations, were known as mega-deals, and they would very often employ literally dozens of lawyers as well as investment bankers and other consultants. It was this transaction-based practice which was, perhaps, the most striking change for many of the Osler lawyers. Because the transactions required a broad range of expertise in a variety of areas, each of which was becoming much more complex, whole teams of lawyers would work together.

A transaction such as the Molson-Carling merger of 1989, in which Oslers represented Molson, required corporate lawyers to provide advice on the terms of the deal, securities specialists to assist with the financing, members of the real estate department for the property considerations, and a host of others to deal with a range of matters including taxation and the federal government's competition regulations.

Marshalling a team of lawyers on a transaction like the Molson merger with Carling is not an easy thing to do. Simply meshing the various fields of law to focus on the deal is one thing, but overcoming lawyers' apparently inherent competitiveness is another. Setting aside for the moment the competition among lawyers representing the various parties on a transaction, and focusing only on those from the same firm, there are powerful economic and professional incentives working against the team.

If questions of profit splits and advancement into and within the partnership are based on client responsibility, individual lawyers' interests arc dependant on maximizing their own roles. In its most extreme form, an individual partner may be tempted to try to control all of the legal work for a client rather than share it where necessary with other members of the firm whose particular skills may be more appropriate. At Oslers, however, this danger has been largely avoided because the culture of the institution has long prohibited coveting of clients. Indeed, this is one of the most significant strengths of the firm.

This strength did not entirely preclude difficulties in determining the value of various practices within the firm, and therefore partners' shares. During the 1980s in particular, mergers and acquisitions represented a very profitable area of practice. Not surprisingly, those partners most active in this area were generally the highest share earners. During the boom years, when there was plenty to spread around, there was relatively little friction in the split process. When the recession hit at the end of the decade, however, it was apparently becoming more difficult to maintain the strong culture of community than it had been during the "fat" years.[10]

In particular, the firm's commitment to what had been termed "full-service" legal practice came into question. As Osler, Hoskin & Harcourt grew and expanded its areas of practice during the 1970s and 1980s, the partners began to describe the firm, with some pride, as a "full-service law firm." Exactly what the term meant, however, was not entirely clear. To most it meant being able to provide expert advice to any client, regardless of the nature of the legal problem. When pressed, however, most would also admit that the term included some implicit limitations.

They would agree that the term probably does not include criminal law. Although during the mid-1970s the Executive Committee gave a young associate permission to try a one-year experiment as a criminal law specialist, and during the early 1980s Allan Beattie and Purdy Crawford made a concerted, but ultimately fruitless, effort to convince a well-known criminal lawyer to join the partnership, the firm does not practise criminal law.[11] This is partly because of the type of clientele involved, but it is also largely a product of the fact that criminal law is generally not a lucrative area of practice.

Except in a very small number of highly publicized cases, such as the 1985-86 Helmut Buxbaum murder trial in which Eddie Greenspan's fee for his ultimately unsuccessful defense totalled some

$1,300,000, criminal law is a relatively unprofitable field.[12] Family law is another area which is relatively less profitable, and until 1986 Osler, Hoskin & Harcourt did not practise family law to any great extent. In that year the partners agreed to merge with an established family law firm, but in the process they had to deal with some fundamental questions about what it meant to be a full-service law firm.

Oslers merged with the Toronto family law firm of MacDonald & Ferrier. That firm dated from 1965 when Jim MacDonald and Lee Ferrier went into partnership together. They met while working with Gordon Ford, a Toronto civil litigator, in a firm known as Ford, MacDonald & Ferrier. MacDonald, who was originally from Western Canada, was called to the British Columbia bar in 1958. He practised for five years with the Vancouver firm Clark, Wilson, but in 1963 he decided to move to Toronto and joined Ford.[13]

When Ferrier, who articled with Ford, finished the Law Society's Bar Admission Course and was called to the bar in 1964, the three men decided to form a litigation firm. Ford, MacDonald & Ferrier only lasted a year, however, and in 1965 the two younger men formed MacDonald & Ferrier.

MacDonald & Ferrier continued as civil litigators, but on the advice of some other lawyers decided that they needed a more narrow specialty. The one they came up with was family law, which was not really a discrete specialty in the mid-1960s. Prior to the Divorce Act of 1968, the only ground for divorce in Canada was adultery, and lawyers who did divorces were anything but the leaders of the profession.[14]

In 1965, however, Prime Minister Lester Pearson struck a special joint committee of Senators and Members of the House of Commons to study the country's divorce laws and recommend reform.[15] By the time Justice Minister Pierre Trudeau introduced the legislation based on this committee's recommendations in early December 1967, it was obvious that Canadian family law was going to drastically change — and family law practice was going to change with it.[16]

The legislative changes introduced by the new Divorce Act of 1968, which included expanded grounds for divorce and significant alterations to spousal and child maintenance, were merely reflective of the social changes taking place at the time, but like virtually all other changes in the law, they brought about a greatly increased demand for legal advice. MacDonald and Ferrier began their specialized practice with this in mind.

The firm of MacDonald & Ferrier was very successful in its practice over the following twenty years. The two also became acknowledged experts in the field by virtue of the fact that they edited the most commonly used practice manual on Canadian divorce law.[17] They were also quite prominent in the legal profession. MacDonald was the director of the Law Society's bar admission program, and Ferrier was a bencher.[18]

By 1986, there were two more partners in the firm in addition to the two name partners.[19] More importantly, and in keeping with what was happening in almost all other areas of the law, their practice was becoming much more complex. Legislative changes such as Ontario's Family Law Reform Act of 1978 and the new federal Divorce Act of 1985 meant that family law practitioners were becoming involved in increasingly wider areas, including matters such as corporate law, tax, estates and securities.[20] Many family law practitioners found themselves retaining outside counsel on these types of matters. The firm that MacDonald & Ferrier most often retained was Osler, Hoskin & Harcourt.

As Ferrier remembered it, they could see that this trend was only going to continue, and from his firm's point of view they had to either bring in some people with more corporate expertise or merge with a firm which had it. From Oslers' point of view, family law was a field of law which they did not really service, and to some — but by no means all — members of the firm, a merger with a firm like MacDonald & Ferrier would be an ideal addition. Representatives of the two firms began informal discussions in the spring of 1986.

The reason that not all of the partners at Osler, Hoskin & Harcourt supported the idea of a merger was that family law was simply not as profitable as what they saw as the firm's mainstream corporate practice. To Allan Beattie, who presented the proposal of a merger to the partners at a special meeting held on June 11, 1986, the addition of an established family law group would help fulfil their commitment to being a full-service firm. Moreover, this was clearly the best family law firm to merge with. It was acknowledged as the leading firm in this new field; it was probably the largest firm solely dedicated to family law in Canada, if not in North America.[21]

Some others apparently did not subscribe to as wide a definition of the term "full-service." As it was put at the meeting, full-service meant that Oslers presented itself as being able to deal with any legal problem which a major Canadian corporation or international company doing business in Canada might have. This they could continue to do quite comfortably without the addition of a less-profitable family law practice.[22]

Nevertheless, after considerable debate the partners accepted Beattie's proposal and agreed to merge with MacDonald & Ferrier.[23] The incident was important in the history of the firm for a number of reasons. Most obviously, it provided another example of the firm's increasingly diversified practice during the 1980s; but more importantly, it showed how fundamental conflict over the very nature of the firm could be resolved — but only partially. Although the debate over the definition of the term ''full-service law firm'' was resolved for the moment, as Allan Beattie proudly put it after the meeting ''without a vote,'' the acceptance of a broad definition of the term did not remain universal, particularly when the boom years of the late 1980s came to an end.[24]

The MacDonald & Ferrier merger was significant in the history of the firm and, as will be outlined below, there were other significant mergers and lateral inductions into the firm. Nevertheless, like those of the 1970s, the majority of the lawyers who joined the firm during the 1980s did so as internal recruits. That is, they articled with the firm and joined as associate lawyers immediately after being called to the bar.[25]

Although articling positions in the major Bay Street firms were considered very prestigious among law students, and about two-thirds of all graduating Ontario LL.B. students applied to article at Osler, Hoskin & Harcourt, the market to attract the best articling students was very competitive.[26] There may have been a very high number of ''buyers'' — students seeking positions — in the market for articling positions, but for only a very small number of them was it truly a buyer's market.

The reason for this is that only a small proportion of the buyers had the necessary features to offer. That is, only that small proportion of students with the highest marks would be considered. The majority of students applying to the large firms were wasting envelopes and stamps. For the medallists and other Dean's list members, the Bay Street firms would pay. In the 1960s, an articling student would be lucky to earn $5,000 a year. By the late 1980s, the going rate was between $30,000 and $35,000. Moreover, virtually all of the law firms continued to pay that salary to students while they were attending the bar admission course, and some, including Oslers, were paying it to all of their students at the bar course, regardless of whether they had been offered associate positions on completion.

Although the salary was very good, the students worked very long hours to earn it. The pressure to work a lot came partly, of course, from the firm. Particularly during the boom years of the mid to late 1980s, the lawyers all had a great deal of work to do, and therefore the students did too. But the students also put pressure on themselves. Not all of them could expect to be asked to return to the firm as associate lawyers after being called to the bar. Although during the 1980s just over two-thirds of the articling students were asked back, few of them wanted to be included in the unlucky third who were not.[27] Students would, therefore, conform to what they saw as the standard workload, and many would try to go beyond it. In an era when some associate lawyers were approaching or even exceeding two thousand billed hours per year, this could make for an exhausting lifestyle.[28]

Many, perhaps most, of the students joining a firm like Osler, Hoskin & Harcourt knew very little about what life in a major firm would be like. Those few who had a parent or other relative who practised law in a downtown firm might have an idea, but the majority would not. None of the students hired at Oslers during the 1980s had a close relative with the firm. Since the early 1970s, the firm had an unwritten, but apparently adhered to, anti-nepotism rule in place.[29] In sharp contrast to the World War II generation, when the Osler and Huycke brothers had a virtually inherited right to join the firm, although many of the senior partners of the 1980s had sons and daughters who became lawyers, none of them joined the firm.

Interestingly, while the children of Oslers lawyers joined other firms, some of the students and junior lawyers who joined Oslers had fathers who were senior partners in other major firms. For example, Douglas Hamilton, who joined the Osler litigation department in 1989, was the son of Fred G. Hamilton of Hicks Morley Hamilton Stewart Storie; Amy Lewtas, who spent the summer of 1987 at Oslers, articled with the firm in 1988-89 and joined the corporate department as an associate after her call to the bar in 1990, was the daughter of James L. Lewtas of Campbell, Godfrey & Lewtas; and Mark Des-Lauriers, who joined the corporate department in 1983, was the son of Bill DesLauriers of Tory, Tory, DesLauriers & Binnington.[30]

There are clearly advantages and disadvantages of an anti-nepotism rule. Among the advantages, incoming associates and those nearing partnership can be confident that at least one formerly powerful subjective criterion will not play a part in determining their fate.

On the other hand, when Osler, Hoskin & Harcourt was still a family firm, it was relatively easy to maintain the common sense of community which has been one of the secrets of its success. Blood was literally thicker than water. In more recent years, the firm has had to work harder at maintaining a sense of collegiality and fairness among the partners and prospective partners.

Of course, as has been demonstrated in other firms, familial relationships are not always a guarantee against divisive acrimony. Moreover, it has not yet been determined what would happen if someone wanted to test the unwritten anti-nepotism rule that developed in the 1970s. It is entirely conceivable that the son or daughter of a senior partner in the firm may one day win a law school graduation medal and apply to work at Oslers. There are some who would argue that the firm is large enough, and the decision-making power spread widely enough, that a decision could be made without the partner/parent taking part.

On the other hand, there are also those who would argue that such a situation would remain very awkward throughout the young lawyer's early career. Because students and associate lawyers are continually evaluated for promotion purposes, and those doing the evaluation may very likely be junior to the partner/parent, such a situation would make their tasks much more difficult. For this reason, apparently the situation has not arisen.[31]

Still, despite the de facto prohibition on nepotism, the firm tried to maintain the values which were inherent in the old, family-based recruitment style. During the 1980s, the firm made very serious efforts to socialize the students into the culture of the firm. This included everything from regular students' and departmental luncheons to the annual Christmas party, where students continued to present skits and musical revues lampooning the partners.

To this end, the trend at Oslers, as at a number of other firms, during the decade was towards students joining the firm for a summer prior to finishing law school. One of the first of these was Clay Horner, who spent the summer of 1982 with the firm, between his second and third years at the University of Toronto law school.

The summer student experience could be a very valuable one for both the student and the firm. For the student, it was a highly prized, well-paying summer job, which provided direct, career-related experience, while most other students were spending their summers painting houses and waiting on tables. For the firm, it could provide an early advantage in recruiting the best students and a head start in the socialization process. On the other hand, it often meant that the student was "locked in" to that particular firm. Some firms, including apparently McCarthy & McCarthy, would not interview a student who had spent a summer with another firm for an articling position.[32]

As important as recruitment of students obviously was during the firm's growth years in the 1980s, it was not the only source of growth. In order to expand its practice as rapidly as it did, the firm needed more established lawyers who could bring not only their experience but their clients into the firm. For this reason, Osler, Hoskin & Harcourt made some serious efforts at both individual lateral recruitment and firm mergers during the 1970s and 1980s. For the most part, this expansion was very positive, but the process was not without danger.

Purdy Crawford, who was a very active participant in the expansion of the firm, felt that growth through mergers and lateral recruitment could be very positive, but he also felt that it had to be approached with extreme caution. There were many examples of firms in Canada and elsewhere which grew too fast and suffered as a result. The most dramatic was probably the New York-based firm of Finley, Kumble, which grew from six partners and ten associates in 1969 to over five hundred lawyers with offices in sixteen cities in 1988. In 1989 Finley, Kumble died in a spectacular and bitter meltdown of greed and venom.[33]

There were many reasons for Finley, Kumble's demise, but it is significant that the bulk of its growth occurred through equity "buy ins" of regional firms. That is, when the firm merged (or rather acquired) another firm, the partners in that firm paid a substantial fee to purchase equity in Finley, Kumble. This is not uncommon among law firms and other professional and business partnerships, nor does it necessarily lead to friction. It is significant, however, that Osler, Hoskin & Harcourt made it a policy never to require the partners of merging firms to contribute any additional equity to the firm.

Being careful about growth did not mean, however, staying small simply out of fear of change. Crawford uses the example of Donald S. Macdonald, the former finance minister, whom Crawford was unsuccessful in recruiting when Macdonald left politics in 1977. Apparently, Crawford and Macdonald were classmates in graduate school at Harvard, and when the latter was looking for a firm to article with in the spring of 1956, he came to Oslers. Norman Strickland, who was responsible for, among other things, interviewing potential articling students, ignored Macdonald's credentials, and told him the firm did not have room for another student.[34]

In Crawford's view, Strickland's response to Macdonald in 1956 was typical of an earlier generation's attitude towards practising law. Two and three decades later, when growth was seen as inevitable — even during slowdowns in the economy — a candidate like Macdonald would be quickly scooped up.

Christopher Portner, himself a lateral addition to the firm, saw the extent of the firm's willingness to recruit lawyers at a senior level as a fundamental difference between Oslers and the other major Canadian firms. This had become quite common in the United States, but until quite recently was uncommon in Canada. The main reason that this phenomenon was uncommon was that the partnership structure itself provides a disincentive to lateral admissions. When a new partner is brought in, his or her share of the profits comes out of the general pot. This means that the other partners must agree to have their own shares diluted. The assumption, of course, is that the admission will increase the overall profits more than his or her own share, but that requires a leap of faith on the part of the existing partners.

Moreover, it requires a willingness to place one's own interests at risk, for a common — albeit calculated — gamble. As Portner put it, "What I think that demonstrates, apart from a lot of foresight, is a high degree of willingness to compromise personal objectives to the greater good of the firm."[35] In addition to the disincentive of profit dilution, and perhaps even more important, is the fact that the lateral recruit will slot into the partnership above some, perhaps many, of the partners. In addition to placing their own economic position at risk, therefore, the partners must be willing to forego some degree of actual and potential power and status within the firm.

Portner pointed to Bob Lindsay in tax, Ed Sexton in litigation and Gordon Marantz in bankruptcy and insolvency as three of the best examples among many of this type of lateral recruitment successes. Like Lindsay and Sexton, both of whom are discussed in the previous chapter, Marantz joined the firm as a well-established practitioner and brought a very important area of expertise to the firm when he joined in 1985.

Gordon Marantz came to Oslers along with three younger colleagues — Arthur Birnbaum, Rupert Chartrand and Steven Golick — from the Toronto firm Smith, Lyons, Torrance, Stevenson & Mayer. Marantz, who was born in Toronto in 1936, grew up in Manitoba and graduated from the University of Manitoba in 1957. He then decided to return to Toronto for law school, and graduated from Osgoode Hall in 1960. After Osgoode, he took another year and did an LL.M. at Yale.

In the summer of 1959, between his second and third years at Osgoode, Marantz tried to find a summer job at a law firm. He asked his uncle, Charles Gavsic, the former president of the St. Lawrence Seaway Authority who had recently joined the Montreal firm then known as Common, Howard, Cate, Ogilvy, Bishop, Cope, Porteous & Hansard, for advice.[36] His uncle apparently made a phone call to Toronto, because some time later Marantz got a call from Dick Meech at Borden, Elliot, Kelley & Palmer. After a brief interview Meech offered him a summer job; Marantz worked there during the summers of 1959 and 1960, and returned for his articling year when he graduated from Yale in 1961.[37]

Marantz did not, however, finish his articles with Borden, Elliot. In the late fall of 1961, a group of partners decided to leave the firm and head out on their own. Borden, Elliot, itself at least partly a break-off firm, most of whose founding partners came from Fraser & Beatty, was then what Marantz termed a first-generation law firm.[38] It had grown to a twenty-eight-man firm and ranked third in the city in terms of size, but most of the decisions were still being made by B.V. (Pete) Elliot and two or three senior partners.

A group of eight of the middle-level partners at Borden, Elliot, therefore, announced in early December of 1961 that as of January 1, 1962 they would form their own firm to be known as Wahn, McAlpine, Mayer, Smith, Creber, Lyons, Torrance & Stevenson.[39] They also asked Marantz to come with them and finish his articles with the new firm. After discussing his options with Ted Creber and John Stevenson of the new firm as well as W. Gibson Gray, who urged him to stay with Borden Elliot, Marantz decided to go.[40]

Marantz was taking a gamble by deciding to go with the upstart firm. This was the first time that such a large group had left an established firm to form a new firm, and there was no assurance that they would be successful. As a student, Marantz might have given himself a bad reputation for leaving. As it turned out, of course, the firm which became known as Smith, Lyons was very successful, and after some twenty-two years in practice with the firm, so was Gordon Marantz.

By the 1980s, Marantz was one of the leaders of the bankruptcy and insolvency bar in Canada. Moreover, his field was becoming a much more important area of corporate legal practice. With the trend towards corporate reorganizations including multiple mergers and takeovers — many of them highly leveraged — fiscal instability was becoming much more common. And as in the other areas of the law, the legislatures and the courts responded to complex problems with complex law. The result was a greater need for expert legal advice. Marantz described the work that he and the rest of the small bankruptcy and insolvency team at Smith, Lyons did as "Everything from bitter partnership fights, shareholder fights in closely held companies to insolvency situations . . . anything that was a mess."[41]

Despite the success of his practice, by the early 1980s Marantz was not happy at Smith, Lyons. Ironically, the firm was much like the one its founders had left twenty years earlier. It was an excellent firm with a good reputation and client list, but it was a first-generation firm which was still very much managed from the top down. During the mid-1970s, they had introduced a two-tiered partnership, and those in the upper group, largely the founding partners, controlled the decision-making power. The most important decision this group had control of involved the partnership splits, which were done on a retrospective basis.[42]

By 1984, Marantz and two of his partners, Arthur Birnbaum and Rupert Chartrand, had decided they wanted to move to another firm. Birnbaum and Chartrand were both ten years younger than Marantz, but had been working closely with him for a number of years.[43] The question was, which firm should they approach? After quietly taking advice from people they knew in the profession and in business, Marantz and the others made up an informal, short list of possible firms. The first firm on the list was Osler, Hoskin & Harcourt.

In December of 1984, Marantz was doing some work with Bernard Wilson, a senior partner with the accounting firm Price Waterhouse. Marantz knew that the Osler firm was general counsel to Price Waterhouse, so he dropped a hint about changing firms. Wilson asked if he might consider moving if the people at Oslers were interested, and Marantz said "sure." A few days later, Marantz got a telephone call from Allan Beattie, and the two met to talk things over.[44]

To Marantz, Birnbaum and Chartrand, Osler, Hoskin & Harcourt was an attractive firm to move to because it had a very good reputation within the legal profession for fairness and collegiality, and an excellent client list; but perhaps most importantly, it was not particularly known for its expertise in bankruptcy and insolvency. The three could, therefore, play an important role in the firm.[45]

From the Osler perspective, the idea of inviting Marantz, Birnbaum and Chartrand to join the firm was also a very good idea, because the three lawyers were among the best in the field. Also, in addition to filling a gap in the firm's practice, bankruptcy and insolvency looked like an excellent hedge against downturns in the business cycle. Diversifying a law firm's practice, like diversifying in any business, is a way to cushion the blows of the market, but bankruptcy is perhaps the best such hedge. Because of the nature of this area of practice, its cycle of demand, unlike most other areas of corporate law, tends to run in inverse relation to the business cycle.

Marantz continued informal discussions off and on throughout the winter of 1985 with Allan Beattie and eventually Ed Sexton, but Marantz, Birnbaum and Chartrand were very concerned that word did not get back to Smith, Lyons that they were looking around. As Marantz put it, "If word had ever gotten out, our partnership distribution would have been about $1.85 for the year. Security had to be at the highest level, because our firm would have cut our hearts out if they'd known."[46] In May, just after the April 30 end of the Smith, Lyons fiscal year, Marantz and Beattie got down to formal discussions. In July, Marantz, Birnbaum & Chartrand came to agreements with Beattie about entering the Oslers partnership.[47]

The problem was, however, that the agreements had to be ratified by the partners at Osler, Hoskin & Harcourt, and the next meeting was not scheduled until September. There were some very tense days during August, and there were some difficult negotiations about what files they could take when Marantz and the others informed the other lawyers at Smith, Lyons that they were leaving. However, there was no problem when the proposal came up at the Osler partnership meeting, and the four lawyers moved into First Canadian Place on October 1, 1985.[48]

Marantz' view of the firm culture was, understandably, very positive. As he put it:

Nobody in this firm could say "This is *my* client." All the clients were here before these guys were born. So you have this tremendous sense that this is an institution. Everybody who is here is a trustee of this thing for the next generation. You come in from outside and [see that] the firm is a living organism. People are really proud of its tradition. Not only that, there's no fear in this place. It's . . . very democratic. You vote according to your share of the partnership, but in the five years I've been here, we've never had to have a vote on that basis.[49]

Marantz's view should, of course, be taken with a grain of salt. He was speaking about his own firm, and he was very happy with it. Nevertheless, it says something significant about the Oslers success. The firm had long since evolved from its founding generation, and by the time that Allan Beattie was chairing the partnership meetings, the firm itself was much more important than any of its individual members.

Significant lateral recruitment and mergers were not a new phenomenon for Osler, Hoskin & Harcourt. The first major merger was the original partnership of Britton Bath Osler and D'Alton McCarthy in 1882, and the tradition of bringing in a lawyer at the partnership level to fill a need in the firm's practice continued with people like Tom Delamere in 1942. During the late twentieth century, however, mergers and lateral recruitment were becoming much more common.

The first major merger of this period occurred in 1974 when the firm concluded agreements with two halves of what had been the old Toronto firm of White, Bristol, Beck. That firm dated to the early twentieth century, when Peter White, K.C., moved from the Ottawa River lumber town of Pembroke to Toronto to join Bain, Bicknell, Macdonell & Gordon. In 1922 that firm was, along with the Blake firm, the largest in Canada, with fourteen lawyers.[50]

Peter White, who became the leader of the firm by the Depression years, was one of the best-known litigation counsel of the first half of the twentieth century. His son, Peter White Jr., began articling with the firm when he graduated from the University of Toronto in 1934 and joined as an associate lawyer when he was called to the bar in 1937. After serving as an officer in the Royal Canadian Artillery during World War II, the junior White rejoined his father's firm as a partner in 1946. In turn, his son (also named Peter) would join the firm which, by 1969, was known as White, Bristol, Beck.

Although this firm was a significant factor in the Toronto legal profession, with clients including American Optical, St. Lawrence Cement, and National Grocers, by 1973 it had shrunk to five lawyers. Peter White (the second of three by that name, by then known as Peter White, Sr.) refused to lay blame on anyone in particular; instead, he pointed to the Osler firm, especially to Britton Osler and Hal Mockridge, as having the secret of success. According to White, the main reason why Osler, Hoskin & Harcourt prospered and grew, while other firms did not, was "generosity and fair dealing among partners and juniors."[51]

What White meant was that Britton Osler built the Osler firm by consciously taking out less than he put in. In other words, he paid a greater reward to junior lawyers and younger partners than they brought into the firm, because in that way he could develop in them a sense of loyalty to the firm. By doing this, and equally importantly, by insuring that no single partner could claim proprietary rights over the work or files of any single client to the exclusion of the rest of the firm, he could create a situation where the members of the firm believed that the whole was greater than the sum of its parts.

Of course, as White and others would be quick to point out, that is an all-too-easy explanation for success. There are a great many other factors involved, including luck, talent and connections. Moreover, it can be and has been a formula for failure as well. A junior lawyer faced with such a generous mentor may simply bide his time, cash his cheques, and wait for the right moment to leave for greener pastures, taking some prized clients with him. Even worse, he may decide when it comes time for him to occupy the senior position, and exercise generosity, to take the lion's share of the spoils. Fortunately for Britton Osler and his successors, neither of those things happened at Osler, Hoskin & Harcourt.

White, Bristol, Beck had been through all of that by the early 1970s, but it was also a very small firm in an age when firms were growing larger and larger. The five lawyers who remained in the firm in late 1973 held no animosity for one another, but decided to divide into two separate firms at the end of the year. As of December 31, 1973, White, Bristol, Beck dissolved, and White, White & Hendrie and Paulin & McDermott were born on January 1, 1974.

The third lawyer who joined the two Whites was Anthony O. Hendrie. Tony Hendrie, a member of an old Toronto family whose name was most closely associated with the Ontario Jockey Club, joined the firm (then known as White, Bristol, Beck & Phipps) as an articling student when he graduated from Osgoode Hall Law School in 1960. After he was called to the bar in 1962, he spent a year in London, England with the solicitors' firm Coward, Chance & Co.

Hendrie spent some time in the Canadian navy before going to law school, and he was very interested in admiralty law; Coward, Chance gave him an opportunity to practise some admiralty law, but within a year of going there he decided that he missed Canada too much and came back to Toronto. He rejoined White, Bristol, Beck & Phipps in September 1963. By 1973, Hendrie was a well- established corporate lawyer largely responsible for the National Grocers account.

Peter White, Jr. graduated from Osgoode Hall Law School in 1963, but he did not article at his father's firm. Rather, he spent his articling year with Osler, Hoskin & Harcourt. He returned to Oslers after his call to the bar in 1965, but in 1969 he decided to join White, Bristol, Beck & Phipps. As of 1973, he had a very healthy commercial real estate practice.

The other two lawyers, who formed their own partnership separate from the Whites and Hendrie in January 1974, were labour law specialists. Bradshaw Paulin was the senior of the two; born in Windsor, Nova Scotia in 1921, he was called to the Ontario bar in 1950. After practising briefly in Toronto, he joined Canadian Petrofina Ltd. in Montreal in the mid-1950s as an assistant solicitor. In the 1960s, he returned to Toronto to practise with a small firm and joined White, Bristol, Beck shortly after Peter White, Jr.

At thirty, Ted McDermott was much younger than his partner, but he was already a very accomplished labour lawyer. After graduating from the University of Toronto in 1964, he went on to law school at Osgoode Hall. While there, he spent a summer as a research assistant to his labour law professor, Harry Arthurs. After graduating from Osgoode in 1967, he articled with the Toronto labour firm, Miller, Thomson, Hicks, Sedgewick, Lewis & Healy; after his call to the bar in 1969, he spent a year as a clerk to Ontario High Court Chief Justice D.C. Wells. He then joined White, Bristol, Beck, and in 1971 he became a partner.

The first notice of the possibility of Osler, Hoskin & Harcourt gaining from the break-up of White, Bristol, Beck came at an Executive Committee meeting on February 12, 1974, when Purdy Crawford mentioned that he had had some preliminary discussions with Peter White Jr. about the possibility of White, his father, and Tony Hendrie coming to Oslers. The committee members knew the younger White quite well because he had practised with them for four years. They also knew the senior White and Tony Hendrie from working on a number of deals together. They encouraged Crawford to pursue the matter.[52]

A week later, Crawford hosted a meeting in the seventeenth-floor conference room in the Prudential Building with the Whites and Hendrie, as well as Allan Beattie, Fred Huycke, Jack Ground and Harry Boylan. Tony Hendrie remembered this meeting as being very informal; they discussed general matters such as firm structure and policy and the name of the firm. Hendrie remembers thinking when this last item came up, ''Ah, oh, I hope this doesn't stand in the way.''

But Peter White, Sr. said in his gruff, gravelly voice, "Well, there's no question; the name will be Osler, Hoskin and Harcourt." The firm was an institution which had existed under that name for almost sixty years, and the addition of three more lawyers wasn't going to make any difference.[53]

On February 26, Beattie reported to the Executive Committee that they had a very positive meeting, but that they had made no commitment. He then added that "the approval of any proposal should in his view be based upon general unanimity within the partnership, and that the existence of any substantial dissent or reluctance to these proposals within the partnership should mean that we should not proceed further."[54] It was quite significant that Beattie should insist on virtual unanimity of the partners regarding the addition of White, White & Hendrie. With fifty-eight lawyers already, thirty-eight of whom were partners, the addition of three more would not dilute the profit pool that much, but Beattie knew that it was essential that the partners be in agreement about the move. This was a firm decision, and all would take part.

As it turned out there was no opposition to the addition of the three men, and they joined the firm on April 1, 1974. One of the first things they learned after joining the firm was that Crawford and C.R. Osler had been conducting similar negotiations with Brad Paulin and Ted McDermott. Since the loss of the Inco labour file to Hicks Morley in 1970, the Osler labour practice had been somewhat in decline, and the addition of Paulin and McDermott's labour practice would be a real bonus.

On March 12, the Executive Committee discussed the possibility of inviting the two to join the firm, and they sent a memo to all partners asking their opinions. At the regular partnership meeting on March 27, the partners gave Crawford the message that they thought it would be a very good thing for the firm.[55]

The firm held a special meeting of the partners on April 3 to discuss the admission of Paulin and McDermott. This was the first meeting that the Whites and Hendrie would attend, and given the topic of discussion, they offered to stay away. Allan Beattie told them, however, that they were needed. They were partners, and in this firm all partners are expected to take part in decisions such as this.[56]

At that meeting, the partners agreed to offer Paulin a partnership, but there was a problem with McDermott. They all agreed that he was an excellent lawyer who would make a substantial contribution to the firm's practice; the problem was that he had only been in practice for five years. He had been a partner at White, Bristol, Beck since 1971, but at Oslers the standard waiting period for partnership was generally more than five years. Would it be fair to offer an outsider a partnership, when there were others in the firm who were just as senior as McDermott, but would have to wait to become partners?[57] There was some fear that Paulin might not agree to join if McDermott was not brought in as a partner, but in the end McDermott agreed to come into the firm as a senior associate lawyer with the prospect of partnership in a year's time.[58]

The most recent lateral appointments to the Osler partnership occurred in 1993 when John Evans, a leading member of the corporate bar, and two of his younger partners, Jean Fraser and Linda Robinson, decided to leave Blake, Cassels & Graydon where they had practised since their calls to the bar.* They approached Oslers as to the possibility of moving their practices across the street. Their admission to the Osler partnership was seen as a significant opportunity for the firm to increase both its profile and reputation in the corporate field and to add to its client base.

By far the largest merger for Osler, Hoskin & Harcourt was that involving the Ottawa firm Herridge, Tolmie in 1985. In the 1960s and 1970s, the trend among law firms in the United States was towards multi-city practices. The New York firms began opening offices in many of the other major cities throughout the country in the 1960s and early 1970s, and the regional firms began to expand outside of their original bases shortly thereafter. Just as the accounting firms had done earlier, American law firms began to compete with each other on a national level.

In the 1980s, this trend came to Canada. McCarthy & McCarthy was the first Canadian firm to expand on a national scale when it opened a satellite firm known as Black & Company in Calgary in 1981. They chose not to name the Calgary firm McCarthy & McCarthy in order not to overtly offend the rules of the Law Society of Alberta, which forbade interprovincial partnerships, but of the fifteen names under Black & Company in Calgary in the 1982 *Canadian Law List*, all but two were also listed under McCarthy & McCarthy in Toronto.

---

* This is indicative of the trend in the 1990s towards greater mobility within the legal profession. In fact, several Osler partners also made moves to other firms in this period.

McCarthys ended up having to fight the Law Society of Alberta in court, but in the end the firm won the right to establish an interprovincial partnership when the Supreme Court of Canada found in its favour in April 1989.[59] Eventually, McCarthy & McCarthy opened branch offices in Ottawa and London, Ontario, and merged with existing firms in Vancouver and Montreal.[60]

At the time, the lawyers at Osler, Hoskin & Harcourt watched what their colleagues at McCarthys were doing with interest. Expansion outside of the main office location was not a new thing. B.B. Osler, whose main office was in Dundas in the 1860s, set up a branch office in Hamilton; and McCarthy, Osler, Hoskin & Creelman had a satellite office in Regina in 1883.[61] Similarly, in the 1970s and 1980s, the Ottawa firm of Gowling & Henderson opened offices in Toronto and Cambridge, Ontario, and Blake, Cassels & Graydon and Fraser & Beatty each had offices in suburban Toronto.

In the 1980s, the Osler partners looked at a number of options for expansion. Following the move to First Canadian Place in 1977, the firm's non-active files were moved to less expensive storage facilities off-site. A few years later, the suggestion was made that some administrative functions of the firm could be treated in the same way. The accounting, printing and mailing departments, for instance, might be located in less expensive office space away from the downtown core. The partners concluded, however, that the cost savings of such an arrangement would not be worth the inconvenience and delays.[62]

Another option was to move certain legal staff outside of the downtown core. The firm could, for instance, set up a branch office in Markham, as Blake, Cassels & Graydon had done, and it could move either a complete department there, or staff it with a cross section of lawyers from the firm. Ultimately, the partners decided that such an office could not serve the firm's major client base, which was largely centred in the downtown core, any better. It was also argued that such a satellite office would, inevitably, be regarded as a second-class operation.[63]

The firm could also follow the McCarthy & McCarthy example and open an office in another province outside of Ontario, but in addition to the legal impediments which McCarthys were dealing with in the courts, the partners at Oslers felt that because their major clients were already national in scope and quite satisfied in dealing with a Toronto legal office. Offices in other provinces would offer no particular advantages.[64] Moreover, interprovincial expansion would certainly bring conflict of interest problems with it. The broader the firm's client base became, the more likely it would be to have to turn potential new clients away because their opponents in litigation or business competitors were already clients.[65]

Nevertheless, the firm was still interested in some form of expansion outside of Toronto; the most logical place to start was Ottawa. It was in Ontario; therefore, there would be no problem with Law Society qualification or rules. More importantly, it was the national capital. Not least because of the free trade agreement of 1987, the 1980s saw dramatically increased integration of Canadian business and trade with the United States. The U.S. model of the major law firm generally included a Washington office, partly to serve a government lobbyist function, but also to provide a federal regulatory practice. American clients expected that a Canadian law firm should have an office in the Canadian capital.

The next question was, should the firm move a few partners to Ottawa to establish a true satellite, or merge with an existing firm there? Oslers began to seriously consider this question late in 1984, when the Practice Development Committee (a committee of the partners first formed in the 1970s) established an Ottawa office sub-committee. In January 1985, this sub-committee submitted a preliminary report suggesting that the firm move two to three partners and three to five associates to Ottawa in order to serve the firm's existing clients in a federal regulatory practice.[66]

At their meeting in early March 1985, the partners discussed this option as well as the possibility of coming to an arrangement with an existing Ottawa firm. In outlining the latter option, Ed Sexton explained to the meeting that such an arrangement could range from a semi-autonomous sharing relationship between the firms to a complete merger of the partnerships. He then told them that informal discussions were already taking place with an Ottawa firm. After some debate, the partners approved continued discussions with a view towards a possible formal relationship.[67] The firm they had opened negotiations with was Herridge, Tolmie.

Herridge, Tolmie was born at the end of World War II. The key founding partner was a young federal government lawyer named Ross Tolmie. Tolmie, who was born in Manitoba in 1908 and was called to the British Columbia bar in 1932, had been a member of the federal civil service since 1935. He was counsel to the Income Tax Division from 1935 to 1941, and a solicitor with the Department of Finance from 1941 to early 1946.

Through his work in the tax field, which included serving as an editor of the CCH Taxation service, Tolmie could see the impact that the unprecedented level of federal government regulation was having on business. This was certainly not going to end with the war; the need for skilled government relations lawyers to help steer business through the regulatory maze in areas such as foreign exchange control, rent and price controls, as well as income tax, would continue. He decided that when the war was over, he wanted to set up a law firm in Ottawa specializing in the new areas of regulation, which he called federal law, and in patent law, the traditional area of government regulation.

During the war, Tolmie talked his idea over with a number of friends and acquaintances, including Glenn McPherson, a fellow federal government lawyer who was then executive assistant to the Secretary of State, and Ross Gray, a young air force officer who had left Osgoode Hall Law School midway through his final year to enlist.[68] Tolmie knew, however, that if the firm was going to get off the ground, it was going to need more than just a few bright young practitioners; it was going to need a name lawyer — someone who was plugged into the Ottawa establishment, and who could give the firm credibility. In fact, Tolmie himself was not even a member of the Ontario bar, and he had spent almost his entire career to that point working in government. The man he decided to approach with his idea was William Duncan Herridge.

The Honourable W.D. Herridge was certainly a name in Ottawa. Born in Ottawa in 1888, Herridge had been Canadian ambassador to Washington during the early 1930s and was former prime minister R.B. Bennett's brother-in-law. He was a politically active Conservative who wrote many of Bennett's speeches for the successful election of 1930, and was widely credited for Bennett's ill-fated "Little New Deal" policy shortly before his defeat by Mackenzie King in 1935. During the early years of the war, he headed a movement known as New Democracy, a federal wing of the Social Credit Party.

Herridge was also a very well-established patent and trademark litigator, whose most famous case was *Coca-Cola Co. of Canada Ltd.* v. *Pepsi-Cola Co. of Canada Ltd.*, which he took to the Privy Council on behalf of Pepsi-Cola in 1942 and won.[69] He was called to the bar in 1912, and after serving in World War I, he set up practice in Ottawa in partnership with George F. Henderson. He stayed with Henderson, Herridge & Gowling (the predecessor of Gowling &

Henderson) until World War II, when he joined Aylen & Maclaren (the predecessor of Scott & Aylen) as counsel.

In addition to his name and connections, and his established trademark litigation practice, Herridge had two key clients to bring into the new partnership. One was General Aniline and Film Corporation, and the other was Pennie, Edmonds, a large New York patent and trademark law firm. Herridge and Tolmie went into partnership in the winter of 1946, with Ross Gray as their associate. McPherson decided not to join them, but instead accepted a post as a member of the Canadian Military Mission to the Allied Control Council in Berlin. He ultimately went into business in British Columbia and became chairman of Okanagan Helicopters Ltd. in Vancouver.[70]

Office space was a major problem for the new firm. Offices were as scarce as refrigerators and cars in the capital right after the war. Herridge still had an office on Sparks Street which he rented from Aylen & Maclaren, and Tolmie was working out of a little office he rented from the Aluminum Company of Canada in the Victoria Building at 140 Wellington Street across from the Parliament Buildings. When they brought Ross Gray in as a junior in March of 1946, he had to use the coffee table in the Alcan waiting room for a desk. They were lucky enough in the early summer, however, to be able to sublet some space in the same building from the New Zealand High Commission.[71]

The new firm was apparently quite busy right from the start, because after the war Canadian business was eager to get back on its feet. This meant lots of patent and federal regulatory work for Ottawa lawyers. For Gray, however, it was not yet an affluent profession. As an air force wing commander, his pay was $12,000 a year, but Herridge, Tolmie paid him $250 a month.[72]

For the first couple of years, Herridge, Tolmie was a three-man firm. Ross Tolmie practised federal law, a largely regulatory practice, and W.D. Herridge practised in the various fields of intellectual property law, with Ross Gray acting as his junior. In 1948, however, they brought in a fourth lawyer; Jack Coyne was the son of James Coyne, a former Winnipeg lawyer who was then on the Manitoba Court of Appeal. Early in his career, Justice Coyne acted for the Crown in the sedition trials following the Winnipeg General Strike of 1919. Justice Coyne's other son, James Jr., was the governor of The Bank of Canada whom Prime Minister John Diefenbaker fired amidst a storm of controversy in 1961.

Jack Coyne was born in Winnipeg on June 20, 1919, in the middle of the general strike. After graduating with a bachelor's degree in history and economics from the University of Manitoba in 1940, and serving in World War II, he took up a Rhodes Scholarship to study law at Oxford. He accepted a B.A. in Honours Jurisprudence from Oxford in 1947, and in the same year was called to the bar of Lincoln's Inn.[73]

Coyne did not practise as a barrister in England, but decided to return to Canada. He was called to both the Manitoba and Ontario bars in 1948 and joined Herridge, Tolmie. He began practice as Ross Tolmie's junior, eventually specializing in federal administrative law and the law of international trade. A year after joining the firm, he was invited into the partnership.

Throughout the 1950s, Herridge, Tolmie did largely intellectual property and federal law, although they also did some local real estate work, and by the late 1950s they were doing some corporate work. Although their patent client list grew substantially from the three or four which Herridge brought in, they remained much smaller than Smart & Biggar and Gowling & Henderson, the two largest intellectual property firms in Canada.

By the mid-1980s, Herridge, Tolmie was a firm of twenty-one lawyers, and it was the third largest in Ottawa.[74] The people at Osler, Hoskin & Harcourt thought it would be a very good candidate for a merger, because it had an excellent reputation and client base, and it seemed to have a good cultural fit with Osler, Hoskin & Harcourt. On May 27, 1985, Ed Sexton reported again to the partners on the discussions taking place with Herridge, Tolmie.

One of the major considerations, Sexton explained, was what to do about potential conflicts between existing clients of the two firms. He did not mean conflicts between litigation clients. The law forbids two members of the same law firm from representing contesting parties in a lawsuit, and if there had been any ongoing litigation in which an Osler lawyer represented one side and a Herridge, Tolmie lawyer represented the other, one or more likely both lawyers would have to step down from the case before a merger could take place. Apparently there were no such obvious conflicts.

What Sexton meant was potential business conflicts. Many clients are uncomfortable using a law firm or advertising firm which has a major competitor as a client. Oslers, for instance, which includes Molson among its clients, has never represented Labatt's; similarly, with General Motors and Coca-Cola as clients, Oslers has not represented Ford or Pepsi Cola. When Procter & Gamble became a client, it was under the explicit understanding that the firm would have no connection with any of the other "soap companies."[75] If such a business conflict between Oslers and Herridge, Tolmie were to appear, it could prove to be difficult to resolve.

Nevertheless, this potential conflict did not materialize; nor did the problem of the post-merger name of the firm. Like the White, Bristol, Beck merger of some eleven years earlier, the name of the new firm could become a sticking point, particularly when the name partners of the smaller firm are still active leaders of the firm. At one point in the negotiations, however, Ross Gray said simply the name should continue to be Osler, Hoskin & Harcourt, and the merger became effective November 1, 1985.

Once the Herridge, Tolmie merger was complete and the firm had an office in Ottawa, the Executive Committee began to look at further expansion. As they saw it, they had two options; they could continue beyond Ottawa and open offices or merge with existing firms in other Canadian cities. Many of their competitors were doing that. In addition to McCarthy & McCarthy, which had offices in Calgary and elsewhere, Stikeman, Elliott, the firm which tax specialist Heward Stikeman started in Montreal after World War II, had offices in Toronto, Ottawa and Vancouver.[76]

Oslers ruled out interprovincial growth, in the short run at least. The major problem was the increased likelihood of client conflicts. Moreover, the firm already had excellent relationships with existing firms in other Canadian cities which brought a great deal of referral and multi-firm transaction work. There was no point in going into direct competition with those firms. Instead, they would step into the international market — eventually in a cooperative venture with two other Canadian firms.

Osler, Hoskin & Harcourt started its international expansion in 1987, when it opened an office in London, England. The lawyers stationed there were neither English solicitors nor barristers; they were, therefore, not qualified to practise law in the United Kingdom. What they were there to do was give advice on Canadian law to British clients interested in doing business in Canada and to act as local facilitators for Canadian clients with interests in the U.K.

The London office was considered a success, and the firm was interested in continuing the international expansion to other cities, but this was a very expensive proposition. The solution to both was to enter into a cooperative venture with another Canadian firm. The

Montreal firm of Ogilvy, Renault had opened its own office in Paris in 1987, and like Oslers it was finding the European experiment a success, but although the idea of expanding to other cities was very attractive, it was also very expensive.

The two firms began negotiations about trying to coordinate their London and Paris offices early in 1989. The problem was how to deal with the fact that these two firms would remain competitors within Canada, while becoming partners outside of Canada. How could each trust the other not to steal a client when the opportunity inevitably arose? Both acknowledged, however, that in order to make the international partnership work they would have to respect each other's domestic client relationships.

Once that hurdle was crossed, the technical details of establishing an international partnership were relatively easy. A press release issued by both firms on May 9, 1989 announced the creation of a new, international law firm, to be known as Osler Renault. Both firms would continue to operate independently within Canada, but each would be a partner in Osler Renault. They would, therefore, share the costs, and the benefits of both the London and Paris offices.

A little over a year later the two firms continued this expansion when they brought the Vancouver firm of Ladner Downs into the international partnership. They announced in August of 1990 that they would take over the office that Ladner Downs had established in Hong Kong, and they would open a new office in New York in October. In only four years, Osler, Hoskin & Harcourt had gone from a single office in First Canadian Place in Toronto to a second full-service office in Ottawa, and membership in an international partnership with offices in London, Paris, Hong Kong and New York. At the end of 1993, Ladner Downs left the partnership; Osler Renault retained the office in Hong Kong, and in October of 1994 opened an office in Singapore.

The international expansion of the firm during the late 1980s was a dramatic manifestation of the general transformation which the firm had undergone during the decades following World War II, but it was only one of many. One of the most profound differences in the firm, one which Hal Mockridge and certainly Britton Osler would find more than a little surprising, was what became known as practice development.

As explained above, Hal Mockridge was from the old school of the legal profession, and he learned most of what he took to be the fundamental values of practising law from his uncle, Britton Osler.

Neither of those men would have approved of, let alone taken part in, a marketing program for the firm. Yet, as even Mockridge realized towards the end of his career, the market for legal services in Canada was fundamentally changing during the 1960s and 1970s. This trend, which saw a much greater degree of liquidity among client/firm relationships, accelerated during the 1980s and into the 1990s.

The fact that lawyers like Purdy Crawford were able to not only adjust to this fundamental change, but compete very successfully in the new marketplace, says a great deal about the firm. During the 1970s and 1980s, Osler, Hoskin & Harcourt not only kept its long-time clients including Inco, Eaton's, General Motors and Kodak, but it gained a number of important new clients, including Nova Corporation and the Oxford Development Group.[77]

The Purdy Crawford style of "rainmaking," which Britton Osler would have undoubtedly considered somewhat distasteful, was, by the 1980s, the norm. In addition, by the late 1980s, Oslers, like many accounting firms and some law firms, had a director of marketing. Although it was still often difficult to convince lawyers to become marketing oriented, there was no doubt that the era when the extent of law firm marketing was lunching at the Toronto Club was long gone.[78] The firm even had its own private box in the SkyDome.[79]

There were also other, less obvious ways which served to market the firm. In 1979, for instance, Ron Atkey, one of the partners in the firm, won a seat in the House of Commons and was appointed to Prime Minister Joe Clark's cabinet. Of course, a partner in the firm serving as a Member of Parliament was not something new. D'Alton McCarthy was an M.P. throughout much of his career, and his nephew Leighton took over the Simcoe North seat after his uncle's death in 1898. But no one in the firm had been an active politician since Leighton left to found McCarthy & McCarthy in 1916.

In fact, there was some evidence to indicate that public political partisanship could be a detriment to the firm. The image it wanted to project was one of impartial, technical expertise. Being tied too closely to one party or another might act as a detriment. Nevertheless, Atkey's position as a cabinet minister brought the firm into public prominence.

Ron Atkey originally came to the firm in 1974. Prior to that, he spent two years in Parliament as the Conservative Member for the Toronto riding of St. Paul's. Although he sat on the opposition benches across from Prime Minister Pierre Trudeau's governing Liberals, he gained invaluable experience as the opposition leader Robert Stanfield's spokesperson on corporate affairs.[80]

Atkey did not have any experience practising law. Prior to his election to Parliament in 1972, he was a member of the faculty at Osgoode Hall Law School, and in July 1974, when he went down to defeat along with a great many of his Conservative colleagues as Prime Minister Trudeau rebounded from his minority position to form a majority government, Atkey had to make some difficult decisions. His first option was to return to Osgoode, where he enjoyed tenure and had been on parliamentary leave. His other option was to go into practice.

He had a prior relationship with McMillan, Binch, for whom he had done some outside consulting on competition law matters. In fact, the day after the election he received a call from some friends there asking if he might like to talk about joining them. Going into practice with a major firm was very attractive. For one thing it would mean a considerably higher income than going back into academics. Moreover, during his time in Ottawa, he found that he very much enjoyed working in the real world. The academic life is a satisfying one, but being a thoughtful observer is not the same thing as being a participant.

Atkey did not, however, accept the offer from McMillan, Binch. Instead, he accepted one from Osler, Hoskin & Harcourt. Jack Ground and Purdy Crawford happened to be Atkey's neighbours; Ground was involved in the Conservative riding association and, although Crawford tended to more often support the Liberal Party, Atkey knew them both relatively well. They both felt that the firm could benefit from the addition of someone with considerable public law expertise and knowledge of federal regulatory law, and they made him an offer. He was well aware of Oslers' reputation, and he found their approach to the future very attractive, so he accepted.

Atkey joined the firm initially as an associate, salaried lawyer. The understanding, however, was that after a year's time he would be considered for admission to the partnership. In September 1975, the partners decided to invite him to become a partner when the current term expired April 1, 1976.[81] He made it clear at the time that he still entertained political ambitions but, in the meantime, he was happy to stay with the firm.[82]

In February 1976, Atkey acted as Flora Macdonald's campaign manager in the Conservative leadership convention, and led her supporters across the arena floor when she withdrew to throw her support behind Joe Clark. The following September he informed his partners at Osler, Hoskin & Harcourt that he intended to seek the Conservative nomination in St. Paul's. In 1978, he received the nomination from his old riding association, and when Prime Minister Trudeau finally called a general election 1979, Atkey won back his seat in Parliament.

When Joe Clark formed his minority government following the election, he asked Atkey to serve as minister of Employment and Immigration. Although D'Alton McCarthy and his nephew Leighton had been able to serve as Members of Parliament while maintaining their partnerships in the firm during the late nineteenth and early twentieth centuries, as a member of the government Atkey would have to resign from the firm. Even to maintain an understanding that he could rejoin the firm when he left politics would be a conflict of interest. He did not, however, expect to be returning to private life nearly so soon as he did.

The events of December 1979 through February 1980 are well known to observers of Canadian politics. After Joe Clark formed a Conservative minority government, his minister of Finance, John Crosbie, introduced a budget. On December 13, during the course of debate over the budget, the government lost a non-confidence motion. As parliamentary practice dictated, Clark and his ministers, including Atkey, were forced to resign.

Pierre Trudeau, who had already announced his intention to resign as leader of the Liberal Party, changed his mind, and in the ensuing election held on February 18, 1980 the Liberals once again won a majority of seats. One of the seats the Liberals won was St. Paul's. On the night of the election, Trudeau opened his victory speech with the words, "Welcome to the 1980s." A few weeks later, Osler, Hoskin & Harcourt said to Ron Atkey, "Welcome back." At a partners' meeting on March 13, 1980, they voted unanimously to invite Atkey back, and he accepted.

In 1985, the firm went through what many feared would be a very difficult period. The fact that it was not nearly as difficult as was feared was very significant. In June of that year, Purdy Crawford left the firm to become president and chief operating officer of Imasco Limited, the Montreal holding company whose primary division was Imperial Tobacco. Crawford was Oslers' leading rainmaker and for fifteen to twenty years the driving force behind much of its growth and evolution. On the day Crawford formally announced to his partners that he was leaving, a special meeting was held at 5:00 p.m. He had tears in his eyes as he told them, and many who had no previous inkling of his decision were in shock. They were afraid of what would be left of the firm after he was gone. But their concerns turned out to be unfounded.

Crawford had been on the Imasco board for a decade, and the idea of accepting an executive office position in the company, with an understanding that he would eventually take over as its chairman, came up quite some time before he made the decision to move. One of the considerations he had to deal with was the effect his leaving would have on his law firm. Although he modestly claimed that his contribution was only one of many, he knew what his role was. More importantly, however, he knew the firm, and he knew that its strengths were its own, not just his or any other individual lawyer's.

Crawford's lifestyle was quite a bit different after leaving Oslers. It was certainly not slack by any estimation, but when asked to compare his working life as chairman of Imasco with that when he was practising law, Crawford thought, and responded, "I don't put the long, long hours in. I miss the friends, the colleagues, but I don't miss being involved in a weekend-long deal."[83] As a corporate executive, he had more time for things such as serving as chancellor of his alma mater, Mount Allison University.

Crawford's departure was certainly traumatic for the firm, but as he put it:

> If I was at Oslers today, I would have been in a nice sort of way pushed aside. The other guys would be getting the clients, and I'd be getting less of that; I'd probably be on a lot of very interesting boards and still playing a significant role, but I think actually it was very good for Oslers that I left. It gave all of these bright young guys a chance to come forward.[84]

What Crawford said is undoubtedly true. His leaving brought about a forced rejuvenation at the top of the firm. Lawyers like Peter Dey and Brian Levitt, who had learned by watching Crawford, became the new corporate rainmakers.[85]

An equally significant, if less dramatic, departure occurred less than two years later when Allan Beattie left the firm to become the vice-chairman of Eaton's of Canada Ltd. His leaving was, in fact, part of another stage in the evolution of the management of the firm. Beattie had been managing partner since the mid-1970s, but in late 1986 the firm decided to eliminate the position and replace it with a four-person Management Committee. Beattie was a member of the

Committee, but it also included Chris Portner, Jim Smellie from the Ottawa office, and Larry Hebb as chairman.[86] Beattie served on the new Management Committee for a few months of orientation, but in early 1987 decided to accept a long-standing offer from Eaton's.

The thinking behind the establishment of a Management Committee to replace the position of managing partner was that the management of the firm had become too much for one person to maintain responsibility for while still retaining at least a limited legal practice. They hoped that by spreading the responsibility among four people no one would become completely removed from practice. After two years, however, they found that the same thing was happening — except there were more people involved. Larry Hebb, in particular, was spending almost all of his time on firm management matters. In early 1989, the partners agreed, therefore, to return to a modified form of the old system and appoint Larry Hebb as the managing partner of the firm.

In effect, the partners had admitted that it was no longer possible to manage a law firm of their size on a part-time basis. As Larry Hebb explained it, "As a practical matter, I ended up getting completely consumed by the thing and Chris [Portner] giving up more than half of his time."[87] If they were going to have the manager(s) of the firm virtually completely removed from practice, they might as well try to limit the effect to as few people as possible.

The problem was that not only would the lawyer/manager lose practice skills and client contacts, he or she would lose the knowledge base provided by active involvement in a rapidly changing legal environment. Even though the theory was that the managing partner would hold the position for a limited period of time before returning to full-time practice, Larry Hebb acknowledged that it could prove to be a difficult task to reacquire the skills for full-time practice.[88]

The logical solution, from the layperson's point of view, would be to hire professional managers and administrators to run the firm, and let the lawyers practise law — but lawyers have been very reluctant to do that. Although throughout the 1980s the firm continually delegated more administrative authority to its senior non-legal staff, the partners still saw themselves as a group of owner-operators. Because they operated in a very high-level corporate environment, and they saw themselves as professionals, they were anxious to make their firm as innovative and efficient as possible, but delegating increasing authority to a management structure in which non-lawyers play a significant leadership role is difficult. Nevertheless, in the late 1980s the firm recognized the need for more sophisticated professional management in creating the non-legal role of managing director.

A formal management structure was an inevitable consequence of growth, just as growth was apparently a prerequisite to survival. By the 1980s, Osler, Hoskin & Harcourt had become a virtual corporation. It was not a corporation in the legal sense. It was still legally a partnership, but in many others it was a functioning bureaucracy. This made it increasingly difficult to maintain the sense of community which had been one of the firm's strongest features since its inception. That tension between increasingly businesslike efficiency to cope with growth and change, and the importance of maintaining a sense of community was one of the most important themes of the 1980s. Nevertheless, the partners, and the managers, continued to strive to maintain the feeling that the whole was greater than the sum of its parts, and at the time of writing they appeared to be succeeding.

FROM COMPACT TO CORPORATION
— AND BEYOND

After more than 130 years, what is historically significant about the law firm Osler, Hoskin & Harcourt? Certainly, there are many things which make it an important part of Canadian history. From the trial of Louis Riel to the modern massive corporate takeover, the firm has been involved in some very significant events in Canadian political, economic and legal history. But perhaps its mere survival is most significant; there are only a small number of institutions of any kind which have survived the great changes this country has experienced since the mid-nineteenth century. Among those are a handful of law firms, including Osler, Hoskin & Harcourt.

Explaining that survival is much more difficult than acknowledging it. The secret of the firm's success is, at least in part, its ability to adapt to change. In 1882, when Britton Bath Osler and D'Alton McCarthy came together to forge their compact, they could see that the growth of Canadian industrial capitalism was going to greatly increase the demand for corporate legal expertise. They were able to take the strength of their own reputations, built on the traditional base of litigation, and develop a comprehensive, corporate law firm. Similarly, as post-World War II Canadian society began to reject established, paternal structures of authority, Hal Mockridge was able to oversee the start of a modern transition in the firm's governance.

In the process, the leaders of the firm — from B.B. Osler and D'Alton McCarthy to Purdy Crawford and Allan Beattie — were able to maintain an essential sense among the members of the firm that the whole was greater than the sum of its parts. To do so, they all had to overcome a fundamental difficulty in any partnership. If any organization is to survive, each member must believe that his or

238

her own interests (monetary and otherwise) are being served more by staying than they would by leaving. In the case of a law firm, if one or more of the partners believe that their contribution to the firm is greater than their rewards, they will be tempted to leave. Maintaining the perception of fairness is a very difficult thing to do, but overall, the lawyers at Osler, Hoskin & Harcourt have apparently been able to do so.

This is not to imply that the Osler method of success is the only one, or that other firms have not employed the same methods. Certainly, there are other successful Canadian law firms — including McCarthy Tétrault, which shares a part of its history with Osler, Hoskin & Harcourt — that have been very successful over a long period of time and may have used many of the same methods. The fact that Britton Osler learned the lesson of not allowing individual lawyers to covet clients from the events leading up to the split of 1916, does not mean that McCarthy & McCarthy followed a different route. In fact, it is likely that the leaders of that firm learned the same lesson.

What is clear, however, is that the Osler firm, probably like the McCarthy firm and others, developed its own collective personality over its history. This, in part, made the task of maintaining a sense that the whole was greater than the sum of its parts easier. The Osler personality, which developed along with the generational evolution of the firm, was largely an extension of its leaders' personalities. In the nineteenth century, B.B. Osler and D'Alton McCarthy gave the firm a professional, but very self-confident — even flamboyant — face. By the mid-twentieth century, Britton Osler and Hal Mockridge gave it a paternal, established and at times stuffy air. By the late twentieth century, however, largely because of Purdy Crawford's style, the Osler firm culture became very informal and unpretentious. Predictably, because the leaders who followed Crawford learned by watching him, they have continued this style into the 1990s.

The evolution of the Osler culture is part of the general evolution of the firm. The organization which began as a compact between Britton Bath Osler and D'Alton McCarthy in 1882 became a clan after the split between the next generation of Oslers and McCarthys. It evolved a little more to become a club, as lawyers from outside of the Osler family began to occupy positions of leadership within the firm, but it was during the transformation of the late twentieth century, which saw the firm take on many of the characteristics of a corporation, when the most significant changes took place.

The evolution of a corporate form of firm organization over the past decade requires more analysis — the changes which the firm has undergone are most profound. The firm experienced enormous change during the 1980s, not least of which was its growth.[1] A service industry like law expands as the need for services grows, and during the 1980s, Oslers grew at a dizzying pace in direct response to the growth in the Canadian — indeed, the global — economy.

Whether the firm, or its clients, or even the rest of the country, actually understood the consequences of such rapid economic growth is doubtful. Taking on more and more lawyers, acquiring more and more space, and expanding a network of international offices, exacted a toll. Among other things, it was becoming increasingly difficult to maintain a common sense of firm culture.

Such growth and change would have to be guided and shaped, and this guidance would be far from easy. Some of the challenges presented by the expansion of the 1980s were relatively obvious; a perennial point of discussion in the partnership from 1977 onwards (when the firm moved into First Canadian Place) was, "How will we find enough space to accommodate all of the lawyers and staff we need to do our work?" The Space Committee was constantly reporting to the partnership about which portions of the building might become available at what time, and on what terms.

Expansion also created the need for a much more disciplined administrative structure. Until the late 1960s, all of the partners could have lunch around a table in a relatively modest boardroom. They made most of the important management decisions during those years at those luncheon meetings, under the unassuming, but forceful, leadership which Hal Mockridge was able to assert among his colleagues.

A partnership which could only be accommodated with great difficulty in a very large boardroom presented a completely different challenge. Questions which would have been discussed, if at all, in private conversations twenty years earlier ("Is this partner managing a particular client relationship effectively?" "Are that partner's docketing and billing practices efficient?") became the topic of detailed recording and regular reporting. The latter years of Mockridge's leadership, and those when Allan Beattie was managing partner, saw an evolution in these kinds of partnership governance matters, but it was not until the mid-1980s that it became impossible to carry on effective firm management on an informal basis through personal relationships. Only as the firm grew to unprecedented levels did it become necessary to make the management of the firm a professional commitment for both the managing partner and a staff of accountants and administrators.

The challenge of management in a rapidly expanding organization is, of course, not unique. But a professional partnership does present some special difficulties. The major challenge is that every partner is, in effect, an owner — and the owners like to direct their affairs. Correspondingly, the owners take responsibility for the decisions which govern the enterprise. A small group of owners, ten or twenty for example, can develop a cohesive and consensual approach to their business. Larger groups have a much more difficult time establishing and sharing a coherent vision and direction. The partners addressed this issue squarely at a firm retreat held at Niagara-on-the-Lake in November 1990. At that point, the firm took some clear steps towards what could be called "the corporation." The partners formally delegated more authority to management and the Executive Committee, and they placed decentralized authority in the hands of firm practice groups. The authority given to these new structures in the firm was, naturally enough, taken away from the partners and the partnership meetings.

The move to a more centralized management structure in the partnership occurred simultaneously with a move to a much more structured management and administrative arrangement under which people who were not trained in law and not eligible to join the partnership took a strong leadership role in the firm's affairs. The role of managing director, a non-legal position first created in 1988, became pivotal in the direction and administration of the firm.

These kinds of administrative changes were the direct consequence of growth, but there were also some other, less obvious, but perhaps more compelling challenges presented by growth. Much of the firm's history revolves around exceptional individuals. B.B. Osler, naturally enough, stands out. His nephew, Britton Osler, is a shadowy figure, but was clearly one of the great builders of the modern firm. Hal Mockridge, Allan Beattie, Purdy Crawford, Fred Huycke and Bertha Wilson remained standards against which many senior members of the firm continued to judge their own performance as they wrestled with the challenges of growth and change. It may be, however, that those people were important for more than their individual accomplishments; they in some ways were the exemplars of firm culture in their times.

"Firm culture" is, to the unbeliever, an oxymoron; to the cynical, merely a cliché. It seems clear, however, that over the course of its history Osler, Hoskin & Harcourt did develop a culture of its own. A closely knit group of colleagues came to accept a set of common values, interests and professional commitments which amounted to a culture and which was shared with (or perhaps imposed upon) those who aspired to join the group. When a group expands as rapidly as the firm did in the 1980s, however, a firm culture becomes much harder to define and very difficult to share.

The attenuation of the old firm culture during the expansive 1980s was not wholly a negative thing. Much of the culture of the smaller firm was derived from the homogeneity of the members of the partnership. The values and practices of the firm were substantially those of middle-class Anglo-Saxon men. The expansion of the firm during the growth years involved recruitment among the best students from every law school in the country — male and female, representing all ethnic and religious groups. These people brought to the firm a very diverse set of backgrounds, talents, and interests. The thrust was not to mourn the loss of an older culture, but create a new one out of the much richer materials at hand.

The growth and expansion which the firm experienced during the 1980s paralleled that experienced throughout Canada, and indeed much of the world. It was clients' work, and the legal services that such work required, that fuelled the firm's progress. But what happens when, as was the case beginning in 1990, the economy contracts, the clients face straitened circumstances and legal advice is sought less frequently? Obviously, a major commercial law firm is not exempted from the rules of economic life that govern its clients. A recession in commerce is necessarily a recession in commercial law. But recessions will sometimes offer opportunities not otherwise available. Also significant — in terms of both challenges and opportunities — was the increasingly competitive market for legal services which predated the recession.

As noted above, the firm culture was difficult to foster, or even define, when the firm was growing at such a dizzying pace during the 1980s. But as the firm moved into a period of somewhat slower growth, the partners had more time to reflect on the standards and values which, they hoped, made Osler, Hoskin & Harcourt unique. During those years, for example, the firm became more focused on such matters as the system of precedents it used, its training of all lawyers in the use of personal computers and computer systems, and its continuing legal education for partners and associates. In the 1960s, Oslers became the first Canadian law firm to establish a research department. In the 1980s, it broke new ground once more by establishing the first full-time director of legal education position. More recently, another lawyer was given responsibility for the development of a computerized precedent system and for the review of opinion letters the firm typically used in commercial transactions.

Each innovation presented a new set of challenges to both the administrators and the lawyers in the firm. Creating a position of director of legal education, for example, necessarily involved acquiring appropriate support staff and educational equipment. It also, however, involved a decision that some portion of the work day of partners and associates, as well as articling students, be devoted to education. A thorough review of precedent materials similarly required allocation of time and effort away from billings and client concerns. Each innovation, if it was to be successful, also had to involve a commitment to a broadened group of priorities.

The firm's relationship with clients also evolved in this period of consolidation. When commercial enterprises are less profitable, they are more careful about expenses, including legal services. There was a time when a law firm was one of the traditional points of reference for any discussion of business objectives and was a frequent consultant on operational decisions. A senior lawyer in the firm would sit on the boards of directors of numerous client companies and in some matters would be almost as familiar with a client's affairs as its senior executives. The more modern approach was for companies to use outside legal services for very specific, and well-defined, tasks.

When clients found themselves in a position to deal with their legal advisors on narrowly defined questions, it became relatively easy to use a variety of law firms. No firm had any advantage over another in terms of detailed long-term knowledge of the client's work. Correspondingly, law firms became intensely competitive in seeking clients' work. The loyalty and goodwill of any client, no matter how long standing, was never taken for granted.

Intense competition for the privilege of offering legal services was a novel concept in the modern era in the profession. Codes of ethics in years gone by prohibited both solicitation and "touting." It was only within the last decade that lawyers in Ontario were permitted to advertise the availability of their services. Even then, the struggle among law firms for the attention and affection of clients remained a relatively discreet one — but it was real and vigorously pursued. They began to reach out to clients with social functions (musical and sports events, for example) and seminars on new legal developments of broad general interest. Osler, Hoskin & Harcourt encouraged all lawyers and associates to be active in client development and to learn, in as much detail as possible, the interests, objectives and concerns of the clients with whom they dealt.

The firm's concern for client interests may take it, in years to come, into apparently novel service delivery and billing arrangements. It is frequently suggested that very large firms provide clients with special value when the firms bring their expertise, and particularly expertise in highly specialized areas of law, to large and complicated transactions. The contribution which a law firm brings to such a transaction may be better represented not by a billing of docketed hours, but rather by what has been termed ''value billing'' associated with the intrinsic contribution of the legal work to the success of the client's project. This is not necessarily a new idea. Until the 1970s, client billing in most law firms was almost an art form. It was very subjective and was often based, at least in part, on the commercial outcome of the advice given.[2] The objective time docketing at a clearly defined hourly rate was a relatively modern phenomenon. The rapid pace of change and the competition of the most recent era required continued flexibility in billing practices.

When asked what should be written in an epilogue to the firm history, one of the partners remarked, only half in jest: ''Well, surely the theme for the last ten years is feasting and indigestion.'' There is, of course, a grain of truth in that remark, but it was not the whole story, or even a major part of the whole story. The real point of significance was the way in which Oslers, even though it remained, among law firms, a giant organization, could still respond quickly and cogently to the dramatic changes in the commercial world around it.

And what of the next century? One of the striking elements of the firm's history was the fact that, at least until very recently, the lawyers there spent very little time in self-examination or long-term planning. An early, but significant, example of such analysis was Hal Mockridge's decision to decline an offer to join the board of Massey-Ferguson.[3] He did so because he felt that the firm did not have enough lawyers at the time to deal with the legal work which that position would likely generate. Perhaps more significantly, he also felt that the firm should not immediately attempt to expand in order to meet such a challenge.

Mockridge's decision to turn down what appears from a more modern perspective to have been a golden opportunity must be considered in its context. The firm would have had fewer than thirty lawyers at the time. He may not have been confident that they could find new associates or partners who could meet the firm's standards, and he did not wish to do work which could not be done both quickly and well. It was also, of course, true that legal work in the decades before electric typewriters, photocopy machines and computers was undoubtedly a great deal more labour intensive than in recent years. The burden to be assumed was obviously a very large one.

How would the firm have responded to a similar proposal in the last decade? Obviously, it has been involved in some of the largest national and international transactions to take place over the last ten years. It was, by that time, a much larger organization than Hal Mockridge could have imagined. No task was too great, no challenge too daunting. Partners and associates were available to meet every need. In the end, however, it was still the clients and their needs that shaped the firm.

It is tempting, particularly in concluding a story which is largely one of success, to predict the future. Historians often drag out Santayana's paraphrased maxim that those who do not understand the past are doomed to repeat it, but it might also be said that those who claim to know the future because they think they understand the past are equally doomed. Canadian historian Michael Bliss issued a similar warning to a workshop on business history in 1991.

After identifying some of what he judged to be the best works in Canadian corporate history, including E.P. Neufeld's 1969 study *A Global Corporation: A History of The International Development of Massey-Ferguson Limited*, Bliss pointed out that Neufeld "got the future of Massey-Ferguson exactly wrong, celebrating its managerial achievements and potential at exactly the moment in history when the stage was being set, through changing markets and managerial dry rot, for the firm's catastrophic decline and fall."

His conclusion is equally appropriate to the study of a law firm: "Our ability to predict the future on the basis of our knowledge of the past is approximately nil."[4]

With this in mind, Osler, Hoskin & Harcourt's future course, ironically, may lie closer to the approach taken in the 1950s; the members of the firm know that they must shape their services rather than be shaped and reshaped by them. They have come to realize, for example, that the expenses generated by a major downtown urban office are probably not appropriate to the needs of clients with, for example, houses to buy, sell and mortgage. Clients with residential files can be more efficiently served in smaller offices. The firm's thinking along this line is becoming more precise and specific. It has developed a work intake policy which is guiding the opening of files. This policy has become an essential element in protecting the firm and its clients from legal and ethical conflicts among the people it serves.

A more thoughtful approach to the services offered at Oslers does not imply an indifference to the needs of the people who seek legal help. The essential question is how legal services can be provided in the most efficient and effective way when dealing with resources as large as those of a firm this size. The Oslers lawyers are also, like their colleagues in other large firms, becoming highly competitive in their approaches to the clients they can serve. They try to shape their practices to the needs of specific clients, and to develop new areas of expertise appropriate to different sectors in the client community. Their recently developed departments in the areas of construction law, pension law and technology law are just a few examples of this type of development.They try to build new clientele within areas in which their expertise is not widely available. As noted above, they used to understand their clients because their partners sat on client companies' boards of directors and were involved on a weekly, or even daily, basis with their executives. Now they are going to teach themselves about the needs and interests of client groups and use new mechanisms to approach these clients and potential clients with ideas for more efficient and more effective delivery of legal services.

The firm's future growth will also reflect an evolution in its approach to the concept of partnership. Without the pressure to expand experienced in the past ten years, the standards with regard to admission to partnership have become more demanding. This trend will probably continue in the future. The role of associate lawyers will evolve correspondingly. They are likely to see, over time, career patterns which emphasize flexibility and lateral movement. Lawyers will move into and out of association with law firms, into and out of positions in corporate law departments, and into and out of government work. Oslers, and large law firms like it, may more commonly be a stage in a career rather than a career itself.

Inside and outside of the partnership, new types of work relationships are developing. Traditional models of practice and progression from associate to partner may be too rigid to meet the needs of the 1990s. Part-time practice arrangements are evolving for both partners and associates. Coupled with these more flexible approaches to practice is a higher degree of accountability among partners. The review of the work and career progress of associates had been taken for granted. A similar review, however, is becoming the norm throughout the partnership.

In the summer of 1994, Osler, Hoskin & Harcourt held a reception at the Art Gallery of Ontario for its alumni — men and women who had been at the firm as associates or partners and had moved on to other positions. Some of the alumni were retired, a number were members of the judiciary, others headed major corporations, and yet others were working with competitive law firms.

The notion that a legal partnership could have ''alumni'' could be regarded as pretentious. Universities and colleges claim that relationship to the people they have touched. But Osler, Hoskin & Harcourt is an institution in its own right. It is larger than any individual partner or collection of partners. Indeed, it is larger than all of the partners, associates and staff existing at any one time. It has a tradition, it develops and redevelops its culture, and it enjoys the affection of members and former members wherever they are. And now, it has a history.

APPENDIX I
LAWYERS AND STUDENTS AT
OSLER, HOSKIN & HARCOURT, 1862-1994*

Abbott, Allyn B.Sc. (University of Toronto, 1978), LL.B. (University of Toronto, 1989); called to the bar 1991; articled with the firm 1989-90; practised with the firm 1991-94.

Abdel-Aziz, Ahab LL.B. (Dalhousie University, 1989); called to the bar 1991; practised with the firm 1991-.

Abugov, Lorne H. B.J. (Carleton University, 1976), B.A. (University of Guelph, 1977), LL.B. (Dalhousie University, 1980); called to the bar 1982; practised with the firm 1994- (partner 1994).

Adsett, Hugh C. B.A. (Mount Allison University, 1987), M.A. (University of Western Ontario, 1988), LL.B. (Queen's University, 1993); articled with the firm 1993-94).

Ahmed, S. Firoz B.Comm. (Carleton University, 1981), LL.B. (Queen's University, 1984); called to the bar 1986; articled with the firm 1984-85; practised with the firm 1986- (partner 1992).

Aitken, David W. B.Eng. (Royal Military College, 1975), LL.B. (McGill University, 1982); called to the bar 1984; practised with the firm 1985- (partner 1990).

Aitken, Melanie L. B.A. (University of Toronto, 1988); LL.B. (University of Toronto, 1991); called to the bar 1993; articled with the firm 1991-92; practised with the firm 1993-94.

Alexander, Bruce B. B.Comm. (Queen's University, 1961), LL.B. (University of Toronto, 1965); called to the bar 1967; articled with the firm 1965-66; practised with the firm 1967-73.

Alexander, Deborah M. B.A. (Queen's University, 1972), LL.B. (University of Toronto, 1975); called to the bar 1977; articled with the firm 1975-76; practised with the firm 1977- (partner 1982).

Ali-Dabydeen, K. Reya D. B.A. (York University, 1986), LL.B. (York University, 1989); called to the bar 1991; articled with the firm 1989-90; practised with the firm 1991-92.

Allen, Francis R. B.A. (University of Toronto, 1973), M.B.A. (York University, 1975), LL.B. (York University, 1978); called to the bar 1980; articled with the firm 1978-79; practised with the firm 1980-88, 1990- (partner 1985-88, resigned 1988, re-admitted 1990).

Allen, Patricia LL.B/B.C.L. (McGill University, 1988); articled with the firm 1988-89.

Allgood, David R. B.A. (Queen's University, 1970), LL.B. (Queen's University, 1974); called to the bar 1976; articled with the firm 1974-75; practised with the firm 1976- (partner 1981).

* Every effort has been made to ensure the accuracy of this information. The listings are as complete as firm records would allow. The author regrets any omissions.

Appleby, Ronald B.Comm. (University of Toronto, 1965), LL.B. (Osgoode Hall, 1968); called to the bar 1970; articled with the firm 1968-69; practised with the firm 1970-71.

Appleton, Barry W. B.A. (University of Toronto, 1985), LL.B. (Queen's University, 1989); called to the bar 1991 (New York), 1992 (Ontario); articled with the firm 1989-90.

Armstrong, Debra B.Comm. (Carleton University, 1987), LL.B. (University of Ottawa, 1990); called to the bar 1992; articled with the firm 1990-91; practised with the firm 1992-94.

Armstrong, John G. B.A. (McGill University, 1966), LL.B. (Osgoode Hall, 1969); called to the bar 1971; articled with the firm 1968-69; practised with the firm 1971-74.

Arnold, Debra B.A. (University of Toronto, 1986), LL.B. (Queen's University, 1989); called to the bar 1991; articled with the firm 1989-90; practised with the firm 1991.

Arnold, Stephen V. B.A., (Queen's University, 1962), LL.B., (University of Toronto, 1965); called to the bar 1967; articled with the firm 1965-66; practised with the firm 1967- (partner 1973).

Arymowicz, Charles B.A. (Queen's University, 1968), LL.B (University of Toronto, 1971), LL.M. (University of Michigan, 1974); called to the bar 1985; articled with the firm 1983-84.

Aston, Helen T. B.A. (University of Toronto, 1983), LL.B. (University of the West Indies, 1986), LL.B. (University of Toronto, 1988), called to the bar 1990; articled with the firm 1988-89; practised with the firm 1990-93.

Atkey, Ronald G. B.A. (University of Western Ontario, 1962), LL.B., (University of Western Ontario, 1965), LL.M., (Yale, 1966); called to the bar 1969; practised with the firm 1974-79, 1980- (partner 1976, resigned 1979, re-admitted 1980).

Au, Nathan S.K. B.Sc. (University of Manchester, 1984), M.Sc. (University of Manchester, 1985), LL.B, (Queen's University, 1988); called to the bar 1990; articled with the firm 1988-89.

Aylward, Sean C. B.A. (University of Ottawa, 1982), LL.B. (York University, 1985), LL.M. (University of London, 1988), called to the bar 1987; practised with the firm 1990-.

Aziz, Andrew W. B.A., (University of Western Ontario, 1983), LL.B. (University of Western Ontario, 1986); called to the bar 1988; articled with the firm 1986-87; practised with the firm 1988-.

Bachinski, Samuel R. B.Comm. (Lakehead University, 1986), LL.B. (University of Victoria, 1989); called to the bar 1991; articled with the firm 1989-90.

Bailey, W. Bruce C. B.A. (Queen's University, 1976), LL.B. (Dalhousie University, 1979); called to the bar 1981; articled with the firm 1979-80; practised with the firm 1981-86.

Bain, Mark W.S. B.A. (University of Toronto, 1984), LL.B. (University of Western Ontario, 1987); called to the bar 1989; practised with the firm 1992-94.

Bajwa, Maya B.A. (Queen's University, 1990), LL.B. (Queen's University, 1993); articled with the firm 1993-94.

Baker, John M. B.A. (University of Toronto, 1970), LL.B. (York University, 1974); called to the bar 1976; practised with the firm 1979-83.

Ball, David B.A. (University of Toronto, 1974), M.B.A. (University of Toronto, 1976), LL.B. (University of Windsor, 1987); called to the bar 1989; articled with the firm 1987-88; practised with the firm 1989-91.

Bannon, David J. B.A. (Wilfrid Laurier University, 1989), LL.B. (York University, 1992); called to the bar 1994; articled with the firm 1992-93; practised with the firm 1994-.

Barker, Grant R.C. B.A. (University of Western Ontario, 1965), LL.B. (University of Western Ontario, 1968); called to the bar 1970; articled with the firm 1968-69; practised with the firm 1970-73.

Barnes, Lyndon A.J. B.A. (York University, 1968), LL.B. (York University, 1971); called to the bar 1973; articled with the firm 1971-72; practised with the firm 1973- (partner 1977).

Barrett, Laurie E. LL.B. (University of Western Ontario, 1980); called to the bar 1982; articled with the firm 1980-81; practised with the firm 1982- (partner 1988).

Bart, Jacqueline R. B.A. (York University, 1987), J.D. (University of Detroit, 1990), LL.B. (University of Windsor, 1990); called to the bar 1992; articled with the firm 1990-91.

Bates, Scott D. B.A. (University of Toronto, 1989), LL.B. (Queen's University, 1992); called to the bar 1994; articled with the firm 1992-93.

Battram, Shelley P. B.A. (University of Guelph, 1973), LL.B. (University of Windsor, 1976); called to the bar 1977 (Ontario), 1979 (New York), 1983 (Michigan); practised with the firm 1986-91.

Bawden, Brian R. B.Sc. (University of Western Ontario, 1972), LL.B. (University of Western Ontario, 1975); called to the bar 1977; practised with the firm 1977- (partner 1982).

Beattie, Allan L. B.A. (University of Toronto, 1948); called to the bar 1951; articled with the firm 1948-51; practised with the firm 1951-86 (partner 1956).

Beatty, Jane M. B.A. (University of Waterloo, 1982), LL.B. (York University, 1985); called to the bar 1987; practised with the firm 1988-91.

Beaumont, D. Robert B.A.Sc (University of Toronto, 1979), LL.B. (Queen's University, 1984); called to the bar 1986; practised with the firm 1988- (partner 1992).

Beckett, David A. B.A. (McMaster University, 1988), M.A. (McMaster University, 1989), LL.B. (University of Windsor, 1994); articled with the firm 1994-.

Beehan, Cathy B.Mus. (University of Ottawa), LL.B. (University of Ottawa); articled with the firm 1982-83.

Begue, Theophilus H.A. Admitted to practise as a solicitor 1863, called to the bar 1876; practised with the firm 1866-80 (partner 1866).

Belecky, Alfred John LL.B. (University of Western Ontario, 1970); called to the bar 1972; articled with the firm 1970-71.

Belfoi, Ronald G. B.A. (University of New Brunswick, 1959), LL.B. (Osgoode Hall, 1963); called to the bar 1964; practised with the firm 1986- (partner 1986).

Belkin, Lyle C. B.A. (University of Toronto, 1977), M.B.A. (York University, 1982), LL.B. (University of Ottawa, 1985); called to the bar 1987; practised with the firm 1989-90.

Bellmore, Brian P. B.A. (University of Toronto, 1963), LL.B. (Osgoode Hall, 1967), LL.M. (Harvard University, 1969); called to the bar 1970; articled with the firm 1968-69; practised with the firm 1970-73.

Bennett, Michael B.A. (University of New Brunswick, 1987), LL.B. (York University, 1990); called to the bar 1992; articled with the firm 1990-91; practised with the firm 1992-.

Berman, Samuel B.Sc. (University of London), LL.B. (McGill University); called to the bar 1984; articled with the firm 1982-83.

Berrill, Fraser R. B.A. (Queen's University, 1971), LL.B. (University of Windsor, 1974); called to the bar 1976; articled with the firm 1974-75; practised with the firm 1976-82.

Best, Gregory O. B.A. (McGill University, 1970), LL.B. (University of Toronto, 1973); called to the bar 1975; practised with the firm 1976.

Binder, Louise D. B.A. (University of Toronto, 1971), LL.B. (Queen's University, 1973); called to the bar 1975; articled with the firm 1974; practised with the firm 1975-77.

Biringer, Monica E. B.A. (Queen's University, 1981), LL.B. (University of Toronto, 1984); called to the bar 1986; articled with the firm 1984-85; practised with the firm 1986-.

Birnbaum, Arthur B.A. (University of Toronto, 1968), LL.B. (University of Western Ontario, 1971); called to the bar 1973; practised with the firm 1985- (partner 1985).

Bishop, John M. B.Comm. (University of Toronto, 1969), LL.B. (York University, 1973); called to the bar 1984; articled with the firm 1982-3; practised with the firm 1984 (partner 1990)

Black, John A. B.A. (University of Western Ontario, 1989), LL.B. (University of Western Ontario, 1992); called to the bar 1994; articled with the firm 1992 93; practised with the firm 1994-.

Blair, Alan S. (Jake) B.Sc. (Queen's University, 1967), M.A. (University of Toronto), Ph.D. (University of Toronto), LL.B. (University of Ottawa, 1977); called to the bar 1981; articled with the firm 1979-80; practised with the firm 1981-82.

Blair, Stephen G. B.A. (University of Waterloo, 1978), LL.B. (University of British Columbia, 1981); called to the bar 1983; practised with the firm 1986- (partner 1989).

Blakey, Jonathan A. B.A. (University of Toronto, 1984), B.J. (Carleton University, 1987), LL.B. (University of Calgary, 1992); called to the bar 1994; practised with the firm 1994-.

Blecher, Roma A. B.A. (Tel Aviv University, 1984), LL.B. (York University, 1986); called to the bar 1988; articled with the firm 1986-87; practised with the firm 1988-89.

Bloom, Glen A. B.A. (Carleton University, 1974), LL.B. (Queen's University, 1978); called to the bar 1980; practised with the firm 1986- (partner 1986).

Blugerman, Brian M. B.A. (University of Toronto, 1975), LL.B. (University of Toronto, 1987); called to the bar 1989; articled with the firm 1987-88; practised with the firm 1989-.

Boast, Keith E. Called to the bar 1973; articled with the firm 1971-72.

Bock, Ian D., LL.B. (York University, 1992), LL.M. (Dalhousie University, 1993). Articled with the firm 1993-94.

Bohnen, Linda Susan B.A. (York University, 1971), LL.B. (University of Toronto, 1974); called to the bar 1976; articled with the firm 1974-75.

Bolan, John B.A. (Queen's University, 1987), LL.B. (Queen's University, 1990); articled with the firm 1990-91.

Boland, Kenneth L.W. B.A. (University of Toronto, 1965), LL.B. (Osgoode Hall, 1968); called to the bar 1970; practised with the firm 1986- (partner 1986).

Bonner, Penelope S. B.A., (Queen's University, 1972), LL.B., (University of Ottawa, 1978); called to the bar 1980; practised with the firm 1984- (partner 1986).

Bookman, Steven Myles B.A. (University of Toronto, 1967), LL.B. (Queen's University, 1970); called to the bar 1972; articled with the firm 1970-71.

Borins, Richard M. B.Sc. (University of Western Ontario, 1990; LL.B. (University of Western Ontario, 1993); articled with the firm 1993-94.

Bortolussi, Felicia B. B.A. (University of Western Ontario, 1988), LL.B. (University of Western Ontario, 1991); called to the bar 1993; articled with the firm 1991-92; practised with the firm 1993-.

Boston, Harold Emerson Called to the bar 1925; articled with the firm 1920-25; practised with the firm 1926-62 (partner 1944).

Boswell, Robert A. B.Sc. (University of Waterloo, 1990), LL.B. (University of Victoria, 1994); articled with the firm 1994-.

Bousfield, Joel A. B.A. (McGill University, 1985), LL.B. (Queen's University, 1989); called to the bar 1991; articled with the firm 1989-90; practised with the firm 1991-93.

Bowman, Michael H.D. B.A. (University of Toronto, 1973), M.S.W. (University of Toronto, 1975), LL.B. (York University, 1981), M.B.A. (York University, 1982); called to the bar 1983; practised with the firm 1988- (partner 1992).

Boylan, Harold K. B.A. (University of Western Ontario, 1950); called to the bar 1954; practised with the firm 1956-90 (partner 1962).

Brace, Paul E. LL.B. (York University, 1986); called to the bar 1978 (Ontario); admitted to practice as a solicitor 1986 (Hong Kong); practised with the firm 1986-89.

Bradbury, Donald Culver B.A. (University of Toronto, 1950); called to the bar 1954; articled with the firm 1952-54; practised with the firm 1954-69.

Brayley, Catherine A. B.A. (University of Toronto, 1979), LL.B. (University of Windsor, 1983), LL.M. (York University, 1986); called to the bar 1985; practised with the firm 1986-88.

Brett, Christopher P. B.Sc. (Queen's University, 1975), LL.B. (Queen's University, 1980); called to the bar 1982; practised with the firm 1985-92 (partner 1988).

Breuls, Morley H. Called to the bar 1925; articled with the firm 1920-25.

Brown, M. Craig G. B.A. (University of Western Ontario, 1979), LL.B. (University of Windsor, 1983); called to the bar 1985; articled with the firm 1983-84.

Brown, S. Andrew B.Comm. (Queen's University, 1987), LL.B. (University of Toronto, 1990); called to the bar 1992; articled with the firm 1990-91; practised with the firm 1992-.

Brownstone, Lisa B.A. (University of Manitoba), LL.B. (University of Toronto, 1988); called to the bar 1990; practised with the firm 1990.

Bruce, David N. B.A. (Queen's University, 1989), LL.B. (University of Western Ontario, 1993); articled with the firm 1993-94.

Bryden, William M. B.A., (McMaster University, 1947); called to the bar 1950; articled with the firm 1948-50; practised with the firm 1950-92 (partner 1955).

Buckley, Francis H. B.A. (McGill University, 1969), LL.B. (McGill University, 1974), LL.M. (Harvard University, 1975); called to the bar 1982; practised with the firm 1982-84.

Bucknall, Brian D. B.A. (McMaster University, 1965), LL.B. (Osgoode Hall, 1968), LL.M. (Columbia University, 1969); called to the bar 1973; articled with the firm 1969-1970; practised with the firm 1977- (partner 1979).

Budd, Robert B. B.A. (University of Toronto, 1971), B.Comm. (University of Windsor, 1973), LL.B. (University of Windsor, 1976); called to the bar 1978; practised with the firm 1987-89.

Burgoyne, Terrence R. B.Comm. (Dalhousie University, 1978), LL.B. (University of Toronto, 1981); called to the bar 1983 (Ontario), admitted to practise as a solicitor 1988 (England and Wales); articled with the firm 1981-82; practised with the firm 1983- (partner 1989).

Burke, Ann E. B.A. (Loyola College (Montreal), 1974), M.A. (York University, 1976), LL.B. (York University, 1982); called to the bar 1984; articled with the firm 1982-83; practised with the firm 1984-87.

Burns, Michael A. B.Comm. (Dalhousie University, 1987), LL.B. (Dalhousie University, 1990); called to the bar 1992; articled with the firm 1990-91; practised with the firm 1992-.

Burnside, Joyce D. B.A. (Queen's University, 1986), LL.B. (University of Ottawa, 1988); called to the bar 1990; articled with the firm 1988-89; practised with the firm 1990.

Burrows, Andrea J. B.B.A. (Wilfrid Laurier University, 1984), LL.B. (University of British Columbia, 1993); articled with the firm 1993-94.

Burt, Mary Elizabeth (Salter) LL.B. (University of Toronto, 1971); called to the bar 1973; articled with the firm 1971-72.

Busche, Janice R. B.P.E. (University of British Columbia, 1989), LL.B. (University of Western Ontario, 1994); articled with the firm 1994-.

Butler, Cyril D. B.Sc. (Carleton University, 1985), M.B.A (Queen's University, 1988), LL.B. (University of Toronto, 1991); called to the bar 1993; articled with the firm 1991-92; practised with the firm 1993-94.

Callaghan, Patrick J. B.A. (Concordia University, 1985); M.A. (McGill University, 1988), LL.B./B.C.L. (McGill University, 1992); LL.M. (University of Toronto, 1993); articled with the firm 1993-94.

Cameron, Wellington Ault B.A. (McGill University); called to the bar 1891; practised with the firm 1910-49 (partner 1910).

Cappell, Franklyn Ephraim Called to the bar 1965 (Nova Scotia), 1969 (Ontario); articled with the firm 1967-68.

Carson, Wayne C. B.Sc.Eng. (University of New Brunswick, 1987), LL.B. (University of New Brunswick, 1990); called to the bar 1994; articled with the firm 1992-93.

Carter, Donald Douglas B.A. (Queen's University, 1963), LL.B. (Queen's University, 1966), B.C.L. (Oxford University, 1968); called to the bar 1970; articled with the firm 1966-67.

Casciano, Lata B.Comm. (University of British Columbia, 1982), LL.B. (University of British Columbia, 1985); called to the bar 1987 (British Columbia) 1989 (Ontario); articled with the firm 1987-88.

Case, William Alfred James Called to the bar 1930; practised with the firm 1940-43.

Caylor, J. Lincoln J. B.A. (University of King's College, 1990), LL.B. (University of Ottawa, 1993); articled with the firm 1993-94.

Ceci, Gina B.A. (York University, 1988), LL.B. (York University, 1991); articled with the firm 1991-92.

Chalifour, Nathalie J. LL.B. (University of Western Ontario, 1994); articled with the firm 1994-.

Chapin, Peter J. B.A. (University of Ottawa, 1971), LL.B. (University of Toronto, 1991); called to the bar 1993; articled with the firm 1991-92; practised with the firm 1993-.

Chaplick, Nancy D. LL.B. (York University, 1973); called to the bar 1975; articled with the firm 1973-74; practised with the firm 1975- (partner 1980).

Charnetski, William A. B.Comm. (University of Alberta, 1985), LL.B. (University of Toronto, 1988); called to the bar 1990; articled with the firm 1988-89; practised with the firm 1990-.

Chartrand, Rupert H. B.A. (University of Ottawa, 1968), LL.B. (Queen's University, 1969), LL.M. (Columbia University, 1970), M.I.A. (Columbia University, 1971), M.B.A. (Columbia University, 1972); called to the bar 1974; practised with the firm 1985- (partner 1985).

Cheng, Ronald C. B.A. (Amherst College, 1970), LL.B. (University of Toronto, 1975); called to the bar 1977; practised with the firm 1986- (partner 1986).

Chiarotto, Lia B.Comm. (University of Toronto, 1989), LL.B. (University of Toronto, 1994); articled with the firm 1994-.

Chik, John B.A. (University of Hong Kong, 1977); called to the bar 1983 (Hong Kong); articled with the firm 1991-92.

Chown, Roger H. B.Sc. (Queen's University, 1985), LL.B. (University of Windsor, 1991); called to the bar 1993; articled with the firm 1991-92.

Christie, Irene P. B.A./B.PHE. (Queen's University, 1981), M.Sc. (University of Illinois at Urbana-Champaign, 1983), LL.B. (Dalhousie University, 1986); called to the bar 1987 (Nova Scotia), 1989 (Ontario); practised with the firm 1989-.

Christie, Katherine B.Sc. (University of Toronto, 1974), LL.B. (York University, 1978); called to the bar 1980; practised with the firm 1986-93 (partner 1990).

Cipparone, Eugene A.G. B.Sc. (University of Toronto, 1988), LL.B. (University of Toronto, 1992); called to the bar 1994; articled with the firm 1992-93; practised with the firm 1994-.

Clare, James A. B.A. (McMaster University, 1936); called to the bar 1939; articled with the firm 1936-39; practised with the firm 1939-40.

Clark, John H. B.A. (York University), LL.B. (York University, 1988); articled with the firm 1988-89, 1994.

Clauzel, Hogarth F. B.Sc. (University of Ottawa, 1989), B.A. (University of Ottawa, 1990); LL.B. (Queen's University, 1993; articled with the firm 1993 94.

Claydon, John E. B.A. (Carleton University, 1967), LL.B. (Queen's University, 1970), LL.M. (University of Virginia, 1971); called to the bar 1973; Director of Legal Education 1987-.

Clayton, Robert J. B.A. (Queen's University, 1970), LL.B. (Queen's University, 1974); called to the bar 1976; practised with the firm 1987- (partner 1988).

Cleland, Edward Gordon B.A. (McGill University, 1970), LL.B. (York University, 1974); called to the bar 1976; articled with the firm 1974-75.

Clement, R.V. Called to the bar 1890; articled with the firm 1886-88.

Clement, William Henry Pope B.A. (University of Toronto, 1878), LL.B. (University of Toronto, 1881); called to the bar 1880; practised with the firm 1882-88 (partner 1882).

Cohen, Oz A. B.Sc. (University of Toronto, 1990), LL.B. (York University, 1993); articled with the firm 1993-94.

Coleman, Richard J. B.Comm. (University of Toronto, 1977), LL.B. (University of Toronto, 1980); called to the bar 1982; articled with the firm 1980 81; practised with the firm 1982- (partner 1988).

Coleman, Ronald B.A. (University of Waterloo, 1978), LL.B. (Queen's University, 1990); articled with the firm (Ottawa), 1990-91.

Collins, Timothy B.Eng. (Concordia University, 1984), LL.B./M.B.A. (University of Ottawa, 1988); called to the bar 1990; articled with the firm 1988-89.

Coombs, Maurice J. B.Sc. (University of Toronto, 1963), LL.B. (Osgoode Hall, 1966); LL.M. (York University, 1970); called to the bar 1970; practised with the firm 1972- (partner 1975).

Cornforth, Jocelyn A. B.A. (Queen's University, 1989), LL.B. (Dalhousie University, 1992); called to the bar 1994; articled with the firm 1992-93; practised with the firm 1994-

Cornish, Diane E. B.A. (Queen's University, 1967), LL.B. (University of Ottawa, 1986); called to the bar 1988; articled with the firm 1986-87; practised with the firm 1988

Cotter, John C. B.A. (University of Western Ontario, 1980), LL.B. (University of Windsor, 1986); called to the bar 1988; articled with the firm 1986-87; practised with the firm 1988-.

Courtney, Nancy J. LL.B. (University of Western Ontario, 1985); called to the bar 1987; practised with the firm 1988-89.

Cox, Wilfrid M. B.A. (Victoria University, 1912); called to the bar 1915; articled with the firm 1912-15; practised with the firm 1915-16.

Coyle, Michael J. LL.B. (University of Western Ontario, 1982); called to the bar 1984; practised with the firm 1986-89.

Coyne, John D. B.A. (Queen's University, 1981), LL.B. (York University, 1984); called to the bar 1986; articled with the firm 1984-85; practised with the firm 1986-92.

Coyne, John M. B.A. (University of Manitoba, 1940), B.A. (Oxford University, 1947), M.A. (Oxford University, 1951); called to the bar 1947 (Lincoln's Inn), 1948 (Manitoba, Ontario); practised with the firm 1986-91 (partner 1986).

Crawford, H. Purdy B.A. (Mount Allison University, 1952), LL.B. (Dalhousie University, 1955), LL.M. (Harvard University, 1956); called to the bar 1956 (Nova Scotia); 1958 (Ontario); articled with the firm 1956-57; practised with the firm 1958-85 (partner 1962).

Creelman, Adam R. Called to the bar 1875 (Ontario), 1902 (Quebec), admitted to practise as a solicitor 1874 (Ontario); practised with the firm 1882-1902 (partner 1882).

Creelman, William F.W. Called to the bar 1885; articled with the firm 1882-85.

Creery, K. Monica B.A. (Queen's University, 1982), B.A. (University of Ottawa, 1986), LL.B. (McGill University, 1993), articled with the firm 1993-94.

Creighton, Jon Leslie B.A. (Waterloo College, 1959), LL.B. (University of Western Ontario, 1962); called to the bar 1964; articled with the firm 1962-63; practised with the firm 1964-69.

Crosby, Howard E. B.A. (St. Mary's University, 1952), LL.B. (Dalhousie University, 1955), LL.M. (Southern Methodist University, 1956); called to the bar 1956 (Nova Scotia); 1966 (Ontario); practised with the firm 1966-67.

Curran, Lisa LL.B. (Queen's University, 1986); called to the bar 1988; practised with the firm 1990-91.

Currie, Linda G. B.A. (University of Western Ontario, 1970), LL.B. (York University, 1980); called to the bar 1982; articled with the firm 1980-81; practised with the firm 1982- (partner 1988).

Curtis, David S. B.Sc. (University of New Brunswick, 1975), LL.B. (University of New Brunswick, 1987); called to the bar 1989; articled with the firm 1987-88; practised with the firm 1989.

Dadson, D. Aleck B.A. (University of Toronto, 1976), B.A. (Oxford University, 1978), LL.B. (University of Toronto, 1980), LL.M. (Yale University, 1984); called to the bar 1982; practised with the firm 1986- (partner 1989).

Dais-Visca, Jacqueline M. B.A. (University of Calgary, 1988), LL.B. (University of Victoria, 1992); called to the bar 1994; articled with the firm 1992-93.

Dale, Lawrence M. LL.B. (University of Toronto, 1986); called to the bar 1988; articled with the firm 1986-87; practised with the firm 1988-91.

Davies, Michael J. B.A. (McMaster University, 1972), LL.B. (York University, 1975); called to the bar 1977; practised with the firm 1986- (partner 1988).

Dawson, William J. B.A. (University of Toronto, 1983), M.B.A./LL.B. (University of Ottawa, 1987); called to the bar 1989; articled with the firm 1987-88.

De Girolamo, Debbie B.A. (University of Toronto, 1982), LL.B. (University of Windsor, 1985); called to the bar 1987; articled with the firm 1985-86; practised with the firm 1987-92.

Delamere, Thomas D. Called to the bar 1925; articled with the firm 1920-25; practised with the firm 1942-74 (partner 1942).

DeLuca, Carl J.A. B.B.A. (University of Western Ontario, 1990), B.A. (University of Western Ontario, 1991), LL.B. (University of Windsor, 1994); articled with the firm 1994-.

DeMarco, Jean M. B.A. (University of Windsor, 1973), LL.B. (University of Windsor, 1974); called to the bar 1976; articled with the firm 1974-75; practised with the firm 1976- (partner 1981).

Dennis, Judith Ann Merle B.A. (University of Toronto, 1976), LL.B. (University of Toronto, 1984); called to the bar 1986; articled with the firm 1984 85.

Denton, Frank B.A. (University of Toronto 1985), M.A. (McMaster University, 1986), LL.B. (McGill University, 1989); called to the bar 1991; articled with the firm 1989-90; practised with the firm 1991.

DesBrisay, H. Jeanne B.A. (Harvard University, 1986), LL.B. (University of Toronto, 1989), LL.M. (Cambridge University, 1991); called to the bar 1992; articled with the firm 1989-90; practised with the firm 1992-94.

Desjardins, Christopher J. B.A. (Carleton University, 1968), LL.B. (University of Ottawa, 1972); called to the bar 1974; articled with the firm 1972-73; practised with the firm 1974-77.

DesLauriers, J. Mark B.Comm. (Queen's University, 1978), LL.B. (York University, 1981); called to the bar 1983; articled with the firm 1981-82; practised with the firm 1983- (partner 1989).

Devir, Anthony J. B.Ec. (Australian National University, 1980), LL.B. (Australian National University, 1983); called to the bar 1983 (Australian Capital Territory), 1989 (New South Wales), 1993 (Ontario); practised with the firm 1993-.

Dey, Peter J. B.Sc. (Queen's University, 1963), LL.B. (Dalhousie University, 1966), LL.M. (Harvard University, 1967); called to the bar 1969; articled with the firm 1967-68; practised with the firm 1969-83, 1985-94 (partner 1973, resigned 1983, re-admitted 1985).

Dickson, Mary Louise B.A. (University of Toronto, 1961), LL.B. (Osgoode Hall, 1964); called to the bar 1966; articled with the firm 1964-65.

Dillon, Ann D. B.A. (Queen's University, 1973), LL.B. (University of Toronto, 1977); called to the bar 1979; articled with the firm 1977-78; practised with the firm 1979-91 (partner 1984).

Dillon, Peter M. LL.B. (Queen's University, 1986); called to the bar 1988; articled with the firm 1986-87.

Dobbin, Terence S. LL.B. (University of Toronto, 1984); called to the bar 1986; articled with the firm 1984-85; practised with the firm 1986- (partner 1992).

Dolman, Jennifer B.A. (University of Toronto, 1986), LL.B. (McGill University, 1989); called to the bar 1991; articled with the firm 1989-90; practised with the firm 1992-.

Donald, Anne K. B.A. (Queen's University, 1984), LL.B. (University of Windsor, 1992); articled with the firm 1992-93.

Doran, James K. B.A. (University of Toronto, 1947); M.A. (University of Michigan, 1951); called to the bar 1956; practised with the firm 1962-91 (partner 1968).

Douglas, J. Ian B.A. (University of Toronto, 1942); called to the bar 1948; articled with the firm 1945-48; practised with the firm 1948-56.

Douglas, William M. Called to the bar 1886; practised with the firm 1888-1901 (partner 1889).

Dover, Edith P. (Meisels) B.Sc. (University of Toronto, 1987), LL.B. (York University, 1990); called to the bar 1992; articled with the firm 1990-91; practised with the firm 1992-.

Drinkwater, David W. B.A. (University of Western Ontario, 1970), LL.B. (Dalhousie University, 1973), LL.M. (University of London, 1974); called to the bar

1976 (Ontario), admitted to practise as a solicitor 1989 (England and Wales); articled with the firm 1974-75; practised with the firm 1976-94 (partner 1981); Managing Partner, Osler Renault 1994-.

Dryden, Kenneth W. A.B. (Cornell University, 1969), LL.B. (McGill University, 1973), LL.D. (Niagara University, 1985); called to the bar 1980; articled with the firm 1973-74.

Dubiner, Jay L. B.A. (York University, 1987), LL.B. (University of Toronto, 1990); called to the bar 1992 (Ontario), 1992 (New York); articled with the firm 1990-91; practised with the firm 1992-93.

Duncan, C. Mark B.A. (Queen's University, 1986), LL.B. (Queen's University, 1989); called to the bar 1991; articled with the firm 1989-90; practised with the firm 1991-93.

Dunlop-Jackson, Colleen B.A. (Queen's University, 1985), LL.B. (Queen's University, 1988); called to the bar 1990; articled with the firm 1988-89.

Dyer, Valerie A.E. B.A. (Dalhousie University, 1976), LL.B. (Dalhousie University, 1980); called to the bar 1982 (Ontario), 1985 (Nova Scotia); articled with the firm 1980-81; practised with the firm 1982- (partner 1988).

Dymond, A. Christopher B.A. (University of Toronto, 1971), LL.B. (Queen's University, 1975); called to the bar 1977; articled with the firm 1975-76.

Dzulynsky, Myron B. B.A. (University of Toronto, 1988), LL.B. (University of Western Ontario, 1991); called to the bar 1993; articled with the firm 1991-92.

Eagan, John J.M. B.A. (Bishop's University, 1963), B.C.L. (University of New Brunswick, 1966); called to the bar 1966 (New Brunswick), 1968 (Ontario); articled with the firm 1966-67; practised with the firm 1968-69.

Edwards, Mark L.J. B.A. (Queen's University), LL.B. (Dalhousie University); called to the bar 1981; articled with the firm 1979-80; practised with the firm 1981-84.

Edwards, W.S. Called to the bar 1909; articled with the firm 1905-09; practised with the firm 1909-11.

Eisen, Sarah A. B.A. (York University, 1985), LL.B. (University of Toronto, 1988); called to the bar 1990; articled with the firm 1988-89; practised with the firm 1990-93.

Eisner, Sherri LL.B. (York University, 1978); called to the bar 1980; practised with the firm 1988-89.

Elliott, Donald J. B.A. (Carleton University, 1966), LL.B. (University of Western Ontario, 1969); called to the bar 1971; articled with the firm 1969-70; practised with the firm 1971-75.

Elliott, William J.S. B.A.(University of Ottawa, 1976), LL.B. (University of Ottawa, 1979); called to the bar 1981; practised with the firm 1984-88.

Ellis, S. Ronald B.A. Sc. (University of Toronto, 1956), LL.B. (University of Toronto, 1962); called to the bar 1964; articled with the firm 1962-63; practised with the firm 1964-75 (partner 1971).

Elston, Harold G. LL.B. (Queen's University, 1986); called to the bar 1988; articled with the firm 1986-87.

Emberley, Cheryl D.M. B.A. (University of Calgary, 1985), LL.B. (University of Ottawa, 1988); called to the bar 1990; practised with the firm 1990-.

Endicott, Timothy A.B. (Harvard University, 1983), M.Phil. (Oxford University, 1985), LL.B. (University of Toronto, 1988); called to the bar 1990; articled with the firm 1988-89; practised with the firm 1990-91.

Erickson, Christian B.L. B.Comm. (University of Calgary, 1986), LL.B. (University of Toronto, 1989); called to the bar 1991; articled with the firm 1989-90; practised with the firm 1991-.

Ernst, Joseph LL.B. (York University, 1994); articled with the firm 1994-.

Evans, Christine S. B.Sc. (McMaster University, 1991), LL.B. (University of Ottawa, 1994); articled with the firm 1994-.

Evans, John T. B.Comm. (University of Toronto, 1961), LL.B. (University of Toronto, 1964); called to the bar 1966; practised with the firm 1993- (partner 1993).

Ewart, Scott L. LL.B. (University of Windsor); called to the bar 1980; practised with the firm 1983-86.

Fairbanks, Edwin Arthur B.A. (McMaster University, 1942); called to the bar 1948; articled with the firm 1945-48.

Farrell, Eleanor K. B.Comm. (McGill University, 1988), LL.B. (McGill University, 1992); articled with the firm 1992-93.

Fay, Paul M. B.A. (Queen's University, 1982), LL.B. (University of Reading, 1990), LL.B. (Queen's University, 1994); articled with the firm 1994-.

Feldbloom, David P. B.Comm. (University of Toronto, 1986, LL.B. (University of British Columbia, 1991); called to the bar 1993; articled with the firm 1991-92; practised with the firm 1993-94.

Fellowes, Karen L. B.A. (University of Manitoba, 1988), LL.B. (University of Western Ontario, 1991); called to the bar 1993, articled with the firm 1991-92; practised with the firm 1993-94.

Ferguson, Robert G. A.B. (Princeton University, 1924); called to the bar 1927; articled with the firm 1927; practised with the firm 1927-79 (partner 1929).

Ferrier, Lee K. B.A. (McMaster University, 1959), LL.B. (University of Ottawa, 1962); called to the bar 1964; practised with the firm 1986-91 (partner 1986).

Field-Marsham, Marilyn M.M. B.A. (McGill University, 1962), LL.B. (York University, 1978); called to the bar 1980; practised with the firm 1980- (partner 1985).

Fine, Sherri R. LL.B. (York University, 1990); called to the bar 1993; articled with the firm 1991-92.

Fischer, Sheryl B.A. (York University, 1981), LL.B. (University of Western Ontario, 1984); called to the bar 1986; practised with the firm 1987-92.

Fisher, Barry D. B.Eng. (McGill University, 1968), LL.B. (York University, 1971); called to the bar 1973; practised with the firm 1973-76.

Fisher, Elizabeth A. B.Sc. (University of Western Ontario, 1970), LL.B. (University of Toronto, 1978); called to the bar 1980; practised with the firm 1986-94 (partner 1988).

Fisher, F. Susan B.A. (University of Western Ontario, 1986); M.B.A. (University of Toronto, 1991), J.D. (University of Detroit, 1994), LL.B. (University of Windsor, 1994); articled with the firm 1994-.

Flak, George B.A. (University of Toronto, 1967), LL.B. (University of Toronto, 1970); called to the bar 1972; articled with the firm 1970-71.

Fogo, James G. B.Sc. (Queen's University, 1951), LL.B. (Dalhousie University, 1954); called to the bar 1954 (Nova Scotia); 1956 (Ontario); practised with the firm 1986- (partner 1986).

Foley, Andrew J. B.A. (University of Toronto, 1985), M.A. (University of Toronto, 1987), LL.B. (University of Toronto, 1991); articled with the firm 1991-92.

Follwell, Rodney Edward B.A. (Queen's University, 1965), LL.B. (Queen's University, 1971); called to the bar 1973; articled with the firm 1971-72.

Fong, Jennifer J. B.N. (Dalhousie University, 1987), LL.B. (Dalhousie University, 1991); called to the bar 1993; articled with the firm 1991-92; practised with the firm 1993-.

Ford, Daniel A.G. LL.B. (University of Ottawa, 1987); called to the bar 1989; articled with the firm 1987-88; practised with the firm 1989-93.

Ford, Frank D.C.L. (University of Toronto, 1909), LL.D. (Université Laval 1946), LL.D. (University of Alberta, 1946); called to the bar 1895 (Ontario), 1906 (Alberta); practised with the firm 1903-06 (partner 1903).

Fordyce, James E. B.A. (University of Toronto, 1970), LL.B. (York University, 1973); called to the bar 1975 (Ontario), admitted to practice as a solicitor (England and Wales) 1990; articled with the firm 1973-74; practised with the firm 1975- (partner 1980).

Forgie, C. Alicia B.A. (University of Toronto, 1958), LL.B. (Osgoode Hall, 1961); called to the bar 1963; practised with the firm 1965-84 (partner 1971).

Forster, David R. B.Comm. (Queen's University, 1985), LL.B. (University of Toronto, 1988); called to the bar 1990; articled with the firm 1988-89; practised with the firm 1990-.

Fox, Sivan B.A. (McGill University, 1990), LL.B./B.C.L. (McGill University, 1994); articled with the firm 1994-.

Fox-Revett, Melissa G. LL.B. (York University, 1991); called to the bar 1993; articled with the firm 1991-92; practised with the firm 1993-.

Francis, Ross W. B.A. (Queen's University, 1979), M.B.A. (Queen's University, 1981), LL.B. (York University, 1986); called to the bar 1988; articled with the firm 1986-87; practised with the firm 1988-93.

Frank, Robert I. B.Sc. (McGill University, 1988), LL.B./B.C.L. (McGill University, 1992); called to the bar 1994; articled with the firm 1992-93; practised with the firm 1994-.

Franklyn, Peter H.G. B.Comm. (Queen's University, 1979), LL.B. (University of Windsor, 1982); called to the bar 1984; articled with the firm 1982-83; practised with the firm 1984- (partner 1990).

Fraser, George Alexander B.A. (University of Toronto, 1969), LL.B. (University of Toronto, 1972), LL.M. (York University, 1979); called to the bar 1974; articled with the firm 1972-73.

Fraser, Jean M. B.Sc. (University of Toronto, 1969), LL.B. (University of Toronto, 1975); called to the bar 1977; practised with the firm 1993- (partner 1993).

Fraser, Megan E. LL.B. (York University, 1994); articled with the firm 1994-.

Frawley, Heather A. B.A. (Dalhousie University, 1965), LL.B. (Dalhousie University, 1968); called to the bar 1970; articled with the firm 1968-69; practised with the firm 1970-92 (partner 1976).

Freedman, Bonnie A. B.A. (American University in Paris), M.A. (Middlebury College, 1986), LL.B. (University of Toronto, 1989); called to the bar 1991; articled with the firm 1989-90; practised with the firm 1991-92.

Friday, Joseph A. B.J. (Carleton University, 1983), LL.B. (University of Ottawa, 1988); called to the bar 1990; articled with the firm 1988-89; practised with the firm 1990-92.

Friedman, Susan E. B.F.A. (Boston University, 1971), LL.B. (University of Toronto, 1983); called to the bar 1985; articled with the firm 1983-84; practised with the firm 1985-91.

Friesen, Ted B.Comm. (University of Manitoba, 1973), M.Sc., (University of British Columbia, 1980), LL.B. (University of Ottawa, 1984); called to the bar 1986 (Ontario), 1987 (British Columbia); articled with the firm 1984-85; practised with the firm 1987-91.

Fry, Robert R.A. LL.B. (University of Ottawa, 1992), LL.M. (University of Ottawa, 1993); articled with the firm 1993-94

Fuke, John M. B.Comm. (University of Toronto, 1960), LL.B. (University of Toronto, 1963); called to the bar 1965 (Ontario); 1982 (Alberta); articled with the firm 1963-64; practised with the firm 1965-69.

Gagan, Sarah K.L. B.A. (McMaster University, 1991), LL.B. (McGill University, 1994); articled with the firm 1994-.

Gagnon-Gravelle, Julie E.M. LL.B. (University of Ottawa, 1984); called to the bar 1987; practised with the firm 1987-91.

Galpern, Karen F. M.A. (University of Glasgow, 1973), LL.B. (University of Glasgow, 1984), LL.B. (University of Western Ontario, 1991); called to the bar 1993, articled with the firm 1992-93; practised with the firm 1993-.

Galway, Laurie A. B.A. (York University, 1986), LL.B. (University of Windsor, 1989); called to the bar 1991; articled with the firm 1989-90; practised with the firm 1991-.

Gameroff, David LL.B. (McGill University, 1986); articled with the firm 1986-87.

Gaudet, Clare M. B.A. (McGill University, 1980), LL.B./B.C.L. (McGill University, 1984); called to the bar 1986; articled with the firm 1984-85.

Gelowitz, Mark A. B.A. (University of Regina, 1983), LL.B. (Queen's University, 1986), B.C.L. (Oxford University, 1989); called to the bar 1987 (Saskatchewan), 1991 (Ontario); practised with the firm 1991-.

Giffen, James Peter B.A. (University of Toronto, 1958), LL.B. (Osgoode Hall, 1961); called to the bar 1963; articled with the firm 1961-62; practised with the firm 1963-65.

Gilchrist, Donald G. B.A. (University of Toronto, 1978), LL.B. (University of Toronto, 1981), B.C.L. (Oxford University, 1984); called to the bar 1985; articled with the firm 1981-82; practised with the firm 1985- (partner 1992).

Gilfillan, John Doherty B.A. (McGill University, 1963), LL.B. (University of Toronto, 1966); called to the bar 1968; articled with the firm 1966-67.

Giulietti, Rosanne M. B.A. (McMaster University, 1985), M.A. (Queen's University, 1987), LL.B. (University of Toronto, 1991); called to the bar 1993; articled with the firm 1991-92.

Glendinning, Deborah A. B.A. (University of Toronto, 1983), LL.B. (University of Ottawa, 1988); called to the bar 1990; articled with the firm 1988-89; practised with the firm 1990-.

Glossop, Peter L. LL.B. (York University, 1983), LL.M. (University of London, 1984); called to the bar 1986; articled with the firm 1984-85; practised with the firm 1986- (partner 1993).

Godson, Robert Gilbert B.A. (University of Toronto, 1953), LL.B. (University of Toronto, 1957); called to the bar 1959; articled with the firm 1957-59; practised with the firm 1959-60.

Goldberg, Barry I. B.A. (McGill University, 1979), LL.B./B.C.L. (McGill University, 1983); called to the bar 1985; practised with the firm 1986- (partner 1991).

Goldberg, Mitchell D. B.A. (University of Western Ontario, 1988), LL.B. (University of Western Ontario, 1991); called to the bar 1993; articled with the firm 1991-92.

Golick, Steven G. B.Comm. (Sir George Williams College, 1979), LL.B. (McGill University, 1982), B.C.L. (McGill University, 1983); called to the bar 1983 (New York), 1985 (Ontario); practised with the firm 1985- (partner 1991).

González-Martin, Clara M. B.A. (University of Toronto, 1988), LL.B. (University of Toronto, 1990); called to the bar 1992; articled with the firm 1990-91; practised with the firm 1992-.

Goodman, Andrew J.; B.S.Sc. (University of Ottawa, 1984), M.A. (Carleton University, 1988), LL.B. (University of Ottawa, 1991); articled with the firm 1991-92.

Goodwin, John G. B.A. (University of Toronto, 1956), LL.B. (Osgoode Hall, 1960); called to the bar 1960; articled with the firm 1958-60; practised with the firm 1960- (partner 1968).

Gorrell, J. David B.A. (University of Toronto, 1965), LL.B. (University of Toronto, 1968); called to the bar 1970; articled with the firm 1968-69; practised with the firm 1970-74.

Gough, Michael J. B.A. (St. Patrick's College, 1965), LL.B. (University of Toronto, 1968), LL.M. (University of London, 1971); called to the bar 1970 (Ontario), admitted to practise as a solicitor 1974 (England and Wales); practised with the firm 1985- (partner 1986).

Grafstein, Laurence S. B.A. (Harvard University, 1982), M.Phil. (Oxford University, 1984), LL.B. (University of Toronto, 1988); articled with the firm 1988-89.

Graif, Michael R. B.S.E. (University of Pennsylvania, 1988), LL.B. (University of Toronto, 1991); articled with the firm 1991-92.

Gray, Margaret A. B.A. (University of Toronto, 1972), M.A. (University of Toronto, 1974), LL.B. (University of Toronto, 1976); called to the bar 1978; articled with the firm 1976-77; practised with the firm 1978-80.

Gray, Ross G. B.A.Sc. (University of Toronto, 1938); called to the bar 1945; practised with the firm 1986-91 (partner 1986).

Greco, Carlo B.A.Sc. (University of Toronto 1985), LL.B. (University of Toronto, 1988); called to the bar 1990; articled with the firm 1988-89; practised with the firm 1990-94.

Green, Lyndsay M. B.A. (University of Waterloo, 1987), LL.B. (Queen's University, 1990); articled with the firm 1990-91.

Greenberg, Mark B.A. (Clark University, 1977), M.A. (University of British Columbia, 1979), LL.B. (Dalhousie University, 1984); called to the bar 1986; articled with the firm 1984-85; practised with the firm 1986-89.

Grier, Alexander Munro Called to the bar 1882 (England), 1884 (Ontario); articled with the firm 1883-84; practised with the firm 1923-45 (Counsel).

Grieve, John N. B.A. (University of Toronto, 1956), LL.B. (Osgoode Hall, 1960); called to the bar 1960; articled with the firm 1958-59; practised with the firm 1960-91 (partner 1968).

Griffiths, Heather P. B.A. (York University, 1974), LL.B. (University of Ottawa, 1985); called to the bar 1987; articled with the firm 1986; practised with the firm 1987- (partner 1993).

Grmovsek, S. Joseph LL.B. (York University, 1993); articled with the firm 1993-94.

Grosfield, Howard M. B.A. (University of Western Ontario, 1990), LL.B. (University of Western Ontario, 1994); articled with the firm 1994-.

Groulx, Rodolph W. B.Sc. Phm. (University of Toronto, 1961), LL.B. (University of Toronto, 1967); called to the bar 1969; practised with the firm 1987- (partner 1987).

Ground, John D. (Jack) B.A., (University of Toronto, 1954), LL.B. (University of Toronto, 1957); called to the bar 1959; articled with the firm 1957-59; practised with the firm 1959-91 (partner 1965).

Guest, Martin T. B.A. (University of Toronto, 1984), LL.B. (University of Toronto, 1987); called to the bar 1989; articled with the firm 1987-88; practised with the firm 1989-94.

Gwyn, Herbert Charles Called to the bar 1876, admitted to practise as a solicitor 1871; articled with the firm 1868-71; practised with the firm 1871-82 (partner 1871).

Gwynne-Timothy, Gordon K. A.B. (Harvard University, 1987), B.A. (Cambridge), LL.B. (University of Toronto, 1991); articled with the firm 1991-92.

Hall, Terence D. B.A. (Queen's University, 1977), LL.B. (University of Toronto, 1981); called to the bar 1983; practised with the firm 1987- (partner 1990).

Halladay, Sheila K. B.A. (University of Windsor, 1974), B.Sc. (University of Windsor, 1974), LL.B. (University of Windsor, 1977), LL.M. (Columbia University, 1978); called to the bar 1980 (Ontario), 1980 (New York); articled with the firm 1978-79; practised with the firm 1980-85.

Halpern, Martin B.A. (University of Toronto, 1985), LL.B. (York University, 1988); called to the bar 1990; articled with the firm 1988-89; practised with the firm 1990-91.

Hambling, Donald V. Called to the bar 1948; articled with the firm 1945-48.

Hamilton, Douglas T. B.Sc. (Queen's University, 1980), LL.B. (Queen's University, 1983), LL.M. (University of London, 1987); called to the bar 1986; practised with the firm 1988- (partner 1994).

Hamilton, Ian T. H. B.A. (University of Toronto, 1962), LL.B. (Osgoode Hall, 1965); called to the bar 1967; articled with the firm 1965-66; practised with the firm 1967-68.

Handy, Francis J.F. B.A. (University of Western Ontario, 1982), LL.B. (University of Windsor, 1988); called to the bar 1990; articled with the firm 1988-89; practised with the firm 1990-94.

Hanna, Donald D. B.A. (Manitoba, 1986), LL.B. (University of Toronto, 1989), B.C.L. (Oxford University, 1991); called to the bar 1992; practised with the firm 1992-.

Hanna, Shenda B.A. (University of Alberta), LL.B. (University of Toronto, 1989); articled with the firm 1989-90.

Hannon, Sally B.A. (Carleton University, 1975), LL.B. (York University, 1986); called to the bar 1988; practised with the firm 1988-91.

Hansell, Carol A. B.A. (University of Western Ontario, 1981), M.A. (University of Toronto, 1982), M.B.A./LL.B. (York University, 1986); called to the bar 1988; articled with the firm 1986-87; practised with the firm 1988-94.

Hanson, W. Jason M. B.A. (University of Toronto, 1977), LL.B. (University of Windsor, 1980); called to the bar 1982; articled with the firm 1980-81; practised with the firm 1982- (partner 1988).

Harcourt, Frederick Weir LL.D. (Queen's University, 1921); called to the bar 1886, admitted to practise as a solicitor 1880; practised with the firm 1882-1932 (partner 1901).

Harnett, Aaron B. B.A. (University of Toronto, 1984), LL.B. (Queen's University, 1990); called to the bar 1992; articled with the firm 1990-91.

Harris, Judith E. B.Sc. (University of Alberta, 1969), LL.B. (University of Toronto, 1982); called to the bar 1984; articled with the firm 1982-83; practised with the firm 1984-88.

Hart, Christopher P. B.A. (Vassar College, 1985), LL.B. (Dalhousie University, 1989); called to the bar 1991; articled with the firm 1989-90; practised with the firm 1991-94.

Hartog, Adrian P. B.Sc., (University of Toronto, 1979), LL.B. (University of Windsor, 1982); called to the bar 1984; articled with the firm 1982-83; practised with the firm 1985- (partner 1990).

Hassell, James R. B.A., (University of Toronto, 1970), LL.B. (York University, 1974); called to the bar 1976; articled with the firm 1974-75; practised with the firm 1976- (partner 1981).

Hawkins, Thomas R. B.A. (Queen's University, 1963), LL.B. (University of Toronto, 1966); called to the bar 1968; articled with the firm 1966-67; practised with the firm 1968-73.

Hay, David D. B.A. (University of Toronto, 1976), LL.B. (York University, 1979); called to the bar 1981; articled with the firm 1979-80; practised with the firm 1981-84.

Heakes, Edward A. B.A (University of Waterloo 1975), LL.B. (University of Western Ontario, 1978); called to the bar 1980; practised with the firm 1981-94 (partner 1985).

Healey, Martha A. B.A. (Wilfrid Laurier University, 1986), M.A. (Carleton University, 1987), LL.B. (University of Western Ontario, 1990); called to the bar 1992; articled with the firm 1990-91; practised with the firm 1992-.

Heath, Philip J.B. B.A. (University of Toronto, 1977), LL.B. (Queen's University, 1981); called to the bar 1983; practised with the firm 1986- (partner 1990).

Hebb, Laurence D. B.A. (University of Toronto, 1959), LL.B. (Dalhousie University, 1962); called to the bar 1963 (Nova Scotia), 1964 (Ontario); articled with the firm 1962-63; practised with the firm 1964- (partner 1971).

Heintzman, Thomas G. B.A. (Harvard University, 1962), LL.B. (Osgoode Hall, 1966), LL.B. (University of London, 1967); called to the bar 1968 (Ontario), 1977 (Newfoundland), 1990 (Alberta); articled with the firm 1966-67.

Hendrie, Anthony O. B.A. (Queen's University, 1955), LL.B. (Osgoode Hall, 1960); called to the bar 1962; practised with the firm 1974-92 (partner 1974).

Herlin, Kenneth B.Comm. (McGill University, 1985), LL.B. (University of Toronto, 1988); called to the bar 1990; articled with the firm 1988-89; practised with the firm 1990-.

Herman, William J. B.Sc. (McGill University, 1979), M.Sc. (McGill University, 1981), B.C.L. (McGill University, 1983), LL.B. (McGill University, 1984); called to the bar 1986; articled with the firm 1984-85; practised with the firm 1986-88.

Herschorn, Arnold B.A. (McGill University, 1968), LL.B. (University of Toronto, 1977); called to the bar 1979; articled with the firm 1977-78.

Hession, Grace M.L.S. (University of Western Ontario, 1987), LL.B. (University of Saskatchewan, 1985); called to the bar 1992; articled with the firm 1990-91.

Hewitt, Gary B.A. (University of British Columbia, 1969), M.Phil. (Yale University, 1971); Ph.D. (Yale University, 1975), LL.B. (University of British Columbia, 1987); articled with the firm 1987-88.

Hicks, Christine F. B.Sc. (Queen's University, 1986), LL.B. (University of Ottawa, 1992); called to the bar 1994; articled with the firm 1992-93; practised with the firm 1994-.

Higgins, Charles L.K. B.A. (University of Toronto, 1974), M.A. (University of Toronto, 1975), LL.B. (University of Ottawa, 1982); called to the bar 1983 (Alberta); 1987 (Ontario); practised with the firm 1986-91.

Hill, Gordon W. B.A. (Carleton University, 1984), LL.B. (Queen's University, 1988); called to the bar 1990; articled with the firm 1988-89.

Hodgson, H. Douglas B.A. (University of Toronto, 1967), M.Phil. (Columbia University, 1973), LL.B. (University of Toronto, 1979); called to the bar 1981; articled with the firm 1979-80; practised with the firm 1981-91 (partner 1987).

Hoffman, Richard C. LL.B. (University of Western Ontario, 1984), M.B.A. (University of Pennsylvania, 1987); called to the bar 1988; articled with the firm 1984-85.

Holmes, Janet A. LL.B. (University of Toronto, 1991), called to the bar 1993; articled with the firm 1991-92.

Hood, John Called to the bar 1930 (Ontario); practised with the firm 1940-45.

Hoppe, Andrew C. B.Comm. (University of Toronto, 1989), LL.B. (Queen's University, 1993); articled with the firm 1993-94.

Horner, H.B. Clay B.A. (Queen's University, 1980), LL.B. (University of Toronto, 1983), LL.M. (Harvard University, 1984); called to the bar 1986; articled with the firm 1984-85; practised with the firm 1986- (partner 1991).

Horton, Edward A. B.A. (University of Western Ontario, 1967), LL.B. (Dalhousie University, 1970); called to the bar 1972; practised with the firm 1987-92 (partner 1987).

Hoskin, John LL.D. (University of Toronto, 1899), D.C.L. (Trinity University, 1904); called to the bar 1863; practised with the firm 1882-1921 (partner 1882-1910).

Houston, J. Alexander (Sandy) B.A. (University of Toronto, 1983), LL.B. (Queen's University, 1990); called to the bar 1992; articled with the firm 1990-91; practised with the firm 1992-94.

Hovland, John M. B.A. (University of Toronto, 1987), LL.B. (Dalhousie University, 1990); called to the bar 1992; articled with the firm 1990-91; practised with the firm 1992-.

Howard, Judith A. B.A. (Hebrew University of Jerusalem, 1976), LL.B. (York University, 1990); called to the bar 1992; articled with the firm 1990-91; practised with the firm 1992-93.

Hsu, Yi-Wen B.B.A. (York University, 1992); LLB. (York University, 1992), LL.M. (Ludwig-Maximilians-Universitaet, 1993); articled with the firm 1993-94.

Huggard, John Joseph Called to the bar 1923; articled with the firm 1918-23.

Hulton, Joy L. B.A. (Queen's University, 1988), LL.B. (Queen's University, 1991); called to the bar 1993; articled with the firm 1991-92; practised with the firm 1993-.

Hurwitz, Paula B. B.Sc. (University of Toronto 1986), LL.B. (University of Toronto, 1989); called to the bar 1991; articled with the firm 1989-90; practised with the firm 1991-.

Huycke, Edward J. M. B.A. (University of Toronto, 1949); called to the bar 1953; articled with the firm 1951-53; practised with the firm 1953-91 (partner 1959).

Huycke, Frederick A. M. B.A. (University of Toronto, 1948); called to the bar 1951; articled with the firm 1948-51; practised with the firm 1951-92 (partner 1956).

Huycke, George Meredith B.A. (University of Toronto, 1918); called to the bar 1920; articled with the firm 1918-20; practised with the firm 1920-70 (partner 1926).

Inwood, William J. B.A. (Carleton University, 1970), LL.B. (University of Ottawa, 1973); called to the bar 1975; practised with the firm 1979-80.

Jalan, Abhimanyu B.Comm. (St. Xavier's College, 1987), LL.B. (University of Delhi, 1990), LL.B. (University of Ottawa, 1993), LL.M. (University of Ottawa, 1993); called to the bar 1993 (Delhi, India); articled with the firm 1993-94.

Jamal, Ferenaz (Farah) S. B.A. (York University, 1990), LL.B./M.B.A. (York University, 1994); articled with the firm 1994-.

Janicki, Peter S. B.A. (Brock University, 1989), LL.B. (York University, 1992); called to the bar 1994; articled with the firm 1992-93; practised with the firm 1994-.

Jenner, Natalie M. B.A. (University of Toronto, 1990), LL.B. (University of Toronto, 1993); articled with the firm 1993-94.

Jennings, John B.A. (University of Toronto, 1896), LL.B. (University of Toronto, 1897); called to the bar 1899; articled with the firm 1896-99.

Jepson, Gordon S. B.A. (Royal Military College, 1986), M.A. (Queen's University, 1991), LL.B. (University of Windsor, 1994); articled with the firm 1994-.

Jobanputra, Sushma LL.B. (University of Toronto, 1988); called to the bar 1990; articled with the firm 1988-89; practised with the firm 1990-.

Johnston, David L. A.B. (Harvard University, 1963), LL.B. (Cambridge University, 1965), LL.B. (Queen's University, 1966), LL.D. (Law Society of Upper Canada, 1980), LL.D. (University of Toronto, 1985), LL.D. (Bishop's University, 1986), LL.D. (Memorial University of Newfoundland, 1986), D.Div. (Montreal

Theological College, 1987), LL.D. (University of British Columbia, 1989), LL.D. (Queen's University, 1991), LL.D. (University of Western Ontario, 1991), LL.D. (Université de Montréal, 1992); called to the bar 1970; articled with the firm 1966-67.

Jordan, Cally B.A. (Carleton University, 1970), M.A. (University of Toronto, 1973), LL.B. (McGill University, 1977), D.E.A. (Université de Paris I, 1978), B.C.L. (McGill University, 1980); called to the bar 1981 (Ontario), 1981 (Quebec), 1984 (California), 1986 (New York); practised with the firm 1989-91.

Josefo, Jay B.A. (McGill University, 1984), LL.B./B.C.L. (McGill University, 1988); called to the bar 1990; practised with the firm 1990-91.

Judge, Thomas R. B.A. (Acadia University, 1952), LL.B. (Dalhousie University, 1955); called to the bar 1956 (Alberta), 1971 (Ontario); practised with the firm 1976-94 (partner 1979).

Julian, George E. B.A. (University of Toronto, 1953), M.A. (University of Toronto, 1956), LL.B. (University of Toronto, 1961); called to the bar 1963; practised with the firm 1965-82 (partner 1972).

Jutras, Ronald H. B.A.Sc. (University of Toronto, 1980), LL.B. (University of Ottawa, 1985); called to the bar 1987; practised with the firm 1987-94.

Kagedan, Barbara Laine LL.B. (University of Toronto, 1979), LL.M. (New York University, 1981); called to the bar 1982 (Ontario); 1983 (New York); practised with the firm 1989-91.

Kalm, John T. B.Sc. (University of Toronto, 1986), M.B.A. (McMaster University, 1989), LL.B. (Dalhousie University, 1992); called to the bar 1994; articled with the firm 1992-93; practised with the firm 1994-.

Kalvin, Neill B.A. (University of Toronto, 1987), LL.B. (University of Western Ontario, 1990); articled with the firm 1991-92.

Karish, Gail D.A. (University of Manitoba, 1985), LL.B./B.C.L. (McGill University, 1989); articled with the firm 1989-90.

Karna, Angie B.Sc. (University of Toronto, 1989), J.D. (University of Detroit, 1993), LL.B. (University of Windsor, 1993); articled with the firm 1993-94.

Karol, Robert H. LL.B. (York University, 1985); called to the bar 1987; articled with the firm 1985-86; practised with the firm 1987-89.

Kay, Sarah A.E. B.A. (Queen's University), LL.B. (University of Windsor, 1991); called to the bar 1993 (Ontario and the Northwest Territories); articled with the firm 1991-92.

Keay, Derek S. B.A. (Carleton University, 1987), M.I.R. (Queen's University, 1989), LL.B. (Queen's University, 1992); called to the bar 1994; articled with the firm 1992-93; practised with the firm 1994-.

Kehl, Krista J. B.A. (University of Toronto), M.L.S. (University of Toronto), LL.B. (York University); called to the bar 1981; articled with the firm 1979-80; practised with the firm 1981-83.

Kelly, Arthur Joseph B.A. (University of Toronto, 1920); called to the bar 1923; articled with the firm 1920-21.

Kelly, John S. B.A. (University of Toronto, 1968), LL.B. (University of Toronto, 1971); called to the bar 1973; articled with the firm 1971-72; practised with the firm 1973-74.

Kempston-Darkes, V. Maureen B.A. (University of Toronto, 1970), LL.B. (University of Toronto, 1973); called to the bar 1975; articled with the firm 1973-74; practised with the firm 1975.

Kennedy, Claire M.C. B.A.Sc. (University of Toronto, 1989), LL.B. (Queen's University, 1994); articled with the firm 1994-.

Kennedy, James F. B.A. (University of Western Ontario, 1957), LL.B. (Osgoode Hall, 1960); called to the bar 1962; practised with the firm 1962- (partner 1971).

Kennedy, Robert A. B.Sc. (Queen's University, 1984), LL.B. (Dalhousie University, 1992); articled with the firm 1992-93.

Kennish, J. Timothy A.B. (Harvard University, 1961), LL.B. (Osgoode Hall, 1964); called to the bar 1966; articled with the firm 1964-65; practised with the firm 1966- (partner 1972).

Kingissepp, Andrew H. LL.B. (York University, 1982); called to the bar 1984; articled with the firm 1982-83; practised with the firm 1984- (partner 1990).

Kirby, Alison B.A. (McGill University, 1981), LL.B. (University of Ottawa, 1987); called to the bar 1989; articled with the firm 1987-88; practised with the firm 1989-92.

Kirby, C.W. Daniel B.A.Sc. (University of Toronto, 1977), LL.B. (York University, 1980); called to the bar 1982; practised with the firm 1986- (partner 1988).

Knowles, Lori P. B.A. (University of Western Ontario, 1987), LL.B. (McGill University, 1992); called to the bar 1994; articled with the firm 1992-93; practised with the firm 1994-.

Knudsen, Jill M. LL.B. (University of Western Ontario, 1986); called to the bar 1988; articled with the firm 1986-87.

Koch, Jeffrey E. B.A. (Wilfrid Laurier University, 1989), LL.B. (York University, 1993); articled with the firm 1993-94.

Kofman, James E. B.Comm. (Queen's University, 1978), LL.B. (Queen's University, 1982); called to the bar 1984 (Ontario), admitted to practice as a solicitor (England and Wales) 1990; articled with the firm 1982-83; practised with the firm 1984- (partner 1990).

Kopparath, Philip G. LL.B. (Queen's University); called to the bar 1979; articled with the firm 1972-73.

Kops, Brenda B.A. (University of Western Ontario, 1982), LL.B. (University of Windsor, 1985); called to the bar 1987; articled with the firm 1985-86; practised with the firm 1987-90.

Korovilas, Konstantina D. LL.B. (York University, 1993); articled with the firm 1993-94.

Kozak, Lubomir B.A. (University of Toronto, 1966), LL.B. (York University, 1969); called to the bar 1971; articled with the firm 1969-70.

Krawitz, Dina B.A. (Tufts University, 1983), J.D. (S.U.N.Y. Buffalo, 1986), LL.M. (University of Ottawa, 1987); called to the bar 1987 (New York); 1987 (Ontario); articled with the firm 1987-88; practised with the firm 1989-91.

Krupat, Kenneth A. B.A. (University of Toronto, 1988), LL.B. (University of British Columbia, 1992); called to the bar 1994; articled with the firm 1992-93; practised with the firm 1994-.

Kruzick, Emile R. B.A. (University of Toronto, 1967), LL.B. (Dalhousie University, 1970); called to the bar 1972; practised with the firm 1986-93 (partner 1986).

Kuwahara, Stephen E. LL.B. (University of Western Ontario, 1988); called to the bar 1990; articled with the firm 1988-89; practised with the firm 1990-94.

Kwasniewski, Bernard J. B.A. (York University, 1985), LL.B. (York University, 1992), M.B.A. (York University, 1992); called to the bar 1994; articled with the firm 1992-93; practised with the firm 1994-.

LaForme, Harry S. LL.B (York University, 1977); called to the bar 1979; articled with the firm 1977-78; practised with the firm 1979.

Laing, R. Gregory B.A. (Queen's University, 1981), LL.B. (University of Windsor, 1985); called to the bar 1987; articled with the firm 1985-86; practised with the firm 1987-91.

Laird, Ian A. B.A. (McGill University, 1987), LL.B. (University of Windsor, 1993); articled with the firm 1993-94.

Lally, A. Michelle B.A. (Queen's University, 1987), LL.B. (University of Western Ontario, 1990); called to the bar 1992; articled with the firm 1990-91; practised with the firm 1992-.

Lambert, John Swanton B.A. (University of New Brunswick, 1969), LL.B. (University of New Brunswick, 1971), LL.M. (University of London, 1974); called to the bar 1971 (New Brunswick); 1975 (Ontario); practised with the firm 1976-78.

Lamont, Stephen B.A. (McGill University, 1985), LL.B. (McGill University, 1990), M.A. (Concordia University, 1993); called to the bar 1992; articled with the firm 1990-91; practised with the firm 1992-.

Lampert, Alvin S. B.A. (University of Toronto, 1972), M.A. (University of Toronto, 1974), LL.B (University of Toronto, 1989); called to the bar 1991; articled with the firm 1989-90; practised with the firm 1991-.

Lando, Robert C. LL.B. (University of Toronto, 1989); called to the bar 1991 (Ontario); 1991 (New York); articled with the firm 1989-90; practised with the firm 1991-.

Landy, Allyson C. B.A. (University of Toronto, 1982), LL.B. (University of Toronto, 1985); called to the bar 1987; articled with the firm 1985-86; practised with the firm 1987 (partner 1994).

Lane, G. Dennis B.A. (University of Toronto, 1954); called to the bar 1958; practised with the firm 1962-89 (partner 1968).

Langford, James Stuart Called to the bar 1977; articled with the firm 1975-76.

Langmuir, Archibald W. Called to the bar 1914; articled with the firm 1909-14; practised with the firm 1914-40 (partner 1914).

Langmuir, A. Woodburn B.A. (University of Toronto, 1937); called to the bar 1940; articled with the firm 1937-40); practised with the firm 1941-81.

Latimer, Bruce R. B.Sc.Eng. (Queen's University, 1983), M.Sc. (Queen's University, 1985), LL.B./M.B.A. (University of Western Ontario, 1992); called to the bar 1994; articled with the firm 1992-93; practised with the firm 1994-.

Latimer, Catherine Called to the bar 1981; articled with the firm 1979-80.

Layton, John F. B.A. (University of Toronto, 1966), M.A. (University of Chicago, 1967), LL.B. (University of Toronto, 1970); called to the bar 1972; practised with the firm 1974- (partner 1977).

Lawrence, Jacqueline G. B.A. (McMaster University, 1990), LL.B. (University of Toronto, 1993); articled with the firm 1993-94.

Leclair, Raymond G. LL.B. (University of Ottawa, 1982); called to the bar 1984; practised with the firm 1988-91.

Lederer, Thomas R. B.A. (York University, 1970), LL.B. (York University, 1973); called to the bar 1975; practised with the firm 1981-92 (partner 1983).

Ledger, J. Brett G. B.A. (University of Toronto, 1974), LL.B. (University of Windsor, 1977); called to the bar 1979; articled with the firm 1977-78; practised with the firm 1979- (partner 1984).

Lee, Julie Y. B.A. (University of Toronto, 1973), M.A. (University of Toronto, 1974), LL.B. (University of Toronto, 1978); called to the bar 1980; articled with the firm 1978-79; practised with the firm 1980- (partner 1986).

Lefas, Agnes S. M.A. (Sorbonne, 1970), M.A. (University of Chicago, 1972), LL.B. (Queen's University, 1979); M.A. (University of Paris XII, 1980); called to the bar 1982; practised with the firm 1985-86.

Lemieux, J. Francois B.A. (University of Ottawa, 1959), M.A. (University of Toronto, 1961), LL.B. (University of Toronto, 1964); called to the bar 1966; practised with the firm 1986- (partner 1986).

Lennox, Toby C.D. B.A. (Trent University, 1984), M.A. (Dalhousie University, 1986), B.A. (Oxford University, 1988), LL.B. (Dalhousie University, 1989); called to the bar 1991; articled with the firm 1989-90; practised with the firm 1991-.

Lester, Nina C. B.A. (Yale University, 1982), LL.B. (University of Toronto, 1986); called to the bar 1988; articled with the firm 1986-87; practised with the firm 1988-91.

Levitt, Brian M. B.A.Sc. (University of Toronto 1969), LL.B. (University of Toronto, 1973); called to the bar 1975; practised with the firm 1976-91 (partner 1979).

Levy, Jimmy Y. B.A. (McGill University, 1980); M.A. (Clark University, 1983), Ph.D. (Clark University, 1990), LL.B. (York University, 1990); called to the bar 1992; practised with the firm 1994-.

Lewis, Donald C. B.A. (Royal Military College, 1960), LL.B. (University of Western Ontario, 1963); called to the bar 1965; practised with the firm 1965-68.

Lewis, Timothy J. B.A. (University of Western Ontario, 1987), LL.B. (University of Toronto, 1990); articled with the firm 1990-91.

Lewtas, Amy C. B.A. (Williams College, 1984), LL.B. (University of Toronto, 1988); called to the bar 1990; articled with the firm 1988-89; practised with the firm 1990-.

Light, Warren B.Comm. (University of British Columbia), LL.B. (University of Toronto, 1990); articled with the firm 1990-91.

Lin, Jolie LL.B. (York University, 1986); called to the bar 1988; practised with the firm 1989-.

Lin, Peter B.A. (McMaster University, 1986), LL.B. (University of Toronto, 1989); articled with the firm 1989-90.

Lindsay, Robert F. B.Comm. (University of Toronto, 1958), M.A. (University of Toronto, 1959), LL.B. (Dalhousie University, 1963); called to the bar 1963 (Nova Scotia); 1968 (Ontario); 1982 (Alberta); practised with the firm 1972- (partner 1973).

Lisson, James H. B.Comm. (McGill University, 1975), LL.B. (Dalhousie University, 1975), LL.M. (Yale University, 1976); called to the bar 1978; articled with the firm 1976-77; practised with the firm 1978- (partner 1983).

Litner, Paul W. B.A. (University of Toronto, 1985), LL.B. (Queen's University, 1988); called to the bar 1990; articled with the firm 1988-89; practised with the firm 1990-.

Little, Andrew D. B.A. (Queen's University, 1987), LL.B. (Dalhousie University, 1990), B.C.L. (Oxford University, 1992); called to the bar 1993; practised with the firm 1993-.

Little, Anthony H. B.A. (University of Western Ontario, 1963), LL.B. (University of Toronto, 1966); called to the bar 1968; articled with the firm 1966-67.

Little, Robert W. LL.B. (Queen's University, 1982); called to the bar 1984; articled with the firm 1982-83; practised with the firm 1984-85.

Livingstone, W.C. Called to the bar 1884; articled with the firm 1883-84.

Lockwood, Thomas J. B.A. (McGill University, 1964), LL.B. (Osgoode Hall, 1967); called to the bar 1969; articled with the firm 1967-68; practised with the firm 1969-73.

Lococo, Richard A. LL.B. (York University, 1975); called to the bar 1977 (Ontario), admitted to practice as a solicitor (England and Wales) 1990; practised with the firm 1983- (partner 1985).

Love, G. Jeffrey B.A. (University of Toronto, 1984), LL.B. (Queen's University, 1987); called to the bar 1989; articled with the firm 1987-88; practised with the firm 1989-92.

Loveland, Norman C. B.Sc. (Queen's University, 1965), LL.B. (University of Toronto, 1972); called to the bar 1974; articled with the firm 1972 73; practised with the firm 1974 (partner 1978).

Lowenstein, Larry P. B.A. (University of Witwatersrand, 1976), B.A. (Juris.) (Oxford University, 1979), LL.B. (University of Toronto, 1981); called to the bar 1983; practised with the firm 1983- (partner 1989).

Ludlow, Gregory C. B.A. (York University, 1976), LL.B. (York University, 1979), called to the bar 1982; practised with the firm 1985-86.

Luff, Stephen W. B.A. (University of Toronto, 1975), LL.B. (University of Western Ontario, 1978); called to the bar 1980; articled with the firm 1978-79; practised with the firm 1980- (partner 1986).

Lyall, Scott H. B.Comm. (Queen's University, 1987), LL.B. (University of Toronto, 1990); articled with the firm 1990-91.

MacDermid, Robert A. B.A. (University of Western Ontario, 1965), LL.B. (University of Western Ontario, 1969); called to the bar 1971; articled with the firm 1969-70.

MacDonald, James C. LL.B. (University of British Columbia, 1957); called to the bar 1958 (British Columbia); 1964 (Ontario); practised with the firm 1986-92 (partner 1986).

MacDonald, John A. B.Sc., (University of New Brunswick, 1980), LL.B. (University of New Brunswick, 1983); called to the bar 1986 (Ontario); 1988 (New Brunswick); practised with the firm 1988- (partner 1993).

Macdonald, P. Dougal B.A. (Queen's University, 1980), LL.B. (York University, 1983); called to the bar 1985; articled with the firm 1983-84; practised with the firm 1985- (partner, Osler Renault, 1991).

MacDougall, Andrew J. B.Comm. (University of British Columbia, 1986), LL.B. (University of Toronto, 1991); called to the bar 1993; articled with the firm 1991-92; practised with the firm 1993-.

MacDougall, Bruce W. B.A. (Acadia University, 1982), B.A. (Oxford University, 1984), LL.B. (Dalhousie University, 1985), B.C.L. (Oxford University, 1986); called to the bar 1988 (Ontario); 1990 (British Columbia); practised with the firm 1988-89.

Macfarlane, John H. B.A. (McGill University, 1986), LL.B. (University of Toronto, 1989); called to the bar 1991; articled with the firm 1989-90; practised with the firm 1991-.

MacGowan, Sheila C. B.A. (Acadia University, 1982), B.Ed. (Acadia University, 1983), LL.B. (University of New Brunswick, 1988); called to the bar 1988 (New Brunswick); 1990 (Ontario); articled with the firm 1988-89.

MacInnes, Charles Stephen B.A. (Trinity University, 1892), M.A. (Trinity University, 1893); called to the bar 1897; articled with the firm 1894-97; practised with the firm 1897-1903 (partner 1897).

MacIntosh, Donald A. B.A. (Brock University, 1976), M.A. (University of Western Ontario, 1978), LL.B. (Dalhousie University, 1983); called to the bar 1985; articled with the firm 1984-85.

MacKinnon, Robert B. B.Sc. (Queen's University, 1984), B.A. (Cambridge University, 1986), B.C.L. (Oxford University, 1987), LL.B. (Dalhousie University, 1988); called to the bar 1990; articled with the firm 1988-89; practised with the firm 1990-91.

Macleod, Brian R. B.Comm. (University of Saskatchewan, 1987), LL.B. (University of Toronto, 1988); called to the bar 1990; practised with the firm 1990-91.

MacLeod, Deborah L. LL.B. (York University, 1986); called to the bar 1988; articled with the firm 1986-87; practised with the firm 1988-90.

MacLeod, Deborah L. B.A. (University of Toronto, 1988), LL.B. (York University, 1991); called to the bar 1993; articled with the firm 1991-92.

MacLeod, L. Douglas H.B.A. (University of Western Ontario, 1983), LL.B. (Queen's University, 1987); called to the bar 1989; articled with the firm 1987-88; practised with the firm 1989-90.

MacMillan, Steven G.R. B.A. (McMaster University), LL.B. (University of Toronto); called to the bar 1986; articled with the firm 1984-85.

MacNaughton, John E. B.C.L. (University of New Brunswick, 1962); called to the bar 1962 (New Brunswick); 1964 (Ontario); practised with the firm 1965-66.

MacPherson, Elizabeth B.A. (McGill University, 1971), LL.B. (University of Ottawa, 1992), articled with the firm 1992-93.

MacTavish, Barry N. B.A. (Concordia University, 1981), LL.B. (Dalhousie University, 1985); called to the bar 1987; articled with the firm 1985-86; practised with the firm 1987-91.

Madden, Rodger B.A. (McGill University, 1985), LL.B. (University of Toronto, 1989); called to the bar 1991; articled with the firm 1989-90; practised with the firm 1991-.

Magidson, Stanley LL.B. (University of Ottawa, 1981), LL.M. (New York University, 1986); called to the bar 1982 (Alberta), 1987 (Ontario); practised with the firm 1986- (partner 1989).

Magnus, Peter A. B.A. (York University, 1973), LL.B./M.B.A. (York University, 1976); called to the bar 1978; practised with the firm 1983-93 (partner 1985).

Magonet, Michael B.A. (McGill University, 1985), LL.B./B.C.L. (McGill University, 1989); called to the bar 1992; articled with the firm 1990-91.

Main, Peter W. B.A. (University of Toronto, 1978), LL.B. (University of Toronto, 1989); called to the bar 1991; articled with the firm 1989-90; practised with the firm 1991-93.

Mallett, Tristram J. B.A. (University of Guelph, 1984), LL.B. (Queen's University, 1987); called to the bar 1989; practised with the firm 1993-.

Malo, Adele S. B.A. (University of Guelph, 1975), LL.B. (University of Windsor, 1986), LL.M. (Cambridge University, 1987); called to the bar 1989; articled with the firm 1987-88; practised with the firm 1989-90.

Manolakis, Emmanuel B.A.Sc. (University of Ottawa); LL.B. (University of Ottawa, 1988); called to the bar 1990; articled with the firm 1988-89.

Manson, Bruce B.A. (University of Waterloo, 1981), LL.B. (University of Windsor, 1984); called to the bar 1986; articled with the firm 1984-85.

Marantz, R. Gordon B.A. (University of Manitoba, 1957), LL.B. (Osgoode Hall, 1960), LL.M. (Yale University, 1961); called to the bar 1963; practised with the firm 1985- (partner 1985).

Marsden, Phillp B.A. (University of Toronto), LL.B. (University of Toronto, 1989); articled with the firm 1989-90.

Marshall, Douglas R. B.A. (University of Western Ontario, 1984), LL.B. (University of Toronto, 1987); called to the bar 1989; articled with the firm 1987-88; practised with the firm 1989-.

Marston, Donald L. B.Sc. (Queen's University, 1963), LL.B. (Queen's University, 1971); called to the bar 1973; practised with the firm 1973- (partner 1977).

Marttila, Robyn L. B.Sc. (University of Toronto, 1988), B.So. (Trent University, 1989), LL.B. (University of Windsor, 1991); called to the bar 1993; articled with the firm 1991-92; practised with the firm 1993-94.

Martyn, J. Scott B.A. (Carleton University, 1984), LL.B. (Dalhousie University, 1990); called to the bar 1992; articled with the firm 1990-91; practised with the firm 1992-.

Mason, Robin I.H. B.A. (Trent University, 1983); LL.B. (Queen's University, 1991); called to the bar 1993; articled with the firm 1991-92; practised with the firm 1993-94.

Matalon, Gary B.A. (Cornell University, 1979), LL.B. (Dalhousie University, 1982); called to the bar 1984; practised with the firm 1987-91.

Mattson, Mark LL.B. (University of Windsor, 1988); called to the bar 1990; articled with the firm 1988-89.

May, Laurie S. B.A. (York University, 1989), LL.B. (University of Toronto, 1993); articled with the firm 1993-94.

McAllister, Anne B. B.A. (Queen's University, 1972), M.P.A. (Queen's University, 1974), LL.B. (Queen's University, 1983), M.A., (Queen's University, 1984); called to the bar 1985; articled with the firm 1983-84; practised with the firm 1985-88.

McArthur, Heather A. B.A. (University of Western Ontario, 1989), LL.B. (University of Toronto, 1992); articled with the firm 1992-93.

McCarthy, D'Alton Called to the bar 1858; practised with the firm 1882-98 (partner 1882).

McCarthy, D'Alton Lally B.A. (University of Toronto, 1892), LL.D. (University of Toronto, 1944); called to the bar 1895; articled with the firm 1892-95; practised with the firm 1895-1916 (partner 1898).

McCarthy, John Francis H. (Frank) Called to the bar 1905; articled with the firm 1903-05; practised with the firm 1905-16 (partner 1905).

McCarthy, Leighton Goldie Called to the bar 1892; articled with the firm 1891-92; practised with the firm 1892-1916 (partner 1894).

McCartney, Helen B. B.A. (University of Toronto, 1983), LL.B. (University of Toronto, 1986); called to the bar 1988; articled with the firm 1986-87; practised with the firm 1988-94.

McCluggage, Robert Douglas B.A. (Queen's University, 1969), LL.B. (York University, 1972); called to the bar 1974; practised with the firm 1974-78.

McCunn, Timothy J. B.Comm. (McGill University, 1982), LL.B. (University of Ottawa, 1985); called to the bar 1987; practised with the firm 1988-93.

McCutcheon, M. Wallace B.A. (University of Toronto, 1926); called to the bar 1930; articled with the firm 1927-30; practised with the firm 1930-34.

McDermott, Edward T. B.A. (University of Toronto, 1964), LL.B. (Osgoode Hall, 1967); called to the bar 1969; practised with the firm 1974- (partner 1975).

McDonnell, Thomas E.J. B.A. (University of Toronto, 1962), LL.B. (Osgoode Hall, 1965); called to the bar 1967; articled with the firm 1965-66; practised with the firm 1967-76 (partner 1972).

McDowell, P. Diane B.A. (Queen's University, 1976), LL.B. (Queen's University, 1979); called to the bar 1981; practised with the firm 1988-94 (partner 1990).

McFall, Mary Jean B.A. (Harvard University, 1984), LL.B. (University of Toronto, 1987); called to the bar 1989; articled with the firm 1987-88; practised with the firm 1989-93.

McFarlane, David S. B.A. (McMaster University, 1981), B.A. (McGill University, 1983), LL.B. (University of Windsor, 1986); called to the bar 1988; practised with the firm 1990-.

McGovern, Ann Marie B.Sc. (McMaster University, 1990), LL.B. (University of Western Ontario, 1993); articled with the firm 1993-94.

McGregor, Barbara J. B.A. (University of Toronto, 1967), LL.B. (University of Toronto, 1972); called to the bar 1974; articled with the firm 1972-73; practised with the firm 1975- (partner 1979).

McGuffin, Andrew S. B.A. (University of Western Ontario, 1982), LL.B. (University of Western Ontario, 1985); called to the bar 1987; articled with the firm 1985-86; practised with the firm 1987- (partner 1993).

McIntosh-Janis, Faye W. B.A. (Queen's University, 1973), LL.B. (Queen's University, 1976); called to the bar 1978; practised with the firm 1979-84.

McKean, Heather R. LL.B. (York University, 1980); called to the bar 1982; articled with the firm 1980-81; practised with the firm 1982- (partner 1988).

McLachlan, Randy B.A. (University of Regina, 1983), LL.B. (Dalhousie University, 1984); called to the bar 1986; articled with the firm 1984-85.

McLean, George R. B.A. (University of Western Ontario, 1990), LL.B./M.B.A. (York University, 1994); articled with the firm 1994.

McLean, K. Scott B.A. (Carleton University, 1972), LL.B. (University of Windsor, 1975), M.A. (University of Windsor, 1976); called to the bar 1977; practised with the firm 1986- (partner 1986).

McMurtry, Harry B.Sc. (Queen's University, 1985), LL.B. (Queen's University, 1989); called to the bar 1991; articled with the firm 1989-90.

McMurtry, Roland Roy Graduate (Royal Military College, 1921), called to the bar 1927; articled with the firm 1922-27.

McPherson, Douglas A. B.A. (York University, 1989), LL.B. (York University, 1993), B.C.L. (Oxford University, 1994); articled with the firm 1994-.

McQuay, M. Kim B.A. (Queen's University, 1982), LL.B. (Queen's University, 1985); called to the bar 1989; articled with the firm 1987-88; practised with the firm 1989-91.

McSweeney, Ian J.F. B.A. (University of Western Ontario, 1975), LL.B. (University of Western Ontario, 1979); called to the bar 1981; articled with the firm 1979-80; practised with the firm 1981- (partner 1987).

McTague, John Charles B.A. (University of Toronto); called to the bar 1948; practised with the firm 1956-71 (partner 1962).

Megoudis, Peter LL.B./B C L. (McGill University, 1989), LL.M. (University of Toronto); articled with the firm 1989-90.

Meighen, Arthur B.A. (University of Toronto, 1896); called to the bar 1902 (Manitoba); 1914 (Ontario); practised with the firm 1927-45 (counsel).

Mendel, Bart Articled with the firm 1989-90.

Menear, John C. B.A. (University of Western Ontario, 1981), LL.B. (York University, 1993); articled with the firm 1993-94.

Menzies, James Marvin B.A. (McMaster University, 1965), LL.B. (Osgoode Hall, 1968); called to the bar 1970; articled with the firm 1968-69; practised with the firm 1970-72.

Meredith, Edmund A. B.A. (University of Toronto, 1948); called to the bar 1951; articled with the firm 1949-51.

Meredith, P. Mark B.A. (University of Western Ontario, 1979), M.A. (University of Western Ontario, 1980), LL.B. (University of Toronto, 1983); called to the bar 1985; articled with the firm 1983-84; practised with the firm 1985- (partner 1991).

Merkur, Ephry N. B.Comm. (University of Toronto, 1964), LL.B. (University of Toronto, 1967); called to the bar 1969; articled with the firm 1967-68; practised with the firm 1969.

Miller, Ronald P. B.Comm. (University of Toronto, 1967), LL.B. (University of Toronto, 1970); called to the bar 1972; articled with the firm 1970-71; practised with the firm 1972-74.

Milne, Christine E. B.A. (York University, 1977), LL.B. (York University, 1981); called to the bar 1983; articled with the firm 1981-82; practised with the firm 1983-84.

Milstone, Joseph S. B.A. (University of Western Ontario, 1988), LL.B. (York University, 1992), M.B.A. (York University, 1992); articled with the firm 1992-93.

Minkowski, Michal E. B.A. (University of Toronto, 1981), LL.B. (York University, 1984); called to the bar 1986; practised with the firm 1993-.

Mitchell, J. Ross B.A. (McMaster University, 1991); LL.B. (University of Toronto, 1994); articled with the firm 1994-.

Mockridge, Britton O. A.B. (Princeton University, 1963), LL.B. (University of Toronto, 1967); called to the bar 1969 (Ontario), 1982 (Alberta); articled with the firm 1967-68; practised with the firm 1969-71.

Mockridge, Harold C.F. B.A. (Princeton University, 1923); called to the bar 1927; articled with the firm 1923-27; practised with the firm 1927-76 (partner 1929).

Moffatt, John R. B.A. (University of Toronto, 1955), LL.B. (University of Toronto, 1958); called to the bar 1960; articled with the firm 1958-59; practised with the firm 1960-74 (partner 1968).

Moffatt, Kelly L. LL.B. (University of Western Ontario, 1990); called to the bar 1992; articled with the firm 1990-91; practised with the firm 1992-.

Mombourquette, David A. B.A. (University of New Brunswick, 1983), LL.B. (University of New Brunswick, 1986), M.I.R. (University of Toronto, 1990); called to the bar 1988; practised with the firm 1990-93.

Moore, J. Patrick B.A. (University of Toronto, 1969), LL.B. (University of Toronto, 1972); called to the bar 1974; practised with the firm 1988-94 (partner 1988).

Moote, Sharon A. (McBroom) B.A. (University of Toronto, 1983), LL.B. (York University, 1986); called to the bar 1988; practised with the firm 1988-89.

Morassutti, Paul J. LL.B. (York University, 1986); called to the bar 1988; practised with the firm 1989-.

Morgan, Brian G. B.A. (University of Toronto, 1973), M.A. (Oxford University, 1976), LL.B. (Dalhousie University, 1977); called to the bar 1979; practised with the firm 1979- (partner 1983).

Morgan, Christopher W. B.A.Sc. (University of Toronto, 1983), LL.B. (University of Toronto, 1981); called to the bar 1983; articled with the firm 1981-82; practised with the firm 1983-85.

Morgan, Donna C. B.A. (Memorial University of Newfoundland, 1972), LL.B. (Dalhousie University, 1978), LL.M. (York University, 1985); called to the bar 1980; articled with the firm 1978-79.

Morgan, Michael F. B.Sc. (Memorial University of Newfoundland, 1983), M.Math (University of Waterloo, 1985), LL.B. (University of Ottawa, 1994); articled with the firm 1994-.

Morison, Frank W.B. B.A.Sc. (University of Waterloo, 1980), M.Sc. (University of Alberta, 1986), LL.B. (University of Toronto, 1990); called to the bar 1992; practised with the firm 1992-.

Morley, George W. B.A. (University of Toronto, 1910); called to the bar 1914; practised with the firm 1918.

Morley, John Scott B.Comm. (Queen's University, 1962), LL.B. (Queen's University, 1966); called to the bar 1968; articled with the firm 1966-67; practised with the firm 1968-72.

Morritt, David S. LL.B. (University of Western Ontario, 1978), B.C.L. (Oxford University, 1979); called to the bar 1984; practised with the firm 1984- (partner 1989).

Morton, John R. B.Comm. (University of Toronto, 1984), LL.B. (University of British Columbia, 1990); articled with the firm 1990-91.

Morton, Wendy J. B.A. (Bishop's University), LL.B. (Queen's University, 1989); called to the bar 1991 (Ontario), 1992 (Alberta); articled with the firm 1989-90.

Moseley, Timothy S. B.A. (University of Toronto, 1983), LL.B. (University of Toronto, 1987); called to the bar 1989; articled with the firm 1987-88; practised with the firm 1989-91.

Mott-Trille, Frank R. B.A. (Oxford University, 1951), B.C.L. (Oxford University, 1953); called to the bar 1953 (England); 1954 (Ontario); articled with the firm 1953-54; practised with the firm 1954-58.

Mraz, Mills LL.B. (University of Toronto, 1959); called to the bar 1961; articled with the firm 1959-60; practised with the firm 1962-92 (partner 1971).

Muirhead, G. Lee B.A. (University of Toronto, 1967), LL.D. (University of Toronto, 1983); called to the bar 1985; practised with the firm 1986- (partner 1992).

Munn, D. Lawrence B.A. (University of Guelph, 1979), M.A. (University of British Columbia, 1982), LL.B. (McGill University, 1986); called to the bar 1989 (Ontario); 1990 (New York); articled with the firm 1987-88; practised with the firm 1989-93.

Murphy, Anne B.Comm. (Memorial University of Newfoundland, 1986), LL.B. (Queen's University, 1989); called to the bar 1991 (Ontario), 1992 (Newfoundland); articled with the firm 1989-90.

Murphy, James J. B.A. (University of Toronto, 1954), LL.B. (University of Toronto, 1957), LL.M. (Columbia University, 1962); called to the bar 1960; practised with the firm 1963-65.

Murray, Blake M. LL.B. (York University, 1973), LL.M. (York University, 1981); called to the bar 1975; articled with the firm 1973-74; practised with the firm 1975- (partner 1981).

Murray, Christopher S. B.A. (Queen's University, 1980), LL.B. (University of Toronto, 1983); called to the bar 1985; articled with the firm 1983-84; practised with the firm 1985- (partner 1994).

Murray, Robert B.M. B.A. (Mount Allison University, 1983), B.Comm. (Mount Allison University, 1983), LL.B. (Dalhousie University, 1986); called to the bar 1988; practised with the firm 1990-93.

Murray, Ross William B.Comm. (Queen's University, 1967), M.B.A. (York University, 1968), LL.B. (University of Toronto, 1975); called to the bar 1977; articled with the firm 1975-76.

Myers, Frederick L. LL.B. (York University, 1983), LL.M. (Harvard University, 1985); called to the bar 1986; articled with the firm 1984-85; practised with the firm 1986- (partner 1992).

Naber-Sykes, Mary F. B.A. (University of Toronto, 1980), LL.B. (University of Toronto, 1983); called to the bar 1987 (Alberta); articled with the firm 1983-84.

Narancic, Perry J. B.A. (McMaster University, 1988), LL.B./B.C.L. (McGill University, 1993); articled with the firm 1993-94.

Nathan, Richard J. A.B. (Dartmouth College, 1983), LL.B. (University of Toronto, 1987); called to the bar 1989 (Ontario), 1989 (New York); articled with the firm 1987-88; practised with the firm 1989-.

Nelson, Clifford S. B.A. (University of Toronto, 1965), LL.B. (Osgoode Hall, 1968); called to the bar 1973; practised with the firm 1986-93 (partner 1986).

Nesbitt, Wallace Called to the bar 1881 (Ontario), 1907 (Nova Scotia); practised with the firm 1883-88, 1889-92, 1905-30 (partner 1883-88, 1889-92; counsel 1905-30).

Newland, James B.A. (University of Toronto, 1977), LL.B. (Queen's University, 1981); called to the bar 1983; practised with the firm 1986-92.

Nicholas, Susan L. (Gillespie) B.A. (Queen's University, 1982), LL.B. (University of Windsor, 1989); called to the bar 1991; articled with the firm 1989-90; practised with the firm 1991-.

Nichols, Laura P. B.A. (University of Western Ontario, 1988), LL.B. (University of Ottawa, 1992); called to the bar 1994; articled with the firm 1992-93; practised with the firm 1994-.

Nickerson, Mara L. B.Comm. (Mount Allison University, 1978), LL.B./M.B.A. (Dalhousie University, 1982); called to the bar 1984; articled with the firm 1982-83; practised with the firm 1984-89; legal education 1989-.

Nield, Laura J. B.A. (Queen's University, 1988); LL.B. (McGill University, 1991); called to the bar 1993; articled with the firm 1991-92; practised with the firm 1993-.

Nieman, Jodine M. B.Mus. (University of Ottawa, 1987), LL.B. (University of Ottawa, 1990); called to the bar 1992; articled with the firm 1990-91; practised with the firm 1992-.

Noonan, James B. B.A. (St. Mary's University, 1966), LL.B. (Queen's University, 1969); called to the bar 1971; practised with the firm 1974-75.

North, Linne M. LL.B. (York University, 1985); called to the bar 1987; articled with the firm 1985-86; practised with the firm 1987-.

Norwood, John George B.Comm. (University of Toronto, 1967), LL.B. (University of Toronto, 1970); called to the bar 1972; articled with the firm 1970-71.

Noss, Elliot B.A. (University of Toronto, 1984), LL.B. (University of Western Ontario, 1988); called to the bar 1990; articled with the firm 1988-89.

Novak, Mark B.Sc. (University of Western Ontario, 1990), LL.B. (University of Western Ontario, 1992); articled with the firm 1992-93.

Obal, Shelley W. B.A. (University of Toronto, 1980), LL.B. (York University, 1983); called to the bar 1985; articled with the firm 1983-84; practised with the firm 1986- (partner 1992).

Obert, Michael B.Sc. (McGill University, 1974), M.A. (Queen's University, 1976), LL.B. (University of Toronto, 1978); called to the bar 1980 (Ontario and Alberta); articled with the firm 1978-79.

Ogilvie, Margaret H. B.A. (University of Toronto, 1971), B.A., (Oxford University, 1976), M.A. (Oxford University, 1976), D.Phil. (Oxford University, 1974), LL.B. (Dalhousie University, 1977); called to the bar 1978 (Nova Scotia), 1984 (Ontario); articled with the firm 1983-84.

O'Leary, Bridget A. B.A. (University of Western Ontario), LL.B. (Queen's University, 1988); called to the bar 1990; articled with the firm 1988-89.

Oliver, Eden M. B.A. (University of Toronto, 1981), LL.B. (York University, 1984); called to the bar 1985 (Alberta), 1992 (Ontario); practised with the firm 1992-.

Opie, David B.A. (University of Toronto, 1984), LL.B. (Queen's University, 1987); articled with the firm 1987-88.

O'Reilly, Hugh M.B. B.A. (University of Regina, 1981), LL.B. (University of Calgary, 1990); called to the bar 1991 (Alberta), 1994 (Ontario); practised with the firm 1994-.

Osler, F. Britton Graduate (Royal Military College, 1894); called to the bar 1897; practised with the firm 1897-43 (partner 1898).

Osler, Britton Bath LL.B. (University of Toronto, 1862); called to the bar 1862; practised with the firm 1862-1901 (partner 1862).

Osler, Britton M. Graduate (Royal Military College, 1931); called to the bar 1934; articled with the firm 1931-34; practised with the firm 1934-84 (partner 1935).

Osler, Campbell R. B.A. (University of Toronto, 1940), D.Cn.L. (College of Emmanuel and St Chad, 1980); called to the bar 1948; articled with the firm 1945-48; practised with the firm 1948-84 (partner 1950).

Osler, Edward Admitted to practice as a solicitor (Ontario) 1866; practised with the firm 1866-71 (partner 1866).

Osler, H.S. Called to the bar 1886; articled with the firm 1883-86; practised with the firm 1889-33 (partner 1889).

Osler, John G. Graduate (Royal Military College, 1934); called to the bar 1937; articled with the firm 1934-37; practised with the firm 1937-78 (partner 1938).

O'Sullivan, Margaret R. B.A. (Queen's University, 1978), LL.B. (Queen's University, 1981); called to the bar 1983; practised with the firm 1983-86.

Pacaud, G.E. Anthony B.Sc. (Bishop's University, 1961), LL.B. (Dalhousie University, 1964); called to the bar 1967; articled with the firm 1965-66; practised with the firm 1967-68.

Paré, Susan M. B.A. (University of Western Ontario, 1990), LL.B. (University of Toronto, 1994; articled with the firm 1994-.

Parkin, Jennifer A.C. B.A. (University of Toronto, 1978), LL.B. (York University, 1982); called to the bar 1984; articled with the firm 1982-83; practised with the firm 1984-87.

Pascutto, Ermanno B.Comm. (University of Toronto, 1974), LL.B. (University of Toronto, 1977); called to the bar 1979; articled with the firm 1977-78; practised with the firm 1979-81.

Patel, Bijal LL.B. (York University, 1994); articled with the firm 1994-.

Pattillo, Laurence A. B.A. (Dalhousie University, 1969), LL.B. (York University, 1972); called to the bar 1974; articled with the firm 1972-73; practised with the firm 1974-77.

Pattison, Donald F. B.A. (University of Toronto, 1949), B.Comm. (University of Toronto, 1951); called to the bar 1957; articled with the firm 1955-57; practised with the firm 1957-88 (partner 1968).

Paul, Margo L. H.B.A. (University of Western Ontario, 1982), LL.B. (University of Western Ontario, 1986); called to the bar 1988; articled with the firm 1986-87; practised with the firm 1988-91.

Paulin, Bradshaw M.W. Called to the bar 1950; practised with the firm 1974-86 (partner 1974).

Payne, Joanne B. B.Ed. (University of Victoria, 1974), B.F.A. (University of Victoria, 1977), LL.B. (University of British Columbia, 1984); called to the bar 1985 (British Columbia); 1987 (Ontario); practised with the firm 1987-89.

Pedinelli, Frank B.A. (York University, 1990), LL.B. (York University, 1993); articled with the firm 1993-94.

Peltomaa, Arthur J. B.A. (Brock University, 1974), LL.B. (York University, 1977), LL.M. (York University, 1981); called to the bar 1981; practised with the firm 1983- (partner 1987).

Penney, Craig J. B.A. (York University, 1988), M.A. (University of Western Ontario, 1989), LL.B. (York University, 1992); called to the bar 1994; articled with the firm 1992-93.

Pepper, Randy A. H.B.A. (University of Western Ontario, 1978), LL.B. (University of Toronto, 1981); called to the bar 1983 (Ontario); admitted to practice as a solicitor 1987 (England and Wales, Hong Kong); articled with the firm 1981-82; practised with the firm 1983-86, 1989- (partner 1991).

Perrault, Bruce M. B.Sc. (Queen's University, 1985), LL.B. (Queen's University, 1988); called to the bar 1990; articled with the firm 1988-89; practised with the firm 1990-92.

Petch, John F. (Jack) B.A. (University of Western Ontario, 1960), LL.B. (University of Toronto, 1963), LL.M. (York University, 1980); called to the bar 1965; articled with the firm 1963-64; practised with the firm 1975- (partner 1975).

Petcher, Katherine E. B.A. (McGill University, 1987), LL.B./B.C.L. (McGill University, 1992); called to the bar 1994; articled with the firm 1992-93; practised with the firm 1994-.

Pether, Terrence K. B.A. (University of Western Ontario, 1984), LL.B./B.C.L. (McGill University, 1988); called to the bar 1990; practised with the firm 1990-91.

Phelan, Michael L. B.A. (Loyola College (Montreal), 1968), LL.B.(Dalhousie University, 1971); called to the bar 1973; practised with the firm 1986- (partner 1986).

Pirie, Andrew J. B.A. (University of Waterloo, 1972), LL.B. (Dalhousie University, 1975), LL.M (University of Victoria (New Zealand) 1977); called to the bar 1978; articled with the firm 1976-77; practised with the firm 1978-81.

Plumb, Thomas Street B.C.L. (Oxford University, 1873); called to the bar 1876 (Ontario and Inner Temple, U.K.); practised with the firm 1882-85 (partner 1882).

Plumley, Kent H.E. B.Sc. (Queen's University, 1960), LL.B. (Queen's University, 1963); called to the bar 1965; practised with the firm 1990- (partner 1990).

Polowin, Melanie A. LL.B. (University of Ottawa, 1991); called to the bar 1993; articled with the firm 1991-92; practised with the firm 1993-.

Ponder, Dale R. B.Sc. (Queen's University, 1976), B.Sc. (University of Western Ontario, 1977), LL.B. (University of Western Ontario, 1980); called to the bar 1982; practised with the firm 1986- (partner 1988).

Portner, Christopher B.Sc. (McGill University, 1967), B.C.L. (McGill University, 1971); called to the bar 1972 (Quebec); 1980 (Ontario); practised with the firm 1980- (partner 1981).

Powrie, Douglas J. B.A. (University of Alberta, 1983), LL.B./M.B.A. (University of Western Ontario, 1987); called to the bar 1989 (British Columbia); articled with the firm 1987-88.

Pratt, Randall W. B.A. (University of Western Ontario, 1984), LL.B. (York University, 1991); called to the bar 1992; articled with the firm 1990-91; practised with the firm 1992-.

Pritchard, J. Andrew B.A. (Trent University, 1974), LL.B. (University of Manitoba, 1980); called to the bar 1982; practised with the firm 1986- (partner 1988).

Purdy, A. David G. B.A. (University of Western Ontario, 1961), LL.B. (Osgoode Hall, 1964); called to the bar 1966; articled with the firm 1964-65; practised with the firm 1966- (partner 1972).

Quinn, Ivan B. B.A. (McGill University); called to the bar 1948 (British Columbia) articled with the firm 1945-48.

Radley, Ronald L. Graduate (Royal Military College, 1955); called to the bar 1959; articled with the firm 1958-59.

Rahilly, Thomas Francis B.A. (University of Toronto, 1966), LL.B. (University of Toronto, 1969); called to the bar 1971; articled with the firm 1969-70.

Rajpal, Deepak B.A. (University of Toronto, 1987), LL.B. (York University, 1990); called to the bar 1992; articled with the firm 1990-91; practised with the firm 1992-94.

Rauenbusch, William R. B.Comm. (University of Toronto, 1968), LL.B. (York University, 1971), LL.M. (Harvard University, 1972), M.B.A. (York University, 1975); called to the bar 1974; practised with the firm 1977- (partner 1978).

Raymond, William Beardsley Called to the bar 1885; articled with the firm 1883-85; practised with the firm 1885-1906 (partner 1889).

Rees, Heidi A. B.A. (University of Western Ontario, 1984), LL.B. (University of Windsor, 1988); called to the bar 1990; articled with the firm 1988-89; practised with the firm 1990-.

Reid, F. Leighton B.A. (University of Toronto, 1971), M.A. (Queen's University, 1973), LL.B. (Queen's University, 1977); called to the bar 1979; articled with the firm 1977-78; practised with the firm 1979-83.

Reid, Vincent P. B.A. (University of Toronto, 1950); called to the bar 1954; articled with the firm 1952-54; practised with the firm 1954-70 (partner 1965).

Reid, Walter Brechin B.A. (University of Toronto, 1938); called to the bar 1941; articled with the firm 1938-41; practised with the firm 1941-53 (partner 1950).

Reilly, Francis Lewis B.A. (Brock University, 1971), LL.B. (University of Toronto, 1974); called to the bar 1976; articled with the firm 1974-75.

Reiner, Laurie A. B.A. (University of Western Ontario, 1986), LL.B. (McGill University, 1991); called to the bar 1993); articled with the firm 1991-92; practised with the firm 1993-.

Resendes, Raymond B.A. (University of Western Ontario, 1977), LL.B. (University of Western Ontario, 1980); called to the bar 1982; articled with the firm 1980-81; practised with the firm 1982-85.

Richards, Cameron B.A. (Queen's University, 1986), LL.B./M.B.A. (York University, 1993); articled with the firm 1993-94.

Richardson, Elinore Jean B.A. (McMaster University, 1967), LL.B. (University of Toronto, 1970); called to the bar 1972 (Ontario), 1977 (Quebec); articled with the firm 1970-71.

Richardson, Sarah B.A. (University of Toronto, 1985), LL.B. (Dalhousie University, 1989); articled with the firm 1989-90.

Rienzo, Douglas J. B.Sc. (University of Toronto, 1985), LL.B. (University of Toronto, 1992); called to the bar 1994; articled with the firm 1992-93; practised with the firm 1994-.

Riggs, Susannah H. B.Comm. (Queen's University, 1991), LL.B. (University of Toronto, 1994); articled with the firm 1994-.

Riley, Nancy M. B.A. (Queen's University, 1975), LL.B. (York University, 1979); called to the bar 1981; articled with the firm 1979-80; practised with the firm 1981-83.

Ritchie, Lawrence E. B.A. (University of Western Ontario, 1983), LL.B. (York University, 1986), LL.M. (University of London, 1988); called to the bar 1989; articled with the firm 1986-87; practised with the firm 1989-.

Roach, Pierre S. B.Comm. (University of Ottawa, 1981), LL.B. (University of Ottawa, 1985); called to the bar 1987; practised with the firm 1988-94.

Roberts, Nancy L. B.A. (McGill University, 1981), LL.B. (University of Toronto, 1994); articled with the firm 1994-.

Roberts, Peter B.A. (Carleton University, 1981), M.B.A. (York University, 1983), LL.B. (Queen's University, 1987); called to the bar 1989; articled with the firm 1987-88.

Roberts, Robert A. LL.B. (York University, 1986); called to the bar 1987 (Alberta), 1988 (Ontario); articled with the firm 1988; practised with the firm 1988-.

Robertson, J. Bruce B.A. (Carleton University, 1980), M.A. (University of Indiana, 1983), LL.B. (McGill University, 1986); called to the bar 1988; articled with the firm 1986-87; practised with the firm 1988-89.

Robertson, Michael S. B.A. (York University, 1974), M.A. (University of Toronto, 1975), LL.B. (York University, 1981); called to the bar 1983; articled with the firm 1981-82; practised with the firm 1983-85.

Robinette, Thomas W. B.A. (University of Toronto, 1954); called to the bar 1958; articled with the firm 1956-58; practised with the firm 1958-59.

Robinson, Christopher B.A. (University of Toronto, 1846), D.C.L. (University of Toronto, 1903); called to the bar 1850; practised with the firm 1901-05 (counsel).

Robinson, Darryl E. LL.B. (University of Western Ontario, 1994); articled with the firm 1994-.

Robinson, Linda D. B.A. (University of Toronto, 1970), M.S.C. (University of London, 1972), L.L.B. (University of Toronto, 1977); called to the bar 1979; practised with the firm 1993- (partner 1993).

Roger, Pierre B.Comm. (University of Ottawa, 1986), LL.B. (University of Ottawa, 1989); called to the bar 1991; articled with the firm 1989-90.

Rogers, Donald H. B.A. (University of Toronto 1965), LL.B. (University of Toronto, 1968); called to the bar 1970; practised with the firm 1988-94 (partner 1988).

Rogers, George Theodore B.A. (University of Toronto, 1939); called to the bar 1942; articled with the firm 1939-42; practised with the firm 1942-44.

Rogers, W. Stewart B.A. (University of Toronto, 1938); called to the bar 1941; practised with the firm 1969-80 (partner 1971).

Rogers, William P. B.A. (University of Toronto, 1941); called to the bar 1948; practised with the firm 1988-93 (partner 1988).

Roland, John M.M. B.Eng. (McGill University, 1960), LL.B. (University of Toronto, 1964); called to the bar 1966; articled with the firm 1964-65; practised with the firm 1966- (partner 1972).

Romano, Domenic B.A. (McGill University, 1988), M.A. (McGill University, 1990), B.A. (Oxford University, 1991), LL.M. (Columbia University, 1992), LL.B. (Dalhousie University, 1994); articled with the firm 1994-.

Roney, David P. B.A. (Queen's University, 1988), LL.B. (University of Toronto, 1991); called to the bar 1993; articled with the firm 1991-92; practised with the firm 1993.

Rook, John F. B.A. (Queen's University, 1968), LL.B. (University of Toronto, 1971); called to the bar 1973; practised with the firm 1990- (partner 1990).

Ross, Alan L. LL.B. (Dalhousie University, 1994); articled with the firm 1994-.

Ross, Donald C. B.A. (University of Toronto, 1969), M.Sc., (University of London, 1970), LL.B. (York University, 1973); called to the bar 1975; practised with the firm 1988- (partner 1988).

Ross, Nancy J. LL.B. (York University, 1982); called to the bar 1984; practised with the firm 1986-88.

Ross, Stephen G. B.A. (University of Western Ontario, 1988), LL.B. (University of Western Ontario, 1991); called to the bar 1993; articled with the firm 1991-92; practised with the firm 1993-94.

Rossiter, Gary S. B.Comm. (Queen's University, 1967), LL.B. (Queen's University, 1971); called to the bar 1974; articled with the firm 1971-72, 73; practised with the firm 1974-75.

Rubinoff, Jeffrey A. LL.B. (York University, 1989); called to the bar 1991; practised with the firm 1993 .

Ruhl, Mary L. B.A. (University of Toronto, 1981), LL.B. (University of Toronto, 1979); called to the bar 1986 (Ontario), 1988 (British Columbia); articled with the firm 1984-85; practised with the firm 1986.

Sagel, J. Frederick B.A. (McGill University, 1970). LL.B (Dalhousie University, 1973); called to the bar 1975; practised with the firm 1984-87 (partner 1986).

Salter, M. Janet B.A. (University of Western Ontario, 1981), M.A (University of Western Ontario, 1982), LL.B. (McGill University, 1987); called to the bar 1989; articled with the firm 1987-88; practised with the firm 1989-.

Sample, Patricia O. B.A. (University of Alberta, 1960), M.A. (Université Laval, 1961), LL.B. (University of Alberta, 1962); articled with the firm 1967-68.

Samuel, Louis Articled with the firm 1921-22.

Sandler, Tracy C. LL.B. (York University, 1989); called to the bar 1991; articled with the firm 1989-90; practised with the firm 1991-.

Sansom, Ronald George B.Sc. (Queen's University, 1965); called to the bar 1970; articled with the firm 1968-69.

Sargeant, Barbara A. B.A. (University of Toronto, 1964), M.A. (University of Toronto, 1966); Ph.D. (University of Toronto, 1974), LL.B. (York University, 1977); called to the bar 1979; practised with the firm 1985-86.

Sargeant, Timothy W. B.A. (Yale University, 1963), LL.B. (Osgoode Hall, 1966), LL.M. (University of London, 1968); called to the bar 1969; articled with the firm 1967-68; practised with the firm 1969-71.

Sasso, William Vincent B.A. (University of Western Ontario, 1965), LL.B. (University of Western Ontario, 1968); called to the bar 1970; articled with the firm 1968-69.

Saunders, Edward B.A. (University of Toronto, 1949); called to the bar 1953; practised with the firm 1954-77 (partner 1959).

Saxe, Neil B.A. (McGill University, 1982), LL.B. (University of Windsor, 1986); called to the bar 1988; articled with the firm 1986-87; practised with the firm 1988-89.

Scarfe, John J. B.A. (University of Western Ontario, 1987), LL.B. (University of British Columbia, 1990); called to the bar 1992; articled with the firm 1990-91.

Scheuermann, Scott L. LL.B. (Queen's University, 1979), LL.M. (York University, 1986); called to the bar 1981; practised with the firm 1984- (partner 1987).

Schindeler, Trevor G. B.A. (Queen's University, 1980), M.A (Queen's University, 1982), LL.B. (Queen's University, 1984); called to the bar 1986; articled with the firm 1984-85.

Schindler, Patrick F. B.A. (McGill University, 1959) M.A. (McGill University, 1963), LL.B. (University of Toronto, 1966), B.Litt. (Oxford University, 1969); called to the bar 1968; practised with the firm 1973-77 (partner 1976).

Schmidt, Preben U. LL.B. (University of Western Ontario, 1967); called to the bar 1969; articled with the firm 1967-68; practised with the firm 1969-93 (partner 1975).

Schumacher, Timothy P. B.E.S. (University of Waterloo, 1980), LL.B. (York University, 1983); called to the bar 1985; articled with the firm 1983-84; practised with the firm 1985- (partner 1992).

Schwill, Robin B. B.B.A. (York University, 1990), M.B.A. (York University, 1991), LL.B. (York University, 1994); articled with the firm 1994-.

Sebastiano, Rocco M. B.A.Sc. (University of Toronto, 1985), LL.B. (York University, 1992); called to the bar 1994; articled with the firm 1992-93; practised with the firm 1994-.

Selfe, Neil M. B.A. (University of Toronto, 1987), LL.B. (York University, 1991); called to the bar 1993; articled with the firm 1991-92; practised with the firm 1993-.

Sellers, Edward A. B.Comm. (McGill University, 1984), LL.B. (University of Toronto, 1987); called to the bar 1989; articled with the firm 1987-88; practised with the firm 1989-.

Sellers, Katherine H. B.A. (Queen's University, 1991), LL.B. (Queen's University, 1994); articled with the firm 1994-.

Sexton, J. Edgar B.Sc. (Queen's University, 1959), LL.B (University of Western Ontario, 1962); called to the bar 1964 (Ontario); 1979 (New Brunswick), 1984 (Alberta); practised with the firm 1977- (partner 1977).

Shamis, Stuart E. B.A. (McGill University, 1980), LL.L. (University of Ottawa, 1983), LL.B. (University of Ottawa, 1984); called to the bar 1986; articled with the firm 1984-85; practised with the firm 1986-94.

Shankman, Howard LL.B. (University of Windsor, 1986); called to the bar 1988; articled with the firm 1986-87.

Shapiro, Murray A. B.A. (Concordia University, 1983), LL.B. (York University, 1986); called to the bar 1988; articled with the firm 1986-87; practised with the firm 1988-89.

Shapley, Harold W. Called to the bar 1907; practised with the firm 1917-52.

Shaul, Jeffrey C. B.Comm. (University of Toronto, 1978), LL.B. (University of Toronto, 1981); called to the bar 1983; articled with the firm 1981-82; practised with the firm 1983-85.

Shaw, Douglas C. B.A. (University of Saskatchewan, 1968), M.A. (University of Toronto, 1970), LL.B. (University of Toronto, 1973); called to the bar 1975; articled with the firm 1973-74; practised with the firm 1975-78.

Shear, Daniel R. B.A. (University of Western Ontario, 1980), LL.B. (York University, 1983); called to the bar 1985; articled with the firm 1983-84; practised with the firm 1985 94.

Shell, Brian A.B. (Brandeis University, 1972), B.A. (Oxford University, 1974), LL.B. (University of Toronto, 1978); called to the bar 1980; articled with the firm 1978-79.

Shiff, Daniel B.A. (University of Toronto, 1980), LL.B. (York University, 1983); called to the bar 1985; articled with the firm 1983-84.

Sigel, Schuyler M. B.Sc. (University of Pennsylvania, 1958), LL.B. (University of Toronto, 1961), called to the bar 1963; articled with the firm 1961-62; practised with the firm 1963-64.

Sigurdson, Stephen P. B.Sc. (University of Manitoba, 1981), LL.B. (Queen's University, 1984); called to the bar 1986; practised with the firm 1989- (partner 1993).

Siller, Philip B.Sc. (City College of New York, 1967), Ph.D. (University of Minnesota, 1973), LL.B. (University of Toronto, 1975); called to the bar 1977; articled with the firm 1975-76; practised with the firm 1981-84.

Silverson, Jack A. LL.B. (York University, 1986); called to the bar 1988; articled with the firm 1986-87; practised with the firm 1988-.

Sim, Janet E. B.A./B.P.H.E. (Queen's University, 1975), B.Ed. (Queen's University, 1976), LL.B. (Queen's University, 1980); called to the bar 1982; practised with the firm 1986- (partner 1990).

Simmons, Kathryn Eleanor B.A. (Queen's University, 1972), LL.B. (Queen's University, 1975); called to the bar 1977; articled with the firm 1975-76.

Simpson, George A.C. B.A. (McMaster University, 1951); called to the bar 1954; articled with the firm 1951-54.

Simpson, J.B. B.A. (McMaster University, 1946); called to the bar 1949; articled with the firm 1946-49.

Simser, Jeffrey R. B.A. (University of Toronto) LL.B. (Queen's University, 1989); called to the bar 1991; articled with the firm 1989-90.

Sinclair, Donald B. B.A. (University of Toronto, 1912); called to the bar 1915; practised with the firm 1920.

Sinnige, Caspar L.P. B.A. (University of Toronto), M.A. (University of Toronto), LL.B. (Queen's University, 1991); called to the bar 1993; articled with the firm 1991-92.

Skrow, Steven R. B.Sc. (University of Toronto, 1986), LL.B. (York University, 1991); called to the bar 1993; articled with the firm 1991-92.

Smart, Stephen B. B.A. (Queen's University, 1965), LL.B. (Osgoode Hall, 1968); called to the bar 1970; practised with the firm 1974- (partner 1977).

Smellie, James H. B.A. (University of Western Ontario, 1970), LL.B. (University of Windsor, 1973); called to the bar 1975; practised with the firm 1986- (partner 1986).

Smith, Steven W. B.Comm. (Queen's University, 1977), LL.B. (University of Toronto, 1980); called to the bar 1982 (Ontario); admitted to practice as a solicitor 1987 (England and Wales); articled with the firm 1980-81; practised with the firm 1982- (partner 1988).

Smith, Walker M. LL.B. (Queen's University, 1962); called to the bar 1964; articled with the firm 1962-63; practised with the firm 1964-65.

Smith, William Morley B.A. (University of Toronto, 1914); called to the bar 1917; articled with the firm 1915-17; practised with the firm 1917-23.

Somer, Bruce B.A. (University of Toronto, 1985), LL.B. (University of Western Ontario, 1991); articled with the firm 1991-92.

Somers, Gregory O. B.Sc. (McGill University, 1977), B.A. (Queen's University, 1982), LL.B. (Dalhousie University, 1986); called to the bar 1988; articled with the firm 1986-87; practised with the firm 1988- (partner 1994).

Somers, William P. B.A. (University of Toronto, 1955), LL.B. (Osgoode Hall, 1959); called to the bar 1959; articled with the firm 1957-59; practised with the firm 1959-65.

Souraya, Abdul B.A. (University of Calgary), LL.B. (McGill University); called to the bar 1991; articled with the firm 1989-90.

Speciale, Anthony M. B.A. (University of Toronto, 1970), LL.B. (York University, 1973); called to the bar 1975; articled with the firm 1974; practised with the firm 1975.

Speirs, Carey R. B.A. (University of Western Ontario, 1986), LL.B. (University of New Brunswick, 1990); called to the bar 1992; articled with the firm 1990-91; practised with the firm 1992-.

Spier, Simeon B.A. (University of Toronto, 1982), M.B.A. (University of Miami (Florida), 1984), M.Sc. (University of Miami (Florida), 1984), LL.B. (University of Ottawa, 1987); called to the bar 1989; articled with the firm 1987-88.

Spiro, Solomon B.A. (Wayne State University, 1954), M.H.L. (Jewish Theological Seminary, 1960), M.A. (Columbia University, 1960), LL.B. (York University, 1970); called to the bar 1972; articled with the firm 1970-71.

Springfield, Roger B.A. (Queen's University, 1985), B.A. (Cambridge University, 1987), LL.B. (University of Toronto, 1989); articled with the firm 1989-90.

Stamp, David A. B.A. (University of Western Ontario, 1987), LL.B. (University of Toronto, 1990); called to the bar 1992; articled with the firm 1990-91; practised with the firm 1992-.

Starchuk, M. Lynn B.A. (Queen's University, 1971); LL.B. (University of Victoria, 1991); called to the bar 1993; articled with the firm 1991-92; practised with the firm 1993-.

Steen, Robert W.J. B.Comm. (University of Toronto, 1989), M.B.A. (York University, 1991), LL.B. (York University, 1994); articled with the firm 1994-.

Stein, Stanley B. B.Comm. (University of Toronto, 1966) M.A., (Yale University, 1967), LL.B. (University of Toronto, 1970); called to the bar 1972; practised with the firm 1986- (partner 1986).

Steinberg, David S. B.A. (University of Western Ontario, 1990), LL.B./M.B.A. (University of Toronto, 1994); articled with the firm 1994-.

Steiner, Joseph M. B.A. (University of Toronto, 1968), M.Phil. (Yale University, 1970), LL.B. (York University, 1975); called to the bar 1977 (Ontario), 1986 (Alberta); articled with the firm 1975-76; practised with the firm 1977- (partner 1982).

Stevens, John W. B.A. (University of Toronto, 1978), LL.B. (Queen's University, 1983); called to the bar 1985; articled with the firm 1983-84; practised with the firm 1985-94 (partner 1991-94), (partner Osler Renault 1994).

Stewart, Andrew M. Called to the bar 1897; articled with the firm 1892-97; practised with the firm 1900-03 (partner 1900).

Stewart, Guthrie J. LL.B. (York University, 1978); called to the bar 1980; articled with the firm 1978-79; practised with the firm 1980-86.

Stitt, Allan J. B.Comm. (University of Toronto, 1984), LL.B. (University of Windsor, 1988), J.D. (University of Detroit, 1988) LL.M. (Harvard University, 1992); called to the bar 1990; articled with the firm 1988-89; practised with the firm 1990-94.

Stitt, Nancy J. B.A. (University of Western Ontario, 1990), LL.B. (University of Toronto, 1993); articled with the firm 1993-94.

Strachan, Ian J. D.A. (University of Toronto, 1966), LL.B. (University of Toronto, 1969); called to the bar 1971; articled with the firm 1969-70; practised with the firm 1971-73.

Strasler, Pandora D. LL.B. (University of Windsor, 1987); called to the bar 1989; articled with the firm 1987-88; practised with the firm 1989-94.

Stratas, David W. LL.B.(Queen's University, 1984), B.C.L. (Oxford University, 1986); called to the bar 1988; practised with the firm 1988- (partner 1994).

Strickland, James Kenneth B.A. (University of Toronto, 1967), M.B.A. (University of Toronto, 1969), LL.B. (York University, 1972); called to the bar 1974; practised with the firm 1974-75.

Strickland, Norman E. Called to the bar 1921; articled with the firm 1918-21; practised with the firm 1921-63 (partner 1923).

Strike, Dan M. B.Comm. (Queen's University, 1983), LL.B. (University of Western Ontario, 1987); called to the bar 1989; articled with the firm 1987-88.

Strung, John D. B.Sc. (University of Toronto, 1969), M.Sc. (University of Toronto, 1971), B.Ed. (University of Toronto, 1972), LL.B. (University of Toronto, 1977); called to the bar 1979; practised with the firm 1988-94 (partner 1988).

Stuart, Robert T. A.B. (Princeton University, 1987), LL.B. (University of Toronto, 1990); called to the bar 1992 (Ontario and New York); articled with the firm 1990-91; practised with the firm 1992-.

Stychin, Carl B.A. (University of Alberta, 1985), LL.B. (University of Toronto, 1988); called to the bar 1990; articled with the firm 1988-89.

Sullivan, Michael B. B.A. (Carleton University, 1969), LL.B. (University of Ottawa, 1981); called to the bar 1983; practised with the firm 1986-87.

Surchin, Mark A. B.A. (Brandeis University, 1978), LL.B. (University of Toronto, 1981); called to the bar 1983; articled with the firm 1981-82; practised with the firm 1985-87.

Swanick, Brent W. B.Comm. (University of Toronto, 1972), LL.B. (University of Toronto, 1975); called to the bar 1977; articled with the firm 1975-76; practised with the firm 1977-78.

Swansburg, Carla R. B.A. (University of King's College/Dalhousie University, 1989), LL.B. (Dalhousie University, 1993); articled with the firm 1993-94.

Swetsky, Eric J. LL.B. (University of Windsor, 1986); called to the bar 1988; articled with the firm 1986-87.

Taber, Geoffrey K. A.B. (Princeton University, 1982), LL.B. (University of Toronto, 1985); called to the bar 1987; articled with the firm 1985-86; practised with the firm 1987-.

Tacit, Christian S. B.Ap.Sc. (University of Waterloo, 1981), LL.B./M.B.A. (University of Ottawa, 1987); called to the bar 1989; practised with the firm 1990-93.

Taggart, Peter Thomas B.Comm. (Sir George Williams College, 1969), LL.B. (Queen's University, 1972), LL.M. (University of London, 1973); called to the bar 1975; articled with the firm 1973-74.

Takahashi, Heather M. LL.B. (University of Toronto, 1992); called to the bar 1994 (British Columbia, Ontario and New York); articled with the firm 1992-93.

Talsky, Marla B.A. (University of Toronto, 1982), LL.B. (University of Windsor, 1985); called to the bar 1987; articled with the firm 1985-86; practised with the firm 1987-89.

Tay, Derrick C.A. LL.B. (University of Toronto, 1979); called to the bar 1981; practised with the firm 1981-92 (partner 1987).

Taylor, Joyce A. B.A. (McMaster University, 1990), LL.B. (University of Manitoba, 1993); articled with the firm 1993-94.

Taylor, Patricia A.A. B.A. (Hillsdale College, 1981), LL.B. (University of Western Ontario, 1985); called to the bar 1987; articled with the firm 1985-86; practised with the firm 1987-93.

Teetzel, James Vernal LL.D. (McMaster University, 1907); called to the bar 1877; practised with the firm 1881-82 (partner 1881).

ten Kortenaar, Lucia B.Sc. (Queen's University, 1980), LL.B. (University of Toronto, 1983); called to the bar 1985; articled with the firm 1983-84; practised with the firm 1985-87.

Tennenhouse Diamond, Carol B.A. (Carleton University, 1974), LL.B. (University of Ottawa, 1979); called to the bar 1980; practised with the firm 1981- (partner 1985).

Tetreault, David T. B.Comm. (McGill University, 1979), LL.B. (University of Toronto, 1982); called to the bar 1984; practised with the firm 1986- (partner 1990).

Thom, Stuart D. B.A. (University of Toronto, 1927), LL.B. (University of Saskatchewan, 1929), LL.D. (Law Society of Upper Canada, 1979), LL.D. (York

University, 1980); called to the bar 1930 (Sask.); 1947 (Ontario); practised with the firm 1954-78 (partner 1954).

Thomas, Caroline L.M. LL.B. (York University, 1985); called to the bar 1987; articled with the firm 1985-86; practised with the firm 1987-.

Thompson, Simon Ian LL.B. (University of Toronto, 1982); called to the bar 1984; articled with the firm 1982-83.

Thompson, Wendy J. B.A. (University of Toronto, 1970), M.L.S. (University of Toronto, 1972), LL.B. (York University, 1977); called to the bar 1979; articled with the firm 1977 78; practised with the firm 1979-86.

Thomson, Bruce M. B.A. (Mount Allison University, 1977), LL.B. (Dalhousie University, 1980), M.S.T. (Harvard University, 1982), M.Div. (University of Toronto, 1984); called to the bar 1984; articled with the firm 1982-83.

Thomson, Kelly Anne B.A. (Queen's University, 1985), LL.B. (Queen's University, 1988); called to the bar 1990 (Ontario), admitted to practice as a solicitor 1993 (England and Wales); practised with the firm 1990 .

Thomson, Kent E. B.A. (Queen's University, 1979), LL.B. (Queen's University, 1982); called to the bar 1984; articled with the firm 1982-83; practised with the firm 1984-85.

Tilley, Sandra J. B.Comm. (Memorial University of Newfoundland, 1991); LL.B (York University, 1994); articled with the firm 1994-.

Todd, Elisabeth (Campin) B.Sc. (University of Toronto, 1975), LL.B. (York University, 1978), called to the bar 1980; articled with the firm 1978-79.

Tolmie, J. Ross B.A. (University of British Columbia), M.A. (University of British Columbia), B.C.L. (Oxford University, 1932); called to the bar 1932 (British Columbia), 1945 (Ontario); practised with the firm 1986-87 (partner 1986).

Tone, Terrence J. LL.B. (York University, 1970), LL.M. (York University, 1977); called to the bar 1972; practised with the firm 1989- (partner 1989).

Trachuk, Mark A. B.A. (Carleton University, 1983), LL.B. (University of Ottawa, 1986), LL M. (University of London, 1987); called to the bar 1989 (Ontario), admitted to practice as a solicitor 1993 (England and Wales); practised with the firm 1990-

Tremayne, Frank A.M. Graduate (Royal Military College, 1954), B.A. (University of Toronto, 1956), LL.B. (Osgoode Hall, 1961); called to the bar 1963; articled with the firm 1961-62; practised with the firm 1963-74 (partner 1971).

Tremblay, Richard G. B.Sc. (University of Ottawa, 1973), LL.B. (York University, 1977), LL.M. (New York University, 1984); called to the bar 1979; practised with the firm 1987- (partner 1989).

Trethewey, Paul R. B.A. (University of Toronto, 1972), LL.B. (York University, 1977), LL.M. (University of London, 1978); called to the bar 1980; articled with the firm 1978-79.

Trudell, William M. B.A. (University of Windsor, 1968), LL.B. (University of Windsor, 1971); called to the bar 1973; articled with the firm 1971-72; practised with the firm 1973-76.

Trumper, Steven J. B.A. (University of Western Ontario, 1975), LL.B. (Queen's University, 1980); called to the bar 1982; articled with the firm 1980-81; practised with the firm 1982- (partner 1988).

Tsampalieros, Gabriel T. B.A. (Sir George Williams College, 1970), LL.B. (University of Ottawa, 1973); called to the bar 1975; articled with the firm 1973-74; practised with the firm 1975-86 (partner 1980).

Tucker, David W. LL.B. (York University, 1993); articled with the firm 1993-94)

Turner, Francis J. LL.B. (University of Victoria, 1991); called to the bar 1993; articled with the firm 1991-92; practised with the firm 1993-.

Valentini, George M. LL.B.(University of Ottawa, 1982); called to the bar 1984; practised with the firm 1987- (partner 1990).

Van Dyck, Christian D. B.A. (University of Toronto, 1982), LL.B. (Dalhousie University, 1985); called to the bar 1987; articled with the firm 1985-86; practised with the firm 1987-90.

Veale, Ronald S. B.A. (University of Toronto, 1967), LL.B. (University of Toronto, 1971); called to the bar 1973 (Ontario), 1973 (Yukon), 1976 (Northwest Territories); articled with the firm 1971-72.

Vesely, J. George B.A.Sc. (University of Toronto, 1973), LL.B. (University of Toronto, 1976); called to the bar 1978; articled with the firm 1976-77; practised with the firm 1978- (partner 1983).

Vine, Ira H. B.A. (University of Toronto, 1979), M.A. (University of Toronto, 1980), M.B.A. (York University, 1984), LL.B. (University of Toronto, 1991); articled with the firm 1992-93.

Wahl, Ruth I. B.A. (McGill University, 1979), LL.B. (York University, 1985); called to the bar 1987; articled with the firm 1985-86; practised with the firm 1987- (partner 1993).

Wahn, Eve R. B.A. (Queen's University, 1980), LL.B. (University of Saskatchewan, 1985); called to the bar 1987; practised with the firm 1990-93.

Wakefield, Donald E. B.A. (University of Toronto, 1959), LL.B. (University of Toronto, 1962); called to the bar 1964; articled with the firm 1962-63; practised with the firm 1964- (partner 1973).

Waldrum, Cheryl L. LL.B. (University of Western Ontario, 1980), M.Jur. (University of Otago, 1991); called to the bar 1982; articled with the firm 1980-81; practised with the firm 1982-85.

Walker, Diane E. B.A. (McMaster University, 1975), LL.B. (University of Western Ontario, 1977); called to the bar 1979; articled with the firm 1977-78; practised with the firm 1979-94 (partner 1984).

Walker, Elizabeth M. LL.B. (University of Ottawa, 1986), B.C.L. (Oxford University, 1987); called to the bar 1989; articled with the firm 1987-88; practised with the firm 1989-91, 1994-.

Walker, Sandra L. B.A. (Queen's University, 1982), LL.B. (University of Toronto, 1986); called to the bar 1988; articled with the firm 1986-87; practised with the firm 1988-90.

Ware, James G. B.A. (Queen's University, 1965), LL.B. (University of Toronto, 1968); called to the bar 1970; practised with the firm 1976-85 (partner 1977).

Warhaft, Wendy D. B.Comm. (McGill University, 1989), LL.B. (University of Ottawa, 1994); articled with the firm 1994-.

Watson, Russell W. B.A. (University of Waterloo, 1984), LL.B. (University of Western Ontario, 1989); called to the bar 1991; articled with the firm 1989-90; practised with the firm 1991-.

Watt, D. Lynn B.A. (York University, 1983), LL.B. (University of Ottawa, 1992); articled with the firm 1992-93.

Waugh, Marilyn R. B.Sc. (University of Toronto, 1972), LL.B. (University of Toronto, 1988); called to the bar 1990; articled with the firm 1988-89; practised with the firm 1990-.

Weatherhead, Rebecca B.A. (University of Manitoba), LL.B. (University of Toronto, 1988); articled with the firm 1988-89.

Webster, Allan Ross B.A. (University of New Brunswick, 1964), B.C.L. (University of New Brunswick, 1966); called to the bar 1966 (New Brunswick), 1969 (Ontario); articled with the firm 1967 68; practised with the firm 1969-72.

Webster, Donald S. B.Sc. (University of British Columbia, 1987), M.Sc. (University of British Columbia, 1989), LL.B./M.B.A. (York University, 1993); articled with the firm 1993-94.

Webster, John David B.A. (University of Toronto, 1954); called to the bar 1956; articled with the firm 1955-56.

Webster, W. Lee B.Sc. (Queen's University, 1976), LL.B. (Queen's University, 1979); called to the bar 1981; practised with the firm 1984- (partner 1987).

Weldberg, Edward B.Sc. (Touro College, 1986), LL.B. (York University, 1990), M.B.A. (York University, 1990); called to the bar 1992; articled with the firm 1990-91; practised with the firm 1992-.

Weinstein, Karen J. B.A. (University of Toronto, 1979), LL.B. (University of Ottawa, 1984); called to the bar 1986; articled with the firm 1984-85; practised with the firm 1986- (partner 1992).

Wells, Allan C. B.A. (University of Manitoba, 1987), LL.B. (Dalhousie University, 1994); articled with the firm 1994 .

Wenger, David J. B.Comm. (University of Calgary, 1985), LL.B. (University of Toronto, 1988); called to the bar 1990; articled with the firm 1988-89; practised with the firm 1990-.

Westcott, Grace A. B.A. (University of Toronto, 1981), LL.B. (University of Toronto, 1981), LL.M. (Columbia University, 1984); called to the bar 1983; practised with the firm 1983.

White, Donna G. B.A. (Carleton University, 1982), LL.B. (University of Ottawa, 1982), LL.M. (University of Ottawa, 1991); called to the bar 1984; practised with the firm 1986 (partner 1994).

White, Peter Sr B.A. (University of Toronto, 1934); called to the bar 1937; practised with the firm 1974 80 (partner 1974).

White, Peter Jr LL.B. (Osgoode Hall, 1963); called to the bar 1965; practised with the firm 1966-70, 1974- (partner 1974).

Whitfield, Linda R. B.F.A. (Queen's University, 1982), LL.B. (University of Western Ontario, 1989); called to the bar 1991; articled with the firm 1989-90.

Whitley, Mark F. B.A. (Queen's University), M.B.A. (University of Toronto), LL.B. (University of Western Ontario, 1990); called to the bar 1992; articled with the firm 1990-91.

Wild, Catharine M. B.A. (Queen's 1979), LL.B. (York University, 1982); called to the bar 1984; articled with the firm 1982-83; practised with the firm 1984-86.

Wilhelmson, Michael D. B.J. (Carleton University, 1987), LL.B./B.C.L. (McGill University, 1992); called to the bar 1994; articled with the firm 1992-93; practised with the firm 1994-.

Will, Gary R. B.A. (York University, 1979), LL.B. (York University, 1979); called to the bar 1984; articled with the firm 1982-83.

Wilson, Bertha M.A. (University of Aberdeen, 1944), LL.B. (Dalhousie University, 1957), LL.D. (Dalhousie University, 1980), LL.D. (Queen's 1983), LL.D. (University of Calgary, 1983), D.C.L. (University of Western Ontario, 1984), D.Hum.L. (Mount Saint Vincent University, 1984), LL.D. (University of Toronto, 1984), D.C.L. (University of Windsor, 1985), LL.D. (University of Alberta, 1985), LL.D. (York University, 1986), LL.D. (University of British Columbia, 1988), D.Litt.S. (Victoria University, University of Toronto, 1990), D.U. (University of Ottawa, 1990), LL.D. (Law Society of Upper Canada, 1991), LL.D. (Mount Allison University, 1991), LL.D. (Carleton University, 1991), LL.D. (Condordia University, 1991), LL.D. (University of Victoria, 1991); called to the bar 1957 (Nova Scotia), 1959 (Ontario); articled with the firm 1958-59; practised with the firm 1959-75 (partner 1968).

Wilson, David K. B.A. (Queen's University, 1980), LL.B. (University of British Columbia, 1983); called to the bar 1985; practised with the firm 1986- (partner 1991).

Wilson, Patricia J. B.A. (Carleton University, 1977), LL.B. (University of Toronto, 1982); called to the bar 1984; practised with the firm 1986- (partner 1990).

Wilson, Peigi B.A. (University of Western Ontario, 1983), LL.B. (University of Victoria, 1990); articled with the firm 1990-91.

Windsor, George F. B.Eng. (McGill University, 1965), LL.B. (Queen's University, 1970); called to the bar 1972; practised with the firm 1988-93 (partner 1988).

Wink, Alexander Stronach Called to the bar 1875; admitted to practice as a solititor 1870; practised with the firm 1876-80 (partner 1876).

Wolfe, Irene L. B.A. (Carleton University, 1987), LL.B. (McGill University, 1990); called to the bar 1992; articled with the firm 1990-91; practised with the firm 1992-.

Wolfond, Henry J. B.A.A. (Ryerson Polytechnic Institute, 1982), LL.B. University of Alberta, 1992); called to the bar 1994; articled with the firm 1992-93; practised with the firm 1994-.

Wong, Doris S.W. B.Sc. (University of Minnesota, 1974), LL.B. (University of Manitoba, 1980); called to the bar 1981 (Manitoba), 1987 (Ontario); practised with the firm 1987-91.

Wong, Lester A. B.Sc. (University of Western Ontario, 1988), LL.B. (University of British Columbia, 1991); articled with the firm 1991-92.

Woodcock, Brent E. LL.B. (University of Western Ontario, 1981; called to the bar 1983; articled with the firm 1981-82.

Woodside, Thane P. LL.B. (York University, 1983); called to the bar 1985; articled with the firm 1983-84; practised with the firm 1985- (partner 1992).

Wortzman, Jeffrey M. B.A. (University of Western Ontario), LL.B. (York University, 1982); called to the bar 1984; articled with the firm 1982-83.

Wortzman, Robert D. B.A. (University of Western Ontario, 1989), LL.B. (York University, 1992); called to the bar 1994; articled with the firm 1992-93; practised with the firm 1994-.

Wotherspoon, Gordon Dorward de Salaberry (Swatty) Graduate (Royal Military College, 1930), D.M.S. (Royal Military College, 1984); called to the bar 1933; articled with the firm 1930-33; practised with the firm 1933-65 (partner 1938).

Wright, J. Craig B.A. (University of Western Ontario, 1981), LL.B. (McGill University, 1985); called to the bar 1987; articled with the firm 1985-86; practised with the firm 1987- (partner 1994).

Wylie, Gregory R. B.A. (Carleton University, 1987), LL.B. (McGill University, 1990); called to the bar 1992; articled with the firm 1990-91; practised with the firm 1992-.

Yakabuski, J. Kimball B.Sc. (University of Waterloo, 1981), LL.B. (Queen's University, 1984); called to the bar 1986; practised with the firm 1988-89.

Yalden, Robert M. B.A. (Queen's University, 1984), B.A. (Oxford University, 1986), LL.B. (University of Toronto, 1988), LL.B. (Université de Montréal, 1991); called to the bar 1991 (Ontario), 1992 (Quebec); articled with the firm 1988-89; practised with the firm 1993-.

Yao, Amy S. LL.B. (University of Hong Kong, 1978); called to the bar 1981 (Hong Kong), 1986 (Ontario); articled with the firm 1984-85.

Young, Karen D. B.A. (University of Toronto, 1978), LL.B. (University of Ottawa, 1984); called to the bar 1986; articled with the firm 1984-85; practised with the firm 1986-92.

Young, R. Alan B.A. (Wilfrid Laurier University, 1978), B.Ed. (Brock University, 1979), LL.B. (York University, 1983); called to the bar 1985; articled with the firm 1983-84; practised with the firm 1985-91, 1994-.

Zaid, Frank B.A.Sc. (University of Toronto, 1968), LL.B. (York University, 1971); called to the bar 1973; practised with the firm 1973- (partner 1977).

Zemans, David H. LL.B. (Dalhousie University, 1991); called to the bar 1993; articled with the firm 1991-92; practised with the firm 1993-.

Zimmerman, Avi B.A.Sc. (University of Toronto, 1983), LL.B. (University of Toronto, 1991); called to the bar 1993; articled with the firm 1991-92.

Zivic, Alexander M.Sc. (University of London, 1989); B.A. (Cambridge University, 1991), LL.B. (Dalhousie University, 1992); articled with the firm 1992-93.

Zitzerman, David B. B.A. (University of Manitoba, 1978), LL.B. (University of Toronto, 1981); called to the bar 1983; articled with the firm 1981-82; practised with the firm 1983-86.

Zytaruk, JoAnn K. B.A. (Laurentian University), LL.B. (University of Toronto, 1987); called to the bar 1989; articled with the firm 1987-88.

APPENDIX II
LARGEST CANADIAN LAW FIRMS, 1862-1992[1]

1862

1. Cayley, Cameron & McMichael (4 lawyers): Hon. William Cayley, M.C. Cameron, Daniel McMichael, Edward Fitzgerald — Church St., Toronto.

2. Crooks, Kingsmill & Cattanach (3 lawyers): Adam Crooks, Nicol Kingsmill, Alexander J. Cattanach — Wellington St., Toronto.

2. Jones Brothers (3 lawyers): Edward C. Jones, Jonas Ap. Jones, Clarkson Jones — Masonic Hall, Toronto.

2. Paterson, Harrison & Hodgins (3 lawyers): James Paterson, Robert A. Harrison, Thomas Hodgins — Ontario Hall, Court St., Toronto.

2. Ross, Crawford & Crombie (3 lawyers): Hon. J. Ross, Q.C., John Crawford, Ernestus Crombie — Masonic Hall, Toronto St., Toronto.

2. Wilson, Paterson & Beaty (3 lawyers): Hon. Adam Wilson, Q.C., Christopher S. Paterson, James Beaty Jr. — 5 King St. W., Toronto.

1872

1. Blake, Kerr & Boyd (6 lawyers): Hon. Edward Blake, Q.C., James K. Kerr, J.A. Boyd, J.W. Fletcher, Walter G.P. Cassels, William R. Mulock — Masonic Hall, Toronto St., Toronto.

2. Harrison, Osler & Moss (6 lawyers): Robert A. Harrison, Q.C., Featherston Osler, Thomas Moss, Q.C., Charles Moss, W.A. Foster, William Glenholme Falconbridge — 36 & 38 King St., E., Toronto.

3. Cameron, Michael & Hoskin (4 lawyers): Hon. Matthew Crooks Cameron, Q.C., Daniel McMichael, Q.C., Charles McMichael, Alfred Hoskin — 44 Church St., Toronto.

3. Crooks, Kingsmill & Cattanach (4 lawyers): Hon. Adam Crooks, Q.C., Nicol Kingsmill, A.J. Cattanach, W. Francis — 17 Wellington St., W., Toronto.

3. Mowat, McLennan & Downey (4 lawyers): Hon. Oliver Mowat, Q.C., James McLennan, Q.C., John Downey, John S. Ewart — Royal Insurance Buildings, Yonge St., Toronto.

3. Macdonald & Patton (4 lawyers): Rt. Hon. Sir John A. Macdonald, Q.C., Hon. James Patton, Q.C., Hugh J. McDonald, Robert M. Fleming — Trust & Loan Companies Building, Toronto.

1882

1. Blake, Kerr, Lash & Cassels (9 lawyers): Hon. Edward Blake, Q.C., Samuel Hume Blake, Q.C., James K. Kerr, Q.C., Zebulon A. Lash, Q.C., Walter G.P. Cassels, C.A. Brough, C.J. Holman, H. Cassels, K. Maclean — Millichamps Buildings, Toronto.

2. Bethune, Moss, Falconbridge & Hoyles (7 lawyers): James Bethune, Q.C., Charles Moss, Q.C., William Glenholme Falconbridge, N.W. Hoyles, Walter Barwick, Allen B. Aylesworth, W.J. Franks — North of Scotland Chambers, 18 & 20 King St., W., Toronto.

2. McCarthy, Osler, Hoskin & Creelman (7 lawyers): D'Alton McCarthy, Q.C., Britton Bath Osler, Q.C., John Hoskin, Adam R. Creelman, Thomas S. Plumb, W.H.P. Clement, Frederick Harcourt — Temple Chambers, 23 Toronto St., Toronto.

4. Bain, McDougall, Gordon & Shepley (5 lawyers): John Bain, Joseph E. McDougall, William S. Gordon, George F. Shepley, Frederic Moffatt — Imperial Bank Building, Toronto.

5. Mowat, Maclennan, Downey & Biggar (5 lawyers): Hon. Oliver Mowat, Q.C., James Maclennan, John Downey, C.R.W. Biggar, Thomas Langton — Queen City Insurance Building, 24 Church St., Toronto.

6. Beatty, Chadwick, Thomson & Blackstock (4 lawyers): W.H. Beatty, E.M. Chadwick, T.G. Blackstock, W.A. Reeve — 58 Wellington St., Toronto.

6. Beaty, Hamilton & Cassels (4 lawyers): James Beaty, Q.C., J.C. Hamilton, Allan Cassels, D.W. Clendenan — Building & Loan Building, Toronto St., Toronto.

6. Crooks, Kingsmill & Cattanach (4 lawyers): Hon. Adam Crooks, Q.C., Nicol Kingsmill, A.J. Cattanach, H. Symons — 17 & 19 Wellington St. W., Toronto.

6. Delamere, Black, Reesor & Keefer (4 lawyers): T.D. Delamere, D. Black, H.A. Reesor, R.W. Keefer — 17 Toronto St., Toronto.

6. Mulock, Tilt, Miller & Crowther (4 lawyers): William Mulock, James Tilt, W.N. Miller, James Crowther Jr. — 99 King St. E., Toronto.

6. McMichael, Hoskin & Ogden (4 lawyers): D. McMichael, Q.C., Charles McMichael, Alfred Hoskin, Albert Ogden — 46 Church St., Toronto.

6. Robinson, O'Brien & Scott (4 lawyers): C. Robinson, Q.C., Henry O'Brien, H.J. Scott, Goodwin Gibson — 68 Church St., Toronto.

6. Rose, Macdonald, Merritt & Coatsworth (4 lawyers): John E. Rose, Q.C., J.H. Macdonald, W.M. Merritt, E. Coatsworth Jr. — Union Loan Building, Toronto.

6. Wells, Gordon & Sampson (4 lawyers): Hon. R.M. Wells, Q.C., W.H.L. Gordon, Alexander Sampson, George T. Blackstock — Front & Scott Streets, Toronto.

1892

1. Blake, Lash & Cassels (11 lawyers): Hon. Edward Blake, Q.C., Samuel Hume Blake, Q.C., Zebulon A. Lash, Q.C., W.G.P. Cassels, Q.C., Alexander Mackenzie, W. H. Blake, Hume Blake, E.F. Blake, A.W. Anglin, T.D. Law, James McGregor Young — Bank of Commerce Buildings, King St. West., Toronto.

2. McCarthy, Osler, Hoskin & Creelman (10 lawyers): D'Alton McCarthy, Q.C., Britton Bath Osler, Q.C., John Hoskin, Adam R. Creelman, Q.C., Frederick Harcourt, Wallace Nesbitt, W.B. Raymond, W.M. Douglas, H.S. Osler, Leighton McCarthy — Temple Chambers, 23 Toronto St., Toronto.

3. Maclaren, Macdonald, Merritt & Shepley (8 lawyers): J.J. Maclaren, Q.C., J.H. Macdonald, Q.C., W.M. Merritt, George F. Shepley, Q.C., W.E. Middleton, R.C. Donald, Arthur E. Lobb, Frank W. Maclean — 28 Toronto St., Toronto.

4. Moss, Hoyles & Aylesworth (7 lawyers): Charles Moss, Q.C., N.W. Hoyles, Q.C., Walter Barwick, Allen B. Aylesworth, Q.C., W.J. Franks, Douglas Armour, H.J. Wright — North of Scotland Chambers, 18 & 20 King St., W., Toronto.

5. Beatty, Chadwick, Blackstock & Galt (6 lawyers): W.H. Beatty, E.M. Chadwick, Thomas G. Blackstock, T.P. Galt, W.H. Brouse, D. Fasken — Bank of Toronto Buildings, 60 Wellington St. E. (at Church St.), Toronto.

5. Abbotts, Campbell, & Meredith (6 lawyers): Hon. J.J.C. Abbott, Q.C., J.B. Abbott, Harry Abbott, Q.C., C.S. Campbell, F.E. Meredith, H.J. Hague — 11 Hospital St., Montreal.

7. Kerr, Macdonald, Davidson & Paterson (5 lawyers): J.K. Kerr, Q.C., W. Macdonald, W. Davidson, J.A. Paterson, R.A. Grant — 18 Toronto St., Toronto.

7. Meredith, Clarke, Bowes & Hilton (5 lawyers): William Ralph Meredith, Q.C., J.B. Clarke, Q.C., J.H. Bowes, F.A. Hilton, C. Swabey — 32 Church St., Toronto.

7. McMurrich, Coatsworth, Hodgins, Urquhart & Geddes (5 lawyers): W.B. McMurrich, Q.C., Emerson Coatsworth Jr., Frank E. Hodgins, D. Urquhart, Walter A. Geddes — 1 Toronto St., Toronto.

7. Robinson, O'Brien & Gibson (5 lawyers): Christopher Robinson, Q.C., Henry O'Brien, Goodwin Gibson, A.H. O'Brien, Colin Fraser — 74 Church St., Toronto.

1902

1. Beatty, Blackstock, Nesbitt, Chadwick & Riddell (15 lawyers): W.H. Beatty, Thomas G. Blackstock, K.C., George T. Blackstock, K.C., E.M. Chadwick, Wallace Nesbitt, K.C., William Renwick Riddell, K.C., T.P. Galt, D. Fasken, A. Munro Grier, H. Armstrong, R. McKay, C.W. Beatty, Alexander Fasken, H.E. Rose, Ross Gooderham — Bank of Toronto Building, 60 Wellington St. E. (at Church St.), Toronto.

2. Blake, Lash & Cassels (13 lawyers): Samuel Hume Blake, K.C. Zebulon A. Lash, K.C., W.G.P. Cassels, K.C., Alexander Mackenzie, W.H. Blake, Hume Blake, E.F. Blake, A.W. Anglin, T.D. Law, W.A.H. Kerr, W. Gow, Miller Lash, R.C.H. Cassels — Bank of Commerce Building, Toronto.

3. McCarthy, Osler, Hoskin & Harcourt (11 lawyers): John Hoskin, K.C., Adam R. Creelman, K.C., F.W. Harcourt, K.C., W.B. Raymond, H.S. Osler, Leighton G. McCarthy, D'Alton Lally McCarthy, C.S. MacInnes, Britton Osler, A.M. Stewart, Christopher Robinson, K.C. — Freehold Building, Victoria St., Toronto.

4. Barwick, Aylesworth, Wright & Moss (6 lawyers): Walter Barwick, K.C., Allen B. Aylesworth, K.C., H.J. Wright, J.H. Moss, Charles A. Moss, J.A. Thompson — Bank of Toronto Buildings, 60 Wellington St. E. (at Church St.), Toronto.

4. McPherson, Clark, Campbell & Jarvis (6 lawyers): W.D. McPherson, J.M. Clark, K.C., R.U. McPherson, G.C. Campbell, F.C. Jarvis, Joseph Montgomery — 16 King St. W., Toronto.

4. Beique, Lafontaine, Turgeon, Robertson & Dessaules (6 lawyers): Frederic L. Beique, K.C., P.E. Lafontaine, K.C., Ed. L. Turgeon, D.C. Robertson, C. Dessaules, L.J. Beique — New York Life Building, Montreal.

4. McGibbon, Casgrain, Ryan & Mitchell (6 lawyers): R.D. McGibbon, K.C., Th. Chase-Casgrain, K.C., Percy C. Ryan, V.F. Mitchell, Ed. Surveyer, L. Macfarlane — Canada Life Building, Montreal.

8. Beaudin, Cardinal, Loranges & St. Germain (5 lawyers): S. Beaudin, K.C., J.T. Cardinal, L. Loranger, P. St. Germain, Joseph-H. Loranger — 1608 Notre Dame St., Montreal.

8. Campbell, Meredith, Allan & Hague (5 lawyers): C.S. Campbell, K.C., F.E. Meredith, K.C., J.B. Allan, H.J. Hague, A.R. Holden — Merchants Bank Chambers, Montreal.

8. Clute, Macdonald, Macintosh & Hay (5 lawyers): R.C. Clute, K.C., G.S. Macdonald, J.A. Macintosh, J.G. Hay, A.R. Clute — McKinnon Building, Toronto.

8. Greenshields, Greenshields, Heneker & Dunn (5 lawyers): J.N. Greenshields, K.C., R.A.E. Greenshields, K.C. R.T. Heneker, J.H. Dunn, W.J. Mitchell — 1724 Notre Dame St., Montreal.

8. Kerr, Davidson, Paterson & Grant (5 lawyers): J.K. Kerr, K.C., W. Davidson, J.A. Paterson, R.A. Grant, E.G. Long — 23 Adelaide St. E., Toronto.

8. Kingsmill, Hellmuth, Saunders & Torrance (5 lawyers): N. Kingsmill, K.C., I.F. Hellmuth, Dyce W. Saunders, W.P. Torrance, E.C. Cattanach — 19 Wellington St. W., Toronto.

8. Maclaren, Macdonald, Shepley & Donald (5 lawyers): J.J. Maclaren, K.C., J.H. Macdonald, K.C., G.F. Shepley, K.C., W.E. Middleton, R.C. Donald — 28 & 30 Toronto St., Toronto.

8. Mills, Raney, Anderson & Halen (5 lawyers): G.G. Mills, W.E. Raney, Alexander Mills, A.J. Anderson, J. Hales — 16 King St. W., Toronto.

8. Thomson, Henderson & Bell (5 lawyers): D.E. Thomson, K.C., D. Henderson, George Bell, John B. Holden, W.N. Tilley; General Trusts Building — 59 Yonge St., Toronto.

1912

1. Beatty, Blackstock, Fasken, Cowan & Chadwick (15 lawyers): W.H. Beatty, G.T. Blackstock, K.C., E.M. Chadwick, K.C., M.K. Cowan, K.C., T.C. Galt, K.C., D. Fasken, K.C., H. Armstrong, Alexander Fasken, H.F. Rose, K.C., Ross Gooderham, W.G. Blackstock, A.G. Ross, G.H. Sedgewick, G.E. McCann, L. Davis — Bank of Toronto Building, Toronto.

2. Blake, Lash, Anglin & Cassels (11 lawyers): Samuel H. Blake, K.C., Zebulon A. Lash, K.C., W.H. Blake, K.C., A.W. Anglin, K.C., T.D. Law, W. Gow, Miller Lash, Glyn Osler, R.C.H. Cassels, George H. Cassels, J.F. Lash — Bank of Commerce Building, Toronto.

3. McCarthy, Osler, Hoskin & Harcourt (9 lawyers): John Hoskin, K.C., F.W. Harcourt, K.C., H.S. Osler, K.C., Leighton McCarthy, K.C., D'Alton Lally McCarthy, K.C., Britton Osler, Wellington Ault Cameron, J.F.H. McCarthy, Wallace Nesbitt, K.C. — Home Life Building, Toronto.

4. Aylesworth, Wright, Moss & Thompson (8 lawyers): Sir Allen B. Aylesworth, K.C., H.J. Wright, J.H. Moss, K.C., C.A. Moss, J.A. Thompson, Featherston Aylesworth, Hugh L. Hoyles, E.R. Lynch — Traders Bank Building, Toronto.

5. Bicknell, Bain, Strathy & Mackelcan (7 lawyers): James Bicknell, K.C., Alfred Bicknell, James W. Bain, K.C., G.B. Strathy, F.R. MacKelcan, M.L. Gordon, T.W. Lawson — corner of Yonge & Adelaide Sts., Toronto.

5. Macdonald, Shepley & Donald (7 lawyers): J.H. Macdonald, K.C., G.F. Shepley, K.C., R.C. Donald, G.W. Mason, H.S. White, A. Foulds Jr., W.W. Davidson — 28, 30 Toronto St., Toronto.

5. Rowell, Reid, Wilkie & Wood (7 lawyers): N.W. Rowell, K.C., Thomas Reid, George Wilkie, S. Casey Wood Jr., C.W. Thompson, E.W. Wright, Irving S. Fairty — 46 King St. W., Toronto.

5. Brown,Montgomery & McMichael (7 lawyers): A.J. Brown, K.C., W. Prescott Sharp, K.C., George H.A. Montgomery, K.C., R.C. McMichael, Rennie O. McMurtry, W.F. Chipman, Walter R.L. Shanks — 164 St. James St., Montreal.

5. Kavanagh, Lajoie & Lacoste (7 lawyers): Sir Alexander Lacoste, K.C., H.J. Kavanagh, K.C., H. Gerin-Lajoie, K.C., Paul Lacoste, Jules Mathier, Alexander Lacoste Jr., T.J. Shallow — 7 Place D'Armes Sq., Montreal.

5. Meredith, Macpherson, Hague & Holden (7 lawyers): F.E. Meredith, K.C., K.R. Macpherson, K.C., H.J. Hague, A.R. Holden, W.J. Shaughnessy, C.J. Heward, C.S. Campbell, K.C. — Merchants Bank Chambers, Montreal.

1922

1. Bain, Bicknell, Macdonell & Gordon (14 lawyers): James W. Bain, K.C., Alfred Bicknell, K.C., A. McL. Macdonell, K.C., Peter White, K.C., M.L. Gordon, E. Bristol, J.M. Forgie, B.H.L. Symmes, J.S. Duggan, C. McKay, J.W. Bicknell, J.F. Lucas, I.M. Macdonald, W.O. Gibson — Yonge and Adelaide Sts., Toronto.

1. Blake, Lash, Anglin & Cassels (14 lawyers): W.H. Blake, K.C., A.W. Anglin, K.C., W. Gow, K.C., Miller Lash, Glyn Osler, K.C., R.C.H. Cassels, K.C., M.C. Cameron, George H. Cassels, J.F. Lash, S.G. Crowell, G.S. Hodgson, G.G. Paulin, G.R. Munnoch, H.C. Walker — Bank of Commerce Building, Toronto.

3. Rowell, Reid, Wood, Wright & McMillan (11 lawyers): Thomas Reid, S. Casey Wood, K.C., E.W. Wright, E.G. McMillan, J.M. Jarvis, E.R. Lynch, A.H.K. Russell, G.S. O'Brian, W.R. Binch, D.J. Nickle, N.W. Rowell, K.C. — 38 King St., W., Toronto.

4. Brown, Montgomery & McMichael (10 lawyers): A.J. Brown, K.C., George H. Montgomery, K.C., Robert C. McMichael, K.C., Warwick F. Chipman, K.C., Rennie O. McMurtry, Walter R.L. Shanks, K.C., G.P. Vanier, G.A. Coughlin, F.B. Common, L.H. Ballantyne — Dominion Express Building, Montreal.

4. Osler, Hoskin & Harcourt (10 lawyers): Frederick W. Harcourt, K.C., H.S. Osler, K.C., Britton Osler, K.C., Wellington Ault Cameron, Harold W. Shapley, Archibald W. Langmuir, Morley Smith, G. Meredith Huycke, Norman E. Strickland, Wallace Nesbitt, K.C. — Dominion Bank Building, Toronto.

6. Aylesworth, Wright, Thompson & Lawr (9 lawyers): Sir Allen B. Aylesworth, K.C., Harry J. Wright, K.C., J.A. Thompson, Waldon Lawr, A.M. Garden, H.J. Stuart, McG. Aylesworth, A.H. Robertson, H.J. Scott, K.C. — Bank of Hamilton Building, Toronto.

6. Davis, Marshall, Macneill & Pugh (9 lawyers): E.P. Davis, K.C., C.B. Marshall, K.C. D.G. Marshall, K.C., J.H. Lawson, J.S.W. Pugh, G. Davis, D.G. Marshall Jr., J.C. Ralston, D.N. Hossie — London Building, 626 Pender St., Vancouver.

6. Donald, Mason, White & Foulds (9 lawyers): R.C. Donald, K.C., G.W. Mason, H.S. White, K.C., A. Foulds Jr., W.W. Davidson, F.C. Carter, R.D. Walter, R.L. Kellock, E.C. Gordon — 60 Victoria St., Toronto.

6. McMaster, Montgomery, Fleury & Co. (9 lawyers): A.C. McMaster, K.C., J.D. Montgomery, R.A. Montgomery, W.J. Fleury, J.H. Fraser, J.M. Bullen, H.L. Steele, N.S. Robertson, G. McG. Willoughby — 901 Temple Building, Toronto.

6.   Munson, Allan, Davis, Haffner & Hobkirk (9 lawyers): G.W. Allan, K.C., D.H. Laird, K.C. G.H. Davis, E.F. Haffner, A.A. Hobkirk, L.J. Loader, K.L. Patton, R.B. MacInnes, J.J. Milne — 392 Main St., Winnipeg.

<u>1932</u>

1.   Brown, Montgomery & McMichael (21 lawyers): A.J. Brown, K.C., G.H.A. Montgomery, K.C., R.C. McMichael, K.C., Warwick F. Chipman, K.C., F.B. Common, K.C., O.S. Tyndale, K.C., T.R. Ker, K.C., W.H. Howard, K.C. L.H. Ballantyne, L.A. Forsyth, K.C., C. Sinclair, K.C., Eldridge Cate, C.R. McKenzie, P. Gauthier, J.L. Bishop, C.S. Richardson, J.A. Ogilvy, F.C. Cope, J.G. Porteous, H. Hansard, G.F. Osler — Royal Bank Building, Montreal.

2.   Blake, Lash, Anglin & Cassels (20 lawyers): A.W. Anglin, K.C., Walter Gow, K.C. Miller Lash, K.C. Glyn Osler, K.C., R.H.C. Cassels, K.C., Geo. H. Cassels, K.C. J.F. Lash, S.G. Crowell, G.S. Hodgson, G.R. Munnoch, H.C. Walker, R.E. Anglin, A.R. Graydon, J.T. Gow, E.C. Snelgrove, R.B.F. Barr, Kenneth Lash, B.B. Osler, J.G. Cassels, T. Mackie — Canadian Bank of Commerce Building, Toronto.

3.   Osler, Hoskin & Harcourt (14 lawyers): H.S. Osler, K.C., F.W. Harcourt, K.C., Britton Osler, K.C., W.A. Cameron, H.W. Shapley, K.C., A.W. Langmuir, G.M. Huycke, N.E. Strickland, H C F Mockridge, R.G. Ferguson, H.E. Boston, M.W. McCutcheon, Rt. Hon. Arthur Meighen, K.C., P.C., A. Munro Grier, K.C. — Dominion Bank Building, Toronto.

4.   Tilley, Johnston, Thomson & Parmenter (12 lawyers): W.N. Tilley, K.C., Strachan Johnston, K.C., R.H. Parmenter, K.C., Arthur J. Thomson, K.C. W.S. Morlock, S F. Wedd, B.V. McCrimmon, C.F.H. Carson, J.G. Middleton, E.P. Tilley, J.S.D. Tory, R.W.S. Johnston — 80 King St., W., Toronto.

4.   Lafleur, MacDougall, Macfarlane & Barclay (12 lawyers): Gordon W. MacDougall, K.C., L. Macfarlane, K.C. G. Barclay, K.C., W.B. Scott, K.C. Hon. Adrian K-Hugessen, W.F. Macklaier, J. Robinson, J F Chisholm, G.M. Hyde, H.L. Smith, E.H. Eberts, H.W. Davis — 507 Place d'Armes, Montreal.

4.   Meredith, Holden, Heward & Holden (12 lawyers). F.E. Meredith, K C LLD., A.R. Holden, K.C., C G Heward, K.C., R.C. Holden, K.C. P.P. Hutchison, E.H. Cliff, C.T. Ballantyne, W.C.J. Meredith, F.T. Collins, A.D.P. Heeney, S.B. Millen, G. Davidson — 215 St. James St., Montreal.

7.   McMaster, Montgomery, Bullen, Steele, Robertson & Willoughby (11 lawyers): A.C. McMaster, K.C., J.D. Montgomery, K.C., R.A. Montgomery, W.J. Fleury, J.M. Bullen, H.L. Steele, N.S. Robertson, G. McC. Willoughby, J.W. McMaster, C.H. Lane, R.M. Fowler — 902 Temple Building, Toronto.

7.   Rowell, Reid, Wright & McMillan (11 lawyers): T. Reid, E.W. Wright, K.C. E.G. McMillan, J.B. Allen, F.R. Lynch, W.R. Binch, F. Wilkinson, H.E. Langford, E.T. Godwin, J.F. Smith, Hon. F.W. Rowell, K.C. — 38 King St., W., Toronto.

8.   Vallee, Vien, Beaudry, Fortier & Mathieu (10 lawyers): A. Vallee, K.C., Thomas Vien, K.C., R. Beaudry, K.C., J.Y. Fortier, K.C. A. Mathieu, K.C. Leon Fairbault, K.C., E.C. Monk, R. Noel, A.A. Macaughton, Y. Pelletier — Themis Building, Montreal.

10.   McCarthy & McCarthy (9 lawyers): Leighton McCarthy, K.C., Frank McCarthy, K.C., H.A. Harrison, W.J. Beittie, W.R. West, S.A. Hayden, W.C. Terry, A. Bissett, F.B. Matthews — Canada Life Building, Toronto.

10. McLaughlin, Johnston, Moorhead & Macaulay (9 lawyers): R.J. McLaughlin, K.C., R.D. Moorhead, K.C., Hon. L. Macaulay, K.C., H.J. McLaughlin, W.W. McLaughlin, D.C. Wells, R.J. May, H.W. Alles, R.H. Soward — 302 Bay St., Toronto.

10. Bain, Bicknell, White & Bristol (9 lawyers): James W. Bain, K.C., Peter White, K.C., Alfred Bicknell, K.C., A. McL. Macdonell, K.C., E. Bristol, K.C., Ian M. Macdonell, Grant Gordon, F.A. Beck, W.M. Vickers — Lumsden Building, cor. Yonge & Adelaide Sts., Toronto.

10. Hudson, Ormond, Swift & Macleod (9 lawyers): A.B. Hudson, K.C., H. Ormond, K.C. H.V. Hudson, K.C. E. Spice, H.E. Swift, C.J. Macleod, W.H. August, I.J.R. Deacon, D.S. Ormond — 303-7 Lombard Building, Winnipeg.

10. Tupper, Hamilton, Adams, McDonald & Campbell (9 lawyers): W.J. Tupper, K.C., W.C. Hamilton, K.C., Sir Charles S. Tupper, K.C., A. Adams, G.C. McDonald, A. Campbell, C.W. Tupper, J.R. Robson, C.P. Wilson, K.C. — McArthur Building, Winnipeg.

10. Foster, Place, Hackett, Mulvena, Hackett & Foster (9 lawyers): J.T. Hackett, K.C., H.R. Mulvena, F.W. Hackett, G.B. Foster, K.C. F.R. Hannen, W.H. Wilson, L.D. L'Esperance, J.E. Mitchell, Hon. P.B. Mignault, K.C. — 507 Place d'Armes, Montreal.

1942

1. Blake, Anglin, Osler & Cassels (25 lawyers): A.W. Anglin, K.C., Walter Gow, K.C., Glyn Osler, K.C., R.C.H. Cassels, K.C., Geo. H. Cassels, K.C. S.G. Crowell, K.C., G.R. Munnoch, K.C., H.C. Walker, K.C., A.R. Graydon, K.C., R.E. Anglin, J.T. Gow, M. Blair, E.C. Snelgrove, R.B.F. Barr, B.B. Osler, J.G. Cassels, T. Mackie, J.T. Garrow, D.G. Guest, A.J.C. Anglin, W.H.C. Boyd, P.S. Osler, T.R. Wilcox, Belva G. Gibson, G.E. Burson — Canadian Bank of Commerce Building, Toronto.

2. Montgomery, Michael, Common & Howard (23 lawyers): George H. Montgomery, K.C. Tobert C. McMichael, K.C. Frank B. Common, K.C. Thomas R. Ker, K.C., Wilbert H. Howard, K.C., Lionel A. Forsyth, K.C., Eldriege Cate, K.C., C. Russell McKenzie, K.C., Paul Gauthier, J. Leigh Bishop, Claude S. Richardson, J. Angus Ogilvy, K.C., F. Campbell Cope, John G. Porteous, Hazen Hansard, John DeM. Marler, George H. Montgomery, Jr., Charles M. Drury, Andre Forget, Thomas H. Montgomery, Paul F. Renault, Warwick F. Chipman, K.C. — Royal Bank Building, Montreal.

3. Osler, Hoskin & Harcourt (19 lawyers): Britton Osler, K.C., H.W. Shapley, K.C., W.A. Cameron, G.M. Huycke, K.C., N.E. Strickland, H.C.F. Mockridge, R.G. Ferguson, T.D. Delamere, B.M. Osler, G.D. Wotherspoon, J.G. Osler, H.E. Boston, W.A.J. Case, J. Hood, A.W. Langmuir, W.B. Reid, G.T. Rogers, Rt. Hon. Arthur Meighen, K.C., P.C., A. Munro Grier, K.C. — Dominion Bank Building, Toronto.

4. McCarthy & McCarthy (17 lawyers): Hon. Leighton McCarthy, K.C., Frank McCarthy, K.C., Hon. S.A. Hayden, K.C., W.R. West, W.C. Terry, A. Bissett, Beverley Matthews, R.M. Fowler, J.W. Walker, W.G. Nield, A.W.H. Kerr, J.K. Webbb, G.M. Ferguson, L.H. Goodwin, M.V. Darte, J.W. Blain, J.H. Ryan — Canada Life Building, Toronto.

5. McMaster, Montgomery, Bullen, Steele, Robertson & Willoughby (13 lawyers): J.D. McMaster, K.C., R.A. Montgomery, W.J. Fleury, J.M. Bullen, K.C.,

H.L. Steele, N.S. Robertson, G.M. Willoughby, J.W. McMaster, C.H. Lane, G.T. Heintzman, J.S. McKinnon, A.E. Robinette, D.A. McKenzie — Temple Building, Toronto.

6. Wright & McMillan (12 lawyers): E.G. McMillan, K.c, W.R. Binch, F. Wilkinson, K.C., H.E. Langford, Peter Wright, E.R. Lynch, N.T. Berry, R.J. Dunn, J.H. Corrigan, W.G.C. Howland, R.G. Parker, D.L. McCarthy, K.C. — 38 King St., W., Toronto.

6. Holden, Heward & Holden (12 lawyers): A.R. Holden, K.C., C.G. Heward, K.C., R.C. Holden, K.C., P.P., Hutchison, K.C., E.H. Cliff, K.C., C.t. Ballantyne, W.C.J. Meredith, K.C., F.T. Collins, K.C. D,R. McMaster, A.M. Minnion, G.R.W. Owen, R.A. Patch — 215 St. James St., W., Montreal.

8. White, Ruel & Bristol (11 lawyers): Peter White, K.C., G. Ruel, K.C., E. Bristol, K.C., T. Moss, K.C., G. Gordon, F.A. Beck, N.E. Phipps, R.W. Armstrong, Peter White, Jr., J.F. Barrett, W.M. Wismer — Imperial Bank Building, Toronto.

8. Aikins, Loftus, MacAulay, Turner, Thompson & Tritschler (11 lawyers): Edwin Loftus, K.C., G.H. Aikins, K.C., J.A. MacAulay, K.C., F.J. Turner, K.C., D.A. Thompson, G.E. Tritschler, T.W.B. Hinch, O.W. Struthers, R.E. Curran, H.M. Pickard, D.C. McGavin — Somerset Building, Winnipeg.

8. Allan, Laird, MacInnes & Burbridge (11 lawyers): D.H. Laird, K.C., R.B. MacInnes, K.C., J.J. Milne, K.C., F.M. Burbidge, K.C., T.G. Wright, J.O. Allison, G.P.R. Tallin, H.E. Carey, D.R. Jackson, W.C. Eyres, D.D. Friesen — 333 Main St., Winnipeg.

1952

1. McMichael, Common, Howard, Ker & Cate (24 lawyers): Robert C. McMichael, Frank B. Common, Thomas R. Ker, Wilbert H. Howard, Lionel A. Forsyth, Eldridge Cate, Paul Gauthier, J. Leigh Bishop, Claude S. Richardson, J. Angus Ogilvy, F. Campbell Cope, John G. Porteous, Hazard Hansard, John deM. Marler, George H. Montgomery, Paul F. Renault, Brock F. Clarke, John G. Kirkpatrick, Robert E. Morrow, Frank B. Common Jr., William S. Tyndale, Kenneth S. Howard — Royal Bank Building, Montreal.

2. Blake, Anglin, Osler & Cassels (22 lawyers): R.C.H. Cassels, G.R. Munnoch, H.C. Walker, Allan Graydon, J.T. Gow, R.B.F. Barr, B.B. Osler, W.E.P. DeRoche, A.S. Pattillo, D.G. Guest, T. Mackie, Belva G. Gibson, W.H.C. Boyd, P.S. Osler, R.A. Kingston, T.R. Wilcox, T.A. King, W.H. Lind, D.M. Grimshaw, N.M. Simpson, A.J. Macintosh, J.M. Hodgson — Bank of Commerce Building, Toronto.

3. McCarthy & McCarthy (17 lawyers): Hon. S.A. Hayden, W.R. West, W.C. Terry, Beverley Matthews, J.W. Walker, A.W.H. Kerr, A. Bissett, G.M. Ferguson, J.W. Blain, Gordon Waldie, P.H.G. Walker, G.F. Hayden, J.H.C. Clarry, John B. Lawson, Frank McCarthy, Harold G. Fox, John J. Robinette — Canada Life Building, Toronto.

3. Osler, Hoskin & Harcourt (17 lawyers): H.W. Shapley, G.M. Huycke, H.C.F. Mockridge, N.E. Strickland, R.G. Ferguson, T.D. Delamere, B.M. Osler, G.D. Wotherspoon, J.G. Osler, H.E. Boston, W.B. Reid, C.R. Osler, A.W. Langmuir, J.I. Douglas, W.M. Bryden, F.A.M. Huycke, A.L. Beattie — Dominion Bank Building, Toronto.

5. Campney, Owen, Murphy, & Owen (15 lawyers): R.O. Campney, W.S. Owen, W. Murphy, D.M. Owen, J.D. Forin, F.H. Bonnell, Geo. S. Clark, F. Read, John I. Bird, W.G. Essex, Michael Spohn, W.R. Mead, C.F. Murphy, M.A. Huel, Geo. H. Shepherd — 744 Hastings St., W., Vancouver.

5. Russell & Du Moulin (15 lawyers): A.M. Russell, L. St. M. Du Moulin, D. McK. Brown, E.D.H. Wilkinson, Wilfrid H. Heffernan, R.G. Wismer, Miss K.I. McArthur, Miss J. McD. Russell, R. E. Osrlund, L.H. Clayton, D.A. Williamson, R.E. Seaton, S.H. Wallace, Allan D. McEachern — 850 Hastings St., W., Vancouver.

7. Borden, Elliot, Kelley, Palmer & Sankey (14 lawyers): B.V. Elliot, W.A.G. Kelley, K.B. Palmer, R.H. Sankey, J.T. Johnson, I.G. Wahn, A.D. McAlpine, H.R. MacEwen, J.A. Renwick, W.G. Gray, W.S. Robertson, W.L.N. Somerville, R.C. Meech, H.B. Mayer — 25 King St., W., Toronto.

7. McMillan, Binch, Wilkinson, Stuart, Berry & Wright (14 lawyers): Gordon McMillan, Hamilton Stuart, Wilfred R. Binch, Nixon T Berry, Peter Wright, Ross Dunn, J.H. Corrigan, W.G.C. Howland, J.M. McPherson, F.O. Gerity, H.M. Lang, W.A. Macdonald, J.S. Farquharson, D.L. McCarthy — 50 King St., W., Toronto.

9. Fraser, Beatty, Tucker, McIntosh & Stewart (13 lawyers): W.G. Tucker, D.A. McIntosh, J.L. Stewart, C.F. Farwell, J.A. Mullin, Z.G.C. Lash, C.H. Stabler, S.E. Edwards, J.W. deC. O'Grady, A. Conway, C.J. Cannon, R.A. Davies, P.W. Beatty — 320 Bay St., Toronto.

10. Aikins, MacAulay, Thompson, Tritschler & Hinch (12 lawyers): G.H. Aikins, J.A. MacAulay, D.A. Thompson, G.E. Tritschler, T.W.B. Hinch, O.W. Struthers, R.G.B. Dickson, D.R. Jackson, H.M. Pickard, D.C. McGavin, R.K. Williams, J.F. Funnell — Somerset Building, Winnipeg.

10. Scott, Hugessen, Macklaier, Chisholm, Smith & Davis (12 lawyers): W.B. Scott, Hon Adrian K-Hugessen, W.F. Macklaier, J.F. Chisholm, H.L. Smith, H.W.Davis, J.P. Anglin, Peter M. Laing, R.D. Weldon, E. Jacques Courtois, Ross T. Clarkson, E. K-Hugessen — Alfred Building, Montreal.

1962

1. Blake, Cassels & Graydon (39 lawyers): Toronto.

2. Howard, Cate, Ogilvy, Bishop, Cope, Porteous & Hansard (35 lawyers): Montreal.

3. Osler, Hoskin & Harcourt (33 lawyers): Toronto.

4. McCarthy & McCarthy (31 lawyers): Toronto.

5. Chambers, Might, Saucier, Peacock, Jones, Black & Gain (24 lawyers): Calgary and Edmonton.

5. Fraser, Beatty, Tucker, McIntosh & Stewart (24 lawyers): Toronto.

5. Russell & DuMoulin (24 lawyers): Vancouver.

8. Borden, Elliot, Kelley & Palmer (22 lawyers): Toronto.

8. Bull, Houser, Tupper, Ray, Guy & Merritt (22 lawyers): Vancouver.

8. Davis, Hossie, Campbell, Brazier & McLorg (22 lawyers): Vancouver.

<u>1972</u>

1. Blake, Cassels & Graydon (67 lawyers): Toronto.

2. Ogilvy, Cope, Porteous, Hansard, Marler, Montgomery, Renault (61 lawyers): Montreal.

3. McCarthy & McCarthy (57 lawyers): Toronto.

4. Osler, Hoskin & Harcourt (54 lawyers): Toronto.

5. Fraser & Beatty (46 lawyers): Toronto.

6. Borden, Elliot, Kelley & Palmer (44 lawyers): Toronto.

6. Thomson, Rogers (44 lawyers): Toronto.

8. Gowling & Henderson (38 lawyers): Ottawa.

9. Davis & Company (37 lawyers): Vancouver.

10. Martineau, Walker, Allison, Beaulieu, Phelan & MacKell (36 lawyers): Montreal.

10. Russell & DuMoulin (36 lawyers): Vancouver.

10. Saucier, Jones, Black, Gain, Stratton & Laycraft (36 lawyers): Calgary and Edmonton.

<u>1982</u>

1. Blake, Cassels & Graydon (123 lawyers): Toronto.

2. McCarthy & McCarthy (112 lawyers): Toronto.

3. Osler, Hoskin & Harcourt (103 lawyers): Toronto.

4, Fraser & Beatty (95 lawyers): Toronto.

5. Ogilvy, Renault (93 lawyers): Montreal.

6. Martineau Walker (85 lawyers): Montreal.

7. Gowling & Henderson (80 lawyers): Ottawa and Toronto.

8. Borden & Elliot (77 lawyers): Toronto.

9. Bennett Jones (76 lawyers): Calgary.

10. Davis & Company (70 lawyers): Vancouver.

<u>1992</u>

1. McCarthy, Tétrault (489 lawyers): Toronto, Montreal, Calgary, Vancouver, Ottawa, London Ont., London Eng., Quebec City, Hong Kong.

2. Osler, Hoskin & Harcourt (285 lawyers): Toronto, Ottawa, London Eng., Paris, Hong Kong, New York.[2]

3. Blake, Cassels & Graydon (275 lawyers): Toronto, Richmond Hill, Ottawa, London Eng.

4. Fasken Campbell Godfrey (246 lawyers): Toronto, London Eng., Brussels.[3]

5. Stikeman, Elliott (233 lawyers): Toronto, Ottawa, Vancouver, Montreal, New York, London Eng., Hong Kong.

6. Fraser & Beatty (224 lawyers): Toronto, North York, Ottawa, Vancouver, Hong Kong.[4]

7. Lang, Michener, Lawrence & Shaw (192 lawyers): Toronto, Vancouver, Ottawa, Mississauga Ont.[5]

8. Borden & Elliot (189 lawyers): Toronto.[6]

9. Milner Fenerty (172 lawyers): Calgary, Edmonton.

10. Tory, Tory, DesLauriers & Binnington (165 lawyers): Toronto, London Eng., Taipei.[7]

APPENDIX III

OSLER FAMILY TREE*

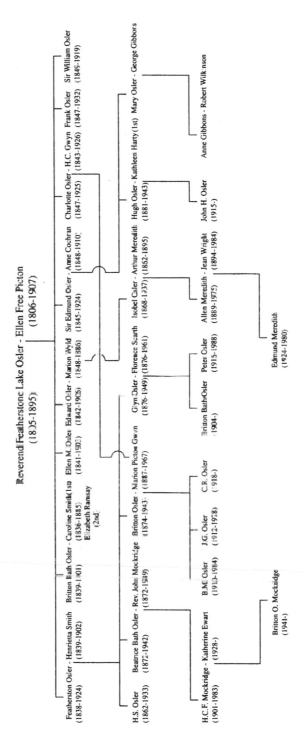

* Note: This is a partial family tree intended to outline the family relationships of individuals referred to in the text and notes.

FOREWORD

---

1. See Brian Bucknall, "My Dear Osler, My Dear Boland: Chronicles of an Early Real Estate Flip," *Law Society of Upper Canada Gazette* 24 (1990), 331.

PREFACE

---

1. *Essays in the History of Canadian Law*, 2 vols. (Toronto, 1981, 1983).
2. Brian Bucknall *et al.*, "Pedants, Practitioners and Prophets: Legal Education at Osgoode Hall to 1957," *Osgoode Hall Law Journal* 6 (1968), 137-229.
3. Curtis Cole, "'A Learned and Honorable Body': The Professionalization of the Ontario Bar, 1867-1929," Ph.D. thesis, University of Western Ontario, 1987.

PROLOGUE: A TRADITION OF "AFFECTION AND ESTEEM"

---

1. Although the lawyer is a common protagonist in popular entertainment, from Spencer Tracy's Clarence Darrow in the original motion picture *Inherit the Wind* to television's *L.A. Law* and *Street Legal*, these depictions often bear little relation to reality. For a series of catalogues of English language theatre and television films with legal themes, see Paul J. Mastrangelo, *Legal References Services Quarterly* III, 4 (1983); V, 4 (1986); VIII, 3,4 (1988).
2. The most recent Canadian law firm histories — all privately published by the firms — are: Gordon McMillan, *McMillan, Binch: A History, 1903-1976* (Toronto, 1976); Douglas H. Tees, *Chronicles of Ogilvy, Renault: 1879-1979* (Montreal, 1979); J.J. Saucier, *The Bennett Firm Revisited* (Calgary, 1982); Doug Mitchell and Judy Slinn, *The History of McMaster Meighen* (Montreal, 1989); Valerie Schatzker, *Borden & Elliot: The First Fifty Years, 1936-1986* (Toronto, 1986); and Stanley E. Edwards, *Fraser & Beatty: The First 150 Years* (Toronto, 1989). There are also a number of similar histories of American law firms, including Albert Boyden, *Ropes-Gray, 1865-1940* (Boston, 1942); William H. Clary, *History of the Law Firm of O'Melveny & Meyers, 1885-1965* (2 vols., Los Angeles, 1966); *Davis Polk Wardwell & Reed: Some of the Antecedents* (privately printed, New York, 1935); Walter K. Earle, *Mr. Shearman and Mr. Sterling and How They Grew* (New Haven, Conn., 1963); Frederick M. Eaton, *Shearman and Sterling, 1873-1973* (New York, 1973); Anne Hobson Freeman, *The Style of a Law Firm: Eight Gentlemen from Virginia* (Chapel Hill, N.C., 1989); Otto E. Keogel, *Walter S. Carter, Collector of Young Masters*; or, *The Progenitor of Many Law Firms* (New York, 1953); Timothy N. Pfeiffer and George W. Faques, *Millbank, Tweed, Hadley & McCloy: Law Practice in a Turbulent World* (New York,

1965); J. Tyson Stokes, *Morgan, Lewis and Bockius: Memoir of a Law Firm, One Hundred Years, 1873-1973* (privately printed, 1973); Robert T. Swaine, *The Cravath Firm and Its Predecessors, 1819-1947* (2 vols., New York, 1946, 1948); Henry W. Taft, *A Century and a Half at The New York Bar: Being The Annals of a Law Firm and Sketches of Its Members* (privately printed, New York, 1938).

3. Swaine, *The Cravath Firm.*

4. The best explanation of the internal and external approaches to legal history appears in Robert Gordon's article, "J. Willard Hurst and The Common Law Tradition in American Legal Historiography," *Law and Society Review* 10 (1975), 9-55. An excellent description of the potential of the latter approach in the Canadian context appears in David Flaherty, "Writing Canadian Legal History: An Introduction," Flaherty (ed.), *Essays in the History of Canadian Law*, Vol. I, (The Osgoode Society, Toronto, 1981), 3-42.

5. New York, 1964.

6. New York, 1988. See also Joseph C. Goulden, *The Superlawyers: The Small and Powerful World of the Great Washington Law Firms* (New York, 1971); Paul Hoffman, *Lions in the Street: An Inside History of the Great Wall Street Law Firms* (New York, 1973); Mark Stevens, *Power of Attorney: The Rise of the Giant Law Firms* (New York, 1987); and James B. Stewart, *The Partners: Inside America's Most Powerful Law Firms* (New York, 1983).

7. Osler, Hoskin & Harcourt and Sullivan & Cromwell have maintained a close relationship, substantially based on Inco, their mutual client, since the early twentieth century.

8. Constance Backhouse, " 'To Open the Way for Others of My Sex': Clara Brett Martin's Career as Canada's First Woman Lawyer," *Canadian Journal of Women and the Law* 1 (1985), 1; Backhouse, *Petticoats and Prejudice: Women and Law in Nineteenth Century Canada* (Toronto, 1991), 308.

CHAPTER ONE: BEGINNINGS: 1862-1882

1. Anne Wilkinson, *Lions in the Way: A Discursive History of the Oslers* (Toronto, 1956), 4-19.

2. This was the origin of what became a traditional given name among Osler men, including Ellen Osler's son Britton Osler, her grandson Featherston Britton Osler, her great-grandson Britton Michael Osler, and her great-great-grandson Britton Osler Mockridge.

3. Wilkinson, 21-28.

4. Wilkinson, 33.

5. Henry Morgan, *Canadian Men and Women of the Time* (Vol. II, Toronto, 1912), s.v. Osler, Featherston.

6. Wilkinson, 68, 80.

7. W. Stewart Wallace, ed., *The Macmillan Dictionary of Canadian Biography* (4th ed., Toronto, 1977), s.v. Osler, Edmund.

8. Wallace, 1977, s.v. Osler, William.

9. Wilkinson, 92.

10. Elmes Henderson, *Some Reminiscences of a Modern Do-the-Boys School* (n.d, n.p.), as quoted in Wilkinson, 91-92.

11. Although the move to Dundas was certainly a step up from Bond Head for Reverend Osler, the family's new home was not a major centre in Upper Canada. The population of Dundas in 1861 was only 2,852, compared to Hamilton's 19,096 and Toronto's 44,821. (*Census of the Canadas, 1860-61*, Vol. I, Personal Census (Quebec, 1863), 480, 500, 510.) For an interesting account of the life of clergymen like Featherstone Osler, see Curtis Fahey, *In His Name: The Anglican Experience in Upper Canada, 1791-1854* (Ottawa, 1990).

12. B.B. Osler to Featherston Osler, June 1857, as quoted in Wilkinson, 108.

13. Wilkinson, 112-13.

14. See Curtis Cole, "'A Learned And Honorable Body': The Professionalization of The Ontario Bar, 1867-1929," Ph.D., thesis, University of Western Ontario, 1987, c.4.

15. Wilkinson, 112-13.

16. Wilkinson, 112-13.

17. Osler, Hoskin & Harcourt, Firm Records, Articles of Clerkship: Britton Bath Osler to George M. Barton, 4 March 1859.

18. Wilkinson, 115.

19. Between 1841 and 1867, the colonial Province of Canada comprised much of what is now Ontario and Quebec. Its legislature consisted of a lower house, the Legislative Assembly, and an upper house, the Legislative Council. Notman, who was called to the bar in 1827, previously sat for Middlesex in the Assembly from 1848 to 1851, and for North Wentworth from 1857 until his death in 1865. (Henry J. Morgan, *The Canadian Parliamentary Companion* (Quebec, 1862) 35; *The Hamilton Times*, 9 June 1866.)

20. The failure rate of this entrance exam in the 1850s was almost fifty per cent. (G. Blaine Baker, "Legal Education in Upper Canada 1785-1889: The Law Society as Educator," in *Essays in the History of Canadian Law* Vol. II, David H. Flaherty, ed. (Toronto, 1983), 49-142 at 78.)

21. Baker, 98.

22. Osler may have decided to leave Notman & Barton because the partners were about to dissolve the firm. This took place in December of 1860. (*The True Banner and Wentworth Chronicle* (Dundas) 12 April 1861.) Although George Barton's name appears in subsequent law lists as practising on his own in Dundas until at least 1891, Notman apparently no longer practised law. He may have decided to retire for health reasons.

23. In later years he was a member of a firm known as Macdonald & Patton, in which his partner was Sir John A. Macdonald. Although the Legislative Council was originally an appointed house, it became an elected body in 1856. In that year, James Patton was elected to an eight-year term representing the district of Saugeen. In 1862 he accepted a post as solicitor-general in the Macdonald-Cartier administration. In those days, however, a member accepting a ministerial portfolio was required to resign his seat and run in a by-election as a member of the government. Patton lost the resulting by-election in 1862 and decided to retire from politics. (Morgan, 1862, 639-40; Wallace, 1977, s.v. Patton.)

24. Moss represented West Toronto from 1873 to 1875 when he was appointed to the Ontario Court of Appeal. He became chief justice of Ontario in 1878

but died at the age of forty-four in 1881. (W. Stewart Wallace, *The Macmillan Dictionary of Canadian Biography* (Toronto, 1963), s.v. Moss.)

25. William Notman to Britton Bath Osler, Osler family papers, Ontario Archives, MU 2303.

26. "Softening of the brain" was the polite term for syphilis.

27. *The Evening Times* (Hamilton), 20 September 1865; *The Spectator* (Hamilton), 21 September 1865.

28. On 24 September 1863 the *Dundas True Banner* published a small advertisement in its professional cards column which read:

    B.B. OSLER, LL.B.

    Barrister & Attorney-at-Law,
    Solicitor, &c.

    Office: Moore's Buildings, Main St., Dundas.

29. Wilkinson, 119.

30. *Waterous* v. *Bishop, Upper Canada Common Pleas Reports* 20 (1869), 29-41.

31. *Consolidated Statutes of Upper Canada* (1859), c.64, s.79(8).

32. *In Re Hutchison And The Board of School Trustees of St. Catharines, Upper Canada Queen's Bench Reports* 31 (1870-71), 214-79, at 276.

33. *In Re Hutchison*, 278-79.

34. *In Re Hutchison*, 279.

35. For an explanation of the reasons for the "fused" legal profession in Ontario, see J.D. Arnup, "Fusion of the Profession," in *Law Society of Upper Canada Gazette* 5 (1971), 71. The lone exception in Canada is, understandably, the civil law jurisdiction of Quebec, where the legal profession is divided between *avocats* and *notaires*, although not along the lines dividing English barristers and solicitors. In Quebec, *avocats* practise as both barristers and solicitors. *Notaires* have a restricted practice. (E.C. Common, "The Role of the Notary in the Province of Quebec," in *Canadian Bar Review* 36 (1938), 33.)

36. On the history of the English legal profession, see generally Brian Abel-Smith and Robert Stevens, *Lawyers and the Courts: A Sociological Study of The English Legal System, 1750 1965* (London, 1967), as well as Raymond Cocks, *Foundations of the Modern Bar* (London, 1983), and David Podmore, *Solicitors and the Wider Community* (London, 1980). The word "attorney," still the more formal term used for a lawyer in the United States, is not generally used in Canada. Prior to the late nineteenth-century fusion of the common law and equity in Britain and Canada, the lower branch of the legal profession consisted of solicitors, who practised in Chancery, and attorneys, who practised in the courts of common law. The term solicitor was not required in Upper Canada until the establishment of the Court of Chancery in the province in 1837. Between then and 1881, when the Judicature Act fused the Court of Chancery and the two common law courts, the Queen's Bench and Common Pleas, into a single Supreme Court of Ontario, the terms solicitor and attorney were used interchangeably, because admission to practice in one court automatically included admission to the other two courts. Since 1881 the term solicitor has been used exclusively. For an outline of the history of the Ontario court structure and an explanation of the Judicature Act, see Margaret A. Banks, "The Evolution of the Ontario Courts, 1788-

1981," in David H. Flaherty, ed., *Essays in the History of Canadian Law*, Vol. II (Toronto, 1983), 492-572.

37.   An act for the better regulating the practice of the law, 37 Geo. III (1797), c.13 (U.C.); An act to repeal part of and amend an act passed in the thirty-seventh year of his late Majesty's reign, entitled "An act for the better regulating the practice of the law," and to extend the provisions of the same, 2 Geo. IV (1822), c.5 (U.C.).

38.   An Act To Amend The Law For The Admission of Attorneys, 20 Vict. (1857), c.63 (United Province of Canada).

39.   See Cole, "'A Learned and Honorable Body,'", c. 3.

40.   B.B. Osler received both his admission to practice as a solicitor and his call to the bar in September, 1862. Featherston passed the solicitor's exam in November 1859 and the barrister's exam in February 1860. (*The Ontario Law List* (Toronto, 1876), 180.)

41.   *The Ontario Law List* (Toronto, 1876), 164.

42.   Wilkinson, 128.

43.   The level of competition in any legal services market is, of course, affected by many more factors than simply the ratio of population to lawyers. Beyond the fact that the courts sat in Hamilton, the larger centre was much more industrialized and offered a thriving mercantile community. It would, therefore, offer much more litigation and more commercial transactions requiring legal assistance. For an interesting discussion of this question see Peter Pashigian, "The Market for Lawyers: The Determinants of the Demand for and Supply of Lawyers," in *Journal of Law and Economics*, 20 (1977), 53-85.

44.   The biography, written by Sir Edmund Osler's granddaughter Anne Wilkinson, was very controversial among the family members. They questioned the accuracy of some of the uncomplimentary commentary about her relatives, including Edward. (Wilkinson, 154.)

45.   Wilkinson, 202.

46.   Alan Stacey, "History Along the Trail: #5: Kionontio (Osler Castle) Blue Mountains 1," *Bruce Trail News* (Spring/Summer 1982), 16-21, at 18.

47.   Herbert Gwyn and Charlotte Osler were married July 3, 1872. One of their children was Marion Picton Gwyn, who married her first cousin, Britton Osler, who was Featherston Osler's second son. This Britton Osler was the senior partner in the firm during the 1920s and 1930s. See Chapter Four.

48.   According to the family biographer, "money did not grow for Charlie. There is an occasional glimpse of him in Ellen's [Osler's mother] letters to her daughter. One ends 'love to Charlie and the *other* children.'" (Wilkinson, 154.)

49.   Morgan, 1912, s.v. Gwyn.

50.   Ontario Archives, MU 2305.

51.   Stacey, 19, from a story in the Dundas *True Banner*, 19 February 1874.

52.   Stacey, 19; Morgan, 1898, s.v. Osler.

53.   Stacey, 19; Morgan, 1898, s.v. Osler.

54.   Stacey, 19.

55.   Like Theophilus Begue before him, there is no evidence to indicate why Alexander Wink left the firm. The *Law Lists* indicate that he practised in Hamilton for a time, but left for Port Arthur some time before 1891.

56. John Honsberger, "The County of York Law Association, 1885-1895: B.B. Osler, Q.C. The First President," *The Law Society of Upper Canada Gazette* 19 (1985), 146-56, at 148.

57. Morgan, 1912, s.v. Teetzel.

58. B.B. Osler diaries, 1882, Ontario Archives, MU 2301.

59. Osler diaries.

60. For an explanation of the Canadian Pacific scandal see, in addition to the first half of Pierre Berton's two-volume work, *The National Dream: The Great Railway, 1871-81* (Toronto, 1970) and the second volume of Donald Creighton's biography of Macdonald, *John A. Macdonald: The Old Chieftain* (Toronto, 1955). For good overviews of Canadian politics during this period, see P.B. Waite, *Canada, 1874-1896: Arduous Destiny* (Toronto, 1971), Joseph Schull's two-volume biography, *Edward Blake: The Man of the Other Way* (Toronto, 1975) and *Edward Blake: Leader in Exile* (Toronto, 1976) and Dale Thompson's *Alexander Mackenzie: Clear Grit* (Toronto, 1960).

61. M.C. Urquhart and K.A.H. Buckley, eds., *Historical Statistics of Canada* (Toronto, 1965), 620.

62. Henry J. Morgan, ed., *The Dominion Annual Register and Review, 1882* (Toronto, 1883), 411.

CHAPTER TWO: THE COMPACT: 1882-1902

1. J. Rordans, *The Upper Canada Law Directory for 1858* (Toronto, 1858), 82.

2. Only one other lawyer appeared in as many; James Bethune of the Toronto firm Bethune, Moss, Falconbridge & Hoyles also appeared in twelve. Bethune's partner, Charles Moss, who later served as chief justice of Ontario, and Christopher Robinson, who edited the *Ontario Reports*, each appeared in ten. No other lawyer appeared in more than five.

3. In 1884, Macdonald offered McCarthy the post of Minister of Justice, but primarily for financial reasons McCarthy declined. (J.R. Miller, *Equal Rights: The Jesuits Estates Act Controversy* (Montreal, 1979), 58.)

4. An Act to restore to Roman Catholics in Upper Canada certain rights in respect to Separate Schools, 26 Vict. (1863), c.5 (Province of Canada); The British North America Act, 1867, 30-31 Vict. (1867) c.3, (U.K.).

5. G.M. Rose, ed., *A Cyclopaedia of Canadian Biography* (Toronto, 1888), 624.

6. Rose, 624.

7. Rose, 624.

8. The contract, signed between the C.P.R. and John A. Macdonald's government in October, 1880, called for a cash payment to the railway of $25 million and a grant of 25 million acres of federal land between Winnipeg and the British Columbia boundary. (Peter B. Waite, *Canada, 1874-1896: Arduous Destiny* (Toronto, 1971), 108; Donald Creighton, *John A. Macdonald: The Old Chieftain* (Toronto, 1955), 303-04.)

9. Canada North-West Land Company Annual Report, 1883, Osler, Hoskin & Harcourt firm records (hereafter OHH).

10. B.B. Osler diaries, Ontario Archives, MU 2301, 23 August 1882 (hereafter BBO); OHH, Articles of Partnership, 1 September 1882.

11. Under the terms of the retainer, McCarthy, Osler, Hoskin & Creelman were to act as Canadian solicitors to the company except in the province of Manitoba, where the Winnipeg firm of Macdonald & Tupper would look after the company's local interests. The political connection here was obvious. The senior partners of this firm were Hugh John Macdonald, the son of the prime minister, and James Stewart Tupper, the eldest son of Sir Charles Tupper, who was briefly prime minister in 1896. (OHH, Retainer Book.)

12. Osler's decision was a wise one; a few weeks later Tupper's Conservatives lost the election to Wilfrid Laurier, who remained as prime minister for fifteen years. (BBO, 23 August 1882; O.D. Skelton, *Life and Letters of Sir Wilfrid Laurier*, Vol. 1 (New York, 1922), 481.)

13. This arrangement lasted until the firm amended its Articles of Partnership after Britton Bath Osler's death in 1901. Until that point, Hoskin's share of the profits was intended to roughly match his earnings from the Official Guardian's office. Under the terms of the new agreement, however, Hoskin became entitled to a share of the firm's profits in addition to his earnings from the Official Guardian's office, which he was not required to pool with the general firm earnings. (OHH, Partnership Agreements, 1882-1901.)

14. John Ross Matheson, "Office of the Official Guardian, 1881-1947," LL.B. thesis, University of Western Ontario, 1949, 55-56.

15. Harcourt's earnings from the Official Guardian's office were treated in the same way which Hoskin's were. His official salary was paid directly to the firm, and he received an equivalent salary from the firm. When Harcourt became a partner in 1901, however, the new partnership agreement permitted him to keep his Official Guardian's office salary as well as his share in the profits of the firm. (OHH, Partnership Agreements, 1882-1901.)

16. The financial information related to the firm as well as its articles of partnership were found in a very large leatherbound ledger book equipped with a brass lock. This volume had apparently been in the firm's dead storage since the turn of the century.

17. M.C. Urquhart, K.A.H. Buckley, eds., *Historical Statistics of Canada* (Toronto, 1965), 93.

18. *The Canadian Law List* (Toronto, 1882, 1892, 1902).

19. *The Canadian Law List*. See also Appendix II.

20. *Goad's 1884 Atlas of Toronto*, reprinted in Lucy Booth Martyn, *The Face of Early Toronto: An Archival Record, 1797-1936* (Sutton West, Ontario, 1982).

21. The 1883 *Ontario, Manitoba and North-West Legal Directory* lists 23 lawyers practising in the North-West Territories, including 12 in Regina, but Hoskin's name is not among them. The firm's name was also not included in the Regina lists.

22. Richard Hoskin to John Hoskin, 7 May 1883, OHH; Draft agreement, Canada North-West Land Company and McCarthy, Osler, Hoskin & Creelman, 1882, OHH.

23. OHH, Articles of Partnership, 1 September 1882.

24. OHH, Articles of Partnership, 1 May 1886.

25. The other partners decided not to enforce McCarthy's payback clause during the 1887-88 and 1888-89 fiscal years, and the new partnership agreement signed 1 June 1889 included a sliding limitation on the payback based on the

other partners' independent incomes. (OHH, Partnership Agreement, 10 June 1889.)

26. See *St. Catharines Milling and Lumber Company* v. *R.*, 10 *Ontario Reports* (1885), 196; 13 *Ontario Appeal Reports* (1886), 148; 13 *Supreme Court Reports* (1886); 14 *Appeal Cases* (1888), 46.

27. This phenomenon provides an interesting contrast to the major firms a century later. During the 1980s, none of the large firms, including Osler, Hoskin & Harcourt, carried on a criminal practice. See Chapter Eight.

28. To a modern observer, the fact that McCarthy would appear before his partner's brother would seem a rather startling conflict of interest. For some discussion of this issue see Chapter Three. (Henry J. Morgan, *The Dominion Annual Register and Review, 1882* (Toronto, 1883), 173-74.) Hereafter *DAR, 18—*.

29. *DAR, 1883*, 202-03.

30. *The Canadian Law Times*, March 1884, 132; *DAR, 1883*, 164.

31. *DAR, 1884*, 334.

32. The names of the accused in these trials do not appear in the firm's account books. Because the trials took place outside of Toronto, it is most likely that McCarthy and Osler were retained by local solicitors to take the cases on. The names of the solicitors would, therefore, appear in the ledgers, but those of the accused would not.

33. There are a great many publications on Louis Riel and the two rebellions he led. Every general survey of Canadian history makes some reference to the events of 1870 and 1885, but the best explanations are still those of W.L. Morton in his introduction to Alexander Begg's *Red River Journal* (Toronto, 1956); *Manitoba: A History* (Toronto, 1957); and G.F.G. Stanley's *The Birth of Western Canada* (Toronto, 1936, 1960) and his biography *Louis Riel* (Toronto, 1963). Thomas Flanagan provides a more recent, although much more inflammatory, analysis in his *Louis "David" Riel: Prophet of the New World* (Toronto, 1979) and *Rebellion in the Northwest: Louis Riel and the Métis People* (Toronto, 1984). Desmond Morton has also written a popular illustrated history of the 1885 rebellion, *The Last War Drum* (Toronto, 1972); he also co-edited with R.H. Roy *Telegrams of the North-West Campaign 1885* (Toronto, 1972) and a transcript of the trial entitled *The Queen* v. *Louis Riel* (Toronto, 1974). The most recent treatment is Maggie Siggins' *Riel: A Life of Revolution* (Toronto, 1994).

34. The Canadian Pacific Railway was completed as far as Calgary by 1883, and the last spike was driven to complete the line in November, 1885. Indeed, it was the rapid pace of settlement which the railway brought to the prairies which was a major complaint of the Métis.

35. See Patrick Brode, *Sir John Beverley Robinson: Bone and Sinew of the Compact* (Toronto, 1984).

36. Because the population of frontier settlements was often very small, North-West law called for criminal juries of only six members rather than the traditional twelve.

37. *Queen* v. *School*, 26 *Upper Canada Queen's Bench Reports*, 212.

38. Whenever Osler or any of the other counsel spoke to the bench, they used the term "Your Honors" to include Richardson and the justice of the peace. It was Richardson, however, who presided over the trial.

39. T.J.W. Burgess, "A Historical Sketch of Our Canadian Institutions for the

Insane,'' in *Transactions of the Royal Society of Canada 1898*, Section IV, 55-57, as cited by Desmond Morton, *The Queen* v. *Louis Riel* (Toronto, 1974), xvii.

40. John Honsberger, ''B.B. Osler, Q.C.: The First President,'' *Law Society of Upper Canada Gazette* 19 (1985), 151-52.

41. *The Queen* v. *Louis Riel*, XI *Manitoba Law Reports* (1885), 329.

42. McCarthy was, of course, a very complex figure; to portray him only as a rabid anti-Catholic and Francophobe would be misleading. He was, until the Jesuits Estates controversy and the Manitoba Schools dispute which followed, a highly respected member of the Conservative Party. For a thorough exploration of the depth of his political thinking see, J.R. Miller, '''As a Politician He Is an Enigma': The Social and Political Ideas of D'Alton McCarthy,'' *Canadian Historical Review* 58 (1977), 399-422.

43. 51 Vict. (1888) c.13, (P.Q.).

44. *Toronto Star*, 2 April 1988.

45. As the table below indicates, between 1884 (the earliest year for which such figures were available) and 1898 (the year of D'Alton McCarthy's death) the firm's income was consistently divided almost equally between litigation and general accounts. (OHH, Ledger Books, 1884-98.)

Year	Litigation	General	Total
1883-84	$42,015.31 (53.5%)	$36,570.23 (46.5%)	$78,585.54
1884-85	$43,245.16 (49.3%)	$44,550.98 (50.7%)	$87,796.14
1885-86	$42,202.68 (48.4%)	$45,039.04 (51.6%)	$87,241.72
1886-87	$36,839.45 (44.7%)	$45,590.22 (55.3%)	$82,429.67
1887-88	$42,482.50 (50.7%)	$41,287.80 (49.3%)	$83,770.30
1888-89	$54,140.51 (53.0%)	$47,939.38 (47.0%)	$102,079.89
1889-90	$46,308.63 (47.0%)	$52,163.82 (53.0%)	$98,472.45
1890-91	$50,831.10 (52.0%)	$46,927.06 (48.0%)	$97,758.16
1891-92	$57,237.84 (48.9%)	$59,764.42 (51.1%)	$117,002.26
1892-93	$52,950.29 (50.2%)	$52,613.35 (49.8%)	$105,536.64
1893-94	$55,421.56 (57.7%)	$40,631.36 (42.3%)	$96,052.92
1894-95	$48,440.00 (51.6%)	$45,420.75 (48.4%)	$93,860.75
1895-96	$39,350.00 (51.8%)	$36,665.02 (48.2%)	$76,015.02
1896-97	$42,905,00 (47.0%)	$48,321.91 (53.0%)	$91,226.91
1897-98	$41,690.00 (51.0%)	$39,362.80 (49.0%)	$81,052.80

46. This firm, which, within a decade was the largest law firm in Canada, was the predecessor of the firm later known as Fasken Campbell Godfrey.

47. James G. Snell and Frederick Vaughan, *The Supreme Court of Canada: History of the Institution* (Toronto, 1985), 89-90.

48. Nesbitt's attitude towards the Supreme Court was not uncommon. As James G. Snell and Frederick Vaughan point out in their book *Supreme Court of Canada: History of the Institution*, the government had considerable difficulty in finding qualified judges to sit on the Supreme Court during the late nineteenth and early twentieth centuries. The salary was very low, and because it was not the ultimate court of appeal for the country — in fact, many appeals went directly from the provincial courts of appeal to the Privy Council — it offered relatively little prestige.

49. The firm changed its name after Adam Creelman left to become in-house counsel for the Canadian Pacific Railway. It was known by this name from 1902 until 1916 when the partners split to form Osler, Hoskin & Harcourt and McCarthy & McCarthy. See Chapter Three.

50. *The Globe* (Toronto) 8 April 1930; *Canadian Bar Review* April 1930; *The Mail & Empire*, 9 April 1930.

51. B.B. Osler had no children of his own. Britton was christened Featherstone Britton Osler, after his grandfather and uncle, but went by the name Britton all of his life.

52. Another McCarthy of this generation, Leighton's younger brother Frank, joined the firm in 1906.

53. *McCarthy & McCarthy: A History* (privately published, Toronto, 1978), 10.

54. BBO, 19 April 1900.

55. BBO, 23-26 April 1900.

56. BBO, 7 September 1900.

57. BBO, 13 December 1900.

58. BBO, 1 January 1901.

CHAPTER THREE: CRISIS, STABILITY AND DIVISION: 1902-1916

1. *The Toronto Daily Star*, 5 February 1901, 9.

2. See the Prologue.

3. *The Globe*, 7 February 1901, 10; *The Toronto Daily Star*, 6 February 1901, 6, 9. A very heavy workload is certainly one of the acknowledged features of modern legal practice, particularly in the largest firms. Fifty- to 60-hour workweeks are not uncommon, but it appears that this is not a new phenomenon. Although some are beginning to question the lifestyle and professional value of this tradition, the pressures of competition make it very difficult to change. This competition is among firms for increasingly demanding clients, but more importantly in this context, it is among young lawyers hoping to advance to partnership level and junior partners hoping to rise within the partnership.

4. B.B. Osler diaries, Ontario Archives, MU 2301, 1-3 January 1899. Unfortunately, these diaries are actually pocket appointment calendars. In them Osler recorded little more than his travel destinations. Unless otherwise indicated, all subsequent information regarding Osler's day-to-day activities is taken from his diaries.

5. In addition to those in Hamilton in January, during 1899 Osler attended assizes in St. Catharines and Cobourg in March, Picton and Ottawa in April, Guelph in May, Cobourg and Picton again in September, Barrie, Guelph and Peterborough in October, Ottawa, London and Chatham in November, and St. Catharines again in December.

6. Nevertheless, he apparently travelled in style. His appointment diaries include numerous notations next to travel destinations which say simply "by private car." If this was a personal railway car he did not own it when he died; it is not included in will or estate inventory. It is possible that he often booked a private car from the railway when he travelled.

7. 6 *Exchequer Court Reports* (1896-1900), 223-35.

8. The others were Chief Justice Sir George William Burton, James MacLennan, James Frederick Lister and Featherston Osler's former law partner, Charles Moss.

9. There is no such thing as a code of judicial conduct for superior court judges in Canada, nor does the Canadian Bar Association's *Code of Professional Conduct*, which applies to lawyers, deal with such a situation. Canon 3C.(1)(d)(ii) of the American Bar Association's *Code of Judicial Conduct* reads: "A judge should disqualify himself in a proceeding in which his impartiality might reasonably be questioned, including but not limited to instances where: . . . he . . . or a person within the third degree of relationship [to him] . . . is acting as a lawyer in the proceeding." A brother is in the second degree of kindred. See *Black's Law Dictionary,* 4th ed. (St. Paul, Minn., 1968), LXXIII, 512.

10. *Dueber Watch Case Manufacturing Company* v. *Taggart,* 26 *Ontario Appeal Reports* (1900), 295-313; *Bicknell* v. *Grand Trunk Railway Company,* 26 *Ontario Appeal Reports* (1900), 431-58.

11. On March 10, 1899 he appeared before the Common Pleas Division of the Ontario High Court to argue *The Bank of Hamilton* v. *The Imperial Bank,* 31 *Ontario Reports,* 100. The Bank of Hamilton was a long-time client of the firm and was identified in the partnership agreements as the firm's bank. In early April he appeared before the weekly sitting of the Ontario High Court in Ottawa and obtained an injunction preventing a railway from expropriating a section of farmland. (*Stewart* v. *Ottawa and New York R.W. Co.,* 30 *Ontario Reports,* 599.)

12. *Stewart* v. *The King,* 7 *Exchequer Court Reports,* 55-93.

13. He left the *Stewart* case in the hands of his nephew Glyn Osler, Featherston's youngest son. Glyn Osler, then only twenty-three years old, was practising in Ottawa with a firm known as O'Gara, Wyld & Osler. The young Osler won the case, but when the government appealed to the Supreme Court he brought in Christopher Robinson, Q.C., to present the case. The appellants were again represented by Samuel Blake, and Stewart won the appeal. (32 *Supreme Court Reports,* 483-505.) Ironically, a few years later Glyn Osler moved to Toronto and joined the Blake firm. Two of Glyn Osler's sons, Britton Bath Osler (named for his great uncle) and Peter Scarth Osler, also practised with the Blake firm.

14. Later in the summer, his partner Adam Creelman wrote to Osler's brother Edmund regarding some stock transfers. "Owing to Mr. B.B. Osler being unable to sign any papers at present, I've been obliged to abandon the plan which I had formed of having the discharge of mortgage and transfers of bank stock executed by the old trustees." (Osler, Harcourt & Hoskin firm records (hereafter OHH), E.B. Osler file.)

15. *The Globe,* 7 February 1901, 10; 8 February 1901, 6.

16. See Appendix II.

17. See Chapter Two.

18. OHH, Ledger Balances, 1897-1902.

19. This firm later became Raymond & Honsberger and still existed under that name in 1994. See John Honsberger, "E.E.A. DuVernet, K.C.: Lawyer, Capitalist," in Carol Wilton, ed., *Beyond the Law: Lawyers and Business in Canada, 1830-1930* (Toronto, 1990), 167-200, for a fascinating account of the early years of that firm.

20. See Chapter Two.

21. See James G. Snell and Frederick Vaughan, *The Supreme Court of Canada: History of the Institution* (Toronto, 1985), 86-89.

22. See, for instance, *Rossiter* v. *Toronto Street Railway*, 15 *Ontario Law Reports* (1908), 297-99.

23. In addition to the CPR, the firm's transportation sector clients included The Toronto Ferry Company, the Toronto BeltLine Railway and The Winnipeg Western Railway. The banks included The Bank of Hamilton and E.B. Osler's Dominion Bank. In manufacturing the firm acted for The Phoenix Appliance Company, John Inglis and Son, and The Collingwood Ship Building Company; in resources, its clients included The Georgian Bay Consolidated Lumber Company, The Caribou Hydraulic Mining Company, The Shepard & Morse Lumber Company and The Spanish River Pulp & Paper Company.

24. The bulk of Harcourt's income came, of course, from his work as Official Guardian, which he did not share with his partners. Hoskin was retired and no longer a partner; he was, however, paid a retainer of $500 for allowing his name to remain on the letterhead. Wallace Nesbitt was still counsel to the firm.

25. See Paul Stevens, *The 1911 General Election: A Study in Canadian Politics* (Toronto, 1970), and R. Craig Brown, *Robert Laird Borden: A Biography*, 2 vols. (Toronto, 1975, 1980).

26. *McCarthy & McCarthy: A History* (privately published, Toronto, 1978), 15.

27. Michael Bliss, *Northern Enterprise: Five Centuries of Canadian Business* (Toronto, 1987), 280.

28. Henry Morgan, *Canadian Men and Women of the Time* (Toronto, 1898), s.v. Osler, Britton Bath.

29. OHH, Ledger Balances, 30 June 1902.

30. OHH, Ledger Balances, 30 June 1903; 30 June 1904; 30 June 1905.

31. OHH, Ledger Balances, 29 June 1906; 29 June 1907; 30 May 1908; 31 May 1909; 31 May 1910.

32. OHH, Ledger Balances, 31 May 1911; 31 May 1912; 31 May 1913; 30 May 1914.

33. OHH, Ledger Balances, 30 May 1915.

34. OHH, Articles of Partnership, 26 May 1913. This paragraph first appeared in the partnership agreement in the version of 1 February 1904.

35. OHH, Articles of Partnership, 1 August 1917 (emphasis added). Interestingly, the 1917 partnership agreement was also the first one to be typewritten.

36. Part of them, it seems, he was putting back into Canada Life. By 1928 he was the largest single shareholder in the company. (*McCarthy & McCarthy: A History* (privately published, Toronto, 1978), 15.)

37. OHH, Articles of Partnership, 26 May 1913.

CHAPTER FOUR: THE CLAN: 1916-1943

1. The partnership agreement, which defined John Hoskin as "a former member of the firm," indicated that he would "be paid the fixed sum or retainer of Five hundred dollars annually but he shall have no interest in the profits of the firm and . . . shall not be liable nor responsible for the acts and liabilities of the firm or any member thereof." (Osler, Hoskin & Harcourt firm records, (hereafter OHH) Articles of Partnership, 26 May 1913; 1 August 1917.)

2. H.S. Osler's share increased from $9,165.00 for the 1 June – 30 November 1915 period to $12,203.40 for the 1 June – 30 November 1916 period. His brother, Britton Osler, saw his share increase from $5,499.00 to $10,169.50, and Frederick Harcourt's went up from $1,222.00 to $1,627.10. (OHH, Ledger Business Statement, 30 November 1916.)

3. OHH, Ledger Balances, 30 November 1915; 30 November 1916.

4. Henry Cartwright, ed., *The Canadian Law List (Hardy's), 1920* (Toronto, 1920), 159; OHH, Ledger Balances, 30 November 1915.

5. OHH, Ledger Balances, 30 November 1916.

6. OHH, Ledger Balances, 30 November 1915; 30 November 1916.

7. OHH, Ledger Balances, 30 November 1915; 30 November 1916; Henry J. Morgan, ed., *The Canadian Men and Women of the Time* (2nd ed., Toronto, 1912), s.v. Cox; W. Stewart Wallace, *The Macmillan Dictionary of Canadian Biography* (4th ed., Toronto, 1978), s.v. Cox.

8. The following table shows the top twelve clients during the 30 June – 30 November 1915 period and the amount they were billed during the same period in 1916. The Canada Life Assurance Company was not among them. In fact, although it was billed $1,000 in the first half of 1915, it does not appear in the ledger for the 30 June – 30 November 1915 period.

	Client	1915	1916
1.	Toronto Railway Co.	$5,129.85	$2,325.00
2.	Canadian Stewart Co.	$2,396.50	$2,500.00
3.	Borden Company Ltd.	$2,045.00	$900.00
4.	Hanna, Hon. W.J.	$2,000.00	$30.00
5.	Dominion Mines & Quarries	$1,687.65	—
6.	Estate of Sen. G.A. Cox	$1,597.00	—
7.	United Cigar Stores	$1,500.00	$459.00
8.	Union Carbide Co.	$1,500.00	—
9.	Wm. H. Biggar	$1,315.40	
10.	Bank of Hamilton	$1,188.00	$1,016.00
11.	Dominion Bank	$1,107.00	$775.00
12.	Cravath & Henderson	$970.00	$4,248.50

(OHH, Ledger Balances, 30 November 1915; 30 November 1916.)

9. OHH, Ledger Balances, 29 June 1906; 31 May, 30 November 1920.

10. OHH, Articles of Partnership, 1 August 1917. There is no document to indicate that the remaining partners drew up a new agreement after the McCarthys left at the end of May 1916. Presumably they simply operated under the terms of the old one until the 1917 agreement came into effect. Although it was signed on August 1 — the day Harold Shapley joined the firm — it was in effect as of 1 June 1917.

11. In 1938, he represented Coca-Cola in a suit with Pepsi-Cola over the use of the word "Cola" as a trade mark. Langmuir won the case at trial in the Exchequer Court of Canada, but this judgement was overturned by the Supreme Court of Canada. Coca-Cola appealed this decision to the Privy Council in London, but lost there as well. See also the discussion of the history of Herridge, Tolmie in Chapter Eight. See *Pepsi-Cola Co. of Canada Ltd.* v. *Coca-Coca Co. of Canada Ltd.* [1938] 4 *Dominion Law Reports*, 145 (Exchequer Court of Canada); [1940] 1 *Dominion Law Reports*, 161 (Supreme Court of Canada); [1942] 2 *Dominion Law Reports*, 657 (Judicial Committee of the Privy Council).

12. OHH, Articles of Partnership, 1 August 1917. Mulock, Milliken, like Oslers,

was a tenant in the Dominion Bank Building. The old McCarthy, Osler firm had moved there in 1913, and Osler, Hoskin & Harcourt remained there when the McCarthys left in 1916.

13. *The Bayer Company Limited* v. *The American Druggists' Syndicate Limited* [1924] *Supreme Court of Canada Reports*, 558-600, at 566.

14. *The American Druggists' Syndicate* v. *The Bayer Company, Limited* [1923] *Exchequer Court Reports*, 65.

15. During 1918 the firm's gross income was $112,787.91. After expenses of $38,002.89, which included salaries for staff and students of $25,928.28, rent of the firm's offices in the Dominion Bank Building of $5,850.00, $1,111.73 for local business taxes, $1,852.25 for stationery, $405.75 for postage, $386.37 for telephone and telegrams, and various other expenses, and after deductions of $889.57 for depreciation of office equipment and $8,896.07 in bad debts charged off, the firm's net earnings were $64,999.38. John Hoskin was paid a retainer of $500 for the continued use of his name, and Wellington A. Cameron was paid a fixed salary of $3,000. As counsel to the firm, Wallace Nesbitt received neither a salary nor a share of the profits. The remaining $61,499.38 were divided into 300 shares and distributed among the five participating partners as follows:

H.S. Osler	130 shares,	$26,649.66
Britton Osler	113 shares,	$23,164.72
Frederick Harcourt	20 shares,	$4,100.00
Harold Shapley.	21 shares,	$4,300.00
Archibald Langmuir	16 shares,	$3,950.00.

(OHH, Ledgers, Partnership Agreement, 1 June 1917.)

16. During 1928 the firm's gross income was $250,200.33. After expenses of $78,977.05, which included salaries for staff and students of $62,963, rent of the firm's offices in the Dominion Bank Building of $9,264.25, $1,211.72 for local business taxes, $2,582.97 for stationery, $715.73 for postage, $842.25 for telephone and telegrams, and various other expenses, and after deductions of $969.25 for depreciation of office equipment and $7,754.94 in bad debts charged off, and an addition of $137.60 in bad debts recovered, the firm's net earnings amounted to $162,636.69. Wellington A. Cameron was paid a fixed salary of $4,333, and as counsel to the firm, Wallace Nesbitt, Arthur Meighen and Munro Grier received neither a salary nor a share of the profits. The remaining $158,303.69 was divided into 310 shares and distributed among seven participating partners as follows:

H.S. Osler	20 shares,	$10,342.00
Britton Osler	154 shares,	$77,635.76
Frederick Harcourt	20 shares,	$10,342.00
Harold Shapley	42 shares,	$21,718.20
Archibald Langmuir	38 shares,	$19,649.80
G.M. Huycke	20 shares,	$10,342.00
N.E. Strickland	16 shares,	$8,273.60

(OHH, Ledgers, Partnership Agreement, 1 June 1928.)

By comparison, an electrician in Toronto could expect to earn about $1.00 per hour, or $2,000 per year in 1928. (M.C. Urquhart and K.A.H. Buckley, eds., *Historical Statistics of Canada* (Toronto, 1965), 86.)

17. *Historical Statistics of Canada*, 304.

18. In fact, the golf clubs they used belonged to Britton Osler. The clubs were a gift from International Nickel; they were made of a material called Monel

Metal, a new alloy which the company began marketing in the 1920s. (Interview by the author with C.R. Osler, 15 November 1988.)

19. Interview by the author with C.R. Osler, 15 November 1988.

20. M.R. Werner and John Starr, *Teapot Dome* (New York, 1959), 175.

21. Quoted by Werner and Starr, 175.

22. Under the new partnership agreement signed in 1920, H.S. Osler's portion dropped from 130 shares to 85. Britton Osler's increased from 113 to 140, Frederick Harcourt's remained at 20, Harold Shapley's increased from 21 to 32, and A.W. Langmuir's increased from 16 to 23. (OHH, Partnership Agreement, 1 June 1920.)

23. Britton Osler's son, C.R., remembered very little about his uncle other than an enormous snake hide trophy which was mounted on the attic ceiling in his Rosedale Road home. The attic was a play room for C.R.'s cousin Philip. H.S. Osler brought back a number of trophy specimens for the Royal Ontario Museum, including a rare, white rhinoceros. After his death the bulk of his trophy collection was apparently donated to the Museum. (Interview by the author with C.R. Osler, 15 November 1988.) At his death in December, 1932, the Toronto *Mail* described him as "Canada's foremost big-game hunter, making numerous trips to Africa where he headed his own safari into the jungles. . . . His home at 1 Rosedale Road Toronto is testimony to his success as a hunter, containing rare heads and skins of lions, tigers, water buffalo and other African game." (The Toronto *Mail*, 9 December 1932.)

24. Werner and Starr, 175-76.

25. Daniel Yergin, *The Prize: The Epic Quest for Oil, Money, and Power* (New York, 1991), 212.

26. Burl Noggle, *Teapot Dome: Oil and Politics in the 1920's* (Baton Rouge, La., 1962), 16-18.

27. Noggle, 38.

28. *The New York Times*, 1 March 1922, 4.

29. Werner and Starr, 29.

30. On Harding's presidency, see Francis Russell *The Shadow of Blooming Grove: Warren G. Harding in His Times* (New York, 1968); Robert K. Murray, *The Harding Era: Warren G. Harding And His Administration* (Minneapolis, 1969); Eugene P. Trani, *The Presidency of Warren G. Harding* (Lawrence, Ka., 1977); and Samuel H. Adams, *Incredible Era: The Life and Times of Warren Gameliel Harding* (Boston, 1939).

31. Harding was reported to have said this in June, 1923, to journalist William Allen White. (Mary Beth Norton, *A People, A Nation: A History of the United States* (2nd ed., New York, 1988), 683.)

32. His other troublesome "friends" included Attorney-General Harry Dougherty, who was implicated in a scheme of accepting bribes and other fraudulent acts, and escaped prosecution only because he refused to testify against himself; Charles Forbes of the Veterans' Bureau, who served time in Leavenworth Prison after being convicted of fraud and bribery in connection with government contracts; and Thomas W. Miller, the Alien Property Custodian, who was jailed for accepting bribes. (Norton, 683-84.)

33. There seems to be some confusion about the date of Fall's admission to practise law. M.R. Werner and John Starr give the year as 1889, while Burl Noggle dates it as 1891. The latter, which cites sources including the Fall

papers in the University of New Mexico Library, seems the more credible source. (Werner and Starr, 5; Noggle, 9.)

34. Noggle, 9-10; Werner and Starr, 6-7. Prior to the ratification of the 17th Amendment in May 1913, Article 3 of the U.S. Constitution provided that senators be chosen by the state legislatures.

35. Werner and Starr, 6.

36. Werner and Starr, 78-79.

37. Noggle, 17-18.

38. Noggle, 36.

39. Noggle, 37.

40. Noggle, 37.

41. Under the terms of the contract, Mammoth was to pay the United States Government 12.5 per cent to 50 per cent of the value of the production of any wells drilled on the property for a lease period of 20 years, or "so long thereafter as oil or gas is produced in paying quantities from said lands." (Noggle, 38.)

42. Werner and Starr, 66.

43. Although La Follette was a Republican, he was associated with the Progressive wing of the party, and he had few friends in the Harding administration. For a discussion of La Follette's political philosophy, see David P. Thelen, *The Early Life of Robert M. La Follette, 1855-1884* (Chicago, 1966) and *The New Citizenship: Origins of Progressivism in Wisconsin, 1885-1900* (Columbia, Missouri, 1972).

44. Noggle, 41-42.

45. Noggle, 51.

46. Despite rumours that Harding had offered Fall a Supreme Court appointment in return for his resignation (the Rio Grande *Republic*, published in Fall's home of Las Cruces, N.M., editorialized on 4 January 1923 that "The fact that President Harding offered Mr. Fall a position on the Supreme Court bench proves the howls of the jackals had nothing to do with his resignation"), the developing scandal was clearly an embarrassment for the president.

47. Francis Russell, *The Shadow of Blooming Grove: Warren G. Harding in His Times* (New York, 1968), 591.

48. Noggle, 68-69.

49. Noggle, 72.

50. *The New York Times*, 12 January 1924, 3.

51. The special counsel appointed were Atlee Pomerene, a former U.S. Democratic Senator from Ohio, and Owen J. Roberts, a prominent Republican Philadelphia lawyer and a professor at the University of Pennsylvania Law School. (Werner and Starr, 142, 152-55.) Roberts became much more prominent six years later when President Herbert Hoover appointed him to the United States Supreme Court. He was one of the justices whom President Franklin Roosevelt described as the "nine old men," and he was the one who, in March 1937, changed his vote on a series of cases upholding the federal regulatory power, thus precluding Roosevelt's plan to "pack" the court by appointing sympathetic justices. (Paul L. Murphy, *The Constitution in Crisis Times, 1918-1969* (New York, 1972), 102, 128-69.) See also Charles A. Leonard, *A Search for a Judicial Philosophy: Mr. Justice Roberts and the Constitutional Revolution of 1937* (Port Washington, N.Y., 1971).

52. Werner and Starr, 160.

53. Werner and Starr, 171.

54. Werner and Starr, 172-74.

55. Werner and Starr, 174-75.

56. Werner and Starr, 178.

57. *Investigation of Activities of Continental Trading Co.*, U.S. Senate Report No. 1326, 70th Congress, 1st Session, 28 May 1928 (hereafter Senate C.T.C. Report).

58. Senate C.T.C. Report.

59. Werner and Starr, 51-2.

60. Werner and Starr, 53.

61. Werner and Starr, 53.

62. *Re United States of America* v. *Mammoth Oil Co.*, 56 *Ontario Law Reports* (1924), 307-18, at 309.

63. Imperial Oil first appeared in the firm ledgers in 1916. Interestingly, however, the initial beside the client name in the ledger was "B" — meaning Britton Osler. Unfortunately, this was the only year in which the ledgers indicated which partners were primarily responsible for particular clients.

64. The firm ledgers indicate that the Midwest Refining Co. was billed $947.00 for the June–November 1920 period.

65. The company's application for incorporation, filed with the Secretary of State in Ottawa on 16 November 1921, indicated that the company's stock was divided into 100,000 shares, but listed only the names of George Meredith Huycke, Norman E. Stickland, Thomas Delany, John J. Huggard and Morley H. Bruels as having subscribed to one share each. Huycke and Strickland were young associate lawyers with the firm. Huycke had been called to the bar in 1920 and Strickland in 1921. Delany, Huggard and Bruels were articling students. Under Canadian company law in force at the time, the remaining stockholders did not have to be identified. In subsequent documentation filed with the Secretary of State, H.S. Osler was identified as the president of the company. The documents also identified Port Perry, Ontario as the company's chief place of business. Osler owned a duck hunting lodge near this little village on the shores of Lake Scucog, some 35 miles northeast of Toronto. (National Archives of Canada, RG95, Vol. 1330, Ch. 2911-21.)

66. In the end, the profit turned out to be substantially less. In the spring of 1923, with the delivery schedule only partially completed, but after Secretary Fall had resigned from Harding's cabinet and the Senate investigation was heating up, the Continental Trading Company sold its contract with Humphreys to the Sinclair Crude Oil Purchasing Company and the Prairie Oil and Gas Company for $400,000. (Carl F. Taeusch, *Policy and Ethics in Business* (New York, 1931), 208.) See also the comment below regarding the U.S. Supreme Court's conclusion about the motive behind this sale.

67. Senate C.T.C. Report.

68. Taeusch, 199.

69. Taeusch, 203; quoting from Senate C.T.C. Report.

70. The Business Profits War Tax Act, 1916, 6-7 Geo. V, c.11; The Income War Tax Act, 1917, 7-8 Geo. V, c.28. On the break-up of Standard Oil, see Yergin, above.

71. Noggle, 190.
72. Werner and Starr 176.
73. Werner and Starr, 179-80.
74. The Companies Act, *Revised Statutes of Canada, 1906*, C.79.
75. Werner and Starr, 182.
76. *United States* v. *Mammoth Oil Co. et al.*, 5 *Federal Reporter* (U.S.), (2d) (1925) 330-54, at 332.
77. Werner and Starr, 187.
78. *The New York Times*, 26 September 1924, 4; *The Globe* (Toronto), 27 September 1924, 13.
79. This was the predecessor of the firm later known as McMillan Binch. McMillan's motion cited the Ontario Evidence Act then in force, which read, in part:

   Where it is made to appear to the High Court Division [of the Supreme Court of Ontario] . . . that any Court or tribunal of competent jurisdiction in a foreign country has duly authorized, by commission . . . the obtaining of the testimony, in or in relation to any action, suit or proceeding pending in or before such foreign Court or tribunal, of a witness out of the jurisdiction thereof and within the jurisdiction of the Court . . , so applied to, such Court . . . may order the examination of such witness before the person appointed, and in the manner and form directed by the commission . . .; and may, by the same or by a subsequent order, command the attendance of any person named therein for the purpose of being examined . . .; and the order may be enforced, and any disobedience thereto punished, in like manner as in case of an order made by the same Court.

   (The Evidence Act, *Revised Statutes of Ontario 1914*, c.76, s.50(1).)
80. Anglin's older brother, Francis A. Anglin, had been appointed chief justice of Canada just eleven days earlier; Rowell was the former leader of the Ontario Liberal Party and had been a member of Prime Minister Sir Robert Borden's wartime Union cabinet and one of the Canadian representatives at the first Assembly of the League of Nations in Geneva in 1920. In 1936 he was appointed chief justice of Ontario. (James G. Snell and Frederick Vaughan, *The Supreme Court of Canada: History of the Institution* (Toronto, 1985) 123, 259; Margaret Prang, *N.W. Rowell: Ontario Nationalist* (Toronto, 1975).)
81. *The Telegram* (Toronto), 27 September 1924.
82. W. Stewart Wallace, *The Macmillan Dictionary of Canadian Biography* (4th ed., Toronto, 1978), s.v. Osler.
83. There is no evidence to explain why Osler switched from A.W Anglin to Wallace Nesbitt as his counsel, but two months later, when the case came before the Ontario Court of Appeal, Osler was once again represented by Anglin (see below).
84. In addition to H.S. Osler, the U.S. government wanted to take evidence from the other directors of the Continental Trading Company. On Osler's instructions, each of these people also refused to answer any of the consul's questions. *Re United States of America* v. *Mammoth Oil Co.*, 56 *Ontario Law Reports* (1924) 307-18, at 310.
85. *Re U.S.A.*, 310-15.
86. *Re U.S.A.*, 317-18.
87. *The Globe* (Toronto), 15 December 1924, 1. *The New York Times* carried the

story on its front page in the Sunday, December 14 issue with the headline "CANADIAN COURT ORDERS H.S. OSLER TO TELL INVESTIGA- TORS FROM THIS GOVERNMENT OF FALL'S CONNECTION WITH SINCLAIR DEAL."

88. *The New York Times*, 16 December 1924, 1, 22; *The Globe* (Toronto), 17 December 1924, 5.

89. *The Globe* (Toronto), 27 September 1924, 13; 9 March 1925, 5.

90. *The Globe* (Toronto), 31 January 1925, 15.

91. *The Globe* (Toronto), 12 February 1925, 12.

92. *Re United States of America* v. *Mammoth Oil Co.* 56 *Ontario Law Reports* 635-52, at 643 (O.C.A., March 11, 1925); affirming 56 O.L.R. 307-18 (S.C.O., Dec. 13, 1924). Interestingly, Ferguson and Osler had nephews who were room-mates at the time. Osler's nephew was Hal Mockridge, who would become the firm's leader in the next generation. Ferguson's nephew Bob Ferguson, then a student with the Mulock, Milliken firm, joined Osler, Hoskin & Harcourt shortly before his call to the bar. He remained with the firm for his entire career. See Chapter Five.

93. *Re U.S.A.* (O.C.A.), 644.

94. *Re U.S.A.* (O.C.A.), 645-46.

95. *The Globe* (Toronto), 12 March 1925, 1.

96. *The New York Times*, 21 February 1925, 5; 1 March 1925, 13. O'Neil and Blackmer, who could also have shed some light on the activities of the Continental Trading Company, were also unavailable to testify. Both had fled to France. In fact, O'Neil remained there until his death in 1932, and Blackmer did not return to the United States until 1949. Robert Stewart was never called to testify in court, but was eventually charged with contempt of Congress for refusing to answer questions put to him before the Senate committee. He was acquitted of both this charge and another of perjury relating to the questions he did answer. (Noggle, 182; Werner and Starr, 273-74.)

97. *The Globe* (Toronto), 29 March 1925, 2; 14 April 1925, 12.

98. *United States* v. *Mammoth Oil Co. et al.* 5 *Federal Reporter*, 2d Series, (1925) 330-54 (District Court, District of Wyoming, June 19, 1925); *The New York Times*, 20 June 1925, 1.

99. *United States* v. *Mammoth Oil Co. et al.* 14 *Federal Reporter*, (2d) (1926), 705-33 (Circuit Court of Appeals, Eighth Circuit, 28 September 1926); *The New York Times*, 29 September 1926, 1.

100. *Mammoth Oil Co. et al.* v. *United States*, 48 *Supreme Court Reporter* (1927), 1-11, at 9.

101. Noggle, 185.

102. Sinclair had hired detectives from the Burns Detective Agency for surveil- lance of the jury. In February, 1928 both he and William J. Burns were convicted of contempt of court for this action. Sinclair was sentenced to six months in prison. This decision was affirmed on appeal by the Supreme Court, and Sinclair began serving his sentence on May 6, 1929. Burns paid a small fine. (Noggle, 185-86; *The New York Times*, 27 November 1927, 1; *Sinclair et al.* v. *United States*, 279 *U.S. Reports* (1928), 749-68; 49 *Supreme Court Reporter* (1928), 471-77.)

103. Noggle, 186.

104. The jury accepted Sinclair's claim that he had given Fall the bonds in payment for a one-third interest in the secretary's New Mexico ranch.

105. Noggle, 201.

106. Werner and Starr, 267.

107. Werner and Starr, 268.

108. Unlike the jury which acquitted Sinclair, this jury apparently did not believe the claim that the bonds were payment for an interest in Fall's ranch.

109. Although he was convicted by a Federal court, Fall was allowed to serve his sentence in the state prison in New Mexico because of his health. He was then suffering from chronic tuberculosis, and his doctors asked that he be allowed to serve his sentence at the high altitude of his home region. He was released in May 1932 after serving nine months of his sentence, almost all of it in the prison hospital. (Noggle, 210-13.)

110. Noggle, 189.

111. Noggle, 189.

112. In order to keep his donations secret, Sinclair used the bonds to pay intermediaries, known supporters of each party, who made the actual donations in cash. (Senate C.T.C. Report.)

113. In 1925, Blackmer and O'Neil travelled separately from Europe to Montreal and summoned representatives of their companies to give them instructions on where to find the bonds. Stewart was more careful. He testified before the Committee that each time Osler delivered a package of bonds he had placed them in a safe in his office, but on April 21, 1928, three days before he concluded his testimony before the Committee, he turned over the bonds to the Sinclair Crude Oil Purchasing Company. (Senate C.T.C. Report.)

114. Werner and Starr, 181.

115. According to the firm's ledgers, the Continental Trading Company was, over a period of two years, the firm's third-largest billing account. Between its incorporation in November, 1921 and its winding up in November, 1923, the company paid Osler, Hoskin & Harcourt a total of $24,023.19. The only clients who were docketed larger amounts during those years were Imperial Oil, which paid $30,552.14, and International Nickel, which paid $28,906.29. During that period, the firm took in a total of just over $400,000; the Continental Trading Company account, therefore, represented about 6 per cent of the firm's gross billings.

116. *The Globe* (Toronto), 27 January 1928, 2; *The New York Times*, 27 January 1928, 1, 8.

117. *The Globe* (Toronto), 14 February 1928, 4.

118. Senate C.T.C. Report.

119. Werner and Starr, 274-75.

120. Senate C.T.C. Report.

121. The Toronto *Telegram* published a series of scathing editorial articles on H.S. Osler's role in the affair in March and April, 1929, and concluded with the comment: "Hal Osler, you should be ashamed of yourself."

122. The firm's gross annual earnings during the 1920s were as follows:

1920:	$163,056.89	1925:	$142,750.48
1921:	$150,912.84	1926:	$150,897.64
1922:	$174,849.39	1927:	$165,313.90
1923:	$169,635.52	1928:	$250,200.33
1924:	$137,839.97	1929:	$284,243.67

(OHH, Ledger Balances, 1920-1929.)

123. The Canadian GNP was $5,952,000,000 in 1926, $6,134,000,000 in 1929, $3,827,000,000 in 1932 and $3,510,000,000 in 1933. By 1937, it had rebounded to $5,257,000,000, and by 1939 it was $5,636,000,000. These economic data, and those which follow, appear in Michael Bliss' *Northern Enterprise: Five Centuries of Canadian Business* (Toronto, 1987), 418-20.

124. The value of Canadian exports were as follows: 1926: $1,261,000,000; 1929: $1,152,000,000; 1932: $490,000,000; 1933: $529,000,000; 1937: $997,000,000: 1939: $929,000,000.

125. Some of these were Abitibi Paper: 98.3%; Bell Telephone: 57.3%; British American Oil: 77.3%; British Columbia Power: 74.2%; Canada Cement: 93.8%; Ford Canada: 91.4%; Hollinger Mines: 54.8%; Imperial Oil: 82.5%; International Nickel: 94.3%; Massey-Harris: 97.4%; National Breweries: 75.2%; and Stelco: 84.1%.

126. The firm's gross annual revenues during the 1930s were as follows:

1930:	$246,301.05	1935:	$231,027.81
1931:	$226,522.15	1936:	$240,890.27
1932:	$201,232.97	1937:	$249,054.56
1933:	$234,237.47	1938:	$231,900.22
1934:	$252,084.68	1939:	$287,741.09

(OHH, Ledger Balances, 1930-1939.)

127. OHH, Ledger Balances, 1929-1939.

CHAPTER FIVE: GROWTH, CHANGE AND BETRAYAL: 1943-1954

1. Interview by Frank Clifford with H.C.F. Mockridge, 1979.

2. Interview by the author with W.M. Bryden, 20 September 1988.

3. Interview by the author with Allan Beattie, 2 February 1989.

4. Interview by Frank Clifford with H.C.F. Mockridge, 1979. After World War I, the Law Society put together an accelerated law school course, including summer classes, which would allow veterans to make up some of the time they had lost in service. Mossey Huycke was the son of E.C.S. Huycke, a county court judge in Peterborough, who was a good friend of Wallace Nesbitt. (Memo from F.A.M. Huycke, 17 April 1995.)

5. Interview by the author with E.J.M. Huycke, 13 September 1988.

6. Interview by the author with W.M. Bryden, 20 September 1989.

7. Mockridge also loved to read. One of the saddest things about his failing health late in life was that his eyesight dimmed and he could no longer read. (Interviews by the author with Allan Beattie, 16 February 1989, and Mrs. Betty Mockridge, 8 March 1990.)

8. Not all of his schooling was in the United States. Before going to high school in Philadelphia, he attended the Lakefield Preparatory School (now known as Lakefield College) near Peterborough, Ontario. He also attended grade schools in Louisville, Kentucky and New York City before his father was posted to Philadelphia. (Interview by Frank Clifford with H.C.F. Mockridge, 1979.)

9. *The New York Times*, 4 January 1944, 23.

10. In addition to Inco, during his career Mockridge's directorships included Anglo-Canadian Mining & Refining Ltd., The Bank of Montreal, Central Scientific Co. of Canada, Ltd., Hudson's Bay Mining & Smelting Co., Ltd., Churchill River Power Co., Ltd., The Royal Trust Co., Confederation Life Association, Canadian Bank Note Co., Ltd., Molson Breweries Ltd., and Northern & Central Gas Corporation Ltd. Huycke's included The Mercantile & General Reinsurance Co. of Canada Ltd., Val d'Or Mineral Holdings Ltd., Cochenour Willans Co., Pickle Crow Gold Mines Ltd., Hasaga Gold Mines Ltd., Harker Gold Mines Ltd. and the Saluda Tea Company.

11. Interview by the author with Donald Pattison, 4 October 1988.

12. According to Allan Beattie, Strickland "always, perpetually seemed to have a cigarette dangling out the side of his mouth. He chain-smoked and he would work away with this cigarette in his mouth to the point where it often wouldn't disappear until it actually burned his lip. Then he would get another one going." (Interview by the author with Allan Beattie, 2 March 1989.)

13. Interview by the author with Donald Pattison, 4 October 1988.

14. Boston remained a fixed-interest partner until 1950, when he became a regular, share interest partner. Even then, however, his share was larger than only three other partners, two of whom had been admitted to the partnership only that year.

15. Interview by the author with C.R. Osler, 15 November 1988.

16. Interview by the author with Allan Beattie, 11 January 1989.

17. Interview by Frank Clifford with H.C.F. Mockridge, 1979.

18. Interview by the author with Mrs. Betty Mockridge, 8 March 1990.

19. See the articles in Irving Abella's edited collection, *On Strike: Six Key Labour Struggles in Canada, 1919-1949* (Toronto, 1974), particularly his own article, "Oshawa 1937," at 93-128; and Desmond Morton's "Aid To The Civil Power: The Stratford Strike of 1933," at 74-91.

20. See Laurel Sefton MacDowell, "The Foundation of the Canadian Industrial Relations System during World War Two," 3 *Labour/Le Travailleur* (1978), 175-96.

21. Interview by the author with Allan Beattie, 2 March 1989.

22. C.R. Osler remembers his father and Colonel Sam McLaughlin as friends during his childhood. (Interview by the author with C.R. Osler, 15 November 1988.)

23. *The Toronto Star*, 1 December 1988. The origin of Wotherspoon's nickname is unknown. Apparently his brother, his children and even his nephews are also known as "Swatty," but no one seems to know why. (Interview by the author with E.J.M. Huycke, 13 September 1988.)

24. In fact, the 1944 *Canadian Law List* included six Oslers practising in Toronto at the time, two at Osler, Hoskin & Harcourt, three at Blakes, and John H. Osler, a second cousin whose grandfather was the original B.B. Osler's brother Edmund. John H. Osler, later an Ontario Supreme Court Justice, practised with Edward Jolliffe, who was the leader of the Official Opposition at Queen's Park from 1943-1945 and led the Ontario CCF from 1942 to 1953, and David Lewis, who led the federal NDP from 1971 to 1975.

25. Their cousin D'Alton Lally, the son of D'Alton McCarthy, who also left McCarthy, Osler, Hoskin & Harcourt in 1916 to form McCarthy & McCarthy had, in turn, left that firm in 1931 because he refused to move with them

from the Canada Permanent Building on King Street to their new offices in the Canada Life Building on University Avenue.

26. A firm with the incredible name of McMaster, Montgomery, Fleury, Mc-Master, Montgomery, Bullen, Steele, Robertson, Willoughby & Lane, who must have had an auctioneer to answer the phone, had 12 lawyers, three of whom were on active service in the armed forces. White, Ruel, Bristol, the predecessor of the firm of White, Bristol, Beck, which merged with Osler, Hoskin & Harcourt in 1974, had 11 lawyers, six of whom were on active service. Wright & McMillan, the predecessor of McMillan, Binch, had 12 lawyers, including Lally McCarthy, with four on active service. Holden, Murdoch, Walton, Finlay & Robinson had 10, with two on active service. Fraser, Beatty, Palmer & Tucker had 10, with three on active service. Mason, Foulds, Davidson & Kellock, a litigation firm which included the Law Society Treasurer Gershom Mason, G.A. Gale (later Chief Justice of Ontario), and John Arnup, later a judge on the Ontario Court of Appeal, had 10, none of whom were serving in the armed forces.

27. Fraser was the author of the then standard treatise *Company Law of Canada*, the fourth edition of which was published by Carswell in 1940.

28. Tory first developed this reputation, which met with the disapproval of many of his fellow lawyers, when he left his partner Strachan Johnston in 1941. Tory articled and began practising with Tilley, Johnston, Thomson & Parmenter. W.N. Tilley, one of the best-known litigators in the country in the 1920s and 1930s, led the litigation side of the firm, and Strachan Johnston led the corporate side. Those two split in 1934; Tilley and Cyril Carson formed Tilley, Carson, a litigation firm, and Tory went with Johnston, but in 1941 he left to form J.S.D. Tory & Associates, taking the most lucrative corporate clients with him.

29. Interview by the author with C.R. Osler, 2 November 1989.

30. Osler also remembers at one time sending a request down to Sullivan & Cromwell in New York to have their printing department produce a set of documents. This was one example of the cooperative relationship between the two firms. In fact, what began during the early twentieth century as a mutually beneficial client referral relationship, had become one of working together very closely on large and complex projects. (Interview by the author with C.R. Osler, 2 November 1989.)

31. Interview by the author with E.J.M. Huycke, 13 September 1988.

32. Interview by the author with W.M. Bryden, 20 September 1988.

33. Interview by the author with W.M. Bryden, 20 September 1988.

34. Interview by the author with Stuart Thom, 11 October 1988.

35. Interview by the author with Stuart Thom, 11 October 1988.

36. Interview by the author with C.R. Osler, 15 November 1988.

37. Interview by the author with Ian Douglas, 5 October 1987. Although Quinn articled in Toronto, he did not practise in Ontario. He was called to the British Columbia bar in 1948.

38. In fact, Meredith was a distant cousin of both Hal Mockridge and the Osler brothers. He was their second cousin, once removed. His great-grandfather was Edward Osler, B.B. and Featherston's younger brother. Edward Osler's daughter, Isobel, married Arthur Meredith, and their son Allen Meredith was the father of Edmund Meredith. Mockridge's mother was Beatrice, the older sister of the Osler brothers' father Britton.

39. Interview by the author with Allan Beattie, 2 February 1989. Dean Cecil Augustus Wright was dubbed "Caesar" by his students.

40. Interview by the author with Allan Beattie, 2 February 1989.

41. Interview by the author with E.J.M. Huycke, 13 September 1988.

42. Interview by the author with C.R. Osler, 2 November 1989.

43. The information on W.B. Reid comes partly from interviews 15 November 1988 and 2 November 1989 with C.R. Osler, who was then a junior partner in the firm, and from the files of the Law Society of Upper Canada.

44. Interview by the author with C.R. Osler, 15 November 1988.

45. This document is in the Law Society's file on Reid. The same file contains other examples of his signature on his 1938 petition of admission to the Law Society as a student and his Articles of Clerkship agreement with Norman Strickland. On these documents his signature is the same, tiny "W.B. Reid" which appears on his confession, but unlike the signature which spelled the end of his career, there was no tremor in his hand when he signed his name to become a lawyer.

46. Swatty Wotherspoon and B.M. and J.G. Osler had also gone to T.C.S., but they were there earlier. The three of them also went to the Royal Military College in Kingston. Kennedy's program was modeled on the ones at Oxford and Cambridge. Although many of its graduates went on to practise law, it was neither a requirement nor an advantage for admission to practise in Ontario. See C. Ian Kyer and Jerome E. Bickenbach, *The Fiercest Debate: Cecil A. Wright, the Benchers, and Legal Education in Ontario, 1923-1957* (Toronto, 1987), especially 114-20 and 148-52.

47. Interview by Frank Clifford with H.C.F. Mockridge, 1979.

48. The 1951 *Financial Post Directory of Directors* lists Reid's father, Walter S. Reid, as a director of International Petroleum, it also lists his home address as 27 Doncliffe Drive, Toronto. The 1954 Toronto city directory also lists a W.S. Reid at that address.

49. Interview by the author with C.R. Osler, 2 November 1989.

50. Interview by the author with Allan Beattie, 2 February 1989. Interestingly, not everyone agreed with this public handling of the affair. C.R. Osler remembers a senior lawyer at another firm severely castigating him at the time for laying criminal charges against a fellow member of the bar! (Memo from C.R. Osler, 2 November 1993.)

51. *Revised Statutes of Canada, 1927*, C.36, ss. 355-358.

52. It is not entirely clear why Harold Boston would be the one to deliver the letter. He was neither a leader in the firm like Mockridge or Huycke, nor did he have any responsibility for running the office, like Strickland. He may have been close to Reid, but there is no evidence to support this.

53. *The Telegram* (Toronto), 16 June 1953, 1.

54. The 1954 Toronto city directory lists a Mrs. Helen E. Reid living in a rented house on Farnham Ave. in north Toronto and working as a secretary, but her name does not appear in subsequent directories. Verna King, a staff member who started as a secretary in the firm a few weeks after Reid left, remembers her mother meeting Mrs. Reid and hearing her sad story in a hairdresser's some time during the mid-1950s. What happened to her after that is a mystery. (Interview by the author with C.R. Osler, 15 November 1988.)

55. In most cases, Reid first forged the payee's signature and then endorsed the cheque himself in order to cash it.

56. Huycke's wife and Bassett's mother were sisters, and the firm had acted for Bassett in his purchase of *The Telegram* less than a year earlier. (Interview by the author with Allan Beattie, 2 February 1989.) The lead story in the final edition involved a battle in the Korean War. (*The Telegram*, 16 June 1953, 1.)

57. *The Toronto Daily Star*, 16-17 June 1953; *The Globe and Mail* (Toronto), 17 June 1953, 5.

58. Interview by the author with Beverley Matthews, 6 November 1989.

CHAPTER SIX: THE CLUB: 1954-1970

---

1. As of 1952, McMichael, Common, Howard, Ker & Cate had 24 lawyers; Blake, Anglin, Osler & Cassels had 22. Osler, Hoskin & Harcourt had 17, as did McCarthy & McCarthy. See Appendix II.

2. The five were Britton Osler's three sons — Britton Michael, John G. and Campbell Revere — his nephew Hal Mockridge, and Mockridge's brother-in-law, Tom Delamere. The three new partners in the 1955 agreement were Mossey Huycke's son Fred, Allan Beattie, whose father Leslie Beattie was the senior Canadian executive at International Nickel, and Bill Bryden.

3. Joseph Schull, *100 Years of Banking in Canada: A History of The Toronto-Dominion Bank* (Toronto, 1956), 197.

4. Interviews by the author with Jim Kennedy, 13 September 1988, and Allan Beattie, 2 February 1989.

5. Interview by the author with Purdy Crawford, 31 January 1991.

6. Interview by the author with John Goodwin, 28 February 1991.

7. The other partners' shares under the 1955 agreement were as follows:

G.M. Huycke	- 57	shares (15%)
T.D. Delamere	- 38.5	shares (10.1%)
N.E. Strickland	- 32	shares (8.4%)
B.M. Osler	- 31	shares (8.2%)
G.D. Wotherspoon	- 31	shares (8.2%)
R.G. Ferguson	- 27.5	shares (7.2%)
S.D. Thom	- 21	shares (5.5%)
H.E. Boston	- 17	shares (4.5%)
J.G. Osler	- 16	shares (4.2%)
C.R. Osler	- 15	shares (4%)
W.M. Bryden	- 13	shares (3.4%)
F.A.M. Huycke	- 12	shares (3.7%)
A.L. Beattie	- 12	shares (3.7%)

8. Interview by the author with Mrs. Betty Mockridge, 8 March 1990.

9. Huycke was called to the bar in 1920, Mockridge was called in 1927. Delamere was called in 1925.

10. Interview by the author with Stuart Thom, 11 October 1988.

11. Stafford Smythe was represented by John Robinette of McCarthy & McCarthy. Between them, the Smythes owned 82.8 per cent of the stock of C. Smythe Limited and had used the tax stripping method to avoid paying income tax on almost three quarters of a million dollars profit they paid

themselves during 1961. (*C.S. Smythe et al.* v. *Minister of National Revenue* [1969] *Canada Tax Cases*, 558-65.)

12.   The first Roman Catholic lawyer with the firm was Vince Reid, who came to the firm as a student in 1952; he was called to the bar in 1954 and became a partner in 1965. The first Jewish lawyer with the firm was Schuyler Sigel, who came as an articling student in 1961. He stayed with the firm for about a year after his call to the bar in 1963, but left to join Stitt & Baker, the firm which eventually became the Toronto office of the giant American firm Baker & Mackenzie.

13.   Interview by the author with Senator David A. Croll, 9 November 1987.

14.   *Plessy* v. *Ferguson* 163 U.S., 537; *Brown* v. *Board of Education* 347 U.S., 483.

15.   Sandra Gwyn, "Madame Justice: How Bertha Wilson's Humanity Is Changing the Last Bastion of Male Power — The Supreme Court of Canada," in *Saturday Night*, July 1985, 13-19.

16.   Gwyn, 16.

17.   Gwyn, 13.

18.   Bertha Wilson, in her comments at swearing-in ceremony, Ontario Court of Appeal, 2 January 1976.

19.   Interview by the author with Madam Justice Bertha Wilson, 18 December 1989.

20.   Gwyn, 17.

21.   Interview by the author with Madam Justice Bertha Wilson, 18 December 1989.

22.   Gwyn, 17.

23.   Interview by the author with Madam Justice Bertha Wilson, 18 December 1989.

24.   Interview by the author with Madam Justice Bertha Wilson, 18 December 1989.

25.   Interview by the author with Stuart Thom, 11 October 1988.

26.   Interview by the author with Madam Justice Bertha Wilson, 18 December 1989.

27.   Interview by the author with Madam Justice Bertha Wilson, 18 December 1989.

28.   Interview by the author with Madam Justice Bertha Wilson, 18 December 1989.

29.   Interview by the author with Madam Justice Bertha Wilson, 18 December 1989.

30.   Interview by the author with Madam Justice Bertha Wilson, 18 December 1989.

31.   Interview by the author with Purdy Crawford, 31 January 1991.

32.   Interview by the author with Purdy Crawford, 31 January 1991.

33.   Interview by the author with Madam Justice Bertha Wilson, 18 December 1989.

34.   Interview by the author with Purdy Crawford, 31 January 1991.

35.   Loss has published a number of books on the subject; see, in particular, his *Fundamentals of Securities Regulation* (Boston, 1983).

36.   Interview by the author with Purdy Crawford, 31 January 1991.

37. [1970] *Supreme Court Reports*, 282-307, at 288-300. The case involved a section of the federal Indian Act, which prohibited intoxication off a reserve, but it was the only instance in which the Supreme Court used the Bill of Rights to protect against racial discrimination. This record contrasts sharply with that of Justice Wilson and her colleagues after the adoption of the Charter in 1982.

38. Interview by the author with Purdy Crawford, 31 January 1991.

39. Interview by the author with Purdy Crawford, 31 January 1991.

40. Interview by the author with Purdy Crawford, 31 January 1991. B.M. Osler, Britton Osler's eldest son, was generally known by the partners as "Brick." The nickname apparently dates to his days at the Royal Military College.

41. Interview by the author with Allan Beattie, 2 March 1989.

42. Interview by the author with Purdy Crawford, 31 January 1991.

43. *Canadian Who's Who* (Toronto, 1990), s.v. Crawford.

44. Interview by the author with John Goodwin, 28 February 1991.

45. See this author's "'A Learned and Honorable Body': The Professionalization of the Ontario Bar, 1867-1929," Ph.D. thesis, The University of Western Ontario, 1987.

46. The best source on this point is Jerrold Auerbach's *Unequal Justice: Lawyers and Social Change in Modern America* (New York, 1976). See also M.S. Larson, *The Rise of Professionalism: A Sociological Analysis* (Berkeley, Cal., 1977), and Terence Johnson, *Professions and Power* (London, 1972).

47. The full name of this firm in the 1960s was Chisholm, Smith, Davis, Anglin, Laing, Weldon & Courtois. It later became Clarkson, Tétrault, and when it merged with McCarthy & McCarthy in 1990, it became McCarthy Tétrault. Molson also retained Heward Stikeman of Stikeman, Elliott, Tamaki, Mercier & Turner on tax and certain corporate matters from time to time. (Interview by the author with Morgan McCammon, 8 July 1991.)

48. Mockridge was invited to sit on the board at Molson because he was very well respected in the Canadian business community and he was a personal friend of Hartland Molson. (Interview by the author with Peter Stewart, 12 June 1991.)

49. Interview by the author with Morgan McCammon, 8 July 1991.

50. Interview by the author with Peter Stewart, 12 June 1991.

51. Interview by the author with Paul McKeown, 23 May 1991.

52. Interview by the author with Purdy Crawford, 31 January 1991.

53. Interview by the author with Purdy Crawford, 31 January 1991.

54. Interview by the author with Jack Ground, 27 September 1988.

55. Interview by the author with Jack Ground, 27 September 1988.

56. The Big Four were the University of Toronto, McGill, Queen's and the University of Western Ontario. The term comes from the name of the football conference the four played in. Likewise, the Little Big Four was the football conference the private high schools played in.

57. Interview by the author with Harry Boylan, 8 November 1990.

58. Interview by the author with E.J.M. Huycke, 13 September 1988.

59. Interview by the author with Madam Justice Bertha Wilson, 18 December 1989.

60. Interview by the author with E.J.M. Huycke, 13 September 1988.

61. Hal Mockridge, B.M. Osler and Bob Ferguson preferred the Toronto Club, and Tom Delamere generally had lunch just down King Street at the King Edward Hotel. (Interview by the author with Allan Beattie, 2 February 1989.)

62. Interview by the author with Allan Beattie, 2 February 1989.

63. Interview by the author with Bill Bryden, 20 September 1988.

64. Somers, who was with the firm as an articling student from 1957 until his call to the bar in 1959, remained with the firm as an associate lawyer until 1965, when he left to set up his own office. In 1991 he was appointed to the Ontario Court of Justice, General Division. Goodwin, who was a year behind Somers, stayed with Oslers throughout his career.

65. Boston was born May 22, 1902. He was still relatively active, but in January 1963 he suffered a heart attack while skiing and died. (Interviews by the author with Bill Bryden, 11 October 1988; Stuart Thom, 11 October 1988; and Allan Beattie, 2 February 1989.)

66. Interview by the author with Stuart Thom, 11 October 1988.

67. Like many of the other lawyers, Saunders was a private school graduate, in his case Upper Canada College. He was also a World War II veteran. He did not, however, article at Oslers. He articled and practised briefly with the firm of McMaster, Montgomery & Co., a medium-sized firm which had a large real estate practice. A few months after his call to the bar in 1954, he moved to the firm after learning from Fred Huycke, with whom he played bridge, that Oslers might be looking for another young lawyer. Saunders stayed with the firm until 1977, when he was appointed to the Supreme Court of Ontario. (Interview by the author with Mr. Justice Edward Saunders, 13 December 1990.)

68. The partnership agreement, which for the first time divided the firm's profits into percentages rather than shares, called for the following division:

H.C.F. Mockridge	- 12.25%
G.M. Huycke	- 12.25%
N.E. Strickland	5.25%
R.G. Ferguson	- 5.25%
T.D. Delamere	- 10.00%
B.M. Osler	- 9.50%
G.D. Wotherspoon	- 10.00%
S.D. Thom	- 6.00%
J.G. Osler	- 3.75%
H.E. Boston	- 3.00%
C.R. Osler	- 4.25%
W.M. Bryden	- 4.00%
F.A.M. Huycke	- 4.00%
A.L. Beattie	- 4.00%
E.J.M. Huycke	- 3.25%
E. Saunders	- 3.25%

In addition, although Boston's share was set at 3 per cent, he was guaranteed a minimum annual share of $12,000. (Osler, Hoskin & Harcourt firm records (hereafter OHH), Partnership Agreement, 31 December 1958.)

69. OHH, Partnership Agreement, 31 December 1958.

70. OHH, Partnership Agreement, 31 December 1958.

71. OHH memorandum re: Articles of Partnership, 21 April 1960.

72. OHH, Partnership Agreement, 31 December 1961.

73. OHH, Articles of Partnership, 1 January 1962.

74. OHH, Articles of Partnership, 1 January 1962.

75. Interview by the author with Allan Beattie, 2 February 1989.

76. Interview by the author with Stuart Thom, 11 October 1988.

77. The trend has continued. The 1990 *RSO* is thirteen thick volumes, and is accompanied by the even more voluminous set of statutory regulations, the *Revised Regulations of Ontario.*

78. The minutes also listed the lawyer to whom bills would be sent based on the subject content of the bill. This list, which Swatty Wotherspoon prepared, provides an accurate picture of the lawyers' primary practice specialties at the time.

BANKRUPTCY:	W.M. Bryden, J.C. McTague, G.D. Lane
BANKS AND BANKING INSURANCE:	F.A.M. Huycke, A.L. Beattie, H.C.F. Mockridge
BUSINESS LAW: (incl. contracts and agency, master and servant, sale of goods, etc.)	W.M. Bryden, G.D. Wotherspoon, B.M. Osler
CONSTITUTIONAL LAW AND COMBINES:	H.P. Crawford, Bertha Wilson, G.D. Wotherspoon
CORPORATION LAW: (incl. companies acts, financing, blue sky laws, special act companies)	A.L. Beattie, F.A.M. Huycke, G.D. Wotherspoon
LABOUR LAW:	T.D. Delamere, B.M. Osler, G.M. Huycke
LITIGATION: (incl. civil, criminal, family and divorce practice and procedure, equity, evidence)	J.C. McTague, G.D. Lane, G.M. Huycke
MINING LAW:	W.M. Bryden, B.M. Osler
MUNICIPAL LAW: (incl. administrative laws, planning and development)	E. Saunders, J.C. McTague, B.M. Osler
PATENTS, COPYRIGHTS AND TRADE MARKS:	R.G. Ferguson, A.W. Langmuir, G.M. Huycke
REAL PROPERTY AND MORTGAGES:	H.K. Boylan, H.E. Boston, V.P. Reid
TAXATION: (excl. estate tax and succession duties)	S.D. Thom, E. Saunders, J.G. Goodwin
WILLS, TRUSTS AND ESTATES: (incl. estate tax and succession duties)	E.J.M. Huycke, Bertha Wilson, J.D. Ground
MISCELLANEOUS AND LEGISLATION GENERALLY:	N.E. Strickland, J.G. Osler, C.R. Osler

79. See the discussion of Purdy Crawford moving to Imasco and Allan Beattie

moving to Eaton's in Chapter Eight, and of Peter Dey's move to Morgan Stanley in the Prologue.

80. Interview by the author with Purdy Crawford, 31 January 1991.

81. See the discussion of the Texas Gulf Kidd Creek strike, below.

82. Interview by the author with Purdy Crawford, 14 March 1991.

83. OHH Executive Committee minutes, 27 February and 10 March 1965.

84. He was born in Cobourg, Ontario on 26 June 1895.

85. Interview by the author with John Goodwin, 28 February 1991.

86. Huycke and Beattie both articled with the firm and were called to the bar together in 1951. Interestingly, Huycke's name always appeared above Beattie's on the firm letterhead, and Beattie occasionally teased Huycke about the nepotism in it: " 'Fred, my understanding always was that the names on the letterhead were in order of seniority at the bar and that because B comes before H, I graduated forty-six seconds before you, so I should be first.' There was another reality, of course, that enabled Fred to sneak in ahead of me." (Interview by the author with Allan Beattie, 11 January 1989.)

87. OHH, Articles of Partnership, 1 January 1965; 1 January 1968

88. Mockridge turned seventy on September 24, 1971, and Beattie was unanimously elected by the Executive Partners as chairman the following January. (OHH, Executive Committee minutes, 12 January 1972.)

89. Interview by the author with Allan Beattie, 16 February 1989.

90. Interview by the author with Allan Beattie, 16 February 1989.

91. While Beattie was clearly trying to build a consensus among the partners, it was equally clear that an individual partner's ability to influence the decision was directly proportional to his standing on the existing share division list. In effect, under Beattie the most important decisions were made by a select few. Although this represented an evolutionary change from the Mockridge regime, as Chapter Seven will discuss, it was not enough of a change to suit some of the younger partners. Under the Partnership Agreement of 1 January 1968, Mossey Huycke and J.G. Osler became fixed-interest partners. Their fixed shares of the profits were $25,000 and $10,000 respectively. The remaining profits were divided as follows:

H.C.F. Mockridge:	6.70%
T.D. Delamere:	6.25%
B.M. Osler:	6.25%
S.D. Thom:	6.25%
F.A.M. Huycke:	6.25%
A.L Beattie:	6.25%
W.M. Bryden:	5.80%
C.R. Osler:	5.10%
E.J.M. Huycke:	5.05%
E. Saunders:	5.05%
J.C. McTague:	5.05%
H.P. Crawford·	4.60%
H.K. Boylan:	4.30%
R.G. Ferguson:	3.75%
J.D. Ground:	3.60%
V.P. Reid:	3.25%
D.F. Pattison:	2.50%
G.D. Lane:	2.50%

J.K. Doran:	2.50%
Bertha Wilson:	2.40%
J.G. Goodwin:	2.20%
J.N. Grieve:	2.20%
J.R. Moffatt:	2.20%

Vince Reid and Jack Ground became partners on January 1, 1965, and Don Pattison, Dennis Lane, Jim Doran, Bertha Wilson, John Goodwin, John Grieve and John Moffatt all became partners on January 1, 1968. The 1968 agreement specified that ''the shares of the net income for subsequent partnership periods (three years) shall be established by agreement among the partners as they are at the commencement of each such partnership period. In the event that a new partner with a percentage interest is taken into the Firm during the course of a partnership period, the shares of the divisible profits for the remaining portion of the partnership year in which the partner is admitted and for any remaining year or years in the partnership period, shall be established by the Executive Partners subject to the concurrence of the partners.''

92. C.R. Osler remembers the meeting taking place prior to the move to the Prudential Building in 1962, but he is unable to pinpoint the year. (Interview by the author with C.R. Osler, 7 March 1991.)

93. Interview by the author with C.R. Osler, 7 March 1991.

94. Interview by the author with C.R. Osler, 7 March 1991.

95. OHH, Articles of Partnership, 1 January 1962.

96. Interview by the author with C.R. Osler, 7 March 1991.

97. Interview by the author with C.R. Osler, 7 March 1991.

98. In the merger of the banks, which took place in 1955, Beverley Matthews acted for the Dominion Bank and Fasken & Calvin represented the Bank of Toronto. The latter firm, which had acted for the Bank of Toronto for many years, remained as the Toronto-Dominion Bank's primary counsel after the merger. (Schull, 197); interviews by the author with Beverley Matthews, 6 November 1989 and C.R. Osler, 7 March 1991.)

99. Interview by the author with Allan Beattie, 2 March 1989.

100. Borden & Elliot, which Beverley Elliot (known generally as ''Pete'') formed during the early years of the Depression of the 1930s with former Prime Minister Robert Borden's nephew Henry Borden, was then known as Borden, Elliot, Kelley & Palmer. Bordens moved into the Bank of Canada Building from their old location in the Bank of Commerce Building at 25 King St. West (south side next to the Dominion Bank building). C.R. Osler remembers the Bank of Commerce building being built in the late 1920s on the eve of the Depression. It was then the most prestigious building in the city. One of its other tenants was the Blake firm, which acted as solicitors to the Bank of Commerce. (Interview by the author with C.R. Osler, 3 November 1989.)

101. The Toronto-Dominion Centre was built by the bank in partnership with Cemp Investments of Montreal, the holding company formed by Sam Bronfman for his children Charles, Edgar, Minda and Phyllis. (Michael Bliss, *Northern Enterprise: Five Centuries of Canadian Business* (Toronto, 1987), 491.)

102. G.P. de T. Glazebrook, *The Story of Toronto* (Toronto, 1971), 249.

103. Interview by the author with Frank Clifford, February 1991.

104. Speaking at Beattie's retirement dinner in 1987, Harry Boylan affectionately

said that other than his support of the New York Yankees and the Liberal Party of Canada, Allan's judgement was impeccable.

105. One of his colleagues in the short-lived Clark cabinet was another (later) Osler partner, Ron Atkey (see Chapter Eight).

106. However, unlike the practice in later years, during the 1950s and 1960s admissions to the partnership were made only every three years when a new partnership agreement was signed. Wilson was, therefore, passed over for partnership in 1965, six years following her call to the bar. McTague was called to the bar in 1948 and joined the firm in 1956. He was passed over for partnership in 1959 and became a partner in 1962. Reid, who articled with the firm, was called to the bar in 1954, but did not become a partner until 1965. In McTague's case, the significant time span is probably the six years between his joining the firm and his admission to the partnership. He was also the son of a former judge. His father, Justice Charles P. McTague, sat on the Ontario Supreme Court from 1935-1944, and he served as Chairman of the Ontario Securities Commission from 1945-1948.

107. Bliss, 481-82.

108. Interview by the author with Bill Bryden, 19 February 1991.

109. In fact, Leitch's claim was that Texas Gulf was holding the property as a constructive trustee. See *Leitch Gold Mines Ltd.* v. *Texas Gulf Sulphur Co.* [1969] *Ontario Reports*, Vol. 1, 469-579.

110. Interview by the author with C.R. Osler, 7 March 1991.

111. Interview by the author with Purdy Crawford, 31 January 1991.

112. Interview by the author with Frank Clifford, 7 March 1991

113. *The Globe and Mail*, 6 November 1969, B2; 15 November 1969, 1; *The Financial Post* (Toronto), 25 October 1969, 3.

114. Interview by the author with John Goodwin, 28 February 1991 Interview by the author with H.P. Crawford, 31 January 1991.

115. Interview by the author with C R. Osler, 7 March 1991.

CHAPTER SEVEN: THE TRANSFORMATION: 1970-1980

1. H.C.F. Mockridge to Erskine Buchanan, Q.C., Buchanan, McAllister, Blakely & Ham, Montreal, 24 June 1970.

2. Osler, Hoskin & Harcourt firm records (hereafter OHH), Executive Committee minutes, 9 January 1972; 21 January 1976. Mockridge's official date of retirement was 1 April 1976.

3. Michael Bliss, *Northern Enterprise: Five Centuries of Canadian Business* (Toronto, 1987), 481.

4. Foreign Investment Review Act, 21-22 Eliz. II (1973), c.64; Anti-Inflation Act, 23-24 Eliz. II (1975), c.75.

5. See Chapter Six. It is significant in the same light that the firm retained the rest of Inco's legal work.

6. On the question of professionalization of lawyers and the flight from competition, see Jerold Auerbach, *Unequal Justice: Lawyers and Social Change in Modern America* (New York, 1976); Raymond Cocks, *The Foundations of the Modern Bar* (London, 1983); and this author's "'A Learned And

Honorable Body': The Professionalization of The Ontario Bar, 1867-1929,''
Ph.D. thesis, University of Western Ontario, 1987.

7. See Chapters Five and Six, respectively.

8. Memorandum to the author from Brian Bucknall, 7 October 1991.

9. The five largest firms in the city in 1911 were Beatty, Blackstock, Fasken, Cowan & Chadwick (15 lawyers), Blake, Lash, Anglin & Cassels (11 lawyers), McCarthy, Osler, Hoskin & Harcourt (9 lawyers), Aylesworth, Wright, Moss & Thompson (8 lawyers), and Bicknell, Bain, Strathy & Mackelcan (7 lawyers). In 1931, they were Blake, Anglin, Osler & Cassels (20 lawyers), Osler, Hoskin & Harcourt (14 lawyers), Tilley, Johnston, Thomson & Parmenter (12 lawyers), McMaster, Montgomery, Bullen, Steele, Robertson & Willoughby (11 lawyers), and Rowell, Reid, Wright & McMillan (11 lawyers). McCarthy & McCarthy (9 lawyers) was the sixth largest in Toronto. See also Appendix II, which outlines the largest firms in Canada between 1862 and 1992.

10. In 1951, the five largest firms in Toronto were Blake, Anglin, Osler & Cassels (22 lawyers), Osler, Hoskin & Harcourt (17 lawyers), McCarthy & McCarthy (17 lawyers), Borden, Elliot, Kelley, Palmer & Sankey (14 lawyers), and McMillan, Binch, Wilkinson, Stuart, Berry & Wright (14 lawyers).

11. In 1961, the five largest Toronto firms were Blake, Cassels & Graydon (39 lawyers), McCarthy & McCarthy (31 lawyers), Osler, Hoskin & Harcourt (29 lawyers), Fraser, Beatty, Tucker, McIntosh & Stewart (24 lawyers), and Borden, Elliot, Kelley & Palmer (22 lawyers).

12. The five largest Toronto law firms in 1971 were Blake, Cassels & Graydon (67 lawyers), McCarthy & McCarthy (57 lawyers), Osler, Hoskin & Harcourt (53 lawyers), Fraser & Beatty (46 lawyers), and Borden, Elliot, Kelley & Palmer (44 lawyers).

13. The five largest Toronto firms in 1981 were Blake, Cassels & Graydon (123 lawyers), McCarthy & McCarthy (112 lawyers), Osler, Hoskin & Harcourt (97 lawyers), Fraser & Beatty (95 lawyers), and Borden & Elliot (77 lawyers). Gowling & Henderson had a total of 80 lawyers, but these were divided between its Ottawa and Toronto offices.

14. The sources of these data are Curtis Cole, ''A Developmental Market: Growth Rates, Competition and Professional Standards in the Ontario Legal Profession, 1881-1936,'' *The Canada-United States Law Journal* 7 (1984), 231-45; Roger Yachetti, ''The Views of the Practising Bar,'' *Canada-United States Law Journal* 6 (1983), 103-12; and the *Census of Canada*, 1981.

15. The retired partners were Bob Ferguson, Hal Mockridge, Brick Osler, Stewart Rogers, Stuart Thom and Peter White, Sr.

16. Seventeen of the 23 partners (73 per cent) articled with the firm, and 26 of the 30 associates (87 per cent).

17. Only 34 of the 56 active partners (61 per cent) and 26 of the 35 associates (74 per cent) articled with the firm. Three of the six retired partners articled with the firm. Stewart Rogers articled with the firm of McLaughlin, Johnson, Moorehead and McCauley in Toronto; Stuart Thom articled with his father's firm, Mackenzie, Thom, Bastedo & Jackson in Regina; and Peter White, Sr., articled with his father's firm, then known as White, Ruel & Bristol.

18. This is further reduced to 3.1 years if Woody Langmuir, who was called to the bar in 1940 but never made partner, is removed from the list.

19. If Woody Langmuir, who died 30 August 1981, is included, this figure is 3.1 years.

20. Bertha Wilson became a partner in 1968; the other two women were Alicia Forgie, who was called to the bar in 1963, joined the firm in 1966, and became a partner in 1971, and Heather Frawley, who articled with the firm during 1968-69, joined the firm after her call to the bar in 1970, and was made a partner in 1976. See also the discussion of student recruitment in this chapter.

21. The five women were Nancy Chaplick, who articled with the firm during 1973-74, joined the firm after her call to the bar in 1975, and became a partner in 1980; Jean DeMarco, who was called to the bar in 1974, joined the firm in 1976, and became a partner in 1981; Barbara McGregor, who articled with the firm during 1972-73, was called to the bar in 1974, joined the firm in 1975 after a year spent as a clerk in the Supreme Court of Ontario, and became a partner in 1979; Alicia Forgie and Heather Frawley.

22. The lone female lawyer at McCarthy & McCarthy in 1971 was Rosemary Hodgins, who was originally called to the bar in British Columbia in 1951. She was called to the Ontario bar in 1959 and practised for a time with the Canada Permanent Trust Co. in Toronto before joining McCarthys.

23. Interview by the author with Harry Boylan, 8 November 1990.

24. Interview by the author with Harry Boylan, 8 November 1990.

25. OHH, Partnership Agreement, 1 January 1968.

26. OHH, Executive Committee minutes, 16 July 1970.

27. OHH, Partnership Agreement, 1 January 1968.

28. OHH, Partnership Meeting minutes, 19 April 1971.

29. OHH, Executive Committee minutes, 26 July 1971.

30. OHH, Articles of Partnership, 1 January 1971.

31. The power to appoint the remaining members lay with the Executive Committee itself.

32. OHH, Executive Committee minutes, 9 December 1971.

33. OHH, Partnership Meeting minutes, 16 March 1972.

34. Interview by the author with Jim Kennedy, 13 September 1988.

35. Beattie began high school in Copper Cliff, but later transferred to St. Andrew's College in Aurora, Ontario. He graduated from St. Andrew's in 1945 and enrolled at Trinity College in the University of Toronto.

36. The two in 1948 were C.R. Osler and Ian Douglas; in 1950, Bill Bryden joined the firm.

37. Interview by the author with Frank Clifford, 9 May 1991.

38. Interview by the author with Frank Clifford, 9 May 1991.

39. Interview by the author with Allan Beattie, 2 March 1989.

40. *Oxford English Dictionary*, 1989, s.v. "troika."

41. Interview by the author with Allan Beattie, 2 March 1989.

42. Interview by the author with Maurice Coombs, 16 February 1989.

43. Interview by the author with Allan Beattie, 2 March 1989.

44. OHH, Executive Committee minutes, 24 April 1973.

45. OHH, Executive Committee minutes, 8, 22 May; 10 July 1973.

46. OHH, Executive Committee minutes, 10 July 1973.

47. OHH, Executive Committee minutes, 10 July 1973.

48. OHH, Executive Committee minutes, 24 July 1973.

49. OHH, Executive Committee minutes, 18 September 1973.

50. OHH, Partnership Meeting minutes, 4 October 1973.

51. Interview by the author with Frank Clifford, 9 May 1991.

52. Interview by the author with Harry Boylan, 8 November 1990.

53. OHH, Articles of Partnership, 1 January 1971.

54. Memorandum, P.J. Dey, L.D. Hebb, E.J.M. Huycke and B. Wilson to The Executive Committee, Osler, Hoskin & Harcourt, 16 July 1975.

55. Memorandum, J.D. Ground to the Executive Committee, Osler, Hoskin & Harcourt, 5 September 1975.

56. OHH, Partnership Meeting minutes, 29 September 1975.

57. OHH, Partnership Meeting minutes, 16 February 1976.

58. In fact, Allan Beattie's share was the same as Fred Huycke's, but as managing partner, Beattie was an ex officio member of the Committee.

59. Richard L. Abel, *American Lawyers* (New York, 1989), vii.

60. The term *pro bono* is an abbreviation of the Latin term *pro bono publico*, literally "in the public good."

61. OHH, Executive Committee minutes, 18 August 1971.

62. Osgoode Hall Law School was the Law Society of Upper Canada's proprietary institution until 1968, when York University took it over. Under the terms of the agreement between the University and the Law Society, however, the latter retained the right to withdraw the name of the law school if it wished.

63. *Re Herbold et al. and Pajelle Investments Ltd.*, 4 *Ontario Reports* (2d), (1975), 133-38 (Ontario Court of Appeal); *Pajelle Investments Limited* v. *Herbold*, [1976] 2 *Supreme Court Reports*, 520-30 (Supreme Court of Canada). The counsel from the clinic in this case was Brian Bucknall, then a member of the faculty at Osgoode Hall Law School. He had articled with Osler, Hoskin & Harcourt, and later left Osgoode to practise in the firm's Real Estate Department.

64. OHH, Executive Committee minutes, 4 April 1972.

65. OHH, Executive Committee minutes, 13 June 1972.

66. OHH, Executive Committee minutes, 16 August 1971.

67. OHH, Executive Committee minutes, 25 January 1972.

68. OHH, Partnership Meeting minutes, 12 January 1972.

69. The other members of the committee were Brian Bellmore, Peter Dey, Ron Ellis, Jack Ground, George Julian, Don Pattison and Stuart Thom. (OHH, Executive Committee minutes, 17 October 1972.)

70. One of the best known of these was the Washington, D.C. firm of Arnold & Porter. (Interview by the author with Ken Dryden, 22 July 1991.)

71. Interview by the author with Ron Ellis, 28 March 1991.

72. OHH, Partnership Meeting minutes, 7 December 1972.

73. OHH, Executive Committee minutes, 28 March 1973.

74. OHH, Executive Committee minutes, 22 May 1973.

75. OHH, Executive Committee minutes, 29 May, 12 June 1973; Partnership Meeting minutes, 18 June 1973.

76. The Canadian Civil Liberties Association had existed for many years in an unincorporated state.

77. Interview by the author with Ron Ellis, 28 March 1991; OHH, Partnership Meeting minutes, 28 November 1974; 1 May 1975.

78. Interview by the author with Ken Dryden, 22 July 1991.

79. Interview by the author with Brian Levitt, 29 November 1989.

80. The 1975 *Canadian Law List* shows a total of four lawyers in Shelburne. Levitt's name is not in the 1975 *Law List*, however, because it was prepared prior to the April call to the bar.

81. Interview by the author with Brian Levitt, 29 November 1989.

82. Interview by the author with Brian Levitt, 29 November 1989.

83. OHH, Executive Committee minutes, 19 October 1976.

84. OHH, Executive Committee minutes, 29 May 1973.

85. Interview by the author with Purdy Crawford, 31 January 1991.

86. Johnston was later in the public eye when he acted as moderator for the televised debates of the party leaders during the federal election of May 1979.

87. OHH, Executive Committee minutes, 19 October 1976.

88. Dey, who was born and raised in Ottawa, graduated in mechanical engineering from Queen's University in Kingston in 1963. He went to Halifax for law school because he won a Sir James Dunn Scholarship to Dalhousie. He also won a scholarship to attend Harvard in 1966.

89. The importance of community involvement has long been recognized at Oslers, both for its business development potential and for its contribution to the individual lawyer's development, not only as a legal technician, but as a well-rounded person. Indeed, for a number of years the firm's partners and associate lawyers have been asked to include in their annual business plans and evaluation forms details of any outside professional or community activities, the thinking being that more is involved in the successful practice of law that the docketing of long hours of chargeable file work.

90. The story of the founding and growth of McCain Foods and the family dispute which erupted in the 1990s has been detailed in court documents and was widely reported in the press. The information respecting the McCains contained in the accompanying text appears in publicly available documents.

91. Interview by the author with Arthur Peltoman, 17 April 1995.

92. Interview by the author with Bob Lindsay, 1 May 1991.

93. Interview by the author with Purdy Crawford, 31 January 1991.

94. Robert Bothwell, Ian Drummond and John English, *Canada Since 1945: Power, Politics, and Provincialism* (Toronto, 1981), 413-14.

95. 19-20-21 Eliz. II (1971), cc. 63,64.

96. By 1994, the Osler tax department consisted of 12 partners and 9 associates. In a survey of in-house tax experts at multinationals in Canada and the United States, conducted that year by the *International Tax Review*, the Olser tax department was rated first among Canadian law and accounting firms, and two Osler tax partners appeared on the list of the six top-rated tax practitioners in Canada.

97. Interview by the author with J. Edgar Sexton, 7 February 1991.

98. Sexton remembers Alex Corry and W.R. Lederman as particularly good.

99. Margaret A. Banks, *Law at Western, 1959-1984* (London, Ont., 1984).

100. *The Gazette* (University of Western Ontario), 8 October 1974, 8; 11 October 1974, 24.

101. Interview by the author with J. Edgar Sexton, 28 March 1991.

102. *Roncarelli* v. *Duplessis* [1959] *Supreme Court Reports* 121; 16 *Dominion Law Reports* (2d) 689.

103. On Duplessis and his government see Robert Rumilly, *Duplessis et son temps* (Montreal, 1973); Pierre Laporte, *The True Face of Duplessis* (Montreal, 1960); or Cameron Nish, ed., *Quebec in the Duplessis Era, 1935-1959: Dictatorship or Democracy?* (Toronto, 1970.) For a more sympathetic view, see Conrad Black, *Duplessis* (Toronto, 1977).

104. *Boucher* v. *The King* [1951] *Supreme Court Reports* 265; *Saumer* v. *City of Quebec* [1953] S.C.R. 299; *Switzman* v. *Elbling* [1957] S.C.R. 285.

105. *Montreal Gazette*, 5 December 1946; as cited by Frank Scott, "Duplessis v. Jehovah," *Canadian Forum* 26 (1947), 222-23; reprinted in Scott, *Essays on the Constitution: Aspects of Canadian Law and Politics* (Toronto, 1977), 193-96.

106. Alcoholic Liquor Act, *Revised Statues of Quebec 1941*, c.255, s.35(1).

107. [1952] 1 *Dominion Law Reports* 680.

108. [1956] *Quebec Queen's Bench Reports* 447.

109. As quoted by Walter Surma Tarnopolsky, *The Canadian Bill of Rights* (2nd. edn., Toronto, 1975), 121-22.

110. *Revised Statutes of Ontario* 1970, c.250; *Revised Regulations of Ontario* 1970, Reg. 563.

111. 5 *Ontario Reports* (2d), (1975), 580-93, at 589.

112. Technically, the injunction applied only to Chairman Mackey and the other officers of the Licence Board as individuals. Under the Crown Agency Act (*Revised Statutes of Ontario* 1970, c.100) and the Proceedings Against the Crown Act (R.S.O. 1970, c. 365), the Board itself, as a Crown agency, could not be made subject to an injunction. Therefore, Keith simply issued a declaratory order against the Board to the same effect. On appeal, the Divisional Court upheld the injunction against the chairman and Board officers, but vacated the order against the Board itself (*MacLean et al.* v. *Liquor Licence Board of Ontario et al.* 9 *Ontario Reports* (2d), 597-613). Interestingly, Robert Sharpe, who acted as Sexton's junior in the initial hearing on the case, later published the leading book on injunctions in Canada. See his *Injunctions and Specific Performance* (Toronto, 1983, 1992).

113. Aziz is not the customer's real name. His name has been changed in order to protect the confidentiality of the client.

114. Interview by the author with J. Edgar Sexton, 28 March 1991.

115. Palmer later co-authored a book on commercial arbitration. See Richard H. McLaren and Earl Edward Palmer, *The Law and Practice of Commercial Arbitration* (Toronto, 1982).

116. OHH, Executive Committee minutes, 15 April 1971.

117. In May 1973, the Executive Committee considered a proposal from the Fairview Corporation offering the firm two floors in the new Commercial Union Tower, but decided not to act on it. (OHH, Executive Committee minutes, 22 May 1973.)

118. Richard Thomson was the chairman and chief executive officer of the Toronto-Dominion Bank.

119. OHH, Executive Committee minutes, 24 October 1974.

120. OHH, Executive Committee minutes, 14 January 1975.

121. OHH, Executive Committee minutes, 4 March 1975.
122. OHH, Executive Committee minutes, 11 September 1975.
123. OHH, Partnership Meeting minutes, 29 September, 7 October 1975.
124. OHH, Partnership Meeting minutes, 16 February 1976.
125. OHH, Partnership Meeting minutes, 10 May 1976.
126. OHH, Partnership Meeting minutes, 10 May 1976

CHAPTER EIGHT: THE CORPORATION: 1980-1994

1. The years 1981 and 1991 have been used rather than 1980 and 1994 in order to provide a comparison across a decade.
2. There were 97 lawyers in the firm in 1981; in 1991 this number had grown to 298. Of that number, 141 were partners (47 per cent), 146 were associates (49 per cent), and the remaining 11 were retired partners (4 per cent). The percentage of partners in the firm was much smaller in 1991 than it had been in 1981, when 56 of the firm's 97 lawyers were partners (58 per cent), because the firm was growing at a substantially greater rate.
3. Of these, 20 were partners (14 per cent of 141), and 55 were associates (38 per cent of 146). All of the 11 retired partners were men. Like 1981, the percentage of female lawyers at Osler, Hoskin & Harcourt in 1991 was comparable to that in the other major firms. At McCarthy, Tétrault 21 per cent of the lawyers in the Toronto office were women, and at Blake, Cassels & Graydon, 23 per cent were women.
4. Interview by the author with Christopher Portner, 5 December 1990.
5. See Harry S. Bray, "Recent Developments in Securities Administration in Ontario: The Securities Act, 1966," in Jacob S. Ziegel, ed., *Studies in Canadian Company Law/Etudes sur le droit Canadien des compagnies*, Vol. I (Toronto, 1967), 415-51.
6. General Graham later resigned from the committee, and in January 1964 the committee's membership was enlarged with the addition of C.W. Goldring, a Toronto investment analyst, T.A.M. Hutchison, a chartered accountant, H.I. Macdonald, then an economics professor at the University of Toronto, and J.S. Yoerger, the senior civil servant in the Ontario Department of the Provincial Secretary and Citizenship. In addition, Martin Friedland, then of Osgoode Hall Law School, served as Legal Associate to the committee.
7. This is what Chris Portner was referring to when he said that Purdy Crawford and Howard Beck "wrote the Securities Act."
8. "Report of the Attorney-General's Committee on Securities Legislation in Ontario," March 11, 1965; The Securities Act, 1966, *Statutes of Ontario* 1966, C.142.
9. The Securities Act, 1978, *Statutes of Ontario* 1978, C.47. For a very thorough analysis of this legislation and the subsequent Act to amend The Securities Act, 1978 (S.O. 1979, C.86), see Victor P. Alboini, *Ontario Securities Law* (Toronto, 1980).
10. Not all of the partners share the positive memory of the so-called "fat years." Brian Bucknall, a real estate partner, seems to echo the kind of sentiment which Bertha Wilson expressed during the early 1970s. He mused that the mid 1980s phenomenon of mergers and acquisitions may soon be seen as a

unique, and perhaps somewhat lamentable anomaly in business history. He pointed out that "much of the popular business literature, including *Barbarians at the Gate*, *The Predators Ball* and *Liar's Poker* . . . demonstrate the manner in which assumptions about a continually expanding (and, in the economic sense, 'inflating') economy generated business decisions which were subsequently proven to be unwise. . . . The decline and fall of the Campeau empire is the most familiar [Canadian] example." He also pointed out that Osler, Hoskin & Harcourt benefitted from the phenomenon, but he wonders whether the mergers and acquisitions of the 1980s, "which we now perceive to have distorted and in some ways damaged many business enterprises," may also have had some negative effects on the firm. (Memorandum to the author from Brian Bucknall, 7 October 1991.)

11. Osler, Hoskin & Harcourt firm records (hereafter OHH), Executive Committee minutes, 26 November 1974, 14 January 1975; interview by the author with Purdy Crawford, 14 March 1991.

12. The actual fee was $1,329,133.94, which included $304,419.44 in disbursements. See *Re Greenspan, Rosenberg and Buxbaum* 17 *Carswell's Practice Cases* (2d), 213-32.

13. Interview by the author with Lee Ferrier, 15 November 1988.

14. Divorce Act, 16 Eliz. II (1968), c.24 (Can.); interview by the author with Lee Ferrier, 15 November 1988.

15. See the *Report of The Special Joint Committee of the Senate and House of Commons on Divorce* (Ottawa, Queen's Printer, 1967).

16. *House of Commons Debates*, 2nd sess., 27th parl., vol. V (1967), 5013-25.

17. James C. MacDonald and Lee K. Ferrier, eds., *Canadian Divorce Law and Practise* (Toronto, 1969, 1986).

18. Ferrier was first elected a bencher in 1979; he was elected treasurer in 1988. This continued a tradition at Oslers; previous Law Society treasurers included John Hoskin, who served in the office from 1916 to 1921; Frederick Harcourt, 1924-27; Wallace Nesbitt, 1927-30; and Stuart Thom, 1974-76.

19. The two new partners were Emile Kruzick, who joined MacDonald & Ferrier when he was called to the bar in 1972 and became a partner in 1974, and Clifford Nelson, who joined the firm when he was called to the bar in 1973. He also became a partner in 1974.

20. Interview by the author with Lee Ferrier, 15 November 1988; Family Law Reform Act, *Statutes of Ontario* 1978, C.2; Divorce Act, 1985, 33-34-35 Eliz. II C.4 (Can.).

21. Memorandum to the author from Brian Bucknall, 7 October 1991.

22. Interview by the author with Brian Bucknall, 29 May 1991.

23. OHH, Partnership Meeting minutes, 11 June 1986. The merger took place as of 1 July 1986.

24. All of the lawyers who came to Osler, Hoskin & Harcourt with the MacDonald & Ferrier merger subsequently left the firm. In 1991, Lee Ferrier accepted an appointment to the Ontario Court of Justice (General Division), and in 1992 Jim MacDonald left to go into private practice.

25. The proportion of external, lateral inductions to the firm during the 1980s was, however, somewhat larger than that of the 1970s. In 1991, 129 of the firm's 298 lawyers (43 per cent) articled with another firm. In 1981, this figure was 37 per cent. In 1991, 79 of 141 partners (56 per cent), 41 of 146 associates (28 per cent), and 9 of the 11 retired partners (82 per cent) articled

outside the firm. For purposes of this analysis, only those who articled with Osler, Hoskin & Harcourt per se were considered to have articled within the firm. Those who articled with subsequently merged firms, such as Herridge Tolmie, were not included in this group.

26. In 1985 the firm received a total of over 640 applications for the 1986-87 articling period. The six Ontario law schools graduated in total between 900 and 1,000 LL.B.s per year during the 1980s. Of the 32 students who articled with the firm during 1988-89, 30 graduated from Ontario law schools.

27. According to the firm brochure published for prospective articling students in 1989, 13 of 15 students were offered associate positions in 1982, 10 of 16 in 1983, 10 of 14 in 1984, 12 of 19 in 1985, 13 of 18 in 1986, 14 of 21 in 1987, and 20 of 29 in 1988. The average over seven years was, therefore, 69.7 per cent; the lowest return percentage was 62.5 in 1983, and the highest was 86.7 in 1982.

28. Between 1986 and 1991, the average billable hours total among associate lawyers in the Toronto office was approximately 1,800 per year. According to a report in *The Globe and Mail* in June 1990, a Vancouver firm had recently lowered the number of expected annual billable hours (that portion of a lawyer's time chargeable to clients) from 1,700 to 1,600. The same story reported, however, that some larger Canadian firms expected their people to bill over 2,000 hours per year, and the standard figure in New York was about 2,500. ("B.C. legal firm bucks workaholic trend, reduces lawyers' workload," *The Globe and Mail*, 7 June 1990, A8.)

29. This anti-nepotism rule was apparently not uncommon. Other firms, including Smith, Lyons, Torrance, Stevenson & Mayer also had the rule. (Interview by the author with R. Gordon Marantz, 24 January 1991.)

30. Others included Martin Guest, who articled with Oslers and then joined the corporate department after his call to the bar in 1989, whose father was Gowan T Guest, formerly a senior partner with the Vancouver firm of Alexander, Guest, Holburn & Beaudin; Sally Hannon, who practised with the real estate department from 1988 to 1991, was the daughter of Matthew Hannon, then the senior partner at Ogilvy, Renault in Montreal; P. Dougal MacDonald, who also articled with the firm and joined the corporate department after his call to the bar in 1985, whose father was William A. MacDonald, the senior partner at McMillan Binch; Robert MacKinnon, who practised with the litigation department from 1990 to 1991, whose father was Justice B.J. MacKinnon, formerly of MacKinnon, McTaggart; John Stevens, who articled with the firm and joined the corporate department in 1985, whose father was Robert Stevens, a senior partner at Blake, Cassels & Graydon; and Allan Stitt, who articled with the firm and practised with the litigation department from 1990 to 1994, whose father was Hubert Stitt, the senior partner in the Toronto office of Baker & Mackenzie.

31. The lone exception to the rule was John D. Coyne, who practised in the corporate department in the Toronto office from 1986 to 1991. His father, Jack Coyne, was a senior partner in the Ottawa office. The younger Coyne was an articling student in the Toronto office when the merger between Osler, Hoskin & Harcourt and his father's firm of Herridge, Tolmie took place in 1985. He was asked back to join the corporate department in Toronto after his call to the bar in 1986. (See the discussion of the 1985 merger with Herridge, Tolmie.) In addition, although the anti-nepotism rule has apparently solved the problem of parent-child conflicts within the firm, there are other, similar, relationships which might pose a problem. For instance, what

should happen when a partner and associate lawyer become involved in a relationship or become married? At one time the precedent was that the associate would leave the firm. In 1983, when Blake Murray, a partner in the Tax Department, married Nancy Riley, an associate in the Corporate/Commercial Department, Riley moved to Fraser & Beatty, where she later became a partner. More recently, however, a different precedent seems to have been set. As of 1991, there were at least two marriages in the firm in which one spouse was a partner and the other an associate. By that point the standard practise in partners' meetings was that a partner would leave the room when personnel matters involving his or her spouse were dealt with. When the partners decided to offer Karen Weinstein, an associate lawyer in the labour department, a partnership, her husband, Jason Hanson, already a partner in the same department, was not present in the meeting.

32. Interview by the author with John Cotter, 30 August 1988.

33. For one insider's view of the Finley Kumble disaster, see Steven Kumble (co-written with Kevin J. Lahart), *Conduct Unbecoming: The Rise and Ruin of Finley, Kumble* (New York, 1990). For a journalist's view, see Kim Isaac Eisler's *Shark Tank: Greed, Politics, and the Collapse of Finley, Kumble, One of America's Largest Law Firms* (New York, 1990). In 1969, the firm, whose office was on Madison Avenue in Manhattan, was Finley, Kumble, Underberg, Persky & Roth. In 1988, as Finley, Kumble, Wagner, Underberg, Manley, Myerson & Casey, it had offices in New York, Los Angeles, Beverly Hills, Newport Beach, Sacramento, San Diego, Miami, Fort Lauderdale, Palm Beach, Tallahassee, Chicago, Baton Rouge, Baltimore, Dallas, Washington and London. It had 227 partners, including Hugh Carey, former governor of New York; Paul Laxalt, former governor of Nevada; Russell B. Long, who served as U.S. senator from Louisiana from 1948-1987; and Robert F. Wagner, former mayor of the City of New York, U.S. ambassador to Spain, and President Jimmy Carter's personal envoy to the Vatican. (*Martindale-Hubbell Law Directory* (Summit, N.J., 1969, 1988).)

34. Interview by the author with Purdy Crawford, 31 January 1991.

35. Interview by the author with Christopher Portner, 5 December 1990.

36. This was the firm which, by the late 1980s, was known as Ogilvy, Renault. In Quebec, law firms can only be named for currently practising members of the firm. When a named partner retires or leaves the firm, its name must change. In Ontario, firms can be named for lawyers who are, *or were*, members. Hence Osler, Hoskin & Harcourt retained its name long after John Hoskin and Frederick Harcourt were dead. As of 1994, there was one remaining Osler with the firm — retired partner Campbell R. Osler, who was Britton Bath Osler's great-nephew.

37. Interview by the author with R. Gordon Marantz, 24 January 1991.

38. Borden, Elliot was formed in 1936, when Henry Borden left Fraser & Beatty to go into partnership with B.V. Elliot. They were later joined by R.H. Sankey, who left Fraser & Beatty in 1938, and Kenneth Palmer, who left Fraser & Beatty at the end of World War II. (Interview by the author with B.V. Elliot, 30 November 1987; Stanley E. Edwards, *Fraser & Beatty: The First 150 Years* (Toronto, 1989), 24.)

39. The eight were Ian G. Wahn, A.D. McAlpine, H.B. Mayer, R.A. Smith, G.E. Creber, J.C. Lyons, J.G. Torrance and J.D. Stevenson. They also brought a young associate lawyer, J.R.C. Cermak, with them.

40. Interview by the author with R. Gordon Marantz, 24 January 1991.

41. Interview by the author with R. Gordon Marantz, 24 January 1991.

42. As Marantz explained it, the firm's year-end was April 30, and a three-man panel of the firm's Executive Committee would deliberate over the summer and tell the rest of the partners what their share was. Their draws would then be adjusted. (Interview by the author with R. Gordon Marantz, 24 January 1991.)

43. Birnbaum was born in 1946; he holds a B.A. from the University of Toronto and an LL.B. from Western. He was called to the bar in 1973. Chartrand was also born in 1946; he holds a B.A. from the University of Ottawa, an LL.B. from Queen's, and an LL.M., an M.I.A., and an M.B.A., all from Columbia. He was called to the bar in 1974.

44. Interview by the author with R. Gordon Marantz, 24 January 1991.

45. Interview by the author with R. Gordon Marantz, 24 January 1991.

46. Interview by the author with R. Gordon Marantz, 24 January 1991.

47. Steven Golick, who was called to the bar in the spring of 1985, was to be brought in as an associate. A year later, Barry Goldberg, who was also called in 1985, came over from Smith, Lyons to join the group. Both Golick and Goldberg became partners at Osler, Hoskin & Harcourt in 1991.

48. OHH, Partnership Meeting minutes, 3 September 1985.

49. Interview by the author with R. Gordon Marantz, 24 January 1991.

50. Osler, Hoskin & Harcourt was one of the four largest in the country. See Appendix II.

51. Interview by the author with Peter White, 21 November 1990.

52. OHH, Executive Committee minutes, 12 February 1974.

53. Interview by the author with Tony Hendrie, 11 October 1990.

54. OHH, Executive Committee minutes, 26 February 1974.

55. OHH, Partnership Meeting minutes, 27 March 1974.

56. Interview by the author with Tony Hendrie, 11 October 1990.

57. The only lawyer called in 1969 who became a partner at Osler, Hoskin & Harcourt in 1974 was Peter Dey.

58. McDermott became a partner 1 April 1975.

59. *Black et al.* v. *Law Society of Alberta*, [1989] 1 *Supreme Court of Canada Reports*, 591-640.

60. The merger with the Montreal firm of Clarkson, Tétrault changed the firm's name to McCarthy Tétrault.

61. See Chapters One and Two.

62. Memorandum to the author from Brian Bucknall, 7 October 1991.

63. Memorandum to the author from Brian Bucknall, 7 October 1991.

64. Memorandum to the author from Brian Bucknall, 7 October 1991.

65. Interview by the author with J. Edgar Sexton, 28 March 1991.

66. OHH, Partnership Meeting minutes, 7 March 1985.

67. OHH, Partnership Meeting minutes, 7 March 1985.

68. Interview by the author with Ross Gray, 19 December 1989.

69. Interestingly, the *Coca-Cola* v. *Pepsi-Cola* case started at Osler, Hoskin & Harcourt in Toronto. A.W. Langmuir, Sr., the patent and trademark law specialist at Oslers, launched suit on behalf of the Coca-Cola Company of Canada, his long-time client, in 1938. [1938] 4 *Dominion Law Reports*, 145-

80 (Exchequer Court of Can.); [1940] 1 *Dominion Law Reports*, 161-79 (Supreme Court of Canada); [1942] 2 *Dominion Law Reports*, 657-62 (Provincial Court).

70. *The Canadian Who's Who*, 1967-69, s.v. McPherson.

71. Interview by the author with Ross Gray, 19 December 1989.

72. Interview by the author with Ross Gray, 19 December 1989.

73. Coyne also received an M.A. from Oxford in 1951.

74. Only Gowling & Henderson, which had 105 lawyers in Ottawa and Toronto, and Soloway, Wright, Houston, Greenberg, O'Grady, Morin, with 31, were larger.

75. Memorandum from C.R. Osler, 2 November 1993.

76. See Appendix II.

77. Interview by the author with Peter Dey, 22 April 1991.

78. Paul McKeown, who joined the firm in 1991, was the former director of marketing with the accounting firm Peat Marwick. He pointed out that ''cross-selling,'' for instance — the marketing term for introducing an existing client or customer to another product or service your organization can supply — was an area which law firms in general were very slow to move into. (Interview by the author with Paul McKeown, 23 May 1991.)

79. According to *The Globe and Mail* (17 June 1991, 1), Skybox rental costs were estimated at between $100,000 and $250,000 per annum on average. There were a total of 161 boxes in the Dome, and the holders included many of the largest corporations in Canada. Osler, Hoskin & Harcourt was one of the few law firms to have one. The decision to lease the box was not, however, an easy one. Like the public debate over the stadium itself, there were some partners in the firm who felt that a luxury box was simply too extravagant. In late 1988 the firm held a plebiscite over the issue, and although it was approved by about 70 per cent of the partners, there were some very strong feelings expressed about it. (Interview by the author with Larry Hebb, 4 October 1991.)

80. Interview by the author with Ron Atkey, 15 November 1990.

81. OHH, Partnership Meeting minutes, 29 September 1975.

82. Interview by the author with Ron Atkey, 15 November 1990.

83. Interview by the author with Purdy Crawford, 31 January 1991.

84. Interview by the author with Purdy Crawford, 31 January 1991.

85. In the next decade both of these men would also leave the firm. Ironically, in 1991, Brian Levitt, the corporate lawyer who took over many of Purdy Crawford's client responsibilities in 1985, followed Crawford to Imasco to take on the position of president of the company. In 1994, Peter Dey left to become president of Morgan Stanley Canada. See the Prologue.

86. Interview by the author with Larry Hebb, 4 October 1991.

87. Interview by the author with Larry Hebb, 4 October 1991.

88. Interview by the author with Larry Hebb, 4 October 1991.

EPILOGUE: FROM COMPACT TO CORPORATION — AND BEYOND

1. One of the changes which the firm was going through at the time of writing

was a decided slowing in the growth which it had experienced during much of the 1980s. As Appendix II indicates, the firm grew from 103 lawyers in 1982 to 285 in 1992; but as the table below indicates, the annual rate of growth during the decade was not consistent. During the early 1980s, the number of lawyers who joined the firm each year continued to grow, reaching a peak of over 25 per cent in 1985. But as the boom years of the 1980s came to an end, the firm's rate of growth was slowing down. By 1991, it was down to 3.5 per cent, and in 1992 the firm actually shrank by 4.4 per cent.

Total No. of Lawyers at OHH and Annual Percentage of Growth, 1982-1992

Year	No. of Lawyers	Annual Growth Rate (Decline)
1982	103	—
1983	113	9.7%
1984	127	12.4%
1985	161	26.8%
1986	188	16.8%
1987	210	11.7%
1988	239	13.8%
1989	265	10.9%
1990	288	8.7%
1991	298	3.5%
1992	285	(4.4%)

2. This should not be confused with a litigation fee contingent upon the outcome of a suit. Unlike in the United States, such an arrangement remained ethically forbidden in Canada.

3. See Chapter Six.

4. "Canadian Business History at the Crossroads," an address to a Business History Workshop, sponsored by the National Centre for Management Research and Development, School of Business Administration, University of Western Ontario, 30 May 1991.

APPENDIX II: LARGEST CANADIAN LAW FIRMS, 1862-1992

---

1. Data are taken from firm records for Osler, Hoskin & Harcourt and predecessor firms. For other firms, where possible annual editions of the *Canadian Law List* published in the year indicated have been used. The 1862 entry includes firms of three or more lawyers; the 1872 entry includes firms of four or more lawyers. The entries for 1872-1992 include the ten largest firms. Entries for 1862-1952 include the names of all lawyers in each firm; entries for 1972-92 include the names of firms only.

2. Osler, Hoskin & Harcourt offices in London, Paris, Hong Kong and New York were operated by the international firm Osler Renault Ladner, in partnership with Ogilvy Renault of Montreal and Ladner Downs of Vancouver. At the end of 1993, Ladner Downs left the partnership, which reverted to the name Osler Renault. In October of 1994, it opened an office in Singapore.

3. Fasken Campbell Godfrey offices in London and Brussels were operated by the international firm Fasken Martineau Davis, in partnership with Martineau Walker of Montreal and Davis & Company of Vancouver.

4. Fraser & Beatty also had a limited domestic affiliation agreement with the Montreal firm McMaster Meighen.

5. The Ottawa office of Lang, Michener, Lawrence & Shaw was operated under the name Lang, Michener, Honeywell, Wotherspoon.

6. Borden & Elliot was affiliated in a national association known as Borden DuMoulin Howard Gervais with the Vancouver firm Russell & DuMoulin, the Calgary firm Howard Mackie and the Montreal firm Mackenzie Gervais.

7. Tory, Tory, DesLauriers & Binnington offices in London, Hong Kong, and Taipei were operated by the international firm Tory Ducharme Lawson Lundell, in partnership with Desjardins Ducharme of Montreal and Lawson Lundell Lawson & McIntosh of Vancouver.

INDEX